# ISLAM
# IN ETHIOPIA

# ISLAM IN ETHIOPIA

*By*

J. SPENCER TRIMINGHAM

GEOFFREY CUMBERLEGE
OXFORD UNIVERSITY PRESS
*London New York Toronto*
1952

*Oxford University Press, Amen House, London E.C. 4*
GLASGOW NEW YORK TORONTO MELBOURNE WELLINGTON
BOMBAY CALCUTTA MADRAS CAPE TOWN
*Geoffrey Cumberlege, Publisher to the University*



PRINTED IN GREAT BRITAIN
AT THE UNIVERSITY PRESS, OXFORD
BY CHARLES BATEY, PRINTER TO THE UNIVERSITY

# PREFACE

THIS book continues the survey of Islam in Africa which was initiated with *Islam in the Sudan.* Its aim is to study as a whole the history and institutions of the Islamic peoples of north-east Africa, that is, the region which embraces the present-day countries of Eritrea, the Empire of Ethiopia, and French, British, and Italian Somalilands. It gives the story of the impact of Islam upon the nomadic and settled peoples of the region, the reaction of the indigenous cultures to that impact, and the existing state of the Islam professed by those peoples who have been won over to it. An attempt has been made to assess the influence of Islam in the history and present-day lives of these peoples, to show how it has moulded their lives, and how they in turn have moulded the Islam which they received. Further, since the Christian state of Ethiopia has for centuries been surrounded by Islamic peoples, it deals with the effect of Islam upon that State and the centuries of conflict between the two civilizations.

This task of giving a clear picture of the influence of Islamic culture in such a vast region is complicated because account must be taken of the fact that its Islam presents the greatest possible diversity, ranging from fanatical orthodoxy to the merest veneer, from the learning of the scholiast to the semi-pagan patterer of a few Arabic formulae. I hope that this study will at least serve to bring together the material upon which a genuine estimate of the depth and influence of Islam in north-east Africa may be based.

To avoid confusion the word 'Abyssinia' is employed to designate the historic kingdom of the highlands which was influenced by the Semitic civilization of South Arabia and afterwards adopted Christianity, and whose peoples expressed themselves through the Semitic languages, Geʿez, Tigriña, and Amharic. The word 'Ethiopia' is used in a much wider sense to embrace the whole region included in this survey. It has also been necessary to use 'Ethiopia' when referring to the modern state of this name founded by Menelik II and ruled today by Hāyla Sellassé. The word 'Abyssinia' is used, therefore, for the historical region of the Christian kingdom and 'Ethiopia' for the wider geographical region, except when it refers to the modern state.

I have given sufficient indication of my sources to enable me to dispense with a bibliography, but in particular I wish to acknowledge my debt to the admirable work done by Italian scholars in various aspects of my subject, and especially to the studies of Carlo Conti Rossini, whose death in August 1949 was a great loss to Ethiopian scholarship, and Enrico Cerulli, now the foremost exponent of Italian scholarship in this field.

J. S. T.

CAIRO
*February* 1951

# CONTENTS

# MAPS

# ABBREVIATIONS

| | |
|---|---|
| *A.A.E.* | *Archivo per l'Antropologia e la Etnologia.* |
| Basset, *Études.* | R. Basset, *Études sur l'histoire d'Éthiopie*, Paris, 1882. |
| *B.G.A.* | *Bibliotheca Geographorum Arabicorum*, ed. de Goeje. |
| Bruce, *Travels* | Bruce, *Travels to Discover the Source of the Nile*, 1790. |
| *B.S.G.I.* | *Bollettino della R. Soc. Geog. Ital.* |
| Cerulli, *E.O.* | E. Cerulli, *Etiopia Occidentale*, Rome, 1933. |
| *C.S.C.O.* | *Corpus Scriptorum Christianorum Orientalium: Scriptores Aethiopici;* series altera: Historica et Hagiographica. |
| *D.A.E.* | E. Littmann, *Deutsche Aksum Expedition*, 1913. |
| *Ency. Is.* | *The Encyclopaedia of Islam.* |
| *Futūḥ* | Shihāb ad-Dīn, *Futūḥ al-Ḥabasha*, ed. and trans. R. Basset, 1897. |
| *Geog. Journ.* | *Journal of the Royal Geographical Society.* |
| *G.S.A.I.* | *Giornale della Società Asiatica Italiana.* |
| *Guida* | *Guida dell' Africa Orientale Italiana*, Milan, 1938. |
| *Ilmām* | Maqrīzī, *al-Ilmām bi akhbār man bi arḍ al-Ḥabasha min Mulūk al-Islām*, ed. G. Zaidān, Cairo, 1895. |
| *J. Asiat.* | *Journal asiatique.* |
| *J.R.A.I.* | *Journal of the Royal Anthropological Institute.* |
| *J.R.A.S.* | *Journal of the Royal Asiatic Society.* |
| *O.M.* | *Oriente Moderno.* |
| *Patr. Gr.* | J. P. Migne, *Patrologiae Cursus Completus*, Series Graeca. |
| *Patr. Lat.* | J. P. Migne, *Patrologiae Cursus Completus*, Series Latina. |
| *Patr. Or.* | *Patrologia Orientalis.* |
| *R.A.S.O.* | C. Beccari, *Rerum Aethiopicarum: Scriptores Occidentales.* |
| *R.M.M.* | *Revue du monde musulman.* |
| *R.R.A.L.* | *Rendiconti della Reale Accademia dei Lincei* (Classe di scienze, morali, storiche e filologiche). |
| *R.S.E.* | *Rassegna di Studi Etiopici.* |
| *R. Sém.* | *Revue sémitique.* |
| *R.S.O.* | *Rivista degli Studi Orientali*, Rome. |
| *S.N.R.* | *Sudan Notes and Records.* |
| *Z.D.M.G.* | *Zeitschrift der Deutschen Morgenländischen Gesellschaft.* |

# INTRODUCTION

As a basis for the genesis and expansion of a higher type of civilization the most favourable areas in Africa in regard to climate, type of soil, and receptivity to the radiations of the eastern civilizations were the Mediterranean and the Ethiopian-plateau regions. But the expansion of the Mediterranean civilizations, Egyptian, Phoenician, Hellenic, Latin, and Islamic, into Africa has always been blocked or diluted to vanishing-point by the desert and the steppe. The physical conditions of the Sudan, the great desert and steppe plain between the Atlantic and the plateau, with its long story of tribal migrations in search of land for stockbreeding or cultivation, have never been favourable to the formation of a civilized society. Thus the Christian, pagan, or Muslim kingdoms of this great plain (Maqurra and ʿAlwa of the Nile, Gāna, Māli, and Songhay of the Niger, Ashanti, Dahomey, and Benin) have never achieved true cohesion, and have remained on the level of derived or primitive cultures.

The plateau region of Ethiopia, however, can offer everything that is conducive to a stable occupation, whilst its position has exposed its inhabitants to the radiations of oriental civilizations. During the first millennium B.C. they had an influx of Semitic colonists which led to the formation of a highly developed civilization. This movement, coming originally from the Yaman, spread throughout the northern Ethiopian highlands, and the bond of a common Semitic civilization was established across the Red Sea. These colonists and the Arabs, associated in a unity of culture, with Arabia as an inexhaustible source of new blood, when united later in the religious unity of Christianity, might well have influenced other parts of Africa. But when Abyssinia and Arabia were indeed associated in religion, a new religious idea came to birth in the seventh century in Arabia which was destined to replace Christianity as the creator of the spiritual unity of the Near East and North Africa. This new religious system, Islam, caused a break between the two associated regions as clear-cut as the physical fracture of the Red Sea, and completely divided Abyssinians and Arabs. These two peoples, opposed from henceforth in mutually hostile camps, barred the road to outside influence upon the interior of Africa until the era of Western expansion, and exhausted their energies in futile struggles with one another.

The two religious cultures did not at first come into decisive conflict.

During one of the most obscure periods of its history the Christianity of northern Ethiopia expanded over the highlands in such a way that it completely claimed the souls of the Hamitic Agao inhabitants. During the same centuries the Arabs also exerted an Islamic influence upon Africans all along the east coast—an influence which spread inland, since the need of many Africans for a system that would integrate life was so great that many were ready to exchange the fear and insecurity of primitive religion for the confident assurance of Islamic citizenship. Islam is a religion which, because of the territorial freedom of its worship and its low êthos, has appealed especially to Hamite or Negroid-Hamite pastoral nomads, and there is scarcely a nomad tribe in Africa north of the Equator which has not accepted it. Christianity, on the other hand, tied to its priesthood and its high êthos, has utterly failed to attract any such tribe. At the same time, with the decay of nomadism, Islam appeals just as vividly and exerts an equally strong hold upon the Hamite when he adopts a settled agricultural or urban life.

North-east Africa was the only African region where Islam had a rival in the presentation of a new religious conception of life to Hamites and Negroes. Consequently, had Abyssinia become Muslim, either violently as a result of the conquest of the Imām Aḥmad Grāñ in the sixteenth century, or pacifically through centuries of gradual infiltration, and had a strong Hamitic–Islamic civilization established itself in the highlands, nothing could have stopped the spread of Islam throughout the whole of the continent, for in North Africa and the Sudan it was the Islamized Hamites who were the most effective missionaries.

Around the Ethiopian plateau stretch vast territories, roamed by nomadic peoples to whom its great bastions have presented an almost insuperable obstacle. The weakest defences are in the north and west, but this wide steppe area has been able to absorb waves of pastoralists who, even after they received driblets of Islamic culture, never built up states sufficiently powerful to constitute an overwhelming menace. The Abyssinians, in the security in their natural fortress, allowed their once vigorous and expanding Christianity to stagnate at a low cultural and spiritual level, and the challenge of Islam did not evoke any response comparable to that which it evoked among the Christians in western Europe. The shock of the Islamic conquest of Aḥmad Grāñ, followed by the still more devastating Galla invasions and the precipitate propaganda of the Jesuits, instead of stimulating the Abyssinians, led to exhausting internal struggles and a withdrawal upon their moribund Christianity as the symbol of their national independence to be guarded at all costs, so that it degenerated still further into a form of higher tribal religion isolated in a sea of Islam.

Yet Abyssinia, by its purely individualistic resistance, for its people had no conception whatever of Christian unity, has helped to change the course of African history. Its highland fastnesses have been a rock against which the waves of expansion of the Islamic civilization from the Arabian Peninsula and East African coast on the one hand, and from the Nile valley on the other, have dashed themselves in vain endeavour, so that Islam could not establish that stable rule on the east coast which would have led to interior expansion and possibly the religious unification of Africa under Islam. A certain inland movement was apparent because many African peoples were ready to respond to the values inherent in the Islamic civilization, but, once the desert and Nilotic Nubia had been conquered, such expansion was chiefly from the north, so that almost the whole of the Sudan from the Atlantic sea-board to the frontiers of Abyssinia is now Muslim. On the other hand, another vigorous religion, Western Christianity, was presented by the forces of Western expansion during the last century and has spread throughout Africa south of the Equator. The rapidity of its expansion and the tenacity with which it is held show that even now, before it has freed itself from what is purely Western and not intrinsic in its heritage, Christianity can fulfil the longings of the African soul and become the unifying force of Southern and Central Africa, as opposed to the unifying force of Islam in the north and the Sudan.

# I

# The Region and its Folk

## I. THE LAND

THE phrase *north-east Africa* is used in such a variety of ways that it is necessary to define the way in which it is used in this survey. For our convenience it is limited to the following political divisions: the former Italian Eritrea, the Empire of Ethiopia, and the French, British, and Italian Somalilands. These form a great triangle bounded on the north-east by the Red Sea and the Gulf of Aden, on the south-east by the Indian Ocean, on the south by Kenya Colony, and on the north-east and east by the Anglo-Egyptian Sudan. This vast area does not constitute any natural homogeneous region, and its peculiar geographical conditions, especially the contrasting cool humid highlands, the home of agriculture and sedentary life, and the hot dry steppe or desert plateaux and plains, the home of animal breeding and the nomadic life, explain much in the Ethiopian history which we shall be treating.

It is necessary to distinguish five principal regions. The first is the Ethiopian-Kaffa plateau, which includes the northern plateau now part of Eritrea and the whole of Tigrai, Amḥara, Gojām, Shoa, and Jimma-Kaffa; that is, the historical region of Abyssinia and of the Sidāma kingdoms. It is a vast irregular tableland of volcanic reefs having a general elevation of 6,500 feet in which terrace rises above terrace to form high wide plateaux. It is clearly defined on the east by the steep edges of a mountain wall which is the western edge of the great East African rift, having an average altitude of 8,000 feet. This acts as a vast retaining wall which drops abruptly into the sea at the Gulf of Arafali or into the low, arid, and hot Dankali depression. A parallel rift runs from Lake Ṭāna along the Blue Nile canyon to the southern lakes. The Ethiopian highland is tilted towards the west and descends more or less regularly in vast terraces towards the plains of the Nilotic Sudan, but in the north-west and south-west there is a rapid descent of several thousand feet. The great line of the escarpment overlooking the Red Sea to the east and the Sudan plains to the west has acted as a barrier protecting the inhabitants against the migratory movements of other peoples. Towards the south-east beyond the Abāy, access is less difficult, the altitude diminishes, the valleys grow more numerous and give an individuality to smaller massifs which is reflected in the history and social life of their inhabitants. Deep ravines divide this great massif into many subordinate plateaux, above which as bases, rise several mountain chains.

The highlands have often been compared with Switzerland, but there is a very characteristic difference:

> In Switzerland, the heights are barren peaks, the valleys fairly broad and fertile. In Abyssinia, all this is reversed. The heights are mostly open plateaux, the valleys jungle-choked gorges or canyons of great depth. The population lives on the plateaux, and the lines of communication follow the high ground, the valleys being formidable obstacles to traffic.[1]

Characteristic of this relief are the *ambas*, which are steep and bare mountain cones whose summits are crowned by plains furnished with abundant water where herds of cattle can pasture and crops can be grown. These *ambas* have played an important part in history, for they form natural self-supporting fortresses whose few approaches could be held by a handful of men. They have been the last strongholds of the original unmodified Hamitic population, of rebels against the central authority, and of Abyssinians themselves when their country has been invaded; whilst they have been used as prisons to segregate males of the royal house and political offenders. Equally characteristic are the abrupt and deep ravines which intersect the surface of these plateaux and have been caused by the concentration of heavy rains in a short space of time. Many of the rivers flow thousands of feet below the general level of the plateaux, sometimes through wide valleys, sometimes through precipitous canyons. These canyons, too, have played their part in history, for movements involve either hazardous descents and climbs or else a long and slow detour. The tremendous gorges which the Abāy and its tributaries have carved for themselves have proved great obstacles to communications between Gojām and the southern highlands and have given it the characteristics of an island. But all the Abyssinian regions and not only Gojām are defined by great river gorges. Thus each region has been a unity in itself whose people have maintained their own individual characteristics. For centuries some of these regions have resisted incorporation into the empire and have often been ready to break away. It is these natural regional divisions which have made the unification of the country such a difficult problem, so that Abyssinia has always been a

[1] *Handbook to Abyssinia* compiled by the British Foreign Office.

federation of countries whose ruler has rightly styled himself 'king of kings'.

Another region is the Eastern Rift valley which runs from the Dankali depression in the north where it is defined by the River Ḥawāsh, through Lakes Zway, Shala, Margherita, and Chamo, which separate the Ethiopian and central massifs, thence through Lakes Stephania and Rudolf to its continuation in the great equatorial lakes. In the north, with the lower course of the Ḥawāsh, the valley enlarges into the third region, the plain known as the Dankali depression which includes Eritrean Dankalia, ʿAfar (or Ethiopian Dankalia), and Aussa. It is defined in the north and east by a mountain chain running along the coast from the Bay of Thio to the Gulf of Tajūra; in the south by the mountains of Harar, and in the west by the formidable line of the escarpment of the Ethiopian plateau. This depression is an arid, sandy, and rocky waste in which some rivers like the Ḥawāsh disappear. It includes volcanic cones, some of which are still active, and encloses a great depression 120 metres below sea-level with a succession of salt lakes at the bottom. In this depression even nomadic tribes can barely exist.

Next comes the central massif between the Rift valley depression and the Galla-Somali plateau. It starts abruptly at the Rift valley fracture with a great wall of basalt, punctuated by peaks, and extends through the high tablelands of Chercher, Boke, and Didda which are incised by numerous deep depressions. Stretching from Lake Chamo to beyond Harar the great chain descends into the last region, the Galla-Somali plateau, in gentle slopes through which flow the river Wēbi Shabēli and the three rivers which form the Jūba. The Galla-Somali plateau has three distinct regions, the interior plateau, a middle steppe, and a coastal region.

The physical structure and relief of north-east Africa explain the directions of the migratory movements of its peoples. It was easy to move about the Galla-Somali plateau or the ʿAfar plain, it was possible to reach the heights of the central massif, but it was a very different matter if migrants wished to attain the Ethiopian massif against the wishes of its inhabitants, for the walls of Tigrai, Shoa, Gurāgē, Gamo, and Barodda offer almost impenetrable obstacles to migratory movements.

If the physical structure has affected the movements of men, the varieties of climate and vegetation in that broken surface have exercised a still more profound influence upon the kind of life lived by its peoples. Its geographical position, the great differences of altitude in the mountain complex, the abundant rainfall of the central region and lack of it in the lowlands, give it every variety of climate from that characteristic of equatorial regions to that of temperate climes.

The region of the Red Sea coast and Gulf of Aden is one of the hottest in the world, where the temperature varies very little, but as one enters the plains inland the climate becomes that of desert regions with great variations between the heat of the day and the cold at night. On the highlands of the Ethiopian plateau and central plateau owing to the abundant rains we get temperatures less high than the first but subject to less variation than the second.

Five climatic regions have been distinguished. In the north-east that of the Gulf of Aden and the Red Sea, affecting the Mijurtin, Warsangali, ʿAfar, and Eritrean coast, is a torrid climate with scanty rains falling in winter. In the south-east the climate of the Indian Ocean affecting much of the Somali plateau is similar except that the weak rains fall in summer. In the centre, south, and west the climate of Ogadēn, Boran, and the basin of Lake Rudolf is characterized by excessive temperatures with low rainfall. In the north-west, the Ethiopian climate, ruling over all the plateau of that name, is distinguished by temperatures varying with the altitude from extreme heat to cold. The people of the plateau, following the height, climate, and vegetable products, recognize three zones: the lowlands (*qolla*) from 2,000 to 5,500–6,000 feet, which are hot, humid, and unhealthy and consequently are the most sparsely populated; the uplands (*woina dega*) from 5,500 to 7,500–8,200 feet, which is the most favourable region for man; and the highlands (*dega*) above 7,500–8,200 feet. The central massif has a similar climate but with less variation in heat and cold, the rains are regular but not so heavy.

In general the plateau regions have a single rainy season from April to September, but the intervention of periods when the rainfall is slighter has caused references to the 'greater' and 'lesser' rains. October to March is generally rainless, except in the south-west (Shoa-Gimira, Kaffa, and Jimma) where it may rain at any time of the year. On the south-eastern slope towards the Indian Ocean and over a large part of Boran the rains are divided into two periods: March–May and October–November.

The general tilt of the Ethiopian plateau being towards the west its drainage is in that direction. The only river that flows east is the Ḥawāsh. This rises near Addis Ababa, flows with a great curve towards the Gulf of Aden, and finally loses itself in the sandy wastes west of

Jibuti. One river, the Omo, flows south into Lake Rudolf. The greater part of the rainfall drains into the Nile which is fed by three tributaries, the Takkazē in the north (called the Setit in its middle and the Atbara in its lower course) flowing into the main Nile, the Sobat in the south flowing into the White Nile, and the Abāy between them. The Abāy flows from Lake Ṭāna some 3,000 feet below the level of the plateau, then turning south-east it describes a huge loop and runs north-west through the Eastern Sudan as the Blue Nile. It is this river which is mainly responsible for the annual rise of the Nile. From the Somali plateau two great rivers flow southwards, the Jūba (Ar. *Al-Jubb*, Som. *Wēbi Ganāna*) which reaches the sea, and the Wēbi Shabēli which is swallowed up in sand-dunes near the coast.

## 2. THE PEOPLE

### (*a*) *Ethnological and Cultural History of the Region*

This region presents a heterogeneous variety of ethnical, cultural, and linguistic types, and Abyssinia has been well styled by C. Conti Rossini *un museo di popoli.*[1] This diversity is in keeping with its morphological and climatic conditions. Although the Arabic term for the Abyssinians, *ḥabash* which means 'a mixture', is not the actual derivation of the word, it does show how they presented themselves to the Arabs.[2] In this region the concept of kinship has little meaning as a guide to the grouping of peoples, rather we have to talk of peoples using a language and culture of Hamitic or Semitic or Nilotic origin, or sometimes of a mixture of cultures.

Our knowledge of prehistory in Ethiopia is yet in its infancy. The earliest inhabitants yet known to us seem to have lived in the lowlands, leaving the plateaux uninhabited. It has been suggested that the pariah caste of primitive hunters scattered all over the region is a remnant of these earlier inhabitants.[3]

At some undetermined epoch Africa was invaded, possibly from South Arabia, by waves of Hamite-Caucasians belonging to the same branch of mankind as most Europeans. The predynastic Egyptians in

[1] C. Conti Rossini, *Etiopia e Genti di Etiopia* (1937), p. 169.

[2] The name is actually derived from the chief tribe of immigrant Arabs who colonized the country about the seventh century B.C. The Arabs of later times as usual tried to give the name a popular derivation.

[3] They are known to the Abyssinians as *Wayṭo*, to the Galla as *Wattā*, to the Kafficho as *Manjo*, to the Gimirra as *Kwayējo*, and to the Somali as Mijān, Tomāl, and Yibir. It is probable that these are all generical names for a low caste and that they are of diverse ethnical groups.

the past and the Beja today are the almost unmodified representatives of this race. The Bani ʿĀmir, who are characteristic representatives of the Beja, show them as long-headed, of medium height, with regular features of European type, nose straight and narrow, skin yellowish to coppery-brown, hair wavy or frizzy but never woolly, lips often thick but never everted, and the beard thin and scanty. These Hamites of north-eastern Africa are usually known under the term of Kushites or Cushites.

These Hamites came in waves and through intermarriage with the aborigines gave rise to groups of hamitized Negroes. Each incoming wave pushed their predecessors farther inland to other negrolands where they formed aristocracies amongst the peoples upon whom they imposed themselves.[1] The purest Hamites today are the Beja of the north, the Bilēn (an Agao migration) of the Keren region of Eritrea, the Agao in the heart of the highlands (northern Kushites); and the various south-western Sidāma tribes (southern Kushites), to mention only the more important. These invaders occupied the Abyssinian highlands proper, and though their lives have been completely changed by Semitic invaders, the mixture was such that Hamitic blood still predominates amongst the Tigreans, Amḥara, Gojāmites, and Shoans to the proportion of 80 per cent. In the course of centuries the Agao peoples came to adopt the languages and outlook on the life of the Semitic invaders but a few have remained almost unmodified and Agao languages still linger on in central Abyssinia (Khamir and Khamta), in the south-west (Dambyā, Wagarā, and Quārā), in Agawmeder south-west of Lake Ṭāna, and in the neighbourhood of Dāmot. The Sidāma tribes once occupied the whole of the western and southern regions of Ethiopia, but they were decimated or absorbed either by waves of Abyssinian conquest or by invading Galla hordes, and reduced to the small groups which now exist around the River Omo.

Some Hamites who mingled more profoundly with the Negroes, like the Gimira of the lowlands south-west of Kaffa, lost their racial identity and are classed by the Abyssinians with Shānqelā

[1] The hamitized Negroes having the largest proportion of Hamitic blood are the pastoral half-Hamites (so called by C. G. Seligman, *Races of Africa*, pp. 157 ff.) such as the Masai, Nandi, Suk, and Turkana, who occupy the greater part of Kenya. The Nilotes (Shilluk, Anuak, Lango, Julus), speaking Sudanic languages, are predominantly Negro in blood, but culturally more Hamitic than Negro. The Bantu are also differentiated from the true Negro by having mixed slightly with Hamites. They once occupied the region between Lakes Margherita and Stephania and a few groups such as the Wa-Gosha and Addōn were left by the Somali invasion and have formed some large federations of agriculturalists in the lower Jūba and middle Shabēli regions.

(Negroes).[1] Negroes of the Nilotic and other stems have also ascended by the middle Nile and live in the strip of land along the whole western frontier of Ethiopia. Amongst the peoples speaking Nilotic, Nilo-Hamitic, Sudanic, and other Negro languages are the Kunāma and Baria in Eritrea, the Gunza, Abigar (Nuēr), Yambo (Anuak), Mekan, Majāño (Masongo), Como, Bakko, Dime, Gayi, Bussa, and Turkana. These peoples have scarcely influenced the ethnography of the region for, except on the borders, they are in no great strength.

Between 1000 and 400 B.C. a third element was introduced by a series of transmarine Semitic migrations from Southern Arabia, which completely modified the whole cultural life of the highlands. These Semites spread over the high plateaux of the north and, since they were agriculturalists, settled down and mingled with the Kushites. One Semitic colony settled farther southwards at Harar in the south-east, from whence some of them later migrated to the Gurāgē country between the Omo and the Rift valley and imposed their language upon the Sidāma amongst whom they settled. Since the Semitic migrants of the northern highlands belonged to a highly developed oriental civilization, they introduced their languages, culture, and racial characteristics of exclusiveness, ferocity, and intensity of faith, and have profoundly changed the cultural life of the highlands. The Abyssinians proper (Tigreans, Amḥara, Gojāmites, and Shoans) who have become the dominant race, are the result of this semitization of the pre-existing Kushitic population, though the Semitic element was not sufficient to modify to any great extent their physical characteristics, which remained Hamitic.

The Semitic element in the culture of these Ethiopian Hamites was further strengthened through the adoption of primitive Judaism by many of the pagan Agao. This religion still lingers on amongst the Falāsha of the north-western provinces whose physical ancestry is Hamitic. Later, some elements of Greek culture were absorbed; but the most profound cultural influence was that of Monophysite Christianity, first introduced into the north in the fourth century A.D. and widely spread during the thirteenth and fourteenth centuries. This religion introduced a new ethos and new cultural elements,

[1] The word *Shānqelā* is employed sometimes in a broader, sometimes in a narrower sense. It is an Amharic term applied by the Abyssinians to any negro tribe or tribe with strongly negroid characteristics, but sometimes the term is limited to those who occupy the lowlands west of the Abyssinian plateau. The Bani Shangūl is the name of a distinct region on the Blue Nile inhabited by Berta and allied peoples who are called by the Abyssinians 'Black Arabs' because they speak Arabic and are Muslims.

whilst at the same time absorbing many pagan Kushite and Jewish elements.

The Somali, Galla, and ʿAfar-Saho also belong to one of the waves of Kushitic migrations which have already been mentioned who crossed the Bāb al-Mandab and the Gulf of Aden in early times into the coastal regions of East Africa. They belong fundamentally to the same Hamitic stem and are usually classified as 'Low Kushite'. Their original African homeland seems to have been between the upper course of the Wēbi and the coast of the Gulf of Aden. In consequence of migrations and fractionings, and through mixing in varying degrees with Negroes, they became differentiated ethnographically into three great groups. Those who spread northwards into the Dankali depression and its coastal region are distinguished by the linguistic group names of ʿAfar and Saho. The Somali, who are probably the most recent Hamitic immigrants into East Africa, were confined for centuries to what is now British Somaliland. From this inhospitable region they began to push south and south-west towards the valleys of the Wēbi Shabēli and Jūba, repelling Galla in the south-west and aboriginal Bantu tribes to the south, absorbing elements of both groups into their own tribal system. Whilst remaining a distinctively Hamitic ethnic group, the Somali, Saho, and ʿAfar have through the spiritual conquest of Islam become subject to a certain Semitic influence. The migration of the Oroma or Galla, as they are more generally called, had a more important effect upon the population of Abyssinia proper. The Galla were living in central Somalia, from whence they had expelled or absorbed the former Bantu inhabitants, from whom they adopted non-Hamitic institutions such as the *gada*-system of 'age-groups'. In the sixteenth century those eastern Kushites (ʿAfar and Somali) who had been islamized from Arabia began a great movement of expansion. The Galla were pushed by the Somali from the valleys of the Shabēli and Jūba southwards towards the River Tana in north-west Kenya and from thence they spread northwards fanwise, following in the wake of the Muslim (Somali-ʿAfar) invasion of Abyssinia in the middle of the sixteenth century. They spread in the east throughout the Arūsi and Harar regions; in the west towards the Diddessa river, overwhelming the existing Sidāma peoples in both directions, whilst the very crest of the wave washed into the highlands of the Shoa and Wallo country, where they settled between Christian peoples as pagan islands. The Galla of the plateau regions (Wallo, Shoa, Jimma, and Harar) became settled agriculturalists and pastoralists in the main, some adopted monarchical institutions from the Sidāma, and later the religion of Islam began to undermine their pagan beliefs. Those of the south (Borana and most of the Arūsi) who remained nomadic pastoralists and those of the west who settled down to agriculture clung to their republican institutions and their paganism.

The history of migrations in the region shows that quite a small group of immigrants can, given certain conditions, completely modify the cultural life of the peoples amongst whom they settle. We have seen that the population of this region possesses a general ethnic unity, being some 80 per cent. Hamitic, but that the Abyssinians proper have been strongly influenced by the Semitic culture of South Arabia, which has made more profound difference than racial origins. Other Kushite tribes, however, have retained their own culture; such are the Beja, Bilēn, and Saho in Eritrea, islands of Agao on the central plateau, and the Kafficho, Walamo, and many other Sidāma tribes in the south-west. The Galla, Somali, and ʿAfar who are Hamites are quite distinct ethnographically from the other Kushites. The nomadic Galla have retained characteristic elements of their own culture; so have the Somali and ʿAfar who have also been subject to a certain Semitic influence, though in quite a different way from the Abyssinians since it came through the Islamic cultural system.

### (*b*) *Social and Economic Life*

To understand the history of religion in north-east Africa we have to distinguish between two great spheres of peoples: the highly developed peoples of the plateau regions (Tigreans, Amḥara, Agao, and Sidāma), and the nomadic pastoralists of the lowlands comprising the Beja, ʿAfar-Saho, Galla, and Somali.

The nomadic and settled life of human societies does not depend upon ethnic factors, but is conditioned by the environment. Mountain and forest dwellers in general tend to be settled whilst the people of the desert and steppes, forced to move about in search of pasture for their flocks and herds, are nomads. The Galla who invaded Ethiopia were formerly all nomadic pastoralists, but those who migrated into plateau regions are now settled herders of cattle and agriculturalists living in villages, whilst those who, like the Boran, migrated into southern Ethiopia, were not affected in their economic and social life. However, between the two extremes are many gradations, for there are intermediate categories of semi-nomads who move only short distances, principally on the peripheries of the mountains, who also have settled abodes.[1] The influence of the environment is shown in the mosaic of tribes who live in the Samhar region of Eritrea.[2] These tribes show great ethnic diversity, but are uniform in their mode of subsistence, social organization, customs, and religion. Most of them are semi-nomadic and pastoral, but cultivate in the winter season.

The plateau is essentially the land of the sedentary peasant who gains his food supply by field culture or animal husbandry, or, more generally, by a combination of the two. The surrounding steppe and desert regions are the domain of the nomads. In the region towards the Red Sea and the Indian Ocean the ʿAfar and Somali, who are true nomads, inhabit the zone between the plateau and the coast. In the west the region which descends from the plateau towards the Nile is traversed by peoples with nomadic or semi-nomadic habits until one comes across settled societies again in the vicinity of the river.

The pure nomad has been called the parasite of the camel, but the camel, the goat, the sheep, and the ox are rather members of his own community like his wife and children, and for the same practical reasons; and his organized life is wholly centred round his flocks and herds. But though he has provided his means of sustenance yet, since they too are food gatherers, he has to wander with them in search of pasture and water. Still he is no aimless wanderer, it is he and not the animal who searches; he leads, not follows, his flocks.

The nomad lives in a tent because it can be easily dismantled and transported; consequently the true nomad possesses great mobility and can traverse vast areas in his search for animal sustenance. With people who live a semi-nomadic life the tribe, or more usually sections, have definite assembly places at wells or rivers to which they return from time to time. Others make periodical migrations with their flocks, spending the winter period in the lowlands or low-lying valleys and the summer on the plateau. This form of semi-nomadism is common amongst the peoples of the Sāḥil and Samhar regions of Eritrea who migrate between the high regions and the low eastern maritime plain

[1] The Italian census of 1931 for Eritrea showed that 73 per cent. of the people were settled and the remainder were nomads and semi-nomads in equal proportion. For Italian Somaliland 17·4 per cent. were sedentaries along the coast and great rivers, 42 per cent. were nomads, and 40·5 per cent. semi-nomads. Nomads, too, prevail in British, French, and Ethiopian Somalilands, and amongst the Southern Galla, whilst many peoples on the western periphery of the plateau are semi-nomads.

[2] The *Samhar* is the coastal region around Maṣawwaʿ extending inland to the foothills and some fifty miles north of Maṣawwaʿ. The region north of the Samhar as far as the Sudan border and deep into the hills to the west is known as the *Sāḥil*, but is called *Bāqla* in Abyssinian books.

or the western and northern plain. The Samhar tribes travel with their flocks and herds in the summer and cultivate along the rivers in the winter.

The kind of animal bred also has its effect on migrations. The ʿAfar, for example, are essentially nomadic herdsmen, but the few cattle-owners among them, such as those of the Buri peninsula, are less mobile than the camel-owners and cannot move far from the richer grazing lands. On the other hand, those who breed camels, which can live on herbage that is almost invisibly scanty, are not so dependent upon seasonal pasture and migrate over great distances from the sea coast to deep within the Abyssinian plateau. Such is the life of the semi-nomadic Bani ʿĀmir of Eritrea, whose camel-owners during the dry season wander far to the east and south towards and into the hills, whilst the cattle-owners have to remain close to the banks of the Gash. But during the rains each has its own well-defined grazing area. Since nomads rarely subsist entirely upon their flocks and herds, they and the cultivators are economically interdependent and exchange their commodities. Some semi-nomads cultivate during certain seasons, others possess slaves who grow crops for them, others have agriculturalists of a different race living amongst them, whilst the loss of their flocks and herds or other reasons may force a section of a tribe to turn to agriculture.

In comparison with the rest of Africa, Abyssinian agriculture is very advanced. The agriculturalists are attached tenaciously to the land, which passes from father to son as patrimony. Two types of farming are found in the region; farming by hand with the hoe, dibble, or mattock; and farming with the plough and livestock. The plough with its ploughshare formed from a heavy spear-head or nail and drawn by bulls or horses is used by the Abyssinians, and the cultivation after ploughing is done by hoes, forks, and mattocks. The implements of people such as the Galla, who have been introduced to agriculture only since they arrived in the country, still remain very primitive; the hoe, for instance, often consists merely of a pole with a nail fixed in its head, but many of the Galla of the highlands have adopted the plough and more advanced implements.

However different the forms of the dwelling in the region may seem they fall into only a few main types. The architecture and form of dwellings are tied to the resources of the country where they are built, to its climate, and to the occupation of its people. In nomadic regions the homes are simple since they must be easy to pull down, transport, and re-erect. The semi-nomadic Somali and the ʿAfar use a hemispherical hut, intermediary between a tent and a house, formed of flexible boughs and palm ribs covered with matting and skins. The prevalent type of permanent house amongst the Abyssinians is the *tukul* (Tigrē *agdo*), a cylindrical structure with a conical roof supported by a centre pole. They also have rectangular stone houses (*hudmo*) derived from the ancient Axumite type. In the highlands the houses are usually found in little groups of from four to six surrounded by a thorn fence, near a spring, and perched on a height well away from main roads. On the highest point the church, which is simply a larger hut, will be seen standing within its own walled enclosure. The sedentary Somali build much the same kind of hut. The Southern Galla make huts of straw, with hemispherical domed roofs, grouped in fives or sixes in a circle and surrounded by a thorn fence. The conditions imposed by their mode of life affect other elements besides their dwellings. The vessels used by nomads must not be fragile, so they use such things as gourds, calabashes, and vessels of wood, skin, or basketry. They do not make their own weapons and a smith-caste is a common thing in nomad society, as, for example, the Tomāl amongst the Somali and Tumtu amongst the Galla.

The social and political organization of the Muslim tribes will be discussed in the sections dealing with the particular tribes, but the main types of organization that are to be found in the region may be sketched.

The pivot of social organization amongst the sedentary Christian tribes on the central Eritrean plateau and the northern part of Abyssinia[1] is the large kinship group (*enda*) which consists of a number of families all claiming descent from a common ancestor whose name the *enda* bears. Because of the hereditary form of land tenure (*resti*), each *enda* is also a definite territorial unit. Social distinction is found between the *restenyatat* (land-owners) and *makhelai-alet* (people amidst) who hold land as tenants (*sedbi*) or by right of purchase (*worki*). Similar to the franchise right in England before the Reform Act of 1832 is the rule that only the *restenyatat* can be elected to the offices of village chief (*cheqa-shum*) and district chief (*shumonya* or *meslanē*, 'prefect'), but this distinction is in no way comparable to that between masters and serfs which we get in the Tigrē-speaking tribes of Eritrea.

Since Imperial Ethiopia dominates much of the region the main principles of political organization may be indicated. The *enda* has no chief and the permanent factor is the traditional autonomy of villages

[1] See S. F. Nadel, 'Land Tenure on the Eritrean Plateau', *Africa*, xvi (1946).

and districts embodied in the village headman and district chief who have just been mentioned. 'These village chiefs,' Miss Perham writes, 'representing continuity of tradition and the sedentary agricultural life, were the stabilizing factor in a system in which changing governors, roving armies, and a distant Emperor played the more dramatic, but often the more superficial, parts.'[1] Then there has always been the leadership of powerful local families which has often cut across all other authority, for the particular form of feudal system which developed neither destroyed the patriarchal system nor completely amalgamated with it. And finally, the direct military or civil administration by the tax-gatherers or regent-delegates who were the representatives of the emperor. The result was that the village chief was in fact under both a local chieftain and the emperor's representative. Today, however, the emperor is ruling by direct administration and the provinces are under governors appointed by him who are not of the old local families.

A completely different type of social organization is that of the Bilēn- and Tigrē-speaking tribes of Eritrea which are tribal federations possessing both a ruling-caste and a serf-caste. These tribal federations (Bilēn, Marya, Mansa, Bait Asgadē, and Bani 'Āmir) are organized as sub-tribes and kinship-groups linked together in a very loose fashion; they are all Muslim and mostly nomadic herdsmen. Since the nomadic organization is one of great fluidity, a continual process of exchange takes place amongst the members and sections of tribes. The serfs (*tigrē*) are the descendants of various groups upon whom a more advanced clan imposed itself, or who, in order to gain protection or for economic reasons, attached themselves to a strong tribe and to which they now regard themselves as belonging by common political association. The relationship between the two classes varies from tribe to tribe, but in general a reciprocal relationship, whereby the serfs received protection and the right to use their master's land and livestock in return for services rendered, kept this system working for centuries. During recent years the system has been undermined in varying degrees by the economic and political changes brought about under the new conditions of European rule. The 'Afar nomads, who like these tribes are a mixture of racial elements, are also a political rather than an ethnic unit. But the two types of 'Afar have coalesced into two classes, noble and plebeian, without too sharp distinctions, rather than into definite castes. Little consciousness of unity exists between the

[1] M. Perham, *The Government of Ethiopia* (1948), p. 275.

various tribes although they possess in common the same language, mode of life, religion, and mutual hatred of Galla and Abyssinian raiders.

The social structure of the pagan Galla tribes again is totally different from the preceding, the contrast between a democratic and an aristocratic organization. They are today under the political organization of the Abyssinians, but they formerly had a highly complex republication organization, much of which still survives, whilst their social organization continues but little modified. Each tribe is divided into a number of 'age-groups', which after a fixed term of years pass successively from one grade of political capacity to another. The group which is in the last grade but one provides the chief and all the minor magistrates. Thus the various offices pass every so many years from one group to another. In contrast to other peoples the organization of the Somali approximates more closely to the historic conception of the Arab tribes. Although the foundation of society is the kinship-group, the individual's loyalty is not confined to this smaller unit but extended to the whole tribe of which it is a part, to which he belongs by birth and in which he has definite rights. The organization of all the Sidāma tribes again varies. The Kafficho, for instance, possessed a highly complex centralized structure. At its head was the divine king, high priest of the State religion, owner of all the land and supreme war-lord. The seven aristocratic clans and their chiefs constituted with the king the summit of the structure of the state. They limited the authority of the king and had power to depose him. The land was divided into crown land and hereditary fiefs, the latter only owned by free Kafficho. Amongst these tribes also the old political organization has suffered considerable change since they came under Amharic rule whilst the general structure of their social life remains much what it was before.

Finally, the organization of the sedentary Kunāma may be mentioned as an example of a more primitive negroid people which has remained uninfluenced by the highly developed peoples who have exploited them. It is based on clans which are exogamous. Descent is counted in the female line and after marriage a man lives in his wife's home until the first child is born. The clans have a totemistic background; the Gumma, for example, have an elephant, the Karka the moon, and the Semma the buffalo, for their symbol. Some clans are invested with magical powers which, though of little political significance, play an important part in the social life of the whole tribe. Sovereignty was formerly based on the assembly of village elders, but today the Kunāma are divided politically into subtribes based on territory, each under its own chief, which are subdivided again into smaller units under chief's deputies. The clans which have been mentioned are scattered throughout the territorial units.

### (c) *Religions and their Distribution*

As north-east Africa is a museum of ethnic types and languages so it is a region of religious confusion. Occupied originally chiefly by pagan Kushites, it has been decisively influenced in its religious complexion by the vicinity of the Near East, the birthplace of the three great monotheistic religions, and the peoples who profess Christianity and Islam are much more numerous than the pagans. The proportion of adherents of the various religions is roughly:

| | *Christians* | *Muslims* | *Jews* | *Pagans* | *Total* |
|---|---|---|---|---|---|
| ERITREA . . | 390,000 | 359,000 | .. | 16,500 | 765,500 |
| ETHIOPIA: | | | | | |
| Abyssinia . | 2,900,000 | 300,000 | 60,000 | .. | 3,260,000 |
| Galla-Sidāma . | 200,000 | 500,000 | .. | 800,000 | 1,500,000 |
| Harar Prov. . | 306,170 | 780,000 | .. | 431,663 | 1,517,833 |
| Dankalia . | .. | 50,000 | .. | .. | 50,000 |
| NW. Margin . | .. | 75,000 | .. | 80,000 | 155,000 |
| SW. Margin . | 50,000 | 40,000 | .. | 400,000 | 490,000 |
| SOMALIA: | | | | | |
| Italian . . | 200 | 750,000 | .. | 10,000 | 760,200 |
| British . . | .. | 345,000 | .. | .. | 345,000 |
| French . . | .. | 46,391 | .. | .. | 46,391 |
| | 3,846,370 | 3,245,391 | 60,000 | 1,738,163 | 8,889,924 |

In treating of the three 'higher' religions we shall find that we have always to take into account a residuum of paganism which gives a distinctive character to the Christianity, Judaism, or Islam which they profess. The essence of religion in this region, as amongst all primitive peoples, is less belief than practice; the primary aim of the Christian and Muslim, as well as the animist, is to act in such a way as to win the assistance of the supernatural or to avert its wrath. Consequently in our study of Islam we shall be concerned not with the whole body of doctrine and practice in orthodox Islam but only with that part of it which actually enters into the lives of the Muslims of north-east Africa. Our aim is to give a picture of the actual religious life and thought of these African Muslims.

# DISTRIBUTION OF RELIGIONS

| | | *Christianity* | *Islam* | *Paganism* | *Judaism* |
|---|---|---|---|---|---|
| HIGH KUSHITES | North | Abyssinians (of Hamasen, Akele Guzai, Shimezana, and Serai)<br>Mansa<br>Bilen (Bogos) | Tigrē-speaking tribes: Bani ʿAmir Bait Asgede Mansa, Bait Juk Marya, &c.<br>Bilen<br>Jabarti | | |
| HIGH KUSHITES | Centre | Abyssinians (of Tigrai, Amhara, Gojam, and Shoa)<br>Agao | Jabarti | Qamant | Falasha (Kayla) |
| HIGH KUSHITES | South | Gurage<br>Sidama (Kafficho, Kambata, Chabo, Walamo, Yamma &c.) | Gurage<br>Eastern Sidama (Tambaro, Hadiya, Garo, and Alaba) | Gurage<br>Sidama (Western, Ometo, some Eastern, Northern) | |
| LOW KUSHITES | Oroma or Galla | Wallo<br>Shoan Tribes (Abichu, Gombichu, Galan, Tulama, Horro, Jimma Rare, Sibu, Chella, Liban, Mecha, Metta, Becheo, Keku, Hillu, Soddo, Chabo, Amaya) | 1. Northern: Wallo, Yejju, Raya<br>2. Galla between Gurage and Abay: Limmu, Gera, Gomma, N. Nonno, Bunno, Jimma<br>3. Harar region: Ala, Nolle, Jaso, Itu, Enia<br>4. Arusi | Leqa tribes<br>Arusi tribes<br>Boran tribes | |
| LOW KUSHITES | ʿAfar-Saho | Saho: Irob and Lab Hale (Debrimela) | ʿAfar (Danakil): Asa Mara and ʿAdo Mara<br>Saho: Asaorta, Hazu, Mini-Fere, Teroʿa, &c. | | |
| LOW KUSHITES | Somali | | Somali: Darod, Hawiya, Rahanwen, &c. | Gubbra Migo, Carrara, Sarar, Gurre | |
| | Negroids | Kunama | Kunama<br>Baria<br>Wayto<br>Bani Shangul (Berta, Watawit Gamosha)<br>Somalized Bantu (Shīdla, Shabeli, &c.) | Kunama<br>Gunza (Gumuz)<br>Gubba<br>Suri<br>Como<br>Gimira<br>Nuer<br>Mao<br>Majaño (Masongo)<br>Yambo (Anuak)<br>Mekan (Shuro)<br>Dama<br>Turkana<br>Konso<br>Gardulla<br>Bantu (various groups) | |

### (a) *Paganism*

D'Almeida, writing about 1620, gives a description of Agao paganism:

> The Agaws of Gojām are pagans and much given to fetishism. They adore a single Creator of Heaven, whom they call Dobān, but have no idols. They also worship river springs, also some species of trees and groves, sacrificing to them and offering cows, milk and butter. They bury their bodies in woods, making chambers for them and placing near their heads hydromel and the cups which they were accustomed to use in drinking when alive.[1]

The chief characteristics of Kushitic paganism from which many of the peoples of the region were converted to monotheistic religions are sketched in this extract. Groups of the Agao retained their paganism until very recent times, but today they are either Jews or Christians with the exception of the *Qamant* who are the last remnants of the pagan Agao. The Qamant live in the mountains around Gondar, in Wogera, Kerker, and Chalga. Most of them are agriculturalists. Emperor Theodore considered forcing them to become Christians[2] and did make them wear the *māteb* cord of the Christians.[3] Little is known about their religion for they are regarded as little better than lepers by Christians and Muslims and consequently conceal it. It has been suggested that it is a form of sun worship, because at daybreak they all turn to the east praying and chanting in celebration of the rising of the sun. Their religious gatherings take place in sacred groves, knowledge of whose existence is jealously guarded since no one other than themselves is allowed to enter. In these groves they gather on their knees around a leader whom they call the *womber* (stool) probably because he is the only one so seated. Their religious ceremony seems to consist of a series of prayers said by the leader and repeated by the others.[4] The residue of the cult of the pagan Agao also survives in many of the customs of the Christian Agao, Amḥara, and Tigreans.

Kushitic peoples which still remain pagan comprise the majority of the Sidāma tribes, many of the Galla tribes of the south-west such as the Lēqa, and the great Boran group of the south between Lake Stephanie and the Jūba. Each of the Sidāma tribes have their own distinctive religion, an amalgam constituted primarily from Hamitic conceptions, together with derived elements such as neo-Sudanese beliefs

[1] Quoted from Weld Blundell, *The Royal Chronicle of Abyssinia* (1922), pp. 513–14.

[2] H. A. Stern, *Wanderings among the Falashas* (1862), pp. 43–5; G. Lejean, *Théodore II*, pp 192–3.

[3] H. Rassam, *British Mission to Theodore*, i. 208–9.

[4] A. Lusana, 'L'Uogherà e l'alto Semien', *Gli Annali dell' Africa Italiana*, I. i. 172.

in a divine king and Christian ideas absorbed from the Abyssinians. Their chief deity is the sky-god, in addition to whom flourishes a supernatural realm of local nature-spirits associated with natural features such as mountain peaks, streams, and trees. Some of these became minor deities such as *Atēte*, the Galla goddess of fertility, and *Ṭalahē*, the Omēti goddess of the River Omo. Many of these spirits become incarnate in the priests who bind them by means of exorcism and magical rites. Since the Shoan conquests between 1890 and 1897 the religion of the Sidāma is in a state of flux, and large numbers have become Christians, but this has simply added to the complexity of their beliefs and practices.

Besides these Kushitic peoples who remain pagan, all the negroid tribes called Shānqelā by the Abyssinians are pagan. These include a remnant of some 3,000 of the Kunāma of south-western Eritrea, the tribes of the north-western margin of Abyssinia bordering on the Sudan (150,000, comprising the Gunza or Gumuz, Gubba, Suri, Tuma, Murle, and Giye), and all the negroid tribes of the south-west (some 500,000, comprising the Como, Abigar (Nuēr), Mao, Majãño (Masongo), Yambo (Anuak), Mekan (Shuro), Dama, Turkana, Konso, and Gardulla). No attempt can be made here to give even a brief sketch of the types of belief amongst these tribes, about which little is known, nor is it necessary as a background to the study of Muslim tribes, and a general sketch of the beliefs of the Kunāma should be sufficient as an example of the paganism of a Nilotic tribe.

The chief feature of Kunāma worship is ancestral conciliation which has as its object the maintenance of the link that secures supernatural support in the conduct of the clan's affairs and has resemblances to the rites of certain Nūba peoples of Kordofān. They have a remnant conception of a high god, *Anna*, who created the heavens and the earth, but having done that takes no further interest in the clan's affairs. Far more effective are the spirits of their dead who, though freed from the body, remain imprisoned on earth and bring good and evil to the living, wherefore they are propitiated with offerings and sacrifices. Their chief rites are agricultural, and two great annual festivals mark the beginning of cultivation and of harvesting. These are the festival of the 'dura' (*kina furda*) and that of the 'feris' at the end of the rains before the harvest, during which beverages are prepared from dura and honey and are placed on the tombs of their ancestors. They have no order of priests, sacrifices and other rites being performed by elders, the second festival by the oldest man of the family, the first by the oldest of the clan who is called *Furda Manna*, chief of customary observances. Certain clans have special functions in controlling the spirits. Such clans are the Awla Manna who control the rain spirits and the Ula Manna who protect against locust migrations.

### (β) *Judaism*

We have seen that the settlement of Semites from overseas has profoundly changed the cultural characteristics of the people of Abyssinia. The languages of the dominant peoples are Semitic and they have adopted the three monotheistic religions, Judaism, Christianity, and Islam. The Semite makes no distinction between the religious and secular aspects of life; for him social, political, and religious institutions have no separate autonomy, but are contained in religion and are aspects of it. Thus the Semite deeply influenced the life of the Kushite because he brought him a unified conception of life embodied in religions based upon revelation.

The first Semites were the pagan colonizers of Axum, but whilst these Semitic colonies were still acquiring cohesion, Judaism was introduced amongst the primitive Agao. Nothing is known about these early Jewish immigrants. Traditionally the judaized people of Abyssinia claim to be descended from the companions of Menelik I, son of Solomon and the Queen of Sheba, and also from those Jews who fled to Egypt under Johanan in 581 B.C. at the time of the Babylonian Captivity, where they reorganized the cult of the Queen of Heaven. The tradition that they are descended from the Egyptian *diaspora*[1] may not be without grounds because they know nothing of the Babylonian and Jerusalem Talmud compiled between the third and fifth centuries A.D., nor do they observe the Feast of Pūrīm, the festival commemorating the deliverance of the Jews from Haman instituted in the days of

[1] Jewish communities were widely scattered over Egypt before Johanan's time (Jer. xliv. 1) from Tahpanhes in the north where he settled (Jer. xliii. 7–9) to Pathros and Elephantine in the south. Aramaic papyri dating from the fifth and sixth centuries B.C. show that there was a Jewish military colony at Elephantine who knew nothing of the religious reform effected by Josiah in 622 B.C., and whose Judaism was full of polytheistic elements (see A. Vincent, *La Religion des Judéo-Araméens d'Éléphantine*, Paris, 1937). One of these papyri is a letter dated 408–407 B.C. which tells of the destruction of the temple of Yahū by the priests of the god Khnum (see A. Cowley, *Aramaic Papyri of the Fifth Century B.C.*, Oxford, 1923, Pap. no. 30, pp. 108–19, Petition to the Governor of Judea). The dispossessed priests and some of their community may well have travelled southwards and so reached Abyssinia. If the interpolation (*c.* 540 B.C.) in the prophecies of Zephaniah is more than empty rhetoric, 'from beyond the rivers of Kush (i.e. Nubia) my suppliants, even my dispersed community, shall bring mine offering' (Zeph. iii. 10), it may refer to Jews in Abyssinia.

Xerxes (465–425 B.C.), whilst the cult of the Queen of Heaven has become the cult of the goddess of the Sabbath.[1]

What is certain is that some Jews, probably pre-exilic, did settle in Abyssinia and eventually converted pagan Agao groups. From the racial point of view they were completely absorbed by the Agao but they left a permanent impress upon their culture. These judaized Agao lived a life of warlike independence in their highland fastnesses of Semēn, continually attacked by the Solomonid monarchs of Amḥara until the last politically independent groups were finally conquered by Susenyos, expelled from Semēn, and scattered over the north-western provinces where the majority still live as villages of agriculturalists.

These groups, who are called Falāsha or Esrā'ēl by the Abyssinians,[2] are pure Kushites. Their beliefs and customs show a mixture of pagan, Christian, and Jewish elements. Evidence of their former paganism is found in their worship of *Sanbat*, goddess of Sabbath, to whom offerings of meat, drink, and incense are made. When a Falāsha *dabtara* was asked by J. M. Flad how they were able to reconcile this with the Second Commandment he replied, 'we fear that if we leave off serving Sanbat she would withdraw her blessing, for she is the goddess of sunshine, rain, and all temporal comforts'.[3] The answer recalls that of the women of Pathros to Jeremiah.[4] Like the Christians and Muslims they retain the universal Agao beliefs in spirit-raisers, rain-makers, and evil-eye-casters, whilst they themselves are credited with a great reputation as sorcerers. Their places of worship (*masjīd*), which are distinguished by a red earthenware pot placed on a pinnacle, are divided into three sections as in the Jewish tabernacles, whilst outside the eastern door is a small enclosure containing an altar of unhewn stone where offerings

[1] If the *diaspora* had then reached South Arabia it would be natural to suppose that the Jews also took part in the South Arabian transmarine migration, but it is fairly certain that the *diaspora* did not reach South Arabia until after the destruction of Jerusalem by Titus in A.D. 70. On the other hand, the only evidence that Jews did reach Abyssinia during the first millennium B.C. is deduced from the arrested stage of the development of their Judaism. In the opinion of the writer the dissemination of Judaism came from the Jews who took such prominent part in the commerce of the later Axumite kingdom, whilst the peculiarities of their religion at the present day would be due to their utter and complete isolation from other Jews for almost 2,000 years. For the first literary mention of the warlike Jews in the highlands of Semēn, see below, p. 54 n. 2, see also p. 57.

[2] The word Falāsha (Ge'ez *falāsyān*) is derived from *falāsi* a stranger or emigrant (cf. הגולה). They are also known as *kāyla*, an Agao word of the same meaning. They do not call themselves by these names, which are convenient distinguishing terms.

[3] J. M. Flad, *The Falashas of Abyssinia* (1869), pp. 6–7.

[4] Jer. xliv. 15–19. If this early *diaspora* carried over vestiges of the worship of 'Astarte, the Canaanite Queen of Heaven, at the phases of the moon, which it has been conjectured was the origin of the Sabbath, the process of assimilation would be simple.

are sacrificed. They are therefore the only Jews in the world whose worship is focused upon the sacrifice on the altar. Their priests, as is the practice of the Eastern Churches, are not allowed to marry a second time. Both sexes are circumcised. Monday and Thursday, the new moon, and the vigil of the Passover are fast days. Their feasts are the Passover, Harvest, and Tabernacles (during which no booths are built), the Day of the Covenant, and Abraham's Day. The Sabbath is very scrupulously observed, their cattle, for instance, being left in the care of Christians. The laws of purification are also strictly enforced by the priests, so much washing being required that their villages are generally situated near a stream.

From Christianity they have adopted a monastic system. This is said to have been introduced in the fourth century by one Abbā Ṣabrā who lived as a hermit in the Cave of Hoharēwa in the Province of Armāchchaho which ever since has been their chief religious centre. Both monks and nuns live strictly regulated lives, they must prepare their own food and no lay person is allowed to enter their huts.

The Falāsha have no knowledge of Hebrew,[1] but their priests, who alone are literate, use the canonical and apocryphal books of the Old Testament in Geʿez, which they have borrowed from the Abyssinians. In the same language they possess a volume of extracts from the Pentateuch; the *Arde'et* which is read during the ceremony of purification of the newly born by immersion (*Ṭemqat*); lives of Abraham (*Gadla Abrehē*), Moses (*Gadla Musē*), and other patriarchs and prophets; a translation of Josephus (*Sana Aihud*), and the Laws of the Sabbath (*Te'zāza Sanbat*)[2] in which the Sabbath is personified as the daughter of God and mediatrix between God and man. With the exception of the last and of collections of prayers, none of the books are of Jewish origin, but are adaptations of Christian Geʿez works.

The Falāsha, who are said to number about sixty or seventy thousand, live as agriculturalists in little villages in the provinces of Dambya, Wogara, and Armāchchaho, but the complete elimination of their independent kingdoms has also led to a dispersion. They thus display the characteristic features of a penalized religious minority. They are found in many of the towns, occupying a separate quarter of their own, despised by the Christian Amḥara with whom they are

[1] An attempt has recently been made to revive their knowledge of Hebrew, and a Falāsha schoolmaster, Tamrat, had fifty young Falāsha from the north-west region learning Hebrew at Addis Ababa at the time of the Italian entry.

[2] Edit. J. Halévy, Paris, 1902.

forbidden to eat and whose houses they are forbidden to enter. They are monogamous, and most people who know them observe that their moral standards are higher than those of their Christian neighbours. They are very industrious workers, skilled in agriculture and the trades such as building, iron-work, weaving, and pottery, but even though they have to this extent left the land they have not adopted the normal characteristic occupation of a Jewish dispersion, that of commerce.

### (γ) *Christianity*

A somewhat fuller account of the Christian Church of Ethiopia will be necessary since Christianity is the official religion of the empire and the bulwark of Ethiopian nationality. Without some knowledge of it the history of Ethiopian Islam would be incomprehensible, whilst the student of living Islam will be confronted by its influence wherever he goes, even in the Muslim citadel of Harar, where the octagonal Church of the Saviour of the World, built upon the site of the chief mosque which was destroyed by the Abyssinians, and the most central object catching the visitor's eye, plays its full part in emphasizing the national aspect of Monophysite Christianity.

Christianity became the official religion of the Axumite kingdom in northern Abyssinia about A.D. 350, largely as a result of the preparation of the field by the diffusion of Greek culture, but it did not spread far beyond its borders. The Axumite Church from the first was in close touch with Alexandrian and to a lesser extent Byzantine and South Arabian Monophysite Christianity, and when the larger part of the Byzantine Empire and the Red Sea coasts were conquered by the Muslim Arabs, its relationships with the Church of Egypt became still closer and have been maintained till this day. During the historically obscure period from A.D. 650 to 1270 Christianity by some miracle spread southwards and the Monophysitism of the defunct Axumite kingdom was, by a process of assimilation and adaptation to Judaic-Agao traditions, turned into an effective medium for the expression of the spiritual aspirations of the Abyssinians. Since the foundation of the 'Solomonid' line in A.D. 1270 Christianity has been dominant in the highland fastness of Abyssinia proper, though outside it Islam has made persistent progress. Cut off from outside influences the vital forces of this Christianity ebbed, it became more and more degenerate, and reached its lowest spiritual level during the disruptive period from the middle of the eighteenth to the middle of the nineteenth centuries. But even after that, when Western influences began to affect the country more and more in other spheres of life, its religious life remained petrified and moribund in its traditional ceremonies and customs, with little influence upon the moral life of the people. At the same time Christianity has been the most important cultural factor in the lives of the Abyssinians; it was the sole repository of traditional learning, it maintained village and monastic schools, it entered fully into the lives of its adherents in the observances of feast or fast, from birth to death, but was rigidly excluded from the moral sphere.

Abyssinia has steadfastly maintained its faith as a remote outpost of the Church, cut off from all relationship with outside churches except that of the Copts. This enforced seclusion, the development of a purely indigenous form of Christianity, and the integration of the Church as the symbol of Abyssinian nationality, enabled it to preserve its faith against many dangers, although at the same time these factors paralysed its spiritual life.

*Distribution.* Reference to the map[1] will show that Christianity is practically coextensive with the homeland of the Abyssinians proper, which is the great plateau divided by the canyons of the Blue Nile and the Takkazē and their lateral rifts. This includes almost all the Tigriña- and Amḥaric-speaking peoples. Tigriña, for instance, is often called *zaravā kheshtan* (or *hēgā kestān* in Tigrē), 'the language of the Christians'. It should be remembered that the Eritrean political boundary is not a natural one, and that the central Eritrean plateau known as the Mareb Mellash, 'Beyond the Mareb' (comprising Ḥamāsēn, Akelē-Guzāi, and Serāi), and the northern part of Abyssinia known as Tigrai, form a large cultural and ethnic block whose people are sedentary agriculturalists, speak Tigriña, and are Ethiopian Christians. In eastern Agamē a large Saho group, the Irōb, is Christian. Amḥara, which is Christian in general except for settlements of Jabarti, Galla blocks, and Jewish remnants, comprises some twenty provinces of which the best known are Angot, Bēgamder with Debra Tabor, Wālqāyt, Dambya, Wagara, and Semēn. Shoa, which has a large Galla population, is Christian. These Galla tribes of Shoa who were christianized during the nineteenth century from the small state of Shoa, comprise the Abbichchu, Gombichchu, and Galān between Ankober and Enṭoṭṭo; the Tulama, Horro, northern Jimma tribes (Rare, &c.),

[1] The actual area distribution of religions shown by the map will not give a correct picture of the strength of the religions unless it is realized that the plateau regions are the most thickly populated areas and the surrounding lowlands very sparsely populated. In Eritrea, for instance, the central plateau which is Christian comprises more than half its total population.

Sibu, Chella, and Liban to the south of the Abāy; the Mecha and Mētta west of Enṭoṭṭo; the Becho, Keku, Hillu, and Soddo in the plains of the upper course of the Ḥawāsh; and the Chabo in the same direction on Mount Dendi; the Gudru near the frontier of Gojām; the Amāya near River Walga; also the Sulu, Jilli, Nonno east of Limmu, Botor, Chora, Agato, Gullallē, and Oborra.

Since Christianity is the official religion of the dominant people, a nominal conformity was enforced upon the chiefs of conquered pagan tribes such as the Sidāma and Galla, but since the conquest of Menelik there have been great movements to Christianity, particularly amongst the Walamo. Also Abyssinian officials and garrisons throughout the whole empire are Christian. In Harar Province, which is predominantly Muslim and where there were no Christians before the conquest of 1887, the Christians number 306,170 out of a total population of 1,517,833. The Wallo Galla of the plateau were forcibly converted from Islam by the Emperor John, but many of them in fact remain Muslim. Official Christianity has also made renewed progress among the Gurāgē, Kambāta, and Kafficho who were first influenced by the early Solominids. Roman Catholic missionary propaganda has spread considerably amongst the Bilēn and other tribes of Eritrea, and amongst groups of Galla and Sidāma of southern Ethiopia. Amongst protestant missions the Swedish mission has advanced farthest in building up an indigenous self-governing Church.

*Aspects of the Church in Ethiopia.* The Abyssinian form of Christianity is that of the Coptic Monophysite Church of Egypt, considerably influenced in its practice by indigenous pagan and Jewish survivals. It is orthodox in doctrine with the exception of its adherence to the Monophysite theory of our Lord's nature. It has the three orders of deacon, priest, and bishop and the seven sacraments, of which the Eucharist (*qeddāsē*) is the most important. Easter is the chief feast, but the festival of the Epiphany (*ṭemqat*),[1] which is celebrated with tremendous enthusiasm, closely follows it.

The canon law is that of the Egyptian Church which constitutes Ethiopia a diocese of that Church.[2] The Bishop of the Ethiopian

[1] *Ṭemqat*, the *ghiṭās* of the Copts, is observed as an annual commemoration of Christ's baptism as is usual in Eastern Churches and is marked by an out-door service which has its own ritual and includes the blessing of water and the sprinkling of the congregation with it. This is the ceremony which was erroneously described by the Jesuits as an annual repetition of the sacramental baptism.

[2] Following the apocryphal canons of the Council of Nicea, Canon 42. We should also note that in certain ways Abyssinian culture, isolated from that of other Christians, has, through

Church (*abūna*)[1] has consequently always been a Copt appointed by the Patriarch of Alexandria from among the monks of the monastery of St. Anthony. Rarely has there been more than one bishop and often long periods have elapsed after the death of one before the see of Alexandria and the Muslim rulers of Egypt could be communicated with and another arrive. The Ethiopian Church is, however, no mere satellite of the Church of Alexandria. It is a mistake to call the Abyssinians, from the religious point of view, Copts, as many people do, for although their Church receives its bishop from the Coptic Church it is a distinct national Church in which the spirit of the nation has found intense expression. This long dependence upon Alexandria is surprising in view of the strong nationalist feeling of the Ethiopians, but in 1929 four Abyssinian bishops were consecrated to serve along with Qerillos, the new Coptic metropolitan. The link with Alexandria was broken during the Italian occupation but restored again on the return of Hāyla Sellassē. After the war a strong party favoured the breaking of this dependence upon Alexandria, and the exact relationship between the two churches remained unsettled for some time until agreement was reached between the Coptic and Ethiopian Churches and signed on 13 July 1948. This agreement provided for the immediate consecration of five Ethiopian bishops by the Patriarch and of any subsequent bishops who might be needed during the lifetime of Archbishop Qerillos; and, after his death, the appointment by the

the medium of Coptic-Arabic literature, been slightly affected by Muslim influence. The Ethiopic *corpus iuris* called the *Fatḥā Nagast* (The Law of the Kings) was translated in the fourteenth century (according to C. Conti Rossini, 'Il Senodos etiopico', *R.R.A.L.*, ser. vii, vol. iii, 1943, pp. 41–48) from the code of the Coptic Church. This code was compiled in Arabic *c.* A.D. 1238 by Aṣ-Ṣafī ibn al-ʿAssāl when the Coptic Church felt the need to collect together the decisions of the Councils and the canonical and civil law governing the Monophysites of Egypt. The compiler, as well as some of his authorities, made use of manuals of the Mālikite *madhhab* for many sections of law for which they had no precedents (see C. A. Nallino, *Raccolta di Scritti*, iv. 371–4; A. d'Emilia, 'Influssi di diritto musulmano nel capitolo XVIII. 2 del Nomocanone arabo cristiano di Ibn al-ʿAssāl', *R.S.O.* xix (1941–2), 1–15). The *Fatḥā Nagast* was only used in the emperor's court and has too artificial a character to have greatly influenced the character, customs, and history of the Abyssinians. Although, as Guidi observes, the collection of Ibn al-ʿAssāl had served merely 'as a guide for the lawyers of his co-religionists, it was regarded by the Abyssinians as a true ecclesiastical and civil code, especially since they regarded it as of Constantinopolitan origin' (I. Guidi, *Fatḥā Nagast*, 1899, p. viii). Since Ibn al-ʿAssāl's code included these apocryphal canons of Nicea the Ethiopians accepted as a genuine decree of the Council the rule that Ethiopia was a single bishopric of the Coptic Church.

[1] *Abūna* (lit. 'our father', the Geʿez title; *abbatachin* in Amharic) denotes bishop, and not metropolitan, and confusion was caused when more bishops were consecrated since they also were *abūnas*.

Patriarch of an Ethiopian as archbishop with authority to consecrate Ethiopian bishops[1]. The link with the Coptic Church is therefore maintained only through the succession of archbishops.

Priests, who are chosen from traditional priestly families, are ordained without any training and are therefore ignorant, greedy, and lazy. A theological college was opened in 1943 but has not yet had time to influence the clergy. These are supported by the voluntary offerings of the people, by tithes, and by the land conceded to them by the State tribute-free as usufruct (the well-known ecclesiastical *gulti*). The regulations for the administration of the Church promulgated in 1942 provide that all landed property belonging to the Church or clergy shall pay land tax which shall go into the Church Treasury and be used for the extension of the Church, for schools, and similar purposes. In spite of these sources of income the reports of the wealth of the churches and monasteries are much exaggerated, and priests and monks do not live at a higher level than the peasants whom they serve. The Church wields great power because it enters into the whole life of the people and the threat of excommunication is greatly feared, but at the same time the peasant of today is well aware of its weaknesses. Economic needs often make him resist many of its claims upon him, land-hunger forces him to encroach upon its property, and land disputes are common.

A church (*bēta kristyān*) may serve one large village or in some parts a group of three or four smaller ones. It is usually perched upon an eminence overlooking the village. The construction of the most prevalent type of church scarcely differs from that of the huts of the people. It is round, often with stone walls, but a thatched roof. The better-built ones in the cities are eight-sided. The sketch (p. 31) shows a typical church. The sanctuary (*maqdas*, sancta sanctorum) into which only priests, deacons, and the king may enter, is in the centre, completely hidden from the view of the communicants in the surrounding ambulatory (the *qeddest*). In the outer ambulatory (*qēnē māhlēt*) are the *dabtara* (choirmen) and the privileged, whilst the mass of the congregation, who are technically 'excommunicate' because they are not sacramentally married, stand outside the church altogether. That not even the communicants should be able to see is of small account for they come 'to assist'. On the 'throne' (*manbar*) is placed the 'ark' (*tābot*), which like the *tabhlītha*, is a portable altar-slab of wood or stone

[1] Qerillos died in October 1950 and the Ethiopian bishop Basilyos was made archbishop on 14 January 1951.

inscribed with symbols and divine names and kept in a flat box. It is the *tābot* and not the church building which is consecrated by the bishop and gives sanctity to the church in which it is placed. At the great festivals it is carried in procession around the church.

Monasticism plays a very important part in the life of the Church. In its form it is at an arrested stage, intermediate between anchoritism and the fully developed conventual life. Theoretically the monks have a rule of life, but it is undeveloped and does not include a rule of prayer. Some are extreme ascetics cut off from the common life, but the majority work on the land or perform the general chores of the monastery such as the preparation of food. Monasteries exist in every region, most of which are of great age, though this does not apply to the visible buildings which consist of groups of ordinary huts. The monasteries used to hold large territorial fiefs but these have now been abolished and all their revenues have to be paid into the general Church Treasury. There are two great orders of monks, those of Takla Hāymānot whose head is the *echaqē*, the Superior of the Monastery of Debra Libānos and the second ecclesiastical dignitary, and those of Ewosṭātēwos who have no vicar-general.

*Pagan and Jewish Elements in Ethiopian Christianity.* The peculiar practices of the Ethiopian Church to which so much attention has been drawn are due to the isolation in which this Christian outpost developed and spread amongst pagan peoples, cut off as it was by its adherence to Monophysitism and its geographical isolation from the developing tradition of the Church. The gods of the pagans were not rooted out of the people's lives, but continued underground in a modified form as good or evil spirits. But Abyssinian Christianity never compromised with paganism; it never attempted to reset pagan elements in its orthodox worship, and they have always remained illegitimate, however much priests have believed in them and acted as witch-doctors. Dr. Cerulli has shown[1] how in recent times the gods of the Kushitic tribes of southern Ethiopia conquered by the Abyssinians continued to be worshipped by both conquered and conquerors, but were changed in the process into minor deities or nature-spirits, whereas the God of the conquerors became supreme even in the religion of the conquered. So it happened that *zār*, the sky-god of the Agao, became a possessive spirit in the popular belief of the Abyssinians. In this way Christianity, having acquired many of the elements of Kushitic paganism, could easily be accepted by subjected peoples. Cerulli writes of the

[1] E. Cerulli, *E.O.* ii. 35.

Chabo of south-west Ethiopia, who speak Oromo but are of mixed Gurāgē and Sidāma origin:

As amongst all the other Galla groups, so also with the Chabo their Monophysite Christianity, accepted as a result of Abyssinian domination, has superimposed itself upon the local paganism without destroying their ancestral beliefs and practices. And I have already noted how, in the same extraordinary syncretism of the Galla, Islam once adopted has always been able to substitute itself for paganism less superficially than Monophysite Christianity. This, on the other hand, depends not only on the character of the Muslim religion but also, and in great part, on the fact that Monophysite Christianity (as it is practised by the Abyssinians) had already acquired by itself many elements of the pre-existent pagansim of the peoples of the northern Ethiopian plateau.[1]

The use in church services of the sistrum (a kind of rattle) has been acquired through the Nubian Church from the pagan worship of Egypt. The sacred groves around the churches have come down from pagan Agao cult. The excessive cult of the Virgin Mary reflects the worship of a pagan goddess, perhaps the Earth-Mother. Mary haunts high mountains, springs, and sycamore trees, the former abodes of pre-Christian genii. Christians, like everyone else, believe in a whole host of evil spirits (*genni*, *jānēn*). The *buda* (*ṭabīb* in Tigriña) is an evil influence which possesses. The devil called *Wadde-genni* in Tigrē and *Tegrida* or *Tigertī* in Tigriña is a spirit in which possesses and makes people mad or ill; whilst *Werzelya*, the Abyssinian Lilith, kills or injures children. For protection against these and other spirits everybody carries amulets, which are magical prayers and formulae written by priests on scrolls or in little booklets and carried in leather cases around the neck and arms, and Muslims will be found wearing these Christian amulets as well as others obtained from their own holy men. Much of the Ethiopian magical literature has been influenced by and even in part translated from Arabic books on magic.[2] The *dabtara* and the priests (or wizards, for the two words are interchangeable according to the type of rite being performed) perform many rites of exorcism; one is by burning the root or branch of the ghost tree with appropriate incantations. At the rite of dedicating a church four oxen, four sheep, and four goats are sacrificed. The book attributed to Abū Ṣāliḥ refers to the sanctioning of this practice by the Patriarch Cyril about A.D. 1080, although such was not the practice of the Coptic Church.[3] Certain feasts (Nativity, Our

[1] E. Cerulli, *E.O.* ii. 165–6.

[2] See C. Conti Rossini, 'Lo ʿAwda Nagast, scritto divinatorio etiopico', *R.S.E.* i. 127.

[3] *Churches and Monasteries of Egypt* (trans. B. T. A. Evetts, 1895), p. 291. This work was actually written by a Copt, Saʿad Allāh ibn Jirjis ibn Masʿūd.

Lady, St. Michael, and others) are celebrated once a month, a practice which probably goes back to the ancient Semitic lunar calendar.

Many Jewish practices are observed by the Christians;[1] such are the distinction between clean and unclean animals, which in the main follows the Old Testament ruling, and the duty of a man to marry his deceased brother's wife. The keeping of the Sabbath (*Qadāmit Sanbat*) as well as Sunday (*Sanbata Krestiyān*) is not a survival from Judaism but a practice which had grown up and was finally enforced by Emperor Zar'a Yāʿqob because controversy over it was upsetting the unity of the Church. It is probable that some of these practices are direct survivals of Judaism as a result of the absorption of Jewish Agao tribes, especially since a number of religious words (e.g., *gahannam*, hell; *ṭāʿot*, idol; *fesh*, Easter; *aṭhara*, purification) were taken directly from Hebrew or Jewish Aramaic. On the other hand, some of these Jewish practices, like the observance of the Sabbath mentioned above, may be due to excessive and uncritical reverence for the Old Testament since their Semitic culture would make much of the Mosaic Law appear natural to the Christians of Abyssinia.

*Roman Catholicism.* The Roman Catholics of the Ethiopian rite should be mentioned. In the eighteenth century an Italian Lazarist, Giustino de Jacobis (d. 1860), realizing how dearly the attempt of the Jesuits to latinize the Ethiopians at the beginning of the seventeenth century had cost them, brought a new spirit into Roman propaganda by retaining the Ethiopian liturgy and insisting only upon the observance of the Roman canons and dogmatic unity. His first concern was to form an indigenous ministry which is the indispensible preliminary to church life of any permanence. In this way he succeeded in spreading a form of Roman Catholicism which was indigenous in liturgy and ministry, depending upon its own Eritrean bishop with his see at Asmara. It has now some 40,000 members in Eritrea chiefly in Akelē Guzāi, Agamē, Serāi, Ḥamāsēn, amongst the Bilēn, and in all the towns. In 1916 a large church was erected over the grave of de Jacobis at Hebo near Saganeti, on the slopes of ʿAddi Gabru, which is visited by both national Church and Catholic Christians to pray for rain. Roman Catholic missions were begun in southern Abyssinia in 1847 by Guglielmo Massaia, the great missionary to the Galla, and strong churches have been built up from pagans in the southern regions.[2]

[1] On Jewish survivals in Abyssinian Christianity see C. Rathjens, *Die Juden in Abessinien* (Hamburg, 1921), pp. 42–59.

[2] The regional distribution of *native* Roman Catholics in 1940 was as follows: Eritrea

(δ) *Distribution of Islam.*

The region which is the subject of our survey is almost entirely surrounded by Muslims, for Islam is the religion of the Northern Sudan, Egypt, Arabia, and the coastal region of Kenya; only in the south and south-west does it border on pagan countries in the Southern Sudan and the north-west frontier province of Kenya. Owing to the proximity of Arabia Islamic influence has been felt since the days of the Prophet Muḥammad, with the result that today half the people of the region are Muslims.

In the north all the indigenous tribes of the low-lying districts of Eritrea and the Red Sea coast are Muslim. They comprise the negroid Baria, Beja tribes such as the Bani 'Āmir and Bait Asgedē (Ḥabāb, Ād Taklēs, and Ād Tamāryām); two-thirds of the Bilēn; the Mansa, Bait Juk, Marya, and Saho; that is, all except the pagan and Christian Kunāma, a minority of the Bilēn, and the Monophysite Christians of the highlands of Ḥamāsēn, Akelē Guzāi, and Serāi. In the Abyssinian highlands of entrenched Christianity there are many villages of Muslims, whilst Muslim colonies are found in all the towns. This Islamic *diaspora* in the highlands we shall call Jabarti for convenience' sake, though the Abyssinians use the term in a much wider sense for any kind of Muslim. In general, except for Yamanite colonies, these highland Muslims are of the same racial stock as the Abyssinians and the islamization of some groups goes back to early waves of Islamic penetration; but though of the same race as the Abyssinians they are psychologically aliens, their difference being that between the son of the house and the child of the ghetto. They are mainly merchants and artisans with some peasants. Apart from the Jabarti a large Muslim block exists in the highlands, comprising the Galla groups known as the Rāya (Azēbo), Yajju, and Wallo. The hunting caste called Wayṭo who live on the southern and western shores of Lake Ṭāna are Muslims, but they are despised by their co-religionists.

In the extreme west the Islamic current from the Sudan has entered into the Bani Shangūl country where most of the Berta of that province and some of the western Galla are Muslims. In the east the nomadic 'Afar (Danākil) and Somali, roaming over vast stretches of desert and steppe, are entirely Muslims. In the southern pagan area a strong influx

40,519, Tigrai 2,724, Amḥara 75, Dessié 150, Shoa 2,500, Wolamo 20,000, Kaffa 6,000, Jimma 10,718, Harar 2,388, Somalia 300, total 85,374 (*Annali dell' Africa Italiana*, iii (1940), 713–20). These figures, even if exaggerated, do give a picture of the relative strength of Roman Catholicism in the various regions.

is found along the line passing from Harar first up the Ḥawāsh, and then south of Addis Ababa through the Gurāgē country to Gorē. Harar in the south-east is a strong Muslim centre which has influenced all the surrounding Galla tribes (Alā, Nōllē, Jāso, Itu, and Enia). Half of the Galla of the provinces of Arūsi and Bāli are at least nominally Muslim. Another strong Islamic centre is found in the region of the River Gibē, consisting of the former kingdoms of Jimma Abba Jifar, Gēra, Limmu Enārya, Gomma, and Guma; whilst in the surrounding areas of Bunno, Nonno, Waliso, Botor, and Gurāgē are Muslim minorities. Amongst the Sidāma tribes only the Hadiya of Qabēna, the Alaba, Gāro, and Ṭambaro are Muslim, and they in little more than name for they actually practice their old Kushitic pagan cult as do their neighbours the Kambāta who are nominally Christian.

The study of Islam amongst the Muslims of north-east Africa which follows is divided into three main sections: in the first, which is historical, we shall try to show how it came, how it spread, and its centuries of conflict with Christian Abyssinia; in the second we shall give a sketch of the mode of life, social structure, and religious characteristics of each of the peoples who have been islamized, together with an account of what is known of their conversion; whilst the third will deal with the special characteristics of Islam in the region as a whole.

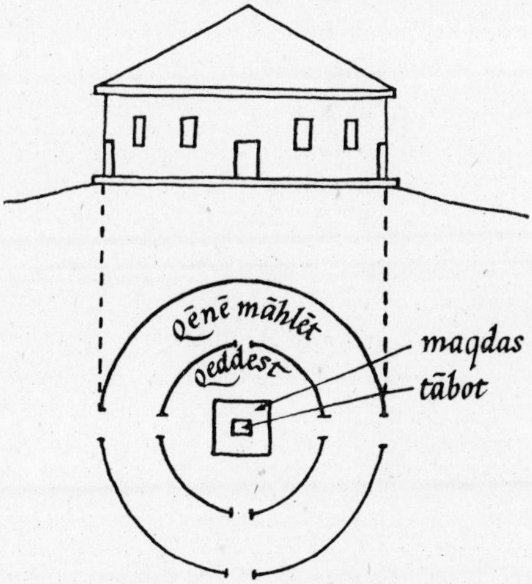


TYPICAL ETHIOPIAN CHURCH
Sketch of Elevation and Plan.

# 2

# The Conflict of Christianity and Islam in Ethiopia

## I. HISTORICAL SKETCH OF THE REGION BEFORE THE RISE OF ISLAM

### (*a*) *Semitic Colonization in Abyssinia*

We have already shown how the pastoral Kushitic tribes who formed the predominant racial element in northern Abyssinia suffered a profound cultural modification through Semitic migrations.[1] The main Semitic influx was around the seventh century B.C. The most important group was the Ḥabashat who, migrating from the Sahartan Province of Yaman,[2] gave their name to the whole country affected by the settlement and occupied the northern parts of Tigrai. Another important group was the Geʿez, whose language was to become the literary vehicle of Christianity,[3] who settled in the Shimezāna, Akelē-Guzāi, and Agamē.

Agriculturalist mountaineers never become nomad shepherds and the Yamanites crossed the plains and settled on the plateau. In Yaman their rural economy depended upon artificial irrigation. Their method of cultivation was by terracing along the steep slopes of the mountains, they had systems of canalization and used elaborate hydraulic devices. The dam of Ma'rib, whose construction is recorded in an early inscription (*c.* 750 B.C.), was particularly famous, and its breaking soon after A.D. 542 is traditionally associated with the failure of irrigation in Southern Arabia, although it was actually the result of the decline of the Sabaean kingdom. The colonization of the northern highlands, therefore, took place when South Arabia was in a high state of civilization, and the colonizers after leaving the inhospitable coastal zone behind them and ascending to the plateau, found a country which pos-

[1] See above, p. 7.

[2] C. Conti Rossini, 'Sugli Ḥabašāt', *R.R.A.L.*, ser. v, vol. xv (1906), pp. 39–59) believes the colonizers to have come, not from the Ḥaḍramawt as Glaser supposed, but from western and south-western Yaman. See also C. Conti Rossini, *Storia di Etiopia* (1928), i. 109.

[3] *Geʿez*, plur. *Agʿāziyān*, 'emigrants' and so, 'the free', from root *gaʿaza*, to emigrate. Ethiopic is known as *lesāna geʿez*, 'the tongue of the Geʿez'. The most ancient text that has been discovered is the inscription on the obelisk of Maṭara, near Senafē, which has been dated in the third century A.D.

sessed the same temperate climate and vegetation as their own land. At the beginning of our era these immigrant Arab tribes had become fused with the original Kushites whom they had infused with Semitic culture. The Sabaean language was changing to the Ethiopic form known as Geʿez. The Ḥabashat had assumed predominance over all the other tribes, and its chief took the title of *negus nagasti* (chief of chiefs). The kingdom of the Ḥabashat consolidated itself about the third century B.C., when its rule extended over the plateau regions of Eritrea and northern Tigrai. An ancient city of this Sabaean civilization was Ava (now called Yeḥā) where monoliths, a temple to the sun-god, and Ḥimyāritic inscriptions dating from the seventh to the fifth century B.C. have been discovered.[1] Axum subsequently became the capital where 'a highly perfected form of stone-worship, associated with sacrifices to the sun',[2] flourished.

The Semitic migrations from Arabia, we have said, were not of nomad tribes but the immigration of peasants and agriculturalists who came as settlers and colonizers. This is shown, not only by the fact that in Yaman they were organized not as tribal but as territorial units (*ashʿāb*) who brought their regional names with them, but also because they settled, not along the coastal plains which would attract nomads, but in the regions most suitable for agriculture on the plateaux of what are now called Eritrea and Tigrai. With them they brought the fully developed civilization of the Sabaeans. They introduced the use of metals, certain domestic animals, new plants, advanced systems of irrigation and agriculture, new forms of communal organization, and the art of writing. Thus these highlands became the diffusion centre of a new civilization. This South Arabian immigration into Africa cannot be compared in any way to the later Muslim Arab infiltrations. By their policy of allowing only Islam in Arabia,[3] the Muslim rulers of Arabia completed the destruction of the Yaman begun by the Abyssinians and Persians. Their action within Arabia differed from their policy in the lands of the former Byzantine and Persian Empires where the Arabs were very tolerant towards 'the People of the Book', taking over much of their civilization, to which Islam gave a new orientation. On the other hand, the Islamic immigrants from Arabia to north-east Africa were relatively small groups of traders, adventurers, and refugees

[1] On the ruins of Yeḥā see Bent, *The Sacred City of the Ethiopians*, chap. viii, and Littmann, *D.A.E.* ii. 78–89; iii. 72–74; iv. 57–61.

[2] Bent, op. cit., p. 191.

[3] The Christians of Yaman were expelled by ʿUmar ibn al-Khaṭṭāb in A.H. 20; cf. Caetani, *Annali dell' Islam*, iv. 354–9.

whose creed had lost the vitalizing elements which gave an irresistible impulse to the earlier Muslim Arab bands and spread them over the civilized lands of the Near East. They were isolated elements which either set up trading colonies or inserted themselves into groups of Hamitic pastoral Beja, ʿAfar, and Somali in the desert and steppe plains. Being without women they took African wives and gave birth to an aristocracy of Arab blood which aided the spread of Islam as a factor in the Arab heritage. This aristocracy soon became a mere fiction, leaving traces in the genealogy and customs of the indigenous folk, but scarcely altering the rhythm of their lives. In contrast to this Islamic immigration, the pre-Islamic, South Arabian Semitic migrations of large groups of agriculturalists together with their women put down deep and permanent roots. The moral force of the civilized Yamanite over the Hamitic tribes permeated and revolutionized the very rhythm of life of the peoples amongst whom they settled and with whom they intermarried, and thereby created a social and cultural order which endures to this day. The cultural achievements of the ancient Axumite kingdom can still be appreciated through the remains of temples and towns, steles and obelisks, reservoirs and dams, scattered over the region where they settled, whilst the influence of its culture was felt in regions which were extremely remote from the original centre of radiation.

The Axumite population was formed by the fusion of the immigrant South Arabians with the original Hamites. Political and social institutions were introduced fully developed from Arabia, and Semitic institutions such as the patriarchate, the right of primogeniture, territorial organization, and collective ownership took the place of the Hamitic social organization based upon the matriarchate, the authority of the maternal brother, and the assembly of elders, still retained by some of the Hamitic tribes of the region. The position of women was high among both the South Arabians and the Hamites with whom they coalesced. The farther away one gets from the original centre of cultural radiation the weaker becomes the strength of the Semitic element in the social life and individual characteristics of the people.

### (*b*) *The Kingdom of Axum*

When the various groups of Semitic, Kushitic, and negroid tribes had fused into a racial and cultural homogeneity and a ruling house had been recognized by the feudal chieftains, the kingdom of Axum, securely established in the mountains, could influence the plains and coastal areas, encourage commerce, develop the Red Sea ports, and make expeditions into the Nubian plains and south-western Arabia.

The colonizing Semites came into contact and conflict with many tribes inhabiting north-eastern Africa who all play an important part in subsequent history. They were in contact with the derived Egyptian civilization of Meroë along the Nile, with nomadic Beja tribes and Nilotics such as Bāryā in the north-western plains, and with Agao tribes in the mountains. These external contacts had little influence upon the social, cultural, and political life of the kingdom, but provided a continual record for the inscriptions of nomadic raids and Axumite punitive or predatory expeditions.

Whilst the Axumites had developed a characteristic indigenous civilization which owed little to outside influences other than the Sabaean civilization from which it was derived, its commercial development was to bring it into more direct touch with the outer world. The two most important external cultural influences on the Axumite world were those of the Greeks and Jews. The profound influence which Greek culture had upon the world in general affected even this region. The Ptolemies founded commercial bases along the Red Sea coast and their very number shows the good relationship that existed between their merchants and the Axumites. Such colonies, acting as centres from which Hellenism was diffused, influenced Axum in a variety of ways. The unknown author of *The Periplus of the Erythræan Sea*, who visited Axum about the middle of the first century A.D., writes of its commercial relations with the Graeco-Egyptians and observes that Zoskales the king was 'acquainted with Greek literature'.[1] Greek influence was especially felt in the organization of commerce and the development of ports and trade-routes, but it also affected the organization of the army and the educational and administrative systems. The Ptolemaic practice of recruiting coloured troops for service in the ports on the Red Sea introduced the Axumites to the Greek military system, whilst Christianity was later introduced through the Graeco-Egyptian commercial colonies.

The influence of the Jews was also considerable, not so much upon Axum itself as upon groups of unsemitized Agao. The Jewish *diaspora* was scattered throughout all the commercial centres of the Ancient World and the activities of these colonies extended along the Red Sea coasts and up the Nile through the kingdoms of Meroë and Axum. These Jewish commercial centres became cells of religious propaganda.

[1] *The Periplus of the Erythræan Sea* (trans. W. H. Schoff, 1912), p. 23.

Perhaps before the consolidation of Axum, but more likely between the first and sixth centuries A.D., Judaism penetrated through the *diaspora* to remote centres in the interior where it became an ethnical characteristic of groups of Agao who continued to maintain their national integrity against the other stream of semitizing influence radiating from Axum. Most of these judaized Agao later became Monophysite Christians and were the primary source of the Jewish customs which are found in Abyssinian Christianity.

These commercial and cultural currents, together with the unsevered link with South Arabia, combined to throw the Axumite kingdom into the wider current of affairs outside its own borders and the result was the undertaking of a number of military expeditions both into the western plains and across the Red Sea. Those into the Sudan against Bāryā, Beja, and Nubians were sometimes predatory, but they were primarily intended to assure the security of the kingdom; those across the Red Sea resulted in their becoming the political masters of their former kinsmen in Yaman from whom they were now strongly differentiated.

For the first three centuries A.D. the kings of Axum had been extending their boundaries westwards and northwards. Their raids reached as far as Meroë where at least one Axumite king set up a throne to celebrate his victory and receive tribute. The first campaign into South Arabia is recorded in the inscription of Adulis (*c.* A.D. 277–90)[1] which relates how the King of Axum waged war from Leukē Komē (al-Ḥawrā') southwards as far as the land of the Sabaeans and from the Land of Incense in the east to the lands of Ethiopia and Sasu in the west. The inscription also records three other expeditions: one towards the east against tribes like the Geʿez and across the Takkazē into Semēn; others were against nomads such as the Beja in the north and the Saho in the south-east. The date and duration of this conquest is uncertain, but an interruption in the series of royal inscriptions in South Arabia from *c.* A.D. 300 to 378 and especially the trilingual inscription of ʿĒzānā,[2] who calls himself 'King of the Axumites, Ḥimyārites, Raydān, Sabaeans, Salḥīn, Ṣiyāmo, Beja and Kāsū', seems to show that a little before the accession of ʿĒzānā[3] the Arabs of Yaman had come under Axumite rule. Their occupation did not last long

[1] *D.A.E.* i. 42–43.

[2] Littmann, *D.A.E.* iv. 4 ff.; A. Kammerer, *Essai sur l'histoire antique d'Abyssinie* (1926), pp. 87–88.

[3] The dates of ʿĒzānā's reign are uncertain, but it probably commenced shortly after A.D. 320 and lasted until after 342.

for records of Yamanite kings reappear on inscriptions in A.D. 378 and last until A.D. 524 when the Axumites again conquered south-western Arabia. 'Ēzānā himself, the greatest of the kings of Axum, turned his energies inland towards the Nile in a number of campaigns recorded on the inscription and included most of the nomadic Beja in his rule. One campaign was directed against the negroid Nūba who by the beginning of the fourth century had occupied the kingdom of Meroë (Eth. *Kāsū*, Meroitic *Q'š*).

We know little about the religion of the Axumites save the names of their chief deities. The deities and cults of the Sabaeans varied from place to place and many could not survive the transmarine migration without suffering profound modification. Deities whose power was coextensive with a particular locality could not emigrate at all; those that could were the more universal ones like planets and the earth and these moulded themselves to suit the new environment. The chief god was probably *'Astar*, god of the sky, who could survive migration. He was a male deity like the *'Athtar* of the Minaeo-Sabaean and Ḥimyārite inscriptions, whereas the North Arabian *'Astarte* (Heb. *'Ashtōrēt*) was feminine. It was probably this god which was by syncretism turned into the Christian 'God of the Heavens' of the later inscription of 'Ēzānā. *Maḥrem*, the god of the royal house, was an important figure in all state functions for the kings call themselves 'Sons of Maḥrem' in their inscriptions. He was also the god of the war and appears in the Greek inscriptions under the name of Ἄρης (Mars). *Beḥēr* is the god of the land and probably of the sea (Arab. *baḥr*) since he is called Ποσειδών in the Greek inscriptions. He also appears to be identified with *Meder*, the Earth-Mother. The Ethiopian Christian word for God, *egzi'a beḥēr*, probably meant originally 'Lord of Beḥēr' as well as 'Lord of the World'. All these names appear together on one inscription of 'Ēzānā in which the throne is dedicated to 'Astar, Beḥēr, and Meder; whilst thanks are offered to Maḥrem, the god 'who begat the king'. Little is known of the practice of the official cult. Certainly the whole of the communal life of the Axumites was impregnated with their religion. Being an agricultural people they accompanied the stages of the year with their appropriate religious ceremonies. The temples were great foundations with colonies of priests, which received the offerings of the people who wished to propitiate and obtain the favours of their gods. 'Thrones' and statues were erected to the various gods and one inscription shows that bulls and captives were sacrificed to Maḥrem.

### (c) *The Introduction of Christianity into the Kingdom of Axum*

During the first centuries of our era Christian communities had grown up in North Africa, and in Egypt, where by the reign of Constantine (A.D. 306–37) the mass of the people had become Christian. In North Africa the Church never became truly indigenous, but in Egypt its triumph over the emasculated cult of the old gods and its absorption by the Egyptians was such that it became an integral part of Egyptian life, stimulated a vernacular Christian literature, and, in its Monophysite form, became the bulwark of Egyptian nationalism.

Christianity was introduced into the kingdom of Axum at an early date through its commercial and maritime relations with the Byzantine Empire, but the actual founders of the Axumite Church were the castaway Syrians, Frumentius and Aedesius, although those early Christian merchants gave them a foundation upon which to build.[1] An unusually good source for their history is the *Ecclesiastical History* of the monk Rufinus[2] (d. A.D. 410), who states that he got his information directly from Aedesius himself (*ipso Aedesio referente*).

Rufinus relates that Meropius, a philosopher (more probably, a merchant) of Tyre, set out on a voyage of exploration in the direction of 'India' accompanied by two young relatives, the elder of whom was Frumentius and the younger Aedesius. During the voyage the boat touched at a port on the African coast of the Red Sea for water. The inhabitants of the place, as a result of injuries received from the crew of a trading vessel, had recently broken their alliance with Byzantium, and massacred Meropius and the whole of the crew, with the exception

[1] Confusion about the foundation of the Church in Abyssinia has often been caused because the term Ethiopia is used by classical writers sometimes in a broader sense to indicate the whole of East Africa south of Libya (Herod. iv. 197), sometimes in a narrower sense to indicate the Nubian kingdoms with a derived Egyptian culture (ἡ Αἰθιοπία ὑπὲρ Αἰγύπτου, Herod. ii. 146). India and Arabia are also often confused with it. The Ethiopian eunuch of Acts viii. 24 ff. was an officer of Queen Candace of the Nilotic kingdom of Meroë, whom Eusebius (*Church History*, II. i, § 13) and others claim as a missionary to his people. Other church historians make one or other of the Apostles the first preachers to the Axumites; thus Jerome (*Cat. Script*.i. 262) gives St. Andrew, Rufinus (*Ecc. Hist*. x. 9) and Socrates (i. 19) give St. Matthew, and St. Chrysostom (*Hom*. 31) gives St. Thomas as the first preacher to the Ethiopians. Origen's remark, 'we are not told that the Gospel has been preached among *all* the Ethiopians' (*Origenis Opera Omnia*, ed. Lommatzsch, 1834, iv. 271) merely implies that Christianity had reached some African people. The term Ethiopians was not appropriated by the Abyssinians until after the time of the Axumite king's inscription quoted by Cosmas Indicopleustes where the king records that he reduced amongst others the peoples 'to the west as far as the country of Ethiopia and Sasu' (*The Christian Topography*, trans. McCrindle, 1897, p. 65; *Patr. Gr.* lxxxviii. 105). Here he refers to the kingdoms of the Nile as Ethiopia.

[2] *Historia Ecclesiastica*, *Patr. Lat.* xxi. 478–80.

of the two boys who were discovered sitting quietly under a tree, reading and meditating. These two were sold as slaves to the king. They quickly gained his interest and won his confidence and he made Aedesius his cup-bearer and Frumentius keeper of his finances and rolls (*rationes suas scriniaque*). On his death-bed the king appointed his wife regent during the minority of his son ʿĒzānā and released the two Syrians, but at the queen's request they agreed to remain to assist in the administration of the country. During his stay in Axum, 'Frumentius was led by some divine impulse (*Deo mentem ejus et animos instigante*) to make diligent enquiry whether there were any Christians among the Greek merchants who frequented or resided in the country, to give them authority and advice about building prayer-houses, . . . and to adopt all necessary and opportune methods whereby the Christian seed might spring up among them'. When the minority of the prince was over the two brothers left the country and shortly afterwards Aedesius became a presbyter of the Church of Tyre where later he met Rufinus and told him the story. Frumentius, however, went to Alexandria where Athanasius had recently been appointed bishop,[1] to urge him to send a bishop to supervise the Christians who had been gathered in Axum. Athanasius in council with his brother bishops carefully considered the request and then appointed Frumentius himself as the most suitable man to build up the Church in the Axumite kingdom.[2]

Within the lifetime of Frumentius and ʿĒzānā Christianity became the official religion of Axum. During the first century and a half after the official conversion the masses do not seem to have been greatly influenced by the new faith and continued in their worship of the old gods. The 'Lord of the Heavens' of ʿĒzānā's inscription would not

[1] Nam is *nuper* sacerdotium susceperat. Athanasius was made bishop in A.D. 328.

[2] Rufinus, loc. cit. I. ix. Frumentius's consecration may be placed between A.D. 341 and 346. Other sources of supporting evidence are: (i) A letter of Constantius II (A.D. 337–61) written to Aizanas and Sazanas, princes of the Axumites, urging them to replace Frumentius by Theophilus, an Arian bishop. This corrects the geographical error and confines the date between A.D. 328, the year of Athanasius's consecration, and A.D. 356 when Athanasius wrote his *Apologia ad Constantium* (see *Patr. Gr.* xxv, 636, and translation by J. H. Newman, *Athanasius: Historical Tracts*, 1843, pp. 182–3). This embassy, which was successful with the King of Sabaʿ but failed to penetrate into Axum, is also mentioned in the *Ecclesiastical History* of Philostorgius (360–430), as epitomized by Photius (trans. E. Walford, 1855, pp. 443–6). (ii) In his earlier inscriptions ʿĒzānā calls himself 'Son of the invincible Maḥrem', whilst in the latest in which he records his victory over the Nūba, no pagan deity is mentioned and he attributes his victory to 'the Lord of the Heavens, who has power over all things in heaven and earth . . . who reigns for ever', Littmann, *D.A.E.* iv. 32–42. (iii) The early coins of ʿĒzānā have the pagan symbol of the crescent and the star whilst the later coins have the symbol of the Cross.

appear to them to be other than ʿAstar. But when about A.D. 480 in the reign Al-ʿAmida the monastic movement reached Ethiopia, the Axumite fusion of immigrants and aborigines, Semites and Kushites, were influenced in such a way that they became intolerant and fanatical adherents of Christianity. Tradition states that nine monks came from Syria as missionaries to reform the faith in Axum.[1] They founded monasteries, introduced the Alexandrine liturgy and liturgical music, translated the Greek-Syrian Gospels into Geʿez, and, after their death, came to play a great role in local hagiography. These monks were Monophysites for this anti-Hellenic reaction was very strong in the district of Edessa and West Syria from whence the 'nine saints' came. They taught the Monophysite doctrine to the Axumite Christians and this cemented a tendency which had commenced earlier, for, from the beginning, Axumite Christianity was dependent upon Alexandria and followed it in dogma and ritual.[2] Cosmas Indicopleustes confirms that at the beginning of the sixth century A.D. the court and country of Axum were mainly Christian.[3]

The conversion to Christianity was the most revolutionary event in the history of Abyssinia. The way had been prepared by the radiation of the Hellenic civilization whereby Axum gained a cultural link with the Mediterranean world. The official conversion of Axum under ʿĒzānā constituted a political link with the Byzantine Empire which regarded itself as the protector of Christendom. At the same time Christianity had been spreading in South Arabia,[4] and this link with its former home once again drew Axum into South Arabian adventures.

[1] See *Acta Sanctorum Yārēd et Panṭalēwon*, ed. C. Conti Rossini, *C.S.C.O.*, *Scr. Aeth.*, ser. ii, vol. xvii (1904), p. 40.

[2] The Church of Egypt seceded in A.D. 452 after the condemnation of the Patriarch Dioscoros for heresy by the Council of Chalcedon. Since the sixth century Monophysites have often been known as Jacobites, after James Baradeus, Bishop of Edessa, but the Monophysites of Egypt should not be called Jacobites since their theological position antedates that of the Syrians.

[3] *Patr. Gr.* lxxxviii, 169; trans. McCrindle, p. 120.

[4] The conversion of South Arabia to Christianity is veiled in obscurity. It is obvious, as Greek and Syriac writers report, that commerce must have carried Christians there at an early date, but the first definite account of a Christian mission is that of the Arian Theophilus in the reign of Constantius II about A.D. 354/5 which has already been mentioned. Theophilus founded three churches: one at the capital *Τάφαρον* (Ẓafār), another at the Roman market of *Ἀδάνον* (Aden), and a third at a colony on the Persian Sea which may have been Hormuz or Kane. As-Samʿāni considers that Theophilus merely converted the Christians who were already there to Arianism (G. S. Assemani, *Bibliotheca Orientalis Clementino-Vaticana*, 1719–28, vol. iii). Other sources (*Chronicle of Seʿert*, *Patr. Or.* v. 330–1) show that Nestorianism was also introduced early in the fifth century through the agency of a merchant of Najrān called Ḥayyān (or Ḥannān). He was converted at al-Ḥīra in ʿIrāq which changed officially from paganism to Nestorianism in A.D. 450.

The Ḥimyārites with their capital at Ẓafār (near Yarīm) had become powerful after the expulsion of the Axumites; and at the same time Judaism, by diffusion from the Ḥijāz colonies of Yathrib and Khaibār, began to make rapid progress in Yaman.[1] During the reign of Justin one Masrūq or Dhū Nuwās[2] became King of the Ḥimyārites, embraced Judaism, and persecuted the Christians. The virtual extermination of the Ḥimyārite Christians of Najrān in A.D. 523[3] caused them to appeal to Ela-Aṣbeḥā,[4] King of Axum, to intervene and defend his persecuted co-religionists. His army crossed the straits in A.D. 524, overthrew Dhū Nuwās, and installed prefects or governors.[5] Axum, now at the height of its power, possessing the richest port in Arabia, whose commercial relations reached as far as Persia, Ceylon, and China, had become a recognized member of the circle of Christian powers.

The Axumite conquest of Yaman as usual was but transitory. Abraha, viceroy of Gabra Masqal son of Kālēb, made himself virtually independent. He built a church at Ṣanʿā which he called al-Qullais (ἐκκλησία) as a counter-attraction to the pilgrimage to Mecca and, according to Muslim tradition, as the result of the assassination of a Ḥijāzian ally of his, attempted an expedition, which included a number of elephants, to destroy Mecca itself. According to one account the Quraish conceded a third of the Tihāma to save the sanctuary; according to another the Black Stone was saved by a miracle. A chapter (Sūra cv) is named after this expedition in the Qur'ān and it plays a great part in later Muslim tradition: the year of the Prophet's birth, for instance, is called 'the year of the elephant', though this does not agree with the chronological facts.[6]

[1] There were numerous Jewish communities in Yaman in the time of Constantius II (337–61), cf. Philostorgius, *Hist. Eccles.*, vol. iii, chap. 4.

[2] He is called 'Masrūq King of the Saracens' in *The Book of the Himyarites* (ed. A. Moberg, Lund, 1924); *Δουναάς*, i.e. Dhū Nuwās, in *Acta S. Arethae*. Professor Moberg regards this episode as nationalistic and political rather than religious, part of the age-long rivalry between Persia and Byzantium, represented in this case by Masrūq and the Axumites (op. cit., p. lxx).

[3] The constancy in faith of the martyrs of Najrān appears to be referred to in the Qur'ān (lxxxv. 4–11), but this interpretation is now proved to be untenable.

[4] In the *Acta S. Arethae* and in *The Christian Topography of Cosmas* he is called Elesbaan and by the Ethiopian chroniclers Kālēb, which does not mean 'dog' as has often been stated, for that is *kalb* in Ethiopic as in Arabic, but is the Ethiopic form of Caleb (Num. xiii. 6).

[5] Procopius, *De Bello Persico*, i. 19–20; Cosmas Indicopleustes, *Patr. Gr.* lxxxviii, 101; trans. McCrindle, p. 55.

[6] This expedition took place between A.D. 540 and 546. Proto-Islamic tradition attributes the campaign to Kālēb (A.D. 514–42), yet dates the Prophet's birth, which was between A.D. 570 and 580, from it. C. Conti Rossini has suggested that al-Fīl has been confounded with the name of the third-century Axumite King Afilas (Af'īl) who conquered Yaman (cf. 'Expéditions et possessions des Ḥabašāt en Arabia', *J.A.*, Juill. 1921, pp. 31–32), but there is no

The expedition of Abraha was a great mistake for it led the Ḥimyārite chiefs to invite the Persians into the country. By A.D. 590 the Persians were masters of Ḥimyār, Aden, Mukha, and other parts of Arabia, and even ports on the African coast. By A.D. 602 they had conquered the whole of Arabia, and Yaman remained in their control until its conquest by the Muslims in the eighth year of the *hijra* (A.D. 629/30). As a result of the Persian conquest of Yaman the Red Sea trade-routes became insecure and from that time began the decline of the kingdom of Axum.

## 2. FIRST CONTACTS WITH ISLAM

### (*a*) *Rise of Islam: Turning-Point in the History of the Region*

The seventh century, which saw the birth and unique expansion of Islam, marked a decisive turn in the history of Axum. Through the influence of their prophet Muḥammad the Arabs were united for the first time by the bond of loyalty to one God. This politico-religious unity cutting across all tribal ties enabled the nomad masses, pressed by the need for expansion, by lightening-swift feats of conquest to occupy the lands of civilized peoples. The two great empires of the day, Byzantium and Persia, which for more than a century had wasted their energies warring against each other and were weakened internally by divided loyalties and religious strife, collapsed under the onslaught of the Arabs, animated and unified by their new and ardent faith. Palestine and Syria were occupied in A.D. 636 and Egypt in 640–2. Under the new unity brought by Islam the conquered peoples were able to construct the new social and religious system which we understand by the term Islam today.

Christian Africa was abandoned to its fate. Egypt remained a Christian country for a long time with the Muslims as the dominant ruling minority, but through the machinery of the State the Church was slowly strangled and more and more of her peoples were absorbed into the new religion until in the course of time Egypt became a Muslim state with the Christians the subject minority they remain to this day. The Monophysite Church and the Christian minority, however, were not eradicated and have maintained their relationship with Christian

reason to suppose that the Axumites did not have trained elephants for Ptolemais (near ʿAqīq) and Adulis (Annesley Bay) were centres during the Ptolemaic period for the export of elephants (cf. *The Christian Topography of Cosmas*, trans. McCrindle, pp. 57–58; *The Periplus*, trans. Schoff, p. 60). These would be of the forest species which could be trained (see Sir W. Gowers, 'African Elephants and Ancient Authors', *African Affairs*, xlvii. 173–80).

Abyssinia throughout the centuries. Christianity had also penetrated to the kingdoms south of Aswān through the missionary enterprise of the Egyptian Monophysite and Melkite Churches. Nobatia, the most northerly of these kingdoms, was converted by Monophysites about A.D. 540–5, the middle kingdom of Makoria by Melkites in A.D. 569–70, whilst the southernmost, Alodia, which bordered on Abyssinia whence Christianity first penetrated into it,[1] was officially converted by Longinus, Bishop of Nobatia, in A.D. 580. These kingdoms defended their independence and their faith for many centuries until finally the northern kingdom of Maqurra (Nobatia and Makoria) came to an end during a period of internal troubles at the beginning of the fourteenth century, whilst that of ʿAlwa (Alodia) was finally destroyed in A.D. 1504 and Christianity was so completely erased from the lives of the Sudanese that not a trace remains.

The conquests of Islam marked a turning-point in Axumite history. Before the rise of Islamic power, although a remote and barbaric country, Axum had been on the margin of a friendly civilization, in touch with the Byzantine Empire whose rulers, though they might persecute Monophysites in their own dominion, regarded themselves as the champions of Christendom. But as a result of the Arab conquests the Christian kingdom of Axum suffered almost complete isolation and Europe so far forgot its existence that for centuries its very geographical position was unknown. 'Encompassed on all sides by the enemies of their religion,' Gibbon writes, 'the Æthiopians slept near a thousand years, forgetful of the world by whom they were forgotten.'[2] Axum's only relations with other Christians were with the Coptic Church of Egypt; those with the Sudanese kingdoms of Maqurra and ʿAlwa were of mutual hostility or indifference, although all were Monophysite Christians threatened by the same menace.[3] Civilization had come to northern Ethiopia from across the sea and once its people lost control of the sea-routes they relapsed into semi-barbarism. Being primarily an agricultural and warrior people with no maritime or commercial instincts

[1] John of Ephesus records (*Eccl. Hist.* pt. iii, trans. R. Payne Smith, 1860, p. 323) that Longinus found in Alodia Abyssinians who had adopted the heresy of Julianus of Halicarnassus.

[2] *Decline and Fall*, chap. xlvii.

[3] In the history of the patriarchs of Alexandria we read that Isaac (A.D. 686–9) sent a message to the Kings of Nubia and Ethiopia exhorting them to concord (*Hist. of Patriarchs of Alex.*, trans. B. Evetts, *Patr. Or.* v, fasc. 1, p. 24). We also read in the *Life of Isaac* (trans. E. Porcher, *Patr. Or.* xi. 377) that the King of Maqurra sent letters to the Patriarch complaining of the diminution of his bishops owing to the difficulties of the journey due to the hostility of the King of Maurotania (Marīs). These notices probably refer to Nubian states and the wars which led to the unification of the kingdom of Maqurra rather than to Abyssinia.

they did not realize the dangers of isolation. The settlements along the trade-routes and the coastal towns were full of Yamanites, Jews, Egyptians, and Greeks who controlled Axumite commerce, and when central control weakened and the pagan Beja and Saho tribes between the plateau and the sea made the trade-routes so dangerous as to be almost impracticable, the whole system broke down. Most of the foreign traders left when the ports fell into the hands of Beja or became lairs of pirates. This completed the isolation of Axum for its economic foundations were based primarily upon control of the trade-routes. Strangled by the isolation caused through the rise of the Islamic Empire, Axum relaxed its grip upon the physical environment and allowed itself to be cut off economically and culturally from its connexions with the outside world by the pressure of Beja tribes; and the ruins of great temples and public buildings point the contrast between its splendid past and the sordid future which it was to experience.

The cultural decline of Axum, due to the atrophy of the constructive ethos of its Christianity cut off from outside stimulus through the isolation caused by Islam, led to the resurgence of the pagan cults which had been forced underground or fossilized in mountain fastnesses and eventually brought about the political ascendancy of the pagan Hamitic Beja and Agao population. At the same time, during these dark ages the cultural translation of the alien Christianity into indigenous terms was proceeding which resulted in its naturalization and ultimate victory in the souls of the Agao.

*First contacts with Islam.* When the Arabian Prophet's followers were being persecuted in Mecca by the Quraish, the Prophet bethought himself of a refuge in the country which had sent such effective help to the persecuted Christian Arabs of Yaman. He told his followers, 'if you go to Abyssinia you will find a king under whom none are persecuted. It is a land of righteousness where God will give you relief from what you are suffering.'[1] So in the fifth year of his call (A.D. 615) refugees began to cross the straits in small groups. This is referred to by Muslim writers as the first *hijra* (emigration).[2] The story goes that the Quraish, dismayed by this defection, sent a deputation to the

[1] Ibn Hishām, *Sīra* (Cairo edn. 1937), i. 343. The number of Ethiopic words in the Qur'ān shows that Muḥammad himself must have been in contact with the Axumite traders, artisans, and soldiers resident in Mecca (see K. Ahrens, 'Christliches im Qoran', *Z.D.M.G.* lxxxiv, 1930, 15–68, 148–90).

[2] The traditions which speak of two *hijras* to Abyssinia are very vague and misleading. It is clear that the refugees did not go in one batch and one group may have been of such proportions that it was called a second *hijra*.

Najāshī[1] to ask that the refugees might be returned. The Najāshī summoned the refugees and said to them, 'What is this religion for which you have abandoned your people and yet have neither adopted mine nor any other known religion?' Jaʿfar b. Abī Ṭālib answered in words which, though apocryphal, reflect the early message of Islam and show the moral revolution wrought by Muḥammad upon pagan Arab life:

O King, we were a barbarous nation, worshipping idols, eating carrion, committing shameful deeds, killing our blood-relations, forgetting our duty towards our neighbours, the strong amongst us devouring the weak. Such was our state until God sent us an apostle, from amongst ourselves, with whose lineage, integrity, trustworthiness and purity of life we were acquainted. He summoned us to God, to believe in His unity, to worship Him and abandon the stones and idols which we and our fathers had worshipped in His stead. He commanded us to speak the truth, to be faithful in our trusts, to observe our duties to our kinsfolk and neighbours, to refrain from forbidden things and bloodshed, from committing immoralities and deceits, from consuming the property of orphans and from slandering virtuous women. He ordered us to worship God and associate no other with Him, to offer prayer, give alms and fast. (Then after ennumerating the duties of Islam he said): So we trusted in his word and followed the teachings he brought us from God. . . . Wherefore our countrymen turned against us and persecuted us to try and seduce us from our faith, that we might abandon the worship of God and return to the worship of idols.[2]

Jaʿfar also quoted appropriate texts from the Qur'ān (iv. 169; xix. 16–34) which made it appear that Islam was a form of Christianity, and after hearing his defence the Najāshī saw no reason to listen to the demands of the Quraish and gave his protection to the refugees. Later, when Muḥammad had exchanged his religious mission for a political career, he arranged for those exiles who wished to return to Arabia. Some of them, however, had become Christians and were therefore the first converts from Islam to Christianity. Sir William Muir remarks: 'if an Arab asylum had not at last offered itself at Medina, the Prophet might haply himself have emigrated to Abyssinia, and Mohammedanism dwindled, like Montanism, into an ephemeral Christian heresy'.[3] Of one of these converts, ʿUbaid Allāh ibn Jaḥsh, we read:

With regard to ʿUbaid Allāh b. Jaḥsh he remained in doubt until he became

[1] Arabic loan-word from Ethiopic ንጉሥ 'king'. Ṭabarī makes no mention of this deputation and Caetani (*Annali*, i. 278) doubts its authenticity. The Quraish were well acquainted with Axum through trading relations (cf. Ṭabarī, i. 1181) and Islamic tradition associated one of their delegations with a demand for the extradition of these refugees.

[2] Ibn Hishām, op. cit. i. 358–9.

[3] W. Muir, *The Life of Mohammed* (1923), p. 70.

a Muslim, then he emigrated with the Muslims to Abyssinia with his wife Umm Ḥabība, daughter of Abū Sufyān, who was a Muslima. But after he married her he became a Christian. Ibn Isḥāq said, M. b. Ja'far b. az-Zubair told me, 'Ubaid Allāh b. Jaḥsh, after he became a Christian, used to pass by the Companions of the Prophet when they were there in Abyssinia and say to them, 'We now see clearly, but you are still blinking'; that is, we have true sight but you are groping for sight and do not yet see clearly. The word he used is applied to a puppy when it tries to open its eyes to see.[1]

The accounts which give the Prophet's references to the Abyssinians are not very trustworthy, but they do show that he held them in considerable affection,[2] for there was nothing fanatical and exclusive about early Islam. 'Leave the Abyssinians in peace', he is reported to have said, 'so long as they do not take the offensive.'[3] At any rate in the great days of the initial impulse which spread the Arabs over country after country no *jihād* was directed against Abyssinia.[4] The Khalīfa 'Umar b. al-Khaṭṭāb is reported to have dispatched a small naval expedition against an Abyssinian fleet in A.D. 640, but the Arab fleet suffered so disastrously that 'Umar would have no more to do with the sea.[5] It is probable that this expedition was really directed against piratical lairs on the Red Sea coasts, but the accounts are too vague for any reliance to be placed upon them. In A.H. 83 Abyssinian pirates raided and sacked Jidda[6] and caused such a scare in Mecca that the Muslims were forced

[1] Ibn Hishām, iii. 417–18. Umm Ḥabība returned to Arabia with other exiles in A.H. 7, after having been first betrothed to the Prophet at his instance by the King of Abyssinia. It was she who described the wonders of the Abyssinian Cathedral of St. Mary to the Prophet on his death-bed (Muir, op. cit., p. 490).

[2] See his words in A.D. 630 on hearing of the death of the King of the Ḥabash (Ṭabari, i. 1720), whose name Hartmann restored to Ella Ṣaḥam ('Der Nağāšī Aṣḥama und sein Sohn Armā', *Z.D.M.G.* xlix (1895), 299–300). Muslim legend says that the Najāshī declared his belief in the Prophet's mission (Ṭabari, i. 1569) and that the Prophet prayed for him at his death (al-Wāḥidī, *Asbāb an-nuzūl*, ed. Cairo, A.H. 1315, pp. 103–4; Bukhārī, *Saḥīḥ*, iv. 254). Another apocryphal report places a nephew of the Najāshī by the Prophet's side at al-Madīna (Ibn al-Athīr, ed. A.H. 1285, ii. 144; v. 273). These legends had considerable effect upon the Muslim attitude towards Abyssinia, whence such eulogies as Ibn al-Jawzī, *Tanwīr al-ghabash fī faḍl as-Sūdān wa 'l-Ḥabash*; As-Suyūtī, *Raf' sha'n al-Ḥubshān*; and M. b. 'Abd al-Bāqī al-Bukhārī (d. A.H. 991), *aṭ-Ṭirāz al-Manqūsh fī maḥāsin al-Ḥabūsh* (Cairo, M.S. No. 2283).

[3] Abū Da'ūd, ii. 133; Ibn Daiba', *Taisīr al-wuṣūl*, iii. 110.

[4] On the painting which adorned the palace of Al-Walīd (A.D. 705–15) at Quṣair 'Amra in Transjordan the Negus is pictured amongst the rulers subjected by the Muslims: Caesar, Chosroes, and Roderick, the last of the Visigothic kings of Spain (see A. Musil, *Kuṣejr 'Amra* (1907); Jaussen and Savignac, *Mission Archéol. en Arabie*; and, for the date, Nöldeke, *Z.D.M.G.* lxi (1907), 222–33). Since, however, no Muslim historians mention any campaign the painting may be part of the fiction that the Negus embraced Islam in the time of Muḥammad.

[5] See Caetani, *Annali dell' Islam*, iv. 219, 366–7.

[6] Wüstenfeld, *Chron. der Stadt Mekka*, ii. 44; Sprenger, *Mohammed*, iii. 430. Jidda took

into taking active measures against them. In order to protect the Red Sea commerce they decided to obtain anchorages on the opposite coast and occupied the Dahlak archipelago which lies off Maṣawwaʿ.[1] Thus Islam established the first bridgehead which was to lead to the occupation of other coastal bases and the gradual penetration of Islam into East Africa.

But the isolation caused by the conquests of Islam was not solely responsible for the decline of Axum and the reorientation of the Christian kingdom southwards in the first half of the eighth century. This decline was also due to the expansion of pagan Beja nomads. The Beja are one of the most important ethnic factors in the region between the Nile and the Red Sea.[2] Owing to the relative poverty of their country, they were subject, like other nomadic tribes, to waves of expansion which carried them into the richer lands of the Nile valley and the northern Ethiopian plateau. One of these waves had resulted in the formation of the Blemmy state on the Nile between Egypt and Nubia which was destroyed by Silko of Nubia about A.D. 543. Towards the end of the seventh century a powerful Beja tribe, the Zanāfaj, had acquired a unified structure and penetrated the Eritrean plateau by way of the valley of the Baraka. They poured over the frontiers and pillaged the villages of the farmers at a time when the Axumite kingdom was at the most depressed period of its history and could do little to maintain its sovereignty over the plains. Much of the Ḥamāsēn was overrun and many of the displaced Axumites dispersed southwards. Axum itself was not abandoned as the cultural capital, but the Beja occupation of the coastal regions and the insecurity of trade-routes westwards to the

the place of Shuʿaiba as the port of Mecca from the caliphate of ʿUthmān; cf. Wüstenfeld, op. cit. ii. 75.

[1] The occupation of Dahlak is confirmed by notices of the exile there of the poet, al-Aḥwaṣ, and the *faqīh* ʿArrāk b. Mālik (*Kitāb al-Aghānī*, ed. Cairo 1350/1931, iv. 239, 246, 248–50, 255) in the time of the Umayyads, and by aṭ-Ṭabarī (*Annales*, III. I. 135) who says that the isles were attacked by Indians in the second half of the eighth century in consequence of the exile there of the sons of ʿAbd al-Jabbār, Governor of Khorasān under Al-Manṣūr (A.H. 136–58). Arabic inscriptions discovered on the island go back to the middle of the ninth century A.D.

[2] The hypothesis that the Blemmyes of the classical writers belonged to the Beja family has been securely established by E. Zyhlarz, 'Die Sprache der Blemmyer', *Zeit. für Eingeborenen-Sprachen*, xxxi, 1940. They are first mentioned in Theocritus (*Idylls*, vii. 114). Eratosthenes (276–194 B.C., in Strabo, *Geography* (Loeb), xvii. I. 2) locates them in the 'lower parts of the country on either side of Meroë, along the Nile and towards the Red Sea... and border on the Egyptians'. Unlike the Libyan Nubae the Blemmyes at that time were 'subject to the Ethiopians'. Strabo's own account (25–24 B.C., xvii. I. 53) shows that some tribes had been advancing northwards along the Nile where later they were to establish the kingdom eventually destroyed by Silko of Nubia.

Nilotic kingdom of Alodia and eastwards to the Red Sea ports strangled its life, and its distinctive culture survived only by a miracle. All connexion with Byzantium being broken, Greek died out as the cultural language of the capital and the Hellenic cultural veneer was soon worn away.[1] Churches and public buildings ceased to be built, the vassal nobles warred against each other, and, still more significant, Judaism, which had probably received new accessions after the expulsion of the Banū Isrā'īl from the Ḥijāz colonies in A.D. 640, gained a greater hold over groups of Agao, whilst pagan cults resurrected themselves from under the veneer of Christianity. The last coins struck were those of Gersem and Hataz II whose dates may be anywhere between the beginning of the eighth and the beginning of the tenth centuries. The Axumites were able to maintain their independence only in the mountain districts of Tigrai, but from thence their influence spread, not as before over the easily accessible plains in the north-west, but into the almost inaccessible regions to the south and south-west occupied by many independent groups of pagan and judaized Agao. The history of the following crucial period is most obscure chiefly owing to the lack of indigenous sources.

## (*b*) *The Birth of the Abyssinian Nation*

These obscure centuries are most important in the history of Abyssinia because out of them the Abyssinians proper emerge. The Agao, inhabiting the highlands of what are now Tigrai, Bēgamder, Dambyā, Gojām (Guažām), Agaw-Meder, Dāmot, and Amḥara, are the most ancient population of the country.[2] Those in the north, as we have seen, had fallen under the influence of Semites from South Arabia who had formed a ruling caste and extended their rule mainly to the west and north over Beja and negroid tribes. During these obscure centuries semitized Axumite peoples driven into the hills of Tigrai by the Beja invasion extended their civilizing activities to the wild regions south of the capital.

[1] The last work to be translated from Greek into Geʿez was the Book of Ecclesiasticus in A.D. 678. It is interesting to note that in this book the word for God is sometimes translated by the pagan *ʿAstar* (iii. 18; xxxvii. 21; cf. Dillmann, *Vet. Test. Aeth.* v. 117). This shows both how the pagan elements persisted and how Axumite Christianity assimilated them.

[2] The Agao are first mentioned by Cosmas Indicopleustes (A.D. 523), 'the king of the Axômites accordingly, every other year, through the governor of the Agau (τοῦ ἄρχοντος τῆς Ἀγαῦ) sends thither (i.e. to the gold country, possibly Fazoqli) special agents to bargain for the gold' (*Patr. Gr.* lxxxviii. 100; *The Christian Topography of Cosmas*, trans. J. McCrindle, 1897, p. 52).

The link between the Axumite Empire and the emergent Abyssinian State was provided by this semitized population of the northern mountains who, dispossessed of their homes by the invasion of Beja nomads, settled in inaccessible districts of the interior of Tigrai, Amḥara, and Shoa (Shāwā) amongst pagan Agao. These Christian peoples, inheritors of the Axumite tradition, spread the Geʿez language and the Christian religion deep into the interior and there began that process of fusion which produced the Abyssinian nation.

The modern Abyssinian type is the result of the complete fusion of the two elements: the Semitic aristocratic class and the indigenous Hamitic peoples, chief amongst whom were the Agao. In this fusion the Semitic languages Geʿez, Tigriña, and Amḥaric prevailed over Agao languages and their social structure was transformed, although from the ethnical point of view the Hamitic element was completely dominant. The Abyssinians, in fact, are the Agao who had never been dominated by the Axumites, but who had received a second-hand Christian heritage from the Axumite fusion of Semite and Hamite.

*The Challenge and the Response: The Conversion of the Abyssinians to Christianity.* Al-Yaʿqūbī, in his history which was composed about A.D. 872, gives a description of the political situation in the north of this region in his own time after the Beja overrunning of part of the Axumite kingdom.[1] Between the Nile and the Red Sea were five independent kingdoms. The first, called Naqīs, extended from the Nile near Aswān to the lower Baraka. Its capital, Hajar, was visited by the Muslims for trading purposes.[2] The various Beja tribes in the kingdom were the Ḥadāreb, Ḥijāb, ʿAmāʿar,[3] Kawbar, Manāsa (Mansa?), Rasīfa, ʿArbarbʿa, and the Zanāfaj.[4] In their country were mines of gold and precious stones worked by Muslims with whom they were on good terms. Next came the Baqlīn (Rora Baqla?), covering the Eritrean Sāḥil, the Rora region of the plateau, and the middle course of the Baraka. Their religion resembled that of the Magians and Dualists.

[1] See al-Yaʿqūbī, *Historiae* (ed. Houtsma, 1883), i. 217–19.

[2] Al-Yaʿqūbī, *Kitāb al-Buldān*, ed. De Goeje, in *B.G.A.*, vii (1892), 336. Hajar has not been identified, but it was probably in the Red Sea hills in the neighbourhood of Sinkāt.

[3] Possibly the Amar'ar who now live in the region around Port Sudan.

[4] In his *K. al-Buldān* (pp. 336–7), which was composed a little later in A.D. 891–2, Al-Yaʿqūbī places the Zanāfaj in the country of Baqlīn, 'the town where the king of the Zanāfija resides is called Baqlīn which the Muslims visit occasionally for trading. Their rite (*madhhab*) is like that of the Ḥadāriba. They have no revealed law and merely worship an idol called *ḥaḥākhawā*.'

They called God *Az-Zabjīr*[1] and the Devil *Ṣahay Ḥarāqa.*[2] The third kingdom was called Bāzīn in the region between the Christian Nūba kingdom of ʿAlwa and the Baqlīn with whom they were formerly at war. The Bāzīn were no doubt the Kunāma who are called Bāzēn by the Abyssinians. The fourth, called Jārīn, had a powerful king whose rule extended from a coastal town called Bāḍiʿ[3] as far as the Baraka and from the kingdom of Baqlīn to a place called Ḥall ad-Dujāj. The fifth, called Qaṭʿa, was the last Beja kingdom and extended from the border of Bāḍiʿ to a place called Faykūn. They were a brave and powerful people and had a military training school called *dār as-sawā* where the young men were trained in arms. These tribes were all pagan with the exception of the southernmost who were Christians subject to the Abyssinian king.

The gradual spread of Islam amongst the Beja began with the settlement of Muslims in the mining district. Maqrīzī records that the excursions of the Beja against Egypt led to the governor of Aswān sending ʿAbd Allāh ibn al-Jahm against them. He concluded a treaty with their chief, Kanūn ibn ʿAbd al-ʿAzīz, whose headquarters was at Hajar, in the year A.H. 216 (A.D. 831).[4] His account shows that the Arab traders and mine owners who were active in northern Beja territory may have influenced the chiefs, and that mosques for the benefit of these Muslims existed, two of which are named, one at Hajar, capital of Naqīs, and another at Ṣinjat.[5]

After describing the five kingdoms which now occupied much of the territory of the former Axumite kingdom, al-Yaʿqūbī goes on to say that south of them was the kingdom of the Najāshī, who was a Jacobite Christian. He ruled an extensive territory which stretched to the coast and included Dahlak.[6] In his kingdom were a number of

[1] v. ll. *az-Zabaḥīr*, *al-Baḥīr*, possibly the Eth. *egzīʾa beḥēr*; cf. Ibn al-Faqīh al-Hamadhānī, *K. al-Buldān*, *B.G.A.* v. 78.

[2] v. l. *Hawāqa.* The first word may be related to Eth. *Ṣaḥāy*, sun.

[3] Crowfoot identifies Bāḍiʿ with Airi (Ar-Rīḥ) near ʿAqīq ('Some Red Sea Ports . . .', *Geog. Journ.* xxxvii, 1911, 542 ff.); whilst Wiet identifies it with Maṣawwaʿ, which even today is called *Bāṣeʿ* in Tigrē and *Bāḍeʿ* in Bedawie (*Khiṭaṭ*, ed. Wiet, iii. 257 n. 10).

[4] *Khiṭaṭ*, ed. Wiet, iii. 274; Cairo edn. A.H. 1324, i. 316–17.

[5] There seems little doubt that Ṣinjat can be identified with the modern Sinkāt. The place is also mentioned by Ṭabarī, in an account of the relations of the Caliphate of Al-Mutawakkil with the northern Beja in A.H. 241 (A.D. 855/6. *Annali*, ser. iii. 1432), and by Ibn Miskawaihi (in *Fragm. Hist.*, ed. De Goeje, p. 551). It was in Khōr Nubt west of Sinkāt that the earliest Arabic inscriptions found in the Sudan were discovered. Two of them which are now in the Khartoum Museum are dated A.H. 147 (764/5) and 153 (A.D. 770), whilst the others belong to the fourth century A.H. The nature of their buildings that have been discovered both at Al-ʿAllāqi and near Sinkāt show that their relationships with the Beja were not very friendly at this early period.

[6] Al-Yaʿqūbī confirms this in *K. al-Buldān*, *B.G.A.* vii. 319.

important cities and many vassal rulers paid him tribute. His capital was an unidentified place called Kaʿbar.[1]

The prosperity of this resurrected Abyssinian State endured throughout most of the tenth century. A treaty of friendship was concluded with the Yamanite sovereign Ibrāhīm b. Ziyād, known as Ṣāḥib al-Harmalay (d. A.D. 901/2), and Yamanite ships from Zabīd did a thriving trade with Abyssinia. Al-Masʿūdi, writing in A.D. 935, confirms these accounts. 'The capital of Abyssinia is Kuʿbar. It is a great city and the seat of the kingdom of the Najāshī. The country has many towns and extensive territories stretching as far as the Abyssinian Sea. To it belongs the coastal plain opposite Yaman where there are many cities such as Zailaʿ, Dahlak, and Nāṣiʿ (i.e. Bāḍiʿ), in which are Muslims tributory (*dhimmī*) to the Abyssinians.'[2] He tells us also that the Ḥadrāba (Ḥadāreb) had now become Muslim through the influence of the Muslims operating the mines in their country, but that the rest of the Beja were pagan. Ibn Salīm al-Aswānī, writing between A.D. 975 and 996, also gives a long descriptive account of the Beja showing that they were divided into many tribes still retaining a matrilinear system.[3] Ibn Ḥawqal, whose book was completed in A.D. 977–8, confirms many of Al-Yaʿqūbī's references to the Beja and gives much additional information.[4] He says that the Beja are all pagans with the exception of the Ḥadāreb who 'are Muslims in name only'. The Baqlīn (whom he calls Taflīn) are situated on the Wādī Baraka. They are camel and cattle nomads and are subject to the kingdom of ʿAlwa. They have a Muslim king who talks Arabic and there are many Muslims amongst them, some of whom even visit Mecca. Adjoining the Baqlīn are the Bāzīn and Bārya, also inhabiting the country around the Baraka. The Bāzīn are settled cultivators ruled over by an assembly of elders. They are pagans but have a high-god called *Anana*. His account gives an exact description of the Kunāma of today, who are called Bāzēn by the Abyssinians and Bāza by the Sudanese, and whose high-god is *Anna*. The Bārya similarly are the tribe still known by that name.[5] He also says that Zailaʿ was in the possession of Abyssinian Christians between

[1] V. l. Kaʿban. C. Conti Rossini identifies Kaʿbar with Aksum (*J. Asiat.* xiv. 263 n. 1). The astronomer Al-Battānī (d. A.D. 929) speaks of 'Kusūmī (Aksūm?), urbs regis Kūsh (Aethiopiae)', *Opus Astronomicum*, ed. Nallino, ii (1907), 47.

[2] Al-Masʿūdi, *Murūj* (ed. Meynard and Courteille, 1863), iii. 34.

[3] His account is preserved in Maqrīzī, *Khiṭaṭ* (edn. A.H. 1324), pp. 313–19.

[4] See the valuable description of the Beja in the edition by J. H. Kramers, *Opus Geographicum auctore Ibn Ḥawḳal* (Leiden, 1938), i. 50–56, which is missing from that edited by De Goeje, *B.G.A.* ii. 27 and 41.

[5] Ibn Ḥawqal, op. cit. i. 55, 57.

whom and the Yamanite Muslims peaceful trading relations existed. He repeats the saying that Abyssinia is territory not subject to the *jihād*.[1]

The new Abyssinian kingdom, no longer confined to the northern part of the plateau, but in the very heart of the Ethiopian massif, was in a state of continuous warfare with the Agao peoples of the interior, whose resistance more than once menaced its very existence. Not only did it survive during these perilous years, but it continued the long process of the conversion of the Agao to Christianity.

It is recorded in the *History of the Patriarchs of Alexandria*[2] that shortly after A.D. 979 the King of Abyssinia wrote a letter to George, King of Nubia, for transmission to the Coptic Patriarch Philotheos (A.D. 979–1003), saying that a queen of the Banī' l-Hamūya was ravaging his country and hunting him and his followers from refuge to refuge. Christians and their clergy were being exterminated and Christianity was in danger of being wiped out.

The contemporary Arabic writer, Ibn Ḥawqal, confirms that there was a queen dominating Abyssinia:

> As regards Abyssinia, for many years it has had a woman as its ruler. It is she who killed the king of Abyssinia who was known under the title of *ḥaḍānī* (Eth. *ḥaḍē*), and she continues to this day to dominate her own country and the neighbouring regions of the land of the *ḥaḍānī* in the west of Abyssinia. It is a vast limitless country, rendered difficult of access by deserts and wastes.[3]

C. Conti Rossini has suggested[4] that the country of this queen may be identified with Grand Dāmot, inhabited by Gurāgē and Sidāma, lying south of the Blue Nile and south-west of Shoa, between it and the Gibē, which country was threatened by the expansion of the Abyssinian kingdom. This invasion, assisted possibly by an uprising of partially

[1] Ibid. 56; *B.G.A.* ii. 27 and 41.

[2] The Arabic text is given by J. Perruchon (*R. Sém.* i, 1893, 360–2), whilst the Ethiopian version which is based upon the Arabic text is found in the Senkessar (*συναξάριον*) for 12 Khedār (trans. E. A. W. Budge, *The Book of Saints of the Ethiopian Church*, 1928, i. 233–4).

[3] Ibn Ḥawqal, op. cit. i. 59. Ibn Ḥawqal finished his book in A.D. 978 and the king must have been killed before then. The Synaxary, which for the most part is based upon the Arabic history of the Patriarchs, also confirms the killing of the king which is not mentioned in the Arabic text (cf. Budge, op. cit. i. 234).

[4] Cf. C. Conti Rossini, *Storia d'Etiopia*, i. 285–6, reading al-Damūta for al-Hamūya; cf. E. Renaudot (*Hist. Patr. Alex.*, Paris, 1713, p. 381) 'Hamovia, vel Amouta'. Traditionally the revolt is ascribed to Esāto (Amharic) or Guedit (Tigrē, i.e. Judith), a Jewish queen of Semēn. On the actual derivation of these names see C. Conti Rossini, *R.S.O.* x. 500–1). She is said to have destroyed Axum and its Christianity and murdered all the royal family except one child who was carried off to Shoa and whose descendants appeared later to restore the Solomonid line.

subjected Agao peoples, was a very grave danger to the embryonic Abyssinian Christianity, far greater even than the Muslim conquest of the sixteenth century when Christianity had become of the very warp and woof of Abyssinian life. In this uprising the kingdom almost came to an end, the country was devastated, churches were burnt, Christians enslaved, and the practice of the cult abandoned. The invasion led to migrations of Agao tribes, amongst them the Bilēn who now live in the Keren district near the river ʿAnsēba and still speak an Agao language.[1] Thus one effect of the invasion was to spread central Abyssinian tribes into regions of the former Axumite Empire which had been occupied by Beja tribes.

This Christian king of Abyssinia[2] who made contact with the Patriarch Philotheos through George of Nubia attributed his desperate position to a long-standing breach between the Patriarchate and the Abyssinian court, for, since Petros who was sent under the Patriarchate of Cosmas (A.D. 923–34), no *abūnas* had been nominated,[3] and in his letter he asked the King of Nubia to induce the patriarch to send another *abūna*. This was done, Abūna Daniel was consecrated and sent to Abyssinia where he was welcomed with great enthusiasm; the queen was subdued and a period of slow recovery ensued. But the power of the kingdom remained weak and its influence restricted for a long time, and it is during this time that Islam made considerable progress in the region.

The challenge of the pagan Agao was met by the embryonic Christianity of the new kingdom in a way which resulted in the fusion of political and religious interests. The conversion of the Agao became a political necessity if the State were to survive. The desperate appeals to Alexandria to send an *abūna*, for these all seem to be connected with dynastic or internal troubles, give the impression of a people living in a messianic atmosphere of crisis in which the overthrow of kings and the scourge of invading armies is regarded as a divine retribution for unfaithfulness, whilst the arrival of a new *abūna* is hailed as a manifestation of divine forgiveness. In such an atmosphere the missionary urge came to life. The vast development and missionary activity of the

[1] Reinisch, *Texte der Bilin-Sprache* (1883), pp. 9–10; C. Conti Rossini, 'Note etiopiche: III, Sovra una tradizione bilin', *G.S.A.I.* x (1897), 153–6.

[2] According to the Ethiopic 'Lives of the Patriarchs' (*Hāymānota Abaw*) he was named Saifa Arʿād and ascended the throne in A.D. 977; see C. Conti Rossini, 'I manoscritti etiopici della Missione Cattolica di Cheren', *R.R.A.L.* ser. v, vol. xiii (1904), p. 266.

[3] See Renaudot, *Hist. Patr. Alex.* pp. 336–41; Perruchon, 'Vie de Cosmas', *R. Sém.* ii (1894), 78–93.

anchorite-monastic system during the later period of the Zāgwē dynasty and the first period of the Solominids which resulted in the victory of Christianity, cannot be understood if the gravity of the threat of Agao paganism to Abyssinian Christianity had not evoked a desperate response from the vital element of Abyssinian Christianity.

Without reading too much into the stereotyped effusions of their later hagiographers, it does seem that these missionaries of the Zāgwē and early Solomonid periods manifested a genuine self-sacrificing zeal for the spread of the Gospel which led to the building up of a new society. But the Abyssinian Agao did not allow Christianity to break up their native tradition; instead they moulded the alien religion to suit their own barbarian religious heritage. The ancient shrines were transformed into Christian sanctuaries, the high places dedicated to saints, and the sacred sycamore trees to the Virgin Mary.[1] The result was a cult deeply steeped in Agao mythology both pagan and judaic.[2] Its ritual and hagiography, its literature and ecclesiastical organization, show the originality of this native Christian cult, against many of whose indigenous practices such as polygamy[3] the Church of Alexandria was

[1] The development of Amharic through the centuries was a similar process in the linguistic sphere, since in Amharic one gets a non-Semitic mode of thought blended with Semitic linguistic usage. Armbruster writes that the Semitic features of Amharic 'give one the impression of having been superimposed on an alien (possibly Hamitic) basis'; *Initia Amharica*, i (1908), p. 3.

[2] Abyssinian tradition asserts that the ancient Abyssinians were converted to Christianity from Judaism. This tradition has been thought to be wrong because the Axumites who were first converted were undoubtedly pagans. But the tradition is partly true in the sense that many of the Agao of the interior, who had never been under Axumite rule and were converted at this period during the birth pangs of a new empire, were adherents of a form of Judaism. The first mention of Jews in Abyssinia is in the strange account of Eldad the Danite who lived in the latter part of the ninth century and wrote a letter to the Jews of Spain in A.D. 883 giving an account of his adventures amongst savage coastal tribes and of the Ethiopian Jews who saved him (see Elkan Adler, *Jewish Travellers*, 1930, pp. 4 ff.). The subjection and conversion of the Agao was a very long process and when the 'Solomonid' dynasty of semitized Agao rulers emerged the process still went on. Dāmot was occupied at the beginning of the fourteenth century, Wagara in the fifteenth, Dambya in the sixteenth, Agao-Meder in the seventeenth, and, most formidable of all, Semēn, in the eighteenth century, after which they were scattered over the north-western provinces. The Abyssinians are these christianized Agao peoples. That explains the association of the old Agao legends, like that of Solomon and the Queen of Sheba, with the Axumite kingdom, which, as Budge remarks, preserves a christianized echo of the belief in the divine origin of the kings of Abyssinia (*The Queen of Sheba*, pp. xi-xiii). It also accounts for many of the pagan and Jewish customs and ritual in Abyssinian Christianity. Certain Agao groups, although they have become Christian, still remain as a distinct element from the surrounding population. They speak various Agao dialects among themselves, but are familiar with the dominant Semitic language of their region, Tigrē, Tigriña, or Amharic.

[3] See Abū Ṣāliḥ, *The Churches and Monasteries of Egypt*, trans. Evetts and Butler, p. 290, and Renaudot, op. cit., p. 453, for the attempt of Sawiros to enforce monogamy on the

to struggle in vain throughout the centuries. At the same time the creative reaction of the Abyssinians to Christianity enabled them to assimilate it naturally and cling to it tenaciously, whilst the symbolical status of the Church in the divinely ordained monarchy enabled the State to rise again and again triumphant over the vicissitudes of fortune.

The missionary activity of the Church was 'cellular', carried out through the monasteries and hermitages scattered about the country. But whilst the work of the monks and anchorites was very effective it lacked true cohesion owing to the weakness of the ecclesiastical organization, and the Church became so completely dependent upon the State that the relationship between them was actually feudal. Consequently the Church of Abyssinia has always felt the repercussions of political crises, and the times when Islam has expanded have corresponded with periods when the State was weak. Islam's first period of expansion was during this time of internal troubles out of which the indigenous Christian State emerged.

During these formative centuries considerable changes took place in the social organization of the Abyssinians. The migrants from Yaman had there been organized by law and locality as territorial units (*ashʿāb*) not as kin-groups, and this type of organization survived migration overseas. But the influence of the Hamitic organization of the partially semitized aboriginals led eventually, during these centuries when the Christian culture was spreading southwards, to the triumph of the more primitive form of the kinship-group (*enda*) as the basic organization of society, whilst the wider organization continued in the village community and regional governors of widely varying functions and authority.

*The Zāgwē Dynasty.* In A.D. 1137 the royal power passed to an Agao family of Lāstā called the Zāgwā who founded their capital at Roḥa in their own homeland.[1] This change of dynasty marked a change of political power from the semitized Abyssinians who had inherited the Axumite tradition to the more recently christianized Agao. It would appear from an incident related in the account of the patriarchs of

Abyssinians about A.D. 1086. Sacramental marriage (*ba qerbān*) which is indissoluble is rarely contracted by the Abyssinians, and the common civil form may be derived from the temporary marriage (*mutʿa*) of the pre-Islamic Arabs. The *mutʿa* union is very common today amongst Arab immigrants into East Africa.

[1] On the Zāgwā see C. Conti Rossini, 'Sulla dinastia Zāguē', *L'Oriente*, ii (1897), 144–59; 'La caduta della dinastía Zagué e la versione amarica del Beʿela Nagast', *R.R.A.L.* ser. v, vol. xxxi (1922), pp. 279–314; and *Storia d'Etiopia*, i. 303–21; J. Halévy, 'Le Pays de Zāguē', *R. Sém.* v (1897), 275–85.

Alexandria that strong resistance was at first offered to the new dynasty by the clergy under Abūna Michael.[1] It is recorded that the first Zāgwē king sent a deputation to Alexandria to ask the Patriarch John (A.D. 1148–67) to appoint a new metropolitan on the grounds that Abūna Michael was too old to exercise his ministry. The patriarch refused since the ecclesiastical canons did not allow him to appoint a new metropolitan whilst his predecessor was still alive, and the king applied to the *wazīr* ʿAlī ibn Ṣalāḥ[2] who put pressure upon the patriarch to get him to agree, and, when he persisted in his refusal, imprisoned him. It seems clear that Michael had at first refused to recognize the new king, who therefore tried to get him replaced. Succeeding members of the Zāgwē dynasty successfully disarmed the opposition of the Church by intensifying missionary propaganda amongst the Agao and building churches and monasteries. At any rate they were soon regarded as legitimate and inheritors of the Solomonid tradition.[3]

In Egypt the period of persecution through which the Copts had been passing was now ended and new commercial relations were being established between Abyssinia and Egypt. Immigrant Copts who had settled in Abyssinia during the persecution of Al-Ḥākim (A.D. 996–1021) contributed in such a way that a literary and religious revival took place. We learn from a Greek source that after Ṣalāḥ ad-Dīn had taken Jerusalem in 1189 he satisfied the request of the Zāgwē king by reserving the Chapel of the Invention of the Cross in the Church of the Holy Sepulchre and an altar in the Church of the Nativity at Bethlehem for the Abyssinians.[4] In spite of the difficulties of the journey pilgrims flocked from Abyssinia to Jerusalem and these contacts with other Christians contributed to the development of the sacred literature of the Ethiopian Church.

Lālibelā (*c.* A.D. 1190–1225), the most celebrated of the Zāgwā and possibly the builder of some of the monolithic churches at Roḥa[5] which now bears his name, has passed into tradition as a great saint. He used

[1] Cf. Renaudot, op. cit., pp. 525–6.

[2] The fact that the *wazīr* ʿAlī was killed shortly afterwards in A.D. 1150 gives us a definite date within the reign of the first Zāgwā.

[3] Abū Ṣāliḥ (op. cit., p. 288), writing during the reign of Lālibelā, definitely regards them as of the true line.

[4] This is not improbable, but it rests solely upon the unconfirmed statement of Neophyte of Cyprus (*c.* A.D. 1844); cf. A. Papadopoulos-Kerameus, *Ἀναλεκτα Ἱεροσολυμιτικῆς Σταχυολογίας ἢ Συλλογὴ ἀνεκδότων* . . . (St. Petersberg, 1894), ii. 409.

[5] Worship in caves was an Agao practice. Besides the ten churches at Lālibelā (Roḥa) there are some 200 other Monolithic churches in the same region; cf. A. Raffray, *Les Églises monolithes de la ville de Lalibela*, Paris, 1882; A. Monti della Corte, *Lalibelà*, Rome, 1940.

the influence of the clergy to consolidate his dynasty, but his policy did not find sufficiently able successors. Church and State became divided, the Church was jealous of the position accorded to Roḥa by the kings, and the way was prepared for the appearance of another adventurer to initiate a new phase in Abyssinian history. This was Yekuno Amlāk, a local chieftain of Geshēn and Amba-Sel whose father was from an ancient Amḥara family and his mother a slave. He revolted against the last Zāgwē king, was joined by dissident elements, defeated and eventually killed the king in the Church of St. Qirqos where he had taken refuge,[1] and ascended the throne as the first of the 'Solomonid' dynasty in A.D. 1270. The stress which the new dynasty laid upon this name meant a return to the semitized Abyssinian tradition. He derived himself from the ancient line of Menelik, a claim which was recognized by the Church, and, thus incorporating in himself the old Agao legends, gave to his line stability and strength.

The Zāgwē rulers could hardly call themselves 'kings of the kings of Ethiopia' for the sphere of their rule was very circumscribed. Tigrai, Lāstā, and Angot were certainly under their control and perhaps part of Bēgamder. In the north on the Eritrean plateau and its lowlands roamed independent pagan Beja tribes amongst whom were interspersed Agao groups such as the Bilēn who had migrated recently from the south. In Geshēn and Amba-Sel reigned the local dynasty from whom came the so-called restorer of the Solomonid line, whilst beyond the Abāy was the powerful independent kingdom of Dāmot. In the north-western regions were strong independent Agao tribes, some of whom were Judaic in religion, about whom Benjamen of Tudela, a Spanish-Jewish traveller who travelled from ʿAidhāb to Aswān in A.D. 1171, gives us some information.[2] The islands of Dahlak and the

[1] Later tradition which does not go back earlier than the seventeenth century says that the last king abdicated peaceably in favour of Yekuno Amlāk at the instance of Abūna Takla Hāymānot of Debra Libānos. On this question see C. Conti Rossini, 'La caduta della dinastía Zagué', p. 38.

[2] From Zabīd, Benjamen writes, 'it is eight days' journey to India, which is on the mainland, called the land of Aden, and this is the Eden which is in Thelasar. The country is mountainous. There are many Israelites there, and they are not under the yoke of the Gentiles, but possess cities and castles on the summits of the mountains, from which they make descents into the plain-country called Lybia, which is a Christian Empire. These are the Lybians of the land of Lybia with whom the Jews are at war. The Jews take spoil and booty and retreat to the mountains, and no man can prevail against them. Many of these Jews of the land of Aden come to Persia and Egypt. Thence to the land of Assuan is a journey of twenty days through the desert. This is Seba on the River Pishon (Blue Nile) which descends from the land of Cush. And some of these sons of Cush have a king whom they call the Sultan Al-Habash' (Elkan Adler, *Jewish Travellers*, 1930, pp. 60–61). The plain country of Lybia upon which these

various coastal settlements were Muslim, whilst in south-eastern Shoa and the whole of southern Ethiopia Islam was progressing with great rapidity.

*Islamic Kingdoms in Eastern Shoa.* New light has been thrown upon the history of Islam in Abyssinia by Dr. E. Cerulli's recent discovery of a short Arabic history of the last days of a Muslim sultanate in eastern Shoa at the end of the thirteenth century.[1] During the Zāgwē period of Christian Abyssinia, eastern Shoa was the seat of a Muslim sultanate under a dynasty called Makhzūmī which had been founded according to tradition in A.H. 283 (A.D. 896/7).[2] This document shows the sultanate in the last stages of decadence, torn by internal strife and weakened by struggles with neighbouring Muslim states which were seeking to throw off their allegiance to Shoa. In A.D. 1277 the Wālī Asmaʿ, sultan of one of these states, made his first attack on Shoa and after some years of struggle deposed the Makhzūmite sultan in A.D. 1285. During the next few years the conqueror ʿAlī ibn Wālī Asmaʿ imposed his rule over other Muslim countries of Adal, Mōra, Hobat, and Jidāya. It was whilst this change of authority was taking place in Shoa that Christian Abyssinia passed from the rule of the Zāgwē dynasty to that of the Solomonids.

The earliest account we possess of the new State of the Walashmaʿ,[3] which was called Ifāt by the Abyssinians and Wafāt or Awfāt by Arabic writers, is that of Ibn Saʿīd (A.D. 1214–87) preserved by Abū'l-Fidā.[4] He says that the region is also called Jabara (i.e. Jabarta). Wafāt is the capital of an autonomous king. Its population, who are Muslim, are very mixed. The city is situated upon an elevated place and below it is a valley through which flows a little stream. The royal palace and citadel are built upon hills. The country is fertile since it rains almost every night and the inhabitants cultivate the banana and sugar cane. He calculates that the astronomical position of the city is 8° lat. 57° long. according to Arab computation, which brings us to the eastern edge of Shoa.

Israelites descended was probably the eastern lowlands of the Sudan roamed over by Beja under the suzerainty of the Christian kingdom of ʿAlwa. Seba (שבא) must be Sōba, the capital of the kingdom of ʿAlwa.

1 See E. Cerulli, 'Il Sultanato dello Shoa nel secolo XIII', *R.S.E.* i (1941), 5–42.

2 The Makhzūmī were the famous Meccan tribe to which Khālid b. al-Walīd, conqueror of Syria, belonged and were great rivals of the Umayyads. The ancestors of the Shoan dynasty are supposed to have emigrated across the sea during the Caliphate of ʿUmar b. al-Khaṭṭāb.

3 So most Arabic writers spell the name. They are called Walasmā by Ethiopic writers (cf. *Chronicle of Ba'eda Māryām*, ed. Perruchon, p. 112).

4 *Géographie d'Aboulféda*, trans. Guyard, ii. 229; cf. Qalqashandī, *Ṣubḥ al-Aʿshā* (Cairo, A.H. 1333), v. 325.

Ibn Khaldūn provides additional information about the early days of the Walashmaʿ, whom he calls Wāṣmaʿ.[1] He does not mention the Sultanate of Shoa, but after stating that Kaʿbar was formerly the capital of the Abyssinian kingdom he writes, 'west of the states of this king (the *Ḥaṭī* of Abyssinia) is the town (principality) of Dāmot where a great chief used to reign in control of a powerful empire'.[2] The pagan kingdom of Dāmot lying south-west of Shoa must have been very powerful for reports to have reached Arab geographers, whilst from Abyssinian sources we read of an expedition made during the thirteenth century by a Zāgwē prince called Zēnā-Pēṭros into Dāmot where he was defeated and killed.[3] At one time the Muslim Walashmaʿ State of Ifāt which had established itself in eastern Shoa paid allegiance to it for Ibn Khaldūn goes on:

> to the north is another of their kings called Ḥaqq ad-Dīn b. M. b. ʿAlī b. Wāṣmaʿ. He inhabits the town of Wafāt and his forebears embraced Islam at some unknown time. Since his ancestor Wāṣmaʿ had recognized the authority of the King of Dāmot, the *Ḥaṭī* was offended and attacked him and took possession of his kingdom. But as the war dragged on the power of the *Ḥaṭī* weakened and the sons of Wāṣmaʿ succeeded in regaining their lands from the *Ḥaṭī* and his sons. They took possession of Wafāt and laid it waste. We have heard that Ḥaqq ad-Dīn has died and has been succeeded by his brother Saʿd ad-Dīn.[4] This family professes Islam; sometimes they recognize the authority of the *Ḥaṭī*, and at others reject it.[5]

By the time Maqrīzī is composing *al-Ilmām* in A.D. 1434/5 the Walashmaʿ claimed an Arab ancestry, for he writes:

> the first of them came from the Ḥijāz and settled in the land of Jabara, now called Jabart, which is part of the regions of Zailaʿ. They settled there and dwelt in the town of Lūfāt (Wafāt). Some of them gained a reputation for their philanthropy and piety, until it came to pass that one ʿUmar, also called Lashmaʿ, was appointed by the *Ḥaṭī* governor of the town of Awfāt and the surrounding country.[6]

[1] Ibn Khaldūn, *Hist. des Berbères*, trans. de Slane, ii. 107–8; *Kitāb al-ʿIbar*, Cairo, vi. 199. He derived most of his material from Ibn Saʿīd, but the reference to Saʿd ad-Dīn brings it up to his own time, the end of the fourteenth century.

[2] Ibn Khaldūn, op. cit. vi. 199; de Slane, *Berbères*, ii. 108. *Ḥaṭī* is derived from Ethiopic *Ḥaḍē* (ሐፄ).

[3] *Gadla Yārēd seu Acta sancti Yārēd*, trans. C. Conti Rossini, *C.S.C.O.*, *Script. Aeth.*, ser. ii, vol. xvii (1904), p. 24.

[4] The death of Ḥaqq ad-Dīn and the succession of Saʿd ad-Dīn occurred in A.D. 1386. The campaigns of these two sultans against Abyssinia will be treated later, see below pp. 74–75.

[5] Ibn Khaldūn, *Berbères*, ii. 108; *ʿIbar*, vi. 199.

[6] *Al-Ilmām*, p. 9. In the Harar Chronicle edited by Cerulli (*R.R.A.L.*, ser. vi, vol. iv, no. 2 (1931), p. 40) the first Walashmaʿ is called ʿUmar b. Dunyā-hūz and died in A.D. 1275/6. He was presumably the father of ʿAlī b. Wālī Asmaʿ who conquered the Shoan king.

He left four or five sons, each of whom succeeded in turn, the last being Ṣabr ad-Dīn b. Nahwī b. Manṣūr b. ʿUmar Walashmaʿ who became King of Ifāt about A.H. 700 (A.D. 1300/1). Maqrīzī continues his account of the history of Ifāt until the reign of Sultan Badlāy (849/1445).

*The First Expansion of Islam.* During this time of troubles which witnessed the emergence of the Abyssinian nation and the triumph of Christianity, when the State had to contend on the home front against pagan or judaized Agao, it had also to defend itself against Muslim penetration, which first cut it off from the sea by securing coastal bases, then gradually converted and organized against it the nomad tribes between the sea and the plateau, and afterwards began to penetrate the Sidāma kingdoms and eastern Shoa. This period between the tenth and twelfth centuries when the Abyssinian kingdom was weak and confined and continually at war with the Agao was the first period of systematic expansion of Islam into north-east Africa. In the north Islam was making but slow progress amongst the Beja. The influence of the Christian kingdoms of Maqurra, ʿAlwa and Abyssinia had introduced Christianity amongst certain of the Beja, for al-Idrīsī wrote in A.D. 1154 that the Baliyyūn, a nomad tribe between the Beja and the Ḥabash, were 'Jacobite Christians as well as all the peoples of Nubia, Abyssinia and most of the Beja'.[1] Yāqūṭ says that Sawākin was inhabited by blacks of the Beja who were Christian,[2] whilst Ibn Saʿīd says they were 'partly Christian, partly Muslim'.[3] Ibn Saʿīd also speaks of 'Abyssinians' who live on the coast being Muslims.[4] But the majority of the Beja still remained pagan, and Maqrīzī (1366–1442) says the only exception was the Hadāreb who 'had become Muslim, though their faith was weak'.[5] Certain groups of the Saho and ʿAfar[6] were converted by the fourteenth century and Somali tribes were being influenced.[7] These tribes, and especially the Somali, all link their

[1] Al-Idrīsī, *Ṣifat al-Maghrib* (ed. and trans. Dozy and de Goeje, 1866), text p. 27, cf. p. 21.

[2] Yāqūṭ, *Geographisches Wörterbuch*, ed. Wüstenfeld, iii. 182.

[3] Ibn Khaldūn, ed. de Slane, ii. 109; Ar. text, vi. 199.

[4] Aboulféda (trans. St. Guyard, 1883), ii, 225.

[5] Maqrīzī, *Khiṭaṭ*, i. 315. See also p. 318 in which he describes the practices of the Shamans of the Hadāreb still retained by those who had become Muslims.

[6] The ʿAfar or Danākil are first mentioned by Ibn Saʿīd, 'Sawākin et ses environs immédiats appartiennent au Bejas; mais tout le pays situé au delà jusqu'à Mandib appartient à une espèce de nègres appelés *Dankal.* Au delà de Mandib, le pays est aux Zailaʿ' (Aboulféda, II. ii. 128). The ʿAfar were therefore on the move northwards whence they gave rise to the Saho groups.

[7] Ibn Saʿīd (1214–87) mentions *barābra* tribes next to the Zanj amongst whom Islam had spread (Aboulféda, ii. 232; Ibn Khaldūn, *Berbères*, trans. de Slane, ii. 106–7). These were

islamization with the coming of an Arab or Arabs from Arabia who married into a leading family and whose descendants formed an aristocracy.

Throughout this period there was a great expansion of the slave-trade and a corresponding development of Muslim coastal trading centres built up by waves of colonizers and traders from across the sea. Such centres were Sawākin, Bāḍiʿ, Dahlak, Zailaʿ, Barbara, Maqdishū, Merka, and Brava, with Mombasa and Zanzibār farther south. These towns were mainly composed of huts of grass with few permanent buildings. This accounts for the rapidity with which towns like Zailaʿ which were within reach of the Abyssinian armies were able to recover and came into use again after their frequent sackings.

The isles of Dahlak from the first became active centres of the trade. Al-Masʿūdī (writing in A.D. 935) and Ibn Ḥawqal[1] (writing in A.D. 977/8) tell us that Dahlak and the towns of the coastal plain were Muslim places tributary to the Abyssinians. At the same time Ibn Ḥawqal, when writing of the revenues of Abū'l-Jaish ibn Ziyād, King of Yaman, in the year 976/7, reports that in token of tribute he received slaves, amber, and leopard skins from the chief of the islands, whilst the queen then dominating Abyssinia sent him gifts.[2] Abū Muḥammad ʿUmāra specifies these slaves as a thousand head, of whom half were Abyssinian and Nūba women.[3] This report conflicts with the statements of Abyssinian sovereignty. The volume of the trade must have been enormous, for there was a dynasty of Abyssinian slave mamlūks (Banū Najāḥ, fl. A.D. 1022–1159) reigning in Zabīd. They and the Banū Ziyād carried on the trade assiduously, thus making many regions of Arabia ethnically similar to the Hamites of the opposite coast. Ibn Saʿīd writes in the thirteenth century that the King of Dahlak was an Abyssinian Muslim who was trying to maintain his independence against the ruler of Yaman.[4] Abyssinian sovereignty over Dahlak must

undoubtedly Somali. He says they possess Maqdishū, 'a town on the Indian Ocean inhabited by Muslim merchants'. South-west of these *barābra* are the 'Damdam, a savage people who wear neither shoes nor clothes. These invaded Abyssinia and Nubia at the time when the Tartars penetrated into ʿIrāq (Jenjis Khān, A.D. 1220) and, after having devastated these countries, returned to their country' (quoted by Ibn Khaldūn, op. cit. ii. 106–7, and Abūʾl-Fidā, p. 163, trans. ii. I. 225). The Arabs used the onomatopoeic Jamjam for any tribe of the cannibal belt. Ad-Dimishqī (A.D. 1256–1327; *Nukhabat ad-Dahr*, ed. M. A. F. Mehren, Leipzig, 1923, p. 162) mentions that the island of Berbera is inhabited by black Muslims who are Zaidites and Shāfiʿites.

[1] *Viae et regna* (ed. de Goeje, 1873), p. 41; cf. Ibn Saʿīd, quoted by Ibn Khaldūn, *ʿIbar*, iv. 213.

[2] Ibn Ḥawqal, ed. Kramers, i. 24.

[3] Abū M. ʿUmāra, *Taʾrīkh al-Yaman* (ed. and trans. H. C. Kay, London, 1892), p. 8.

[4] *Géographie d'Aboulféda* (ed. Reinaud and de Slane, 1840), p. 371; trans. ii. 128.

have been but transitory. Zailaʿ was also lost[1] and became a great centre for the slave-trade and Islamic propaganda, influencing the ʿAfar and some Somali. Farther south Maqdishū and Kilwa were founded by waves of Qarmatians from al-Aḥsā, the first between A.D. 900 and 950 and the second in A.D. 984.[2] Merka is first mentioned by al-Idrīsī who states that the fertile banks of the near-by river (Wēbi-Shabēli) are 'subject to flooding like the Nile'.[3] Ibn Saʿīd says that Merka, capital of the Hawiyya Somali, is a Muslim town.[4] Brava is mentioned by al-Idrīsī under the form *Baruwat*. He also says that the Barbar (i.e. Somali) possess the towns of Qarfawa, Marka, an-Najā, and Ba<u>dh</u>ūna which marks the border between them and the Zanj.[5]

The link with the Islamic world was strong along the coast through the slave-trade, the pilgrimage, and the common practice of those who sought religious posts travelling to centres like Al-Madīna and Cairo for study. A *riwāq* (portico) in the Azhar and a section of the Mosque of the Umayyads at Damascus were reserved for students from Zailaʿ.[6]

At the same time, as we have seen, Islam was spreading inland from the coast throughout the Sidāma kingdoms of southern Ethiopia and into the highlands of eastern Shoa where a sultanate seems to have existed for a long time. In the document describing its last days mention is made of the conversion to Islam in A.D. 1108, of the country of Jubbah (Argobba) which was included in the sultanate. This Shoan dynasty was succeeded in A.D. 1285 by that of the Walashmaʿ of the neighbouring Muslim State of Ifāt. Other Muslim states which are mentioned are those of Adal, Mōra, Hōbat, and Jidāya. Farther south what may have been slavery expeditions developed into regular conquests, and a whole series of Muslim states (Hadya, Faṭajār, Ifāt, Dawāro, Bāli, and Māra) grew up along the coast and inland in ʿAfar

[1] Al-Yaʿqūbī is the first Arabic writer to mention Zailaʿ (*Kitāb al-Buldān*, trans. G. Weit, 1937, p. 159); then in the second half of the tenth century we find references by al-Iṣṭakhrī, *B.G.A.* i. 36; Ibn Ḥawqal, ed. Kramers, i. 43, 56; and al-Muqaddasī, *B.G.A.* iii. 102, 242. Ibn Saʿīd describes its heat, the bad quality of the water, its lack of gardens and fruit, and says that it is governed by shaikhs (quoted in Maqrīzī, *Ilmām*, pp. 25–6; Abūʾl-Fidā, *Géog.* ii. 161). Al-Idrīsī (writing before A.D. 1154) mentions it under the name of Zālagh as a port frequented by the ships of Qulzum who export slaves from Abyssinia (*Description de l'Afrique et de l'Espagne*, text, p. 25). Abūʾl-Fidā writes of the people of Zailaʿ as Muslims in the first half of the 14th century (*Géog.* ii. 231–2).

[2] João de Barros, *Da Asia* (1777–8), dec. i, liv. viii, cap. iv, pp. 211–12, 224–5; Muḥyī ad-Dīn, *Kitāb as-Sulwa fī akhbār Kilwa*, ed. S. A. Strong; *J.R.A.S.*, 1896, p. 399.

[3] Al-Idrīsī, *Géographie* (trans. P. A. Jaubert, Paris, 1836–40), pp. 44–45.

[4] *Géographie d'Aboulféda*, ii. 232.

[5] Al-Idrīsī, *Kitāb al-muhaj wa rawḍ al-faraj* (588/1192), see *R.S.O.* ix. 450–2.

[6] Ibn Baṭūṭa, *Riḥla* (Cairo, 1939), i. 73.

regions, in Harar and Arūsi territory as far as the lakes, thus ringing the east and south of the Ethiopian massif.[1]

Muslim colonies had even established themselves in the Christian part of the highlands, as is shown by references in the *History of the Patriarchs of Alexandria* and by epigraphic evidence.[2] Abū Ṣāliḥ (fl. *c.* A.D. 1170–1220) mentions that there were many Muslims in Abyssinia in the early years of the thirteenth century, each of whom was required to pay a tax of three *afiqaḥīs* (ingots of iron), which was the Abyssinian currency.[3] The struggle with Islam was further embittered by the fact that the Coptic Church in its dark days sometimes took the side of Islam. Acting in collusion with the Muslim rulers of Egypt, the Church sometimes appointed abūnas who worked for the promotion of Islamic interests in Abyssinia itself. For instance, after the death of the Abūna Daniel mentioned above, the Patriarch Christodulos (A.D. 1047–78), during a fresh wave of persecution, professed himself unable to fill the vacancy and an adventurer named ʿAbdūn got himself recognized in Abyssinia by means of forged documents.[4] The next Patriarch Kierlos II (A.D. 1078–92) wished to nominate a bishop regularly consecrated, but Badr al-Jamālī, the *wazīr* of Al-Mustanṣir bi'llāh (A.D. 1035–94), openly intervened in the choice in favour of his nominee, one Abbā Sawiros (*c.* A.D. 1080). When this bishop arrived in Abyssinia where he was welcomed with great rejoicings, he proceeded to fulfil the terms of his agreement with the *wazīr* to favour the propagation of Islam by constructing mosques. A general uproar followed. The bishop tried to appease it by saying that mosques for the use of Arab merchants compromised nothing, whilst refusal to build would draw reprisals upon the Copts of Egypt. But hatred of the *abūna* reached such a pitch that the king put him in prison and destroyed the seven mosques that had been built. Restrictions were placed on the activities of Muslim merchants which led to reciprocal action

[1] This is confirmed by the epigraphic evidence from the Arūsi region collected by P. Azaïs, *Cinq Années de recherches archéologiques en Éthiopie*, appendix, 'Stèles et inscriptions arabes du Harar' (1931), pp. 283–309. Two Arabic inscriptions are dated A.H. 666 and 675 (A.D. 1267/8 and 1276), during the last days of the Shoan sultanate.

[2] Gravestones bearing Arabic inscriptions have been discovered at Woger Hariba in Enderta (southern Tigrai), one of which is dated 8 Dhū'l-qaʿda 396 (6 Aug. 1006); see C. Conti Rossini, 'Necropoli musulmana ed antica chiesa cristiana presso Uogrì Haribà', *R.S.O.* xvii (1938), 399–408; C. Pansera, 'Quattro stele musulmane presso Uogher Hariba nell' Enderta', *Studi Etiopici* raccolti da C. Conti Rossini (1945), pp. 3–6.

[3] *The Churches and Monasteries of Egypt* (trans. B. T. A. Evetts, 1895), p. 290.

[4] *Hāymānota Abaw*, in C. Conti Rossini, 'I manoscritti etiopici della Missione Cattolica di Cheren', *R.R.A.L.*, ser. v, vol. xiii (1904), p. 267.

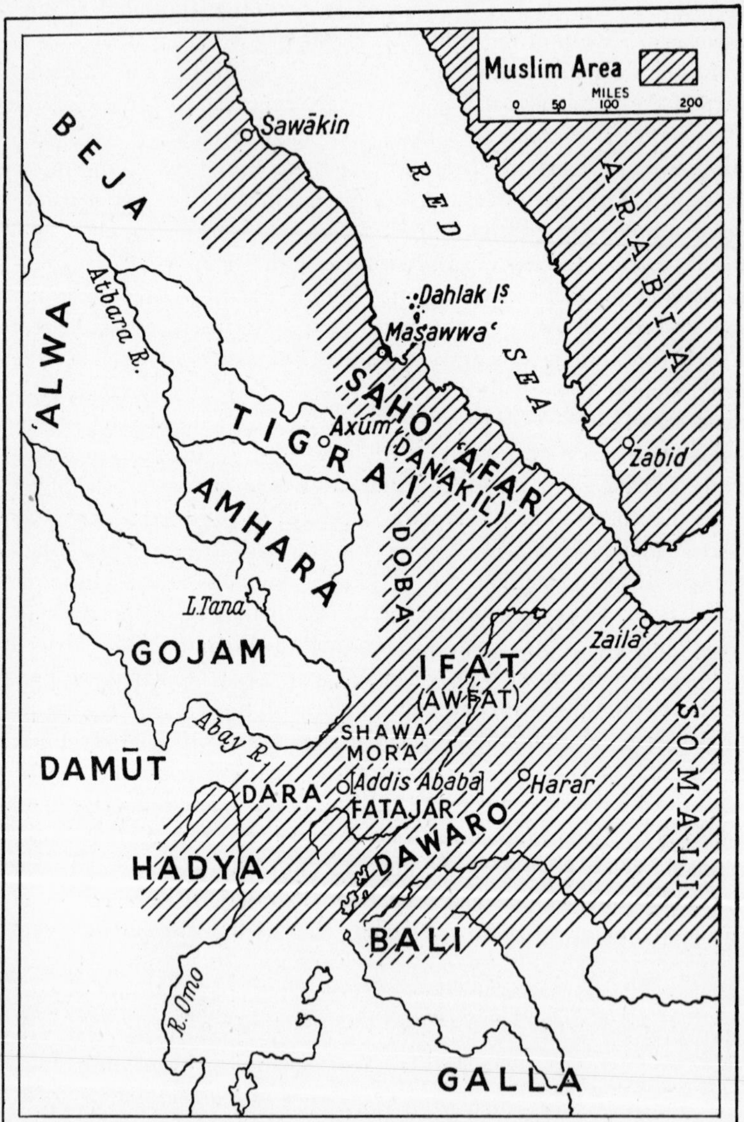


MUSLIM STATES IN THE TIME OF ʿAMDA SYŌN I
(A.D. 1314–44)

being taken in Egypt and a rupture in the relationship of the two countries.[1]

Whilst open propagation of Islam within the Christian kingdom itself did not have much success, commercial relations with the Red Sea ports and Egypt and the influence of Muslims in eastern Shoa did result in the conversion of families or small groups of Abyssinians in the interior, some of whom, like the Walashmaʿ, were of noble families. But as the Abyssinian State gradually consolidated itself after the end of this period of historical obscurity, it began to expand southward over Muslim regions and a protracted struggle broke out between Christians and Muslims, the chief cause of which was not zeal for religion but territorial expansion.

### (c) *The 'Solomonid' Dynasty*

The period of Abyssinian history for which we have native chronicles begins with Yekuno Amlāk (1270–85), the first of the Solomonid line of 'kings of kings' of Ethiopia. The stabilization of the rule of the new dynasty was accomplished rapidly and the centre of the State changed from Lāsta to Amḥara, but the policy of the early Solomonids was directed less towards the consolidation of the highlands under one rule than towards containing the menacing expansion of the Sultanate of Ifāt over the fertile regions of Shoa. The struggle which broke out between the Christian and Muslim kingdoms was not a war of religion but a struggle for political predominance, and the consequent expansion of Amharic sovereignty which led to the formation of a great empire was the result of the challenge of islamized-pagan societies which caused it to seek to dominate those societies.

The conversion of the Abyssinians, who were still largely pagan in the thirteenth century, received a great impulse under the early Solomonids. A missionary who began the conversion of the pagan regions of western Shoa and Dāmot beyond the Abāy was St. Takla Hāymānot (d. *c.* A.D. 1312), the Benedict of Abyssinia, in whose name, fifty-seven

[1] See Renaudot, *Hist. Patr. Alex.*, pp. 461–2. No credence can be attached to the various legends circulating in Egypt at this time which attribute exceptionally low Niles resulting in famine to Abyssinian interference with its source, and their restoration to a visit of the Patriarch to Abyssinia. Such a patriarchal visit in the year A.H. 451 (A.D. 1059/60) is recorded by Ibn Iyās on the authority of Ibn Wāṣif Shāh (*Nashq al-Azhār fī ʿAjāʾib al-Aqṭār*, ed. L. Langlès in *Notices et Extraits des Manuscrits de la Bibliothèque Impériale*, vol. viii, pt. 1 (1810), pp. 47–48, 78–79. Another in the time of the Patriarch Michael (IV) al-Ḥabīs (1092–1102) is mentioned by al-Makīn (Ibn al-ʿAmīd, *c.* 1205–73), reproduced by Maqrīzī, see *Geschichte der Kopten*, ed. Wüstenfeld, p. 27; *Khiṭaṭ*, ii. 476. Qalqashandī (*Ṣubḥ*, ed. A.H. 1333/1915, v. 323), who also derives his material from Ibn al-ʿAmīd, denies its accuracy.

years after his death, the great monastery of Dabra Libānos in Shoa was founded. Another founder of a monastic order and missionary to pagans was St. Ewosṭātēwos (d. *c.* A.D. 1332) who we are told destroyed twelve sacred groves dedicated to pagan deities.[1] At the same time the new orders set themselves with equal energy and some measure of success to reform Abyssinian Christianity and social life.

*The Muslim Sultanates.* We have seen that whilst Christianity was slowly expanding throughout the highlands Islam had been making more rapid strides from the coastal regions over the southern part of the country and a line of sultanates now extended from the Red Sea to the region of the great lakes, pressing into southern Shoa. These, had they been united, would have been a menace to the very existence of the resurrected Christian kingdom in the highlands, surrounded and interpenetrated by pagan Agao groups entrenched in impregnable fastnesses. In the reign of Yekuno Amlāk this kingdom was still of little account for he had to devote his energies to the consolidation of his rule, but under his successors it became the dominating power throughout the whole of Ethiopia, the Negus being literally a king of kings; al-ʿUmarī, for instance, speaks of him figuratively as reigning over ninety-nine kings.[2]

The most westerly of the Muslim principalities was that of Hadya which covered a very large extent of territory between the rivers Ḥawāsh and Gibē. Its ruling class were Muslim but their subjects, who were Sidāma and included the semitized Gurāgē and the Chabo, a fusion of Gurāgē and Sidāma, were pagan.[3] Hadya was noted in Muslim lands as an important supplier of eunuchs, a practice forbidden by the

[1] 'Die quodam, cum doceret, audivit silvestria delubra idolorum esse, in quibus homines idololatrae adorant. Et eo ivit, cum esset aemulator legis Dei, sicut Honorius rex, qui cecidit et igne ussit silvam matris suae, in qua adorabat et sacra faciebat. Ita et hic Mar Eustathius has silvas cecidit et eas igne ussit, quoad cinis fierent; et ventus cinerem earum dissipavit ibi, quo erant. Et numerus delubrorum silvestrium quae igne ussit erat XII, in Ṣalmā et in omnibus regionibus' (*Acta S. Eustathii*, *C.S.C.O.*, vol. xxi (1906), trans. Turaiev, p. 31).

[2] Al-ʿUmarī, *Masālik al-Abṣār* (trans. Gaudefroy-Demombynes, 1927), p. 25; al-Qalqashandī, *Ṣubḥ*, v. 332; viii. 39.

[3] West of the Gibē-Omo were pagan Sidāma kingdoms. The Sidāma had migrated to this region at some remote epoch in distinct groups who imposed themselves first on the aboriginal negro tribes and then on former Sidāma settlers. In their evolution they lost their Hamitic democratic organization and developed into monarchical states. The ruling classes of the Sidāma east of the Gibē adopted Islam, but those west of the river who extended northwards well beyond the Abāy maintained their independence and their paganism in a number of states. One of the strongest kingdoms, by reason of the external threat from the Muslim states, was Yamma or Zinjaro, west of the Gibē, who were considerably mixed with negroes; then came the Mansho (in Kaffa region) west of the Omo, south of the Gogeb; Bosha in the Jimma region; Enārya to the north-west; Affillo between the Baro and the Abāy; the Gafat, who now spoke a Semitic language, on the banks of the Abāy; and the Shināsha in the Wallegga region.

King of Amḥara.[1] Two small kingdoms, 'Arābabni and Sharkha, seem to have intervened between Hadya and Dawāro.

On the western loop of the Ḥawāsh was Faṭajār occupying the extreme south-eastern buttresses of Shoa. North of Faṭajār was the sultanate of Ifāt. Ifāt proper was the plateau region of eastern Shoa which included the slopes down to the valley of the Ḥawāsh, but its sphere of influence was much wider and extended to the region around Zaila' on the Gulf of Aden,[2] whilst the nomadic 'Afar tribes of the plain of Aussa also paid its ruler some kind of allegiance. Ifāt was the most powerful of the Muslim kingdoms by reason of its control of the trade-routes connecting the interior with Zaila', and as we have seen was governed by a dynasty of Abyssinian origin (though they now claimed to be 'Alids) having the title of *qāṭ* and the family name of Walashma', who had their seat in eastern Shoa. By the middle of the thirteenth century the majority of the population, who spoke a Semitic language,[3] were Muslims. Included in Ifāt were two emirates called Mōra and Adal. These three kingdoms, Hadya, Faṭajār, and Ifāt, were the bridgehead of Muslim expansion into Shoa.

Of the other Muslim-Sidāma kingdoms, Dawāro was situated south of Shoa, bordering on Ifāt on the right bank of the Ḥawāsh, stretching southwards as far as the river Wēbi which marked the border with the neighbouring state of Bāli. Dawāro therefore corresponded roughly to the present Arūsi region. Although not as large as Ifāt it is said to have been able to raise an army equal to that of Ifāt. South of Dawāro was Bāli, between the Wēbi in the north and the Ganālē Doria in the south, thus controlling the Somali plain. It was inhabited chiefly by Sidāma with Galla nomads to the south of them. In the interior of this region was a mountain (later called Abū'l-Qāsim) which had been a famous place of pilgrimage from early times whose cult was to be associated with

[1] Cf. Aboulféda, p. 229; Al-'Umarī, op. cit., pp. 16–17.

[2] Al-'Umarī, op. cit., p. 5. Ibn Baṭūṭa who visited the town of Zaila' about 1330 describes it in most unflattering terms, 'It is the capital of the Berbers (*barābra* as he calls the Somali), a type of blacks who are Shāfi'i in *madhhab*. Their land is desert for a two months' journey from Zaila' to Maqdishū. Their beasts are camels and they have sheep renowned for their fat. The people of Zaila' are black and most of them Rāfiḍa (Zaidī-Shī'ite). It is a large town with an important market. On the other hand, it is the filthiest and most wretched town in existence and possesses the most awful stench. The cause of its stench is the quantity of fish and the blood of the camels they slaughter in its alleys. When we arrived there we chose to sleep on board ship in spite of the strong swell and never slept in the town on account of its filthiness' (*Riḥla*, 1939, i. 195).

[3] Al-'Umarī (op. cit., p. 7; cf. Maqrīzī, *Ilmām*, p. 7) says of the people of Ifāt, 'their language is Abyssinian and Arabic'. The people of Argobba, part of former Ifāt, still speak an Ethiopic-Semitic language; cf. M. Cohen, *Études d'éthiopien méridional* (Paris, 1931), pp. 354 ff.

Islam. On the extreme buttresses of the Ahmar mountains was Harar; an ancient city which must originally have been founded either by a Semitic military colony from the north or by immigrants from Arabia, because its people to this day speak a Semitic language.[1] The inhabitants of Harar had been converted to Islam and it was soon to become an important centre of commerce and Islamic propaganda. In Egypt the whole region was known as the country of Zailaʿ. Al-ʿUmarī writes, 'this is the region which is called in Egypt and Syria "the land of Zailaʿ". This, however, is only one of their coastal towns and one of their islands, whose name has been extended to the whole'.[2] Along the coast of the Somali-Galla territory were a whole string of Muslim trading-colonies, of which Maqdishū was already ruled by a hereditary sultanate.[3] These colonies were influencing some of the Somali tribes.

The actual area of these Muslim kingdoms was much larger than that of the Christian kingdom, and the Muslim rulers, as we shall see, were in touch with unsubjected Agao, always ready to make common cause with invaders. In the coming struggle, however, the Abyssinians had the advantage of being able to move on interior lines, whilst the Muslims were dispersed over a vast region with poor communications, much of it sparsely populated by nomads, the more fertile regions cultivated by peace-loving Sidāma. The Muslim powers were not well organized, mobilization was difficult, they had little power of resistance, and were liable to sudden collapse. Ifāt, which so far had been subject to no external threat since the Sidāma kingdoms were on the defensive, had assumed predominance amongst the states and was in process of organization towards a more consolidated power. Ifāt was a good base for attack, but only if it kept the initiative. In the reign of ʿAmda Ṣyōn, however, the initiative passed to the Christians and Ifāt found itself exposed to the shock of the whole Abyssinian army. Whenever it was attacked by surprise without being able to bring up allies it was forced

[1] Harar is first mentioned in the chronicle of ʿAmda Ṣyōn (Perruchon, pp. 52, 90). The language is today confined to the city itself and is called *gey sinān*, 'the city language', by its speakers and *afan aḍāri* (language of the citizens; Ar. *ḥaḍarī*) by the Galla.

[2] Op. cit. p. 4; cf. Maqrīzī, *Ilmām*, p. 6.

[3] The Qarmatian and Persian groups which colonized Maqdishū had united in face of the perpetual threat of the nomadic tribes which hemmed in their settlement. One of the clans, the Muqrī, adopted the *nisba* of al-Qaḥṭānī and formed a ruling class of ʿ*ulamā* (Yāqūṭ, ed. Wüstenfeld, 1869, iv. 602; i. 502). In the second half of the thirteenth century Abū Bakr b. Fakhr ad-Dīn established a hereditary sultanate, though the Muqrī retained the right to elect the qāḍī. In A.D. 1331 the town was visited by Ibn Baṭūṭa, who found there a sultan of Somali origin who spoke Maqdishī (Somali?) but also knew Arabic (*Riḥla*, 1939, i. 196–9). Zar'a Yāʿqob fought a battle at Gomut with the reigning sultan in A.D. 1445.

to capitulate and the other kingdoms were destroyed one after another. All the campaigns of the Abyssinians against the Walashmaʿ resulted in continual reverses to the latter and the situation only changed when Harar became the chief Muslim base, for then the Abyssinians were far from their own highlands, Harar was in direct contact with the warlike ʿAfar and Somali tribes ever seeking to expand out of their inhospitable regions, and the offensive was again taken up successfully by the reorganized forces of Islam.

*The Struggle with the Sultanates.* Abyssinia had been without an *abūna* since A.D. 1250 and one of the first acts of Yekuno Amlāk, the founder of the new dynasty, was to correspond in 1274/5 with Rukn ad-Dīn Baybars through the Hamdānid sultan of Yaman concerning the appointment of an honest bishop who would not be solely concerned with amassing money.[1] He also took immediate precautions on the frontier menaced by Ifāt.[2] This caused Baybars to break off relations with the kingdom and refuse to allow an *abūna* to be consecrated. The next king, Yāgbe'a Ṣyōn (1285–94), if we can trust Marco Polo,[3] began

[1] Mufaḍḍal b. Abī'l-Faḍā'il, *Hist. des Sultans Mamlouks.* trans. Brochet in *Patr. Or.* xiv (1920), 383–6. See also Maqrīzī, *Hist. des Sultans Mamlouks* (trans. Quatremère, 1837), ii. 122, 151 n. The account of the correspondence between Baybars and Yekuno Amlāk recorded by Mufaḍḍal b. Abī'l-Faḍā'il, a Coptic clerk in the employ of the Sultan of Egypt, gives some information about Abyssinia: 'Amḥarā is one of the regions of Abyssinia and it is the largest. Its lord rules over the greater part of Abyssinia such as the countries of Dāmūt and Ḥarlā. The ruler of Amḥarā is called *Ḥaṭī*, that is to say *khalīfa*, and all who have ruled over it have borne this title. One of the kings of Abyssinia was Yūsuf ibn Arsamāya who was lord of Jidāya, Shawā, Qalḥūr, and their dependencies, which are all Muslim principalities. As for the region of Zailaʿ and its tribes, they have no kings but are divided into seven tribes. These are Muslims and their preachers recite the *khuṭba* in the name of their seven chiefs' (op. cit., pp. 386–7). Yūsuf ibn Arsamāya is not mentioned elsewhere and it is impossible to say whether he was one of the kings of the Muslim dynasty in Shoa or one of the Walashmaʿ.

[2] C. Conti Rossini, 'Appunti ed osservazioni sopra i re Zāguē', *R.R.A.L.*, ser. v, vol. iv, p. 464.

[3] Marco Polo obtained some information about Abyssinia from Arab pilots: 'Its principal king is a Christian. Of the others, who are six in number, and tributary to the first, three are Christians and three are Saracens' (*Travels*, Everyman's ed., p. 398). He mentions that the Jews are also numerous there. The capital of the Negus is in the interior whilst the dominions of the Muslims are near the Province of Aden. The people of Abyssinia are constantly engaged in wars with the Sultan of Adal, the people of Nubia, and other neighbouring countries. He says also that in the year 1288 the Negus sent a bishop to Jerusalem whom the Sultan of Adal tried to convert to Islam when he passed through his dominions, and when he refused had him forcibly circumcised (this is impossible since he would already be circumcised). After his return to Abyssinia the Negus invaded Adal with the assistance of two of his Muslim tributary princes and sacked the city of Adal (presumably Zailaʿ) (op. cit., pp. 398–401). Although Marco Polo confuses Aden and Adal it is certainly the latter which is meant here. That Yāgbe'a Ṣyōn sent an embassy to Jerusalem which arrived in Cairo A.H. 689 (A.D. 1290) is confirmed by Arab sources (cf. 'Life of Qalā'ūn', quoted by Quatremère, *Mémoires géographiques et historiques sur l'Égypte* (Paris, 1811), ii. 267–8.

his reign with a successful campaign against Adal (presumably Zailaʿ). Later he accepted a truce with his powerful neighbours and reopened the frontier to Muslim merchants in consequence of which Abyssinia reacquired its sites in the Holy Land and an *abūna* was consecrated. The Amḥara kingdom was not yet securely established and the years 1294–9 saw a succession of five of Yāgbe'a Ṣyōn's sons. The internal troubles are reflected in the following story from Muslim sources. In A.H. 698 (A.D. 1298/9) a Muslim shaikh called Muḥammad Abū ʿAbd Allāh was inspired by angelic visitants to collect a considerable army and conquer Abyssinia. The invasion fizzled out and the king arranged a treaty with him whereby he conceded several frontier districts to the Muslims on condition of the recognition of his suzerainty.[1] It is impossible to tell from the text where this took place; it may have been an incident in the conflicts with Ifāt or with the Muslim Balaw of Walqayt.

Yāgbe'a Ṣyōn's policy of appeasement with the Islamic world showed itself ineffective to stop the steady advance of Islamic influence. The people of Ifāt, taking it to be a sign of weakness, changed their policy to one of open aggression. Islamic pressure, however, evoked in the Abyssinians a dogged nationalism which was to prove more than a match for Ethiopian Islam.

The new Amḥara kingdom was stabilized and began to expand in the reign of ʿAmda Ṣyōn I (1314–44)[2] who may well be called the founder of the Abyssinian State. The Mamlūk sultan, An-Nāṣir Muḥammad b. Qala'ūn, began a new persecution of the Copts of Egypt and demolished many churches. This brought forth a strong protest from the Abyssinian king who sent envoys to Cairo in A.H. 726 (A.D. 1321) to ask the sultan to restore the churches and refrain from persecuting the Copts; otherwise, he threatened, he would take reciprocal measures against the Muslims in his dominions and starve the

[1] Mufaḍḍal b. Abī'l-Faḍā'il, *Patr. Or.*, xx. 56–58. Maqrīzī dates the incident in the year A.D. 1300 which would put it in the reign of Wedem Raʿād (1299–1314) who restored the stabilityof the throne; cf. *Histoire des Sultans Mamlouks* (trans. Quatremère, Paris, 1837–45), iv. 183.

[2] Our sources for ʿAmda Ṣyōn's campaigns against the Muslims are primarily the Ethiopic Chronicle translated by Dillmann, *Die Kriegsthaten des Königs ʿAmda-Ṣyōn*, Berlin, 1884; Perruchon, 'Histoire des Guerres d'Amda Ṣyon', *J. Asiat.* (Paris, 1889), ser. viii, vol. xiv, pp. 271–363, 381–493; Ducati, *La Grande Impresa di Amda Siôn*, Milan, 1939. On the Muslim side we have Maqrīzī, *Al-Ilmām bi akhbār man bi arḍ al-Ḥabasha min mulūk al-Islām*, composed in A.H. 829 (A.D. 1434/5). This was edited and translated by Rinck, *Historia regum Islamiticorum in Abyssinia*, Leyden 1790, and edited by G. Zaidān, Cairo, 1895. It is Zaidān's edition which is cited below under *Ilmām*. Maqrīzī's descriptive material is based chiefly on Al-ʿUmarī's *masālik al-abṣār*.

peoples of Egypt by diverting the course of the Nile. The sultan was only amused and dismissed the envoys.[1] This again came as a pretext to Ḥaqq ad-Dīn, Sultan of Ifāt, to change his policy from one of casual raids and gradual penetration to a definite war of aggression. He invaded Christian territory, burnt churches, and forced Christians to apostatize. He captured an Abyssinian ambassador returning from Cairo and, after failing to make him abjure his faith, killed him. This act roused the Abyssinians. In 1328 ʿAmda Ṣyōn overwhelmed the outposts of Ifāt and then sent columns in all directions, paralysing Muslim opposition. Ḥaqq ad-Dīn was taken prisoner and both Ifāt and Faṭajār annexed as one vassal state under Ṣabr ad-Dīn, brother of Ḥaqq ad-Dīn.

The other Muslim states of Hadya and Dawāro now rallied around Ṣabr ad-Dīn who planned to overthrow the long and narrow kingdom of Amḥara by attacking it from as many points as possible. He therefore invited the co-operation of the judaized Agao in Wagarā, Dambya, and Bēgamder, who were to divert the attention of the king whilst the Muslims were to invade at three points into Amḥara, Angot, and Shoa simultaneously. But the king learnt of his plans and attacked his enemies separately. One army attacked Hadya whose sultan Amano was being incited by a 'false prophet in the guise of Balaʿam'; the country was ravaged, many of its people carried off captive, and 'the false prophet then fled to Ifāt where he continued to spread his false doctrines'.[2] Faṭajār was next reduced, followed by Dawāro and Ifāt, whose sultan was forced to submit though his life was spared.

Thus ended the independence of Hadya, Faṭajār, Dawāro, and Ifāt which were all placed under Jamāl ad-Dīn, another brother of Ṣabr ad-Dīn, as ruler tributary to Abyssinia. The boundaries of Ethiopia proper were carried to the edge of the plateau along the River Ḥawāsh. At the same time some Shoan regions such as Manz (Manzeḥ) and Zēga were definitely annexed by the Christian kingdom.[3] Islam must have declined very rapidly amongst the imperfectly islamized Sidāma for the mass of the people were pagan,[4] though Muslim colonies still

[1] Al-Maqrīzī, *Histoire des Sultans Mamlouks*, trans. Quatremère, Paris, 1837–44; cf. R. Basset, *Études*, notes 63, 68. It was no doubt this incident which caused Al-ʿUmarī to write, 'the Abyssinians claim that they are the guardians of the course of the Nile for its descent to Egypt and that they further its regular arrival out of respect for the sultan of Egypt', Al- Umarī, op. cit., p. 30.

[2] Perruchon, op. cit., p. 334.

[3] Ducati, op. cit., p. 8.

[4] C. Conti Rossini, *Acta S. Baṣalota-Mikāʾēl et Anorēwos*, *C.S.C.O.*, ser. ii, vol. xx, p. 33.

existed near Lake Zway during the early decades of the fourteenth century.[1]

Between A.D. 1332 and 1338 the Muslims of Ifāt sent an embassy under ʿAbd Allāh az-Zailaʿī to Cairo to ask the Sultan of Egypt, An-Nāṣir Muḥammad, to intervene with the Abyssinians on their behalf. The sultan asked the Coptic Patriarch to write a letter to the Negus, on which Al-ʿUmarī comments, 'ses exhortations furent excellentes, mais cet incident est charactéristique de la situation'.[2]

We will dispense with any detailed account of the wars of ʿAmda Ṣyōn which make tedious reading. The two petty Shoan chieftaincies of Mōra[3] and Adal had become alarmed at this expansion of Abyssinian power at the expense of Muslim kingdoms and now joined in, together with Ṭīqō, Pāgūma, Labakalā, Wārgār, and Gabalā, which were probably nomad tribes nominally subject to the two kingdoms.[4] All were defeated and the kings of Mōra and Adal took council with the Imām Ṣāliḥ, son of a Mekkan *sharīf*, who had great influence as a holy man in the Harar region. The new alliance was joined by Jamāl ad-Dīn. Again they were defeated and ʿAmda Ṣyōn marched triumphantly through Ifāt, captured and killed its king and Imām Ṣāliḥ, and destroyed its town and mosques.

ʿAmda Ṣyōn now ruled a conglomeration of principalities with hereditary vassal princes. The central kingdoms in the highlands which were still being conquered were reduced to the status of provinces whose governors were not necessarily hereditary. The king had no fixed capital, but always went to the holy city of Axum to be crowned. The most valuable account of the tributary Muslim sultanates is that of Ibn Faḍl Allāh al-ʿUmarī who wrote his *masālik al-abṣār* between A.D. 1342 and 1349, which was towards the end of the reign of ʿAmda Ṣyōn. He obtained his information from Shaikh ʿAbd Allāh az-Zailaʿī, leader of the embassy mentioned above, and tells us that:

The Muslim kingdoms in Abyssinia were seven in number: Awfāt, Dawāro,

[1] B. Turaiev, *Acta S. Aaronis et S. Philippi*, *C.S.C.O.*, ser. ii, vol. xx, pp. 208–10.

[2] Al-ʿUmarī, op. cit., pp. 2–3.

[3] Mōra is first mentioned in the document discovered by Cerulli on the early Shoan sultanate (*R.S.E.* i. 13) and appears in the Chronicle of ʿAmda Ṣyon (tr. Perruchon, pp. 44, 346–70) as situated beyond the Ḥawāsh near the River Yās.

[4] Ducati, op. cit., p. 27. Cerulli identifies the Wārgār with the Warjiḥe, who, with the Gabalā and Zallān, are referred to as nomadic pastoralists in the Chronicle of ʿAmda Ṣyōn (tr. Perruchon, p. 331). Some Muslim groups who now speak Galla and claim a Tigrean origin still exist scattered over southern Shoa and in the region between the Ḥawāsh and the Gibē (see Cerulli, *E.O.* i. 14–15, *R.S.E.* i. 18). The inscription of Adulis mentions *Γαβαλα* north of Axum (*D.A.E.* i. 42–43).

ʿArābabni,[1] Hadya, Sharkhā,[2] Bāli, and Ḍāra.[3] These kingdoms, which belonged to seven kings, are weak and poor, because the cohesion between the inhabitants is weak, the produce of the country is not abundant and the king of Amḥara imposes his authority on the other kings of Abyssinia; not to mention the religious antipathy which exists between them and the disputes which separate Christians and Muslims. Thus the authority of each is isolated and their unity is changed in its very essence. I heard from Shaikh ʿAbd Allāh az-Zailaʿī and other learned men of this country that if these seven kings maintained a united front and replaced their rivalry by a solid union, they would have the power to defend themselves and to resist; but, in addition to their weakness and the dispersion of their authority, they are jealous of each other. Some of them throw themselves into the arms of the king of Amḥara and are under his authority; and in their abasement and poverty, they pay him a fixed tribute.[4]

He says of the Islam of these kingdoms, 'they have cathedral mosques and ordinary mosques, where they perform the *khuṭba*, the Friday prayer, and congregational prayer. They observe the precepts of religion, but they have neither *madrasa*, *khānaqāh*, *ribāṭ*, nor *zāwiya*'.[5] The King of Ifāt and most of his subjects were Shāfiʿī, the other kingdoms were all Ḥanafī.[6]

The extension of Abyssinian power by ʿAmda Ṣyōn had repercussions in the surrounding Muslim lands and his successor, Sayfa Arʿād (A.D. 1344–72), who consolidated his work, appears to have assumed the role of protector of the Patriarchate of Alexandria. The account which has come down to us is very unreliable, but it is related that when Amīr Shaikhūn, tutor of Sultan al-Malik aṣ-Ṣāliḥ, persecuted the Christians and imprisoned the Patriarch Marcos in A.D. 1352, Sayfa Arʿād retaliated by seizing the Egyptian merchants in his dominions, putting some to death, and forcing others to embrace Christianity.

[1] ʿArābabni (v. l. ʿArābīnī) is corrected to Arā'ini and identified with the Ar'ēñ of the Ethiopic chronicles by C. Conti Rossini, *Historia regis Sarṣa Dengel*, *C.S.C.O.*, *Scr. Acth.*, ser. ii, vol. iii (1907), p. 95.

[2] Sharkhā is probably the Sārkā mentioned in the wars of ʿAmda Ṣyōn (Perruchon, p. 481) which took part in the revolt of the people of Dawāro. Sharkhā may have been part of the kingdom of Enārya whose capital was Sāka. Sarṣa Dengel on his way to attack Muḥammad of Adal in 1577 passed through Wāj (Gurāgē country) and then Sharkā (*C.S.C.O.*, vol. iii (1907), p. 57). This would place it just east of Hadya and is the more likely identification.

[3] Ḍāra, which is mentioned in the *Gadla Anorēwos* (d. 1374; *C.S.C.O.*, *Scr. Aeth.*, ser. ii, vol. xx, pp. 1, 54, 76–7) as a Muslim province (*tanbalāt*), was probably situated east of the Abāy, cf. Weld Blundell, *The Royal Chronicle of Abyssinia*, p. 538. Al-ʿUmarī (op. cit., p. 19) says it bordered on Bāli.

[4] Al-ʿUmari, *Masālik* (trans. Gaudefroy-Demombynes, 1927), pp. 1–2; cf. Qalqashandī, *Ṣubḥ* (1333/1915), v. 332–3.

[5] Ibid., p. 3; quoted by Qalqashandī, *Ṣubḥ*, v. 324.

[6] Ibid., pp. 5, 14, 15, 18, 19; cf. Qalqashandī, v. 324.

An-Nāṣir Ḥasan (d. A.D. 1361), one of the puppet Baḥrī sultans of the time, asked the patriarch once more to intervene. An embassy of bishops was sent and the Negus was so delighted with them that he refused to allow them to return.[1]

In A.D. 1376 internal struggles between pretenders to the throne of Ifāt[2] resulted in the accession of Ḥaqq ad-Dīn II who declared himself independent of the Abyssinians, but was conquered and killed in battle against them in A.H. 788 (A.D. 1386/7). His successor Saʿd ad-Dīn II recommenced hostilities. He gained initial successes, but the Negus Dāwit I (A.D. 1382–1411) sent an expedition against him under a general called Bārwā. Maqrīzī writes in terms which make the campaign sound like a *jihād*:

> With Saʿd ad-Dīn were jurisconsults, dervishes, peasants, and all the inhabitants of the country. They all made a death-covenant. A fierce battle took place between them. Four hundred godly shaikhs, each with his ablution jug and having under him a great number of dervishes, fell martyrs. The slaughter of the Muslims continued until the majority had perished and the remainder were broken to pieces.[3]

Saʿd ad-Dīn took refuge on the island of Zailaʿ where he was besieged and killed in A.H. 817 (A.D. 1415) during the reign of the Negus Yesḥāq.[4] The occupation of Zailaʿ brought to an end the kingdom of Ifāt which was permanently occupied by the Abyssinians and is heard of no more.[5] The ten sons of Saʿd ad-Dīn took refuge with Aḥmad b. al-Ashraf Ismāʿīl, King of Yaman. When shortly afterwards they returned to Africa the Walashmaʿ dynasty took the title of kings of Adal and chose a lower platform for their capital at Dakar, farther removed from the threat of Abyssinian armies.[6] Thenceforth the protagonist of the struggle against Abyssinia was this kingdom of Adal,[7]

[1] Cf. J. Perruchon, *R. Sém.* i (1893), 177–82; Renaudot, pp. 607–10. Qalqashandī (*Ṣubḥ*, v. 333) mentions another intervention of the patriarch in the early years of the reign of Sultan Barqūq (A.D. 1382–98). It is possible that both accounts refer to the same event.

[2] See Maqrīzī, *Ilmām*, pp. 10–11.

[3] Ibid., p. 13.

[4] This date is according to the History of the Walashmaʿ edited by Cerulli, *R.R.A.L.* ser. vi, vol. iv (1931), p. 45. Maqrīzī gives the date of the death of Saʿd ad-Dīn as A.H. 805 (A.D. 1402) during the reign of Dāwit I.

[5] *Ilmām*, pp. 11–14; R. Basset, *Études*, p. 239 n. 93; *Futūḥ*, p. 306 n. 1.

[6] Tradition places Dakar south-east of Harar near Fiyambiro. Maqrīzī (*Ilmām*, p. 20) says that it was the residence of Sultan Badlāy (A.D. 1432–45). It was destroyed by Iskander (A.D. 1478–94) and finally abandoned by Sultan Abū Bakr in A.H. 926 (A.D. 1519/20).

[7] Adal is first mentioned in the Arabic account of the last days of the Shoan sultanate as being conquered along with Mōra in A.D. 1288 (*R.S.E.* i. 9). Marco Polo refers to it about A.D. 1295. The Chronicle of ʿAmda Ṣyōn speaks of the numerous peoples of Adal and Mōra (Perruchon, pp. 346–7). Al-ʿUmarī, writing in the same century (14th), mentions the

inheritor of the tradition of Ifāt, which also came to be called *Barr Saʿd ad-Dīn*, 'the land of Saʿd ad-Dīn', in memory of the martyr in the holy war.[1]

Relations with Egypt became friendlier during the reign of Dāwit I, since we read that in A.H. 788 (A.D. 1387) he sent an embassy to the court of Barqūq which was accompanied by twenty camel-loads of gifts.[2] During the reign of Dāwit's second son, Yesḥāq (A.D. 1414–29), Turkish mamlūks settled in Abyssinia and established workshops for making coats of mail, swords, and other weapons; an exiled Egyptian mamlūk, aṭ-Ṭabungha (Altunbuga) Mufriq, reorganized Yesḥāq's army and taught the Abyssinians to make Greek fire; whilst a Copt, Fakhr ad-Dawla, reorganized the system of tax collection.[3] Ṣabr ad-Dīn II (d. A.H. 825/A.D. 1422), son of Saʿd, returned from Arabia, but was defeated after some initial victories.[4] The same happened with his successors, Manṣūr (d. A.D. 1424/5) and Jamāl ad-Dīn (d. A.D. 1433).

The Solomonid dynasty reached the peak of its power in the long reign of Zar'a Yāʿqob (A.D. 1434–68). He consolidated the conquests of his predecessors, built numerous churches, endowed monasteries, and encouraged literature and art. He was involved in the usual struggle with Adal whose sultan, Badlāy b. Saʿd ad-Dīn, after a successful preliminary campaign, in A.H. 849 (A.D. 1445) invaded the Province of Dawāro, but was defeated and killed.[5] Zar'a Yāʿqob realized the danger to the State of these endemic incursions from Adal, for although con-

climate (i.e. region) of *ʿAdal al-Umarā*, 'the ʿAdal of the *amīrs*'. Whilst not referring to any actual State of Adal, he mentions an ʿAdal as one of the 'mother cities' of the kingdom of Ifāt, like Shawā and Baqul-zar, which implies that it is a region of Ifāt like Shoa. One may conjecture that Adal then was a district or a nomad tribe more or less subject to Ifāt, and that when the Walashmaʿ dynasty were eventually dispossessed of Ifāt they took the title of sultans of ʿAdal. Alvarez says the Adal kingdom in 1520–7 bordered on Faṭajār and Shoa and extended as far south as Cape Guardafui (*Narrative of the Portuguese Embassy to Abyssinia*, trans. Lord Stanley of Alderley, 1881, p. 346). Later a Roman Catholic missionary writes of Adal as the region west of Zailaʿ, 'orientale (latus) regna Dancalinum et Adalense, australe patrius Gallarum nidus' (Beccari, *R.A.S.O.* viii. 26).

[1] It is so called in the *Futūḥ-al-Ḥabasha* (text, p. 5). The tomb of Saʿd ad-Dīn was on Zailaʿ island, site of the ancient Zailaʿ where he was killed, but it has now been washed away; cf. R. F. Burton, *First Footsteps in East Africa*, pp. 72–73.

[2] Abū'l-Maḥāsin ibn Taghrī-Birdī, *An-Nuzūm az-Zāhira*, ed. Popper, v. 383.

[3] Maqrīzī, *Ilmām*, p. 4.

[4] This may be linked with events recorded by Abū'l-Maḥāsin in A.H. 826 (A.D. 1423) when Yesḥāq, annoyed by the closing of the Church of the Holy Sepulchre at Jerusalem, massacred the Muslims of his country, destroyed their mosques, and raided the country of the Jabarta. The Mamlūk Sultan Barsabay thought of taking reprisals on the patriarch and Copts in Egypt but refrained; Abū'l-Maḥāsin b. Taghrī-Birdī, op. cit. vi. 572; see also p. 398.

[5] J. Perruchon, *Les Chroniques de Zar'a Yaʿeqob et de Baʾeda Māryām* (Paris, 1893), p. 88.

tinually defeated the sultanate could always recover because of its links with the wider Islamic world. To counteract its influence the king made great endeavours to reform and unify the religion of his own kingdom[1] and to establish relationships with the wider Christian world.[2] The death of Zar'a Yāʿqob ends the first period of the Solomonid dynasty—the period of conquest and expansion—and a defensive phase begins.

## 3. THE MUSLIM CONQUEST OF THE SIXTEENTH CENTURY

### (a) *Introductory*

*Ottomans and Portuguese in the Arabian Sea.* New factors now come into play upon the East African scene. When the brilliant period of exploration inaugurated by Prince Henry the Navigator reached its peak with the discovery of the sea-route to the east, Portugal had opened a new page in African history. In 1499 Vasco da Gama bombarded the

[1] The conversion of many of the Agao, carried out partly by force and partly by the work of the monks, had been purely nominal, they still retained allegiance to their old gods, whilst many pagan islands had been left in the hills. In the time of Alvarez (1520–7) Gojām and Dāmot, for instance, were still largely pagan (*Narrative*, p. 348). Zar'a Yāʿqob waged a cruel and implacable campaign to try and wipe out the Agao religion and national resistance. The king forced all his subjects to be tattooed with an amulet affirming belief in the Trinity and condemning idolatry, and the persecution was such that many groups were forced to emigrate to more inaccessible hills.

[2] Muslim pressure on Europe, which had been restrained by the Mongol threat, had now become more menacing and led to the fall of Constantinople in A.D. 1453. The sense of common danger forced the Christians to try to achieve closer unity and the abortive Council of Florence met in A.D. 1439–41 to try and heal the breach between Rome and Constantinople. The Egyptian Church also joined in this attempt at reconciliation and an envoy of Zar'a Yāʿqob is mentioned as being present at the Council (Hardouin, *Acta Conciliorum* (Paris, 1714), vol. ix, fol. 1183). That direct relationships had already taken place between Ethiopian kings and the rulers of western Mediterranean powers is shown from both Arabic and Western sources. Maqrīzī records that shortly before his death Yesḥāq, 'wrote to the kings of the Franks urging them to ally themselves with him in order to eliminate the Islamic Power. He made arrangements with them to that end and began preparations in the regions between his own and Islamic territory by winning over the *bedāwīn* tribes' (*Ilmām*, p. 5). There may be some foundation to this story because Ibn Taghrī-Birdī, in connexion with the Egyptian expeditions against Cyprus in 1425 and 1426, mentions a Persian merchant called al-Ḥājj Nūr ad-Dīn ʿAlī who acted as intermediary between the Negus and Frankish kings (op. cit., vol. iii, pt. ii, p. 637). Further, according to the archives of Naples, Yesḥāq addressed an appeal to Alphonso V of Aragon (1416–58) proposing that they should co-operate against the Muslims of whom those of Adal menaced his kingdom. The king replied proposing an exchange of princely marriages to cement the alliance (cf. C. de la Roncière, *La découverte de l'Afrique au moyen âge* (1924–5), ii. 116. That such an exchange of envoys had taken place is confirmed by a letter of Alfonso to Zar'a Yāʿqob dated 1450 proposing an alliance in which he refers to earlier relationships between the two kingdoms; cf. F. Cerone, 'La politica orientale di Alfonso di Aragona', *Archivio Storico per le Province Napoletane*, xxvii (1902), 39–43, 65–66.

port of Maqdishū, and in 1507 a settlement was made on the island of Socotra, near the entrance to the Red Sea. All the Muslim powers surrounding the Arabian Sea then combined to make one effect to crush the Portuguese, but failed. Qanṣūh al-Ghawrī, the last Mamlūk ruler of Egypt, organized expeditions as far as India in 1507 and 1515. Lope Suarez took and burnt Zailaʿ in 1517 and Saldanha sacked Berbera the following year. But now they came up against a new and vigorous power, that of the Ottoman Turks, and Portugal embarked upon a naval war with the greatest military power in the world.

During the first quarter of the sixteenth century the invasion of Islamic territory by the nomad horde of the Ottoman Turks had resulted in the political unification of a large part of the Islamic world. By the conquest of Syria, Egypt, North Africa, and the Arabian coasts between 1512 and 1519, the Ottomans acquired a combination of strategic and commercial points of vantage of which they failed to make effective use because, on the one hand, they did not proceed to the conquest of the Maghrib which might have enabled them to close the sea-route round Africa; and, on the other, when they did arrive in the Red Sea and the sea-route to India was for the first time open to them they found the Portuguese already holding strategic points in the Indian Ocean. The failure of the siege of Diu in A.D. 1538, which left the Portuguese in command of the open waters of the Indian Ocean, finally brought to an end the Ottomans' dream of universal empire.

The struggle between the Portuguese and Ottomans for mastery of the Arabian Sea was destined to have a profound effect upon the fate of the Christian kingdom of Ethiopia. Although they did not secure control of the Indian Ocean the Ottomans maintained their power in the Red Sea, as was shown in 1641, when the Portuguese viceroy, Estevão da Gama, attacked the Turkish naval port of Suez. This expedition, which failed in its main purpose, was destined to contribute, through the quixotic but heroic adventure of Christovão da Gama, to the preservation of Ethiopia from destruction at the hands of coastal nomadic tribes who had been furnished with firearms by the Turks.

*The Empire of Ethiopia.* Christian Abyssinia approached the most dramatic stage of its history as a composite human aggregate with an autochthonous civilization under an autocratic ruler. The State was supra-national, its bonds of allegiance were loyalty to the person of the sovereign and the Ethiopian Church. The masses were barbarous, uncultured, and fanatical, deeply dyed with the outward forms of their indigenized Christianity, and equally deficient in its spirit; but clinging to their independence and destined to be equally resistant to Islam and to Roman Catholicism.

During the period of expansion which we have been considering the Negus had acquired a vast empire. In the north it extended as far as Maṣawwaʿ and the Sudan plain, overawing the nomadic Tigrē and Beja tribes of the Sāḥil and upper Baraka. The southern provinces included the former Muslim kingdoms of Ifāt, Faṭajār, Dawāro, and Bāli. In the rich and fertile south-western region it ruled the former Sultanate of Hadya and the numerous pagan Sidāma kingdoms as far as and including the Walamo, most of which had been conquered by the Negus Yesḥāq (1414–29).

With the death of Zar'a Yāʿqōb a new phase begins. Over many of these outlying regions the sovereignty of the Negus was but nominal, fear of reprisals alone holding the governors to an allegiance expressed merely by the payment of a yearly tribute. The primitive political organization of the Abyssinians was unable to cope with this vast expansion. As a rule, each conquered Muslim territory was self-governing, under a Muslim governor called *al-jarād*. In many cases he was a member of the family of the former ruler, with the result that the governorship was often hereditary. The inhabitants of the conquered territories were not compelled to become Christians, though some of their rulers did so from motives of policy. Muslims were still found in Shoa and even eastern Tigrai for Alvarez observes: 'in this country there are villages of Moors, separated from the Christians; they say that they pay much tribute to the lords of the country in gold and silk stuffs. They do not serve in the general services like the Christians: they have not got mosques because they do not allow them to build or possess them.'[1]

The Province of Hadya, in addition to other forms of tribute, was required to hand over every year a maiden who had to become a Christian. When this province was taken by the Imām Aḥmad,

> he questioned them concerning their practice, although they were Muslims, of handing over every year a maiden chosen for her beauty, grace and noble birth. They answered, 'He (i.e. the Negus) imposed this on our forefathers for he was the stronger. He forbade us to wear war-apparel, bear arms, or ride saddled horses though we might ride bare-back. He enacted that we should hand over a maiden, and this we did for fear he would put us to death and

[1] Alvarez, *Narrative*, p. 95, see also pp. 103–4. The locality of these Muslim villages was about a day's journey from Agroo (i.e., Wogoro) where was the tomb of Muḥammad an-Najāsh, patron saint of the Jabarti. That the tomb goes back to this period we know from the statement that it was visited by the Imām Aḥmad (*Futūḥ*, tr., pp. 419–20).

destroy our mosques. When he sent his people to collect the girl and the tribute we used to place her on a bed, wash her, cover her with a shroud, recite the prayers of the dead over her, and then hand her over.'[1]

The organization of Abyssinian territory proper was little more unified than that of subject provinces. At first the kin group had been the only stable unity in the social structure, but in time districts and then regions began to acquire regional consciousness under some local chief. In these days of expansion the peculiar form which feudalism took was successfully dragooned into the service of the Negus, but the social and economic differentiation which the system entailed, allied with regional animosities, was to cause internal stresses and strains which hindered the formation of a stable and peaceful highland society. Whenever the grip of central authority began to relax, feudal chieftains, such as those of Tigrai and Lāsta, raised their heads aggressively against the central authority. It is true that unless of royal blood they never aspired to the throne because the aureola of the divine origin of the monarchy exercised such a powerful hold over the hearts and minds of the masses, but a regency period or the rule of a weak king was inevitably a time of troubles.

At this time the struggle with the Muslims chiefly occupied the attention of the king and forced him to be near the threatened frontier; and the more the external threat intensified the more the feudal barons profited to make themselves virtually independent, so that feudalism came more and more to exercise an effective influence in internal affairs. The empire therefore presented but a superficial appearance of strength and vigour and the initiative in the struggle began to pass to the Muslim coastal powers whose force of expansion was the nomad tribes ever seeking to escape from their inhospitable homeland.

*The Jihād and Tribal Movements.* Behind all these struggles between Ethiopia and the Muslims was a movement of expansion of the ʿAfar (Dankali) and Somali. The movement appears to have been initiated by the ʿAfar who lived in the region of the oasis of Aussa and the valleys descending from the eastern districts of Shoa. Their seasonal migrations carried the tribes westwards and they were ready, given the required stimulus, to burst out of their desert plains and flood over the sedentary societies on the plateaux.

This irruption of ʿAfar and Somali hordes failed because it was primarily a military operation led by fanatical leaders seeking to extend their domain by imposing their political and religious dominion upon

[1] *Futūḥ*, text, pp. 275–6.

equally fanatical Christian highlanders who could never be subjected by armies operating far from their home base. Only secondarily was this eruption of nomads a displacement and migration of population. The Galla migration, however, which immediately followed, succeeded because the Galla had been so utterly uprooted that the very whereabouts of their former home can only be conjectured and they migrated *en masse* to find new ranges.

The leaders of this ʿAfar tribal movement were not the old hereditary sultans of Adal, but fanatical Muslim *amīrs* who began by carving out for themselves principalities within the Sultanate of Adal itself in the regions between Harar and the sea and relegated the Walashmaʿ dynasty to the position of nominal rulers. Shihāb ad-Dīn, the historian of the Muslim conquest, writes, 'it was the custom in the country of Saʿd ad-Dīn that every *amīr* had power to prosecute or withhold action, to carry out raids, and to make holy war. Most of the soldiers were under him and the sultan had nothing but his share of the taxes.'[1] These *amīrs* first recruited their forces from the ʿAfar tribes who were feeling the urge to expand and were lured by visions of loot, but they were soon joined by the Habr Maqadi, Jirri, Zerba, and Marrēḥān Somali tribes, followed later, as the movement accelerated, by the Harti and many others. These leaders, of whom the most famous were Maḥfūẓ and Aḥmad b. Ibrāhīm, did not have the feudal title of *amīr*, but the religious title of *imām*.[2] Shihāb ad-Dīn was told by a friend of his dream of two saints who said of Aḥmad b. Ibrāhīm, the future conqueror of Abyssinia, ' "Call him neither Sulṭān, nor Amīr, but call him the Imām of the true believers." "The Imām of the Last Days?" I asked, and they answered, "yes".'[3] This change of title signified a change in the character of the war against Ethiopia. It was transfigured by an ardent fanaticism and transformed into a *jihād*, a religious war. The invisible meanings which lay behind the 'vain repetitions' of the Islamic formulae now struck a responsive spark in the hearts of the populace and kindled fire to emulate the swift conquests of early Islam.

With the rise of these *amīrs* and the firing of the spirit of the populace, two parties grew up in Harar State: the one a popular party,

[1] Ibid. p. 12.

[2] Legally the *Imām* is the leader of the whole Muslim community as *khalīfa* of the Prophet. The title, however, was normally used by the Shīʿa sects which recognized the rights of the descendants of ʿAlī. At this time it was used in Abyssinia to denote 'the elected one', the leader of the *jihād*, but in its later use in the region came to mean no more than tribal leader.

[3] Ibid. p. 13. *Imām ākhir az-zamān* is the Mahdī, but there is no evidence other than this that Aḥmad was ever regarded as such.

fanatical and militaristic, whose leaders were these *amīrs*; and the other an aristocratic party, whose concern was with commerce and the cultivation of the arts of peace, which surrounded the court of the sultan. This internal split was to be the cause of the final break-up of Islamic power in this region.

## (*b*) *Abyssinia before the Conquest*

Ba'eda Māryām (1468–78) who succeeded Zar'a Yā'qob, pursued the traditional Solomonid policy of converting the pagan Agao of the interior both by force and propaganda and repressing the Muslim coastal powers. The Adalite sultanate was now worn out after the continuous wars and to ensure a respite from the wearisome round of raids and counter-raids Muḥammad ibn Badlāy (1445–71) sent a delegation to Ba'eda Māryām at the beginning of his reign to promise the payment of an annual tribute.[1] This truce enabled Ba'eda Māryām to send an expedition against the Falāsha and lead one himself against the Dob'a, an islamized-pagan tribe inhabiting the mountain region of Woggerāt around Amba Alāgi and infesting the caravan routes.[2]

The new Adalite policy of equilibrium did not appeal to the more intransigent Muslim elements in the sultanate with whom the *jihād* ranked as the primary duty of Islam and political power began to pass

[1] In this account the Ethiopian chronicler for the first time calls the Walashma' King of Adal, instead of Ifāt (Perruchon, *Chron. de Zar'a Ya'eqob*, pp. 131–3.)

[2] Cf. Perruchon, op. cit., pp. 144–6. The Dob'a are first mentioned in the Acts of St. Mārqorēwos (fifteenth century?) which refers to one Yaḥyā, a Muslim chief of the Dob'a during the thirteenth century (cf. *Acta Mārqorēwos*, *C.S.C.O. Scr. Aeth.* ser. ii, vol. xxii, 1904, p. 18). They are mentioned by Alvarez (op. cit., pp. 108–12, 346) in 1520 as occupying the extreme eastern edge of the plateau and infesting the route from Debarwā to Lake Ḥayq. He says that they are called Dobaas after the name of their country and that they were all Moors (i.e. Muslims). From his description they are obviously nomads and a captain called Xuum Janamora (i.e. the Shum of Zān Amorā, the name of a district) had the duty of keeping them in order. Barradas (A.D. 1633) writes of them as subject to the emperor, 'são os mouros obedientes . . , os mouros Dobâs todos sogeitos ao Emperador' (*R.A.S.O.* iv, 1906, 83–85). They are often mentioned in the Ethiopian chronicles (cf. Pereira, *Hist. de Minas*, n. 146; Pereira, *Susenyos* (1900), ii. 65) as bitter adversaries of the Abyssinians and of their religion. They were defeated by the army of Iyāsu II (1730–55, I. Guidi, *Annales Regum Iyāsu II et Iyo'as*, *C.S.C.O.* ser. ii, vol. vi, pp. 141–2, 159) after which they seem to have been absorbed into the Yajju Galla who were established amongst them in the time of Barradas (cf. *R.A.S.O.* iv. 85). Remnants still existed in the Samhar in the time of Bruce (*Travels*, iv. 135, 204) and south of Woggerāt in the time of Pearce (cf. Salt, *A Voyage to Abyssinia*, 1814, p. 275). After that they disappear completely. They were probably of 'Afar stock who had penetrated the eastern spurs of the plateau where they maintained a precarious existence, enemies of all the world including the 'Afar of the deserts below, subjected to expedition after expedition by the Abyssinians whose routes they menaced, until they were finally displaced by the Galla and disappear from history. The Muslim population just north of Quoram are still shown on some maps as Doba, but it is doubtful if this represents more than the name of the district.

from the less resolute hands of the Walashmaʿ to that of the new *amīrs*. The first of these was Ladāʿi ʿUthmān, governor of Zailaʿ, who began preparations for renewing the war in 1471 immediately after the death of Sultan Muḥammad. Ba'eda Māryām took the offensive, routed the Adalite army and captured many of its *amīrs*. But the battle was not decisive for soon afterwards the semi-pagan ʿAfar who had been subjected by Ba'eda Māryām made common cause with the Muslims and the whole eastern frontier flared up in revolt. Two Abyssinian armies were sent into Adal in 1473/4 and both were defeated. This marked the turning-point in the military supremacy of the Abyssinians.

Ba'eda Māryām's young son Eskender (1478–94) also took the field against the Adalites, then under Shams ad-Dīn b. Muḥammad (1472–87), but in spite of some ephemeral successes, during which he sacked their capital Dakar, he was surprised and defeated.[1] From that time the raids of Muslim *amīrs* were continuous. During his reign (1481) an embassy was sent to Cairo to demand a new *abūna* from the Sultan Qā'it Bāy. The embassy, which afterwards went on pilgrimage to Jerusalem for the Easter festival, obtained concessions for the Ethiopian community in Jerusalem.[2]

The next king Nā'od (1494–1508) was a mature and experienced man who made use of the advice of the Empress Helena (Illēni). This queen was a daughter of al-Jarād Ābūn, tributary King of Dawāro, who had become a Christian when she became one of the four wives of Ba'eda Māryām.[3] Brought up in contact with the wider Islamic world she was conscious of the dangers to which Abyssinia was exposed through its isolation. At first she sought alliances with the Muslims, but when this method failed through the intensified Islamic propaganda of the fanatical *amīrs* who had acquired control of Adal, she made contact with the Western Christian power which was now operating in the Indian Ocean.

During the reign of Nā'od, Muḥammad ibn Aẓhar ad-Dīn, who reigned over Adal for thirty years (1488–1518), tried to remain at

[1] J. Perruchon, 'Histoire d'Eskender, d'Amda Seyon II et de Nā'od', *J. Asiat.* (1894), pp. 43–44.

[2] *Ibn Iyās*, ed. Kahle; events of Muḥarram A.H. 886 (A.D. 1481); Al-ʿUlaimī (wrote 1494/5), *Kitāb al-ins al-jalīl bi ta'rīkh al-Quds wa'l-Khalīl* (Cairo, A.H. 1283), pp. 657–8.

[3] Zar'a Yāʿqob was the first Negus to take a wife from a Muslim tributary, that of Hadya. Another wife of Ba'eda Māryām, Romane-Warq, mother of Eskender, had also been a Muslima. Alvarez writes, 'the preceding Presters, until the father of this one who now reigns (i.e. Lebna Dengel) always had five or six wives, and they had them from the daughters of the neighbouring Moorish kings, and from the Pagans . . . and from the King of Dankali another; and from the King of Adel, and the King of Adea (Hadya)', *Narrative*, p. 110.

peace with the Christian kingdom; but, according to Alvarez,[1] his efforts were nullified by the raids which Maḥfūẓ, *amīr* of Harar, constantly made into Christian territory during the strict Abyssinian Lent when the people were weak through fasting. Nā'od, determining to put an end to this, reorganized the Abyssinian army, cleansed it of Muslim elements, led it against the *amīr*, and defeated him decisively. The Sultan Muḥammad hastened to assure Nā'od of his neutrality. An uneasy truce followed; both adversaries were weary of war, the Muslims were divided, and, though Maḥfūẓ still made spasmodic raids on Christian territory, the policy of Helena appeared to have gained some degree of success when Lebna Dengel (1508–40) came to the throne at the age of eleven and she was made regent. Muḥammad was still on the throne of Adal and both he and Helena preferred peace and the commercial prosperity which resulted. Missions were sent to other countries along with great trading caravans, one of which was to the last Mamlūk Sultan of Egypt, Qanṣūh al-Ghawrī, in 1516.[2]

But Helena realized that the uneasy peace would not long endure and her outstanding political project is her attempt to form an alliance with Portugal. This was first suggested by Pedro da Covilhã, an envoy sent by John II of Portugal in 1487 when he first heard of the existence of a Christian kingdom in Africa. Pedro had eventually (1494) reached Abyssinia, but was not allowed to return. He suggested that it was to the interests of Abyssinia that a great naval power like Portugal should occupy the coastal commercial centres and cut off the Muslims of Abyssinia from contact with the Islamic world. So in 1509 Helena sent an Armenian called Matthew to Dom Manuel I. A Portuguese mission was eventually sent, but it did not arrive until 1520 when the situation had changed.

In the meantime Lebna Dengel had come of age and reversed the policy of Helena. The frontier situation had deteriorated. Since the death of Nā'od, Maḥfūẓ, who was governor of Zaila' and *de facto* ruler of Adal, having recovered from his defeat, had renewed his raids into Abyssinian territory. In this he was stimulated by emissaries sent from Arabia who proclaimed the *jihād*, presented him with a green standard and a tent of black velvet and brought help in arms and trained men. In 1516 the Adalites under Sultan Muḥammad moved into Faṭajār for a regular invasion, but Lebna Dengel was prepared and organized a

[1] *Narrative*, pp. 304–10.

[2] Cf. *Die Chronik des Ibn Ijâs*, ed. P. Kahle, Leipzig, 1932, Bibliotheca Islamica, vol. v$^e$, pp. 9–11; G. Wiet, 'Les relations égypto-abyssines sous les Sultans Mamlouks', *Bull. de la Société d'Archéologie Copte*, iv (1938), 136–9.

successful ambush. The Adalite army was decisively defeated, Maḥfūẓ was slain, and the emperor invaded Adal and destroyed the castle of the sultan at a place called Zankar. At the same time the fleet of Lope Suarez surprised Zailaʿ whilst its garrison was away with Maḥfūẓ and burnt the town.[1] It seemed then that the Muslim menace was eliminated for some time to come.

When the Portuguese mission arrived, therefore, it met a king flushed with success and suspicious of Portuguese motives. The old Queen Helena had retired to her domain of Gojām and the king denied that the Armenian Matthew had received any official sanction to solicit an alliance. The mission remained in Abyssinia six years[2] and it sailed away in 1526 shortly after a youth of nineteen named Aḥmad ibn Ibrāhīm had won a notable victory over an Abyssinian expedition at a time when Adal had relapsed into a state of anarchy.

### (*c*) *The Great Conquest*[3]

After the victory of Lebna Dengel the internal weaknesses in the kingdom of Adal soon showed themselves. The older generation of Muslims headed by the Walashmaʿ, living in settlements and towns, interested in commerce, indifferent in religion, and ready to come to terms with Abyssinia, were opposed by newly converted ʿAfar and Somali tribes, moved by motives both religious and migrational and led by warlike fanatical *amīrs*. The Sultan Muḥammad was murdered in 1518 on his return from a campaign against Lebna Dengel, and Adal was torn by intestinal struggles during which five sultans succeeded in two years, which we do not need to consider in detail.

One outstanding figure who brought order out of chaos for three whole years was that of al-Jarād[4] Ābūn b. Ādash who

re-established law and order, affirming the right and forbidding the wrong.

[1] João de Barros, *Decada terceira da Asia* (Lisbon, 1628), ff. 11–14.

[2] The account of this mission by its chaplain Alvarez (*Narrative*) gives us a valuable description of the country before the Muslim invasion.

[3] The sources for the history of the conquest are Shihāb ad-Dīn, *Futūḥ al-Ḥabasha*, ed. and trans. by R. Basset (*Histoire de la conquête de l'Abyssinie*, 1897), quoted as *Futūḥ*. This account, which is incomplete, was written shortly after 1559 by a Yamanite who was an eyewitness of many of the events which he records. E. Cerulli, 'Documenti Arabi per la storia dell' Etiopia', *M.R.A.L.*, ser. vi, vol. iv (1931), pp. 39–101; the Abyssinian chronicle, ed. and trans. by R. Basset, *Études sur l'histoire d'Ethiopie*, 1882, also translated by F. Béguinot, *La Cronaca abbreviata d'Abissinia* (Rome, 1901), pp. 15–26; C. Conti Rossini, 'Storia di Lebna Dengel', *R.R.A.L.*, iii (1894) (Bodl. MS.).

[4] *Jarād* was a title carried by governors of Muslim provinces tributary to Abyssinia, but seems to have been adapted by Muslims with a general sense of feudal governor. It is still in use amongst the Karanla (Hawiya) and the Ḍūlbahanta (Darod).

He exterminated highway robbers, forbade drinking carousals, gambling and dancing with drums, in consequence of which the country prospered. He loved the *ashrāf* (descendants of the Prophet), jurisconsults, dervishes and shaikhs. He really controlled the country and cared for his subjects.[1]

But Sultan Abū Bakr ibn Muḥammad, who had transferred his military headquarters from Dakar to Harar in 1520, profiting by the prestige which the hereditary monarchy still held, collected a band of Somali brigands, surprised Ābūn at Zailaʿ, and killed him (931/1525). Another period of disorder followed and Shihāb ad-Dīn, who is somewhat biassed, contrasts his rule with that of the zealot Ābūn quoted above:

He ruined the country; highway robbery and drunken carousals reappeared. In his time his subjects used to hold up travellers and plunder them. Vices reappeared and no one in his time could get restitution for injustices.[2]

As in all times of trouble visions of a reformer make their appearance. Shihāb ad-Dīn writes:

Men upon whose word I can rely, such as ʿAlī b. Ṣalāḥ al-Jabalī and Aḥmad b. Ṭāhir al-Marʿuwi, informed me that they heard a man called Saʿd b. Yūnis al-ʿArjī recount, 'One night whilst I was sleeping I saw the Prophet with Abū Bakr aṣ-Ṣiddīq on his right and ʿUmar b. al-Khaṭṭāb on his left; whilst ʿAlī b. Abī Ṭālib was beside him, and beside ʿAli was the Imām Aḥmad b. Ibrāhīm. I said, "O Prophet of God, who is this man beside ʿAlī b. Abī Ṭālib?" He said, "Through this man God intends to reform Abyssinia."' At the time of this vision the Imām was but an ordinary soldier and had never been seen by the dreamer except in this dream at ʿAlī's side. In the time of al-Jarād Ābūn this dreamer visited Harar and related his vision to the people of the town who asked him, 'Was it he (Ābūn) whom you saw in your dream?' But he answered, 'No'. The *amīrs* succeeded one after another until the time came when Imām Aḥmad gained control. And when he saw him he recognized him as the one he had first seen in his dream when he was with ʿAlī. Thereupon he said to the townsfolk, 'This is the man whom I saw'.[3]

This Imām Aḥmad ibn Ibrāhīm al-Ghāzī (1506–43), nicknamed Grāñ, 'the left-handed', by the Abyssinians,[4] was the leader who was destined to reconstitute Muslim political power in south-eastern Ethiopia and embark on a conquest which brought three-quarters of Abyssinia into his power. His earlier years were passed in Hūbat (the region between Gildessa and Harar) which later became the base for his military operations. His father placed him under the care of a freed slave called ʿAdlī

[1] *Futūḥ*, text, p. 6. [2] Ibid., pp. 6–7. [3] Ibid., pp. 13–14.
[4] See 'Storia di Lebna Dengel', C. Conti Rossini, p. 24; *Futūḥ*, p. 207.

(ʿAdolē) who became his most fervent supporter. His marriage to Bāti Del Wanbara, daughter of the Imām Maḥfūẓ of Zailaʿ, assured to him the loyalty of Maḥfūẓ's partisans. After the death of Ābūn he did not immediately attempt conclusions with Sultan Abū Bakr, but retired to Hūbat to build up his power.

Meanwhile Ottomans and Portuguese had come into conflict for the control of the sea-routes. The Portuguese had destroyed Arab commerce between the Red Sea and the Persian Gulf, whilst their mission in Abyssinia was causing apprehensions to the Ottomans, who as a counter-measure occupied Sawākin and Zailaʿ and established relations with the Muslims in Portuguese-occupied Maṣawwaʿ. At Zailaʿ, where Catalan merchants, rivals of the Portuguese, were supplying them with arms,[1] the Muslims were building up a fleet.

Aḥmad's early years were spent in struggles with Sultan Abū Bakr. For some time they shared the country, but ultimately Aḥmad killed the sultan and replaced him by his brother, ʿUmar Dīn, as puppet king. Once in complete control he could turn to the task for which he felt himself the divinely appointed *Imām*, the conquest of Abyssinia. His first act was to refuse tribute and that made war inevitable. In 1527 the Abyssinian army invaded Adal under Dēgalhān, Governor of Bāli, and was decisively defeated by Aḥmad at ad-Dīr. Fervour for the *jihād* had not yet overcome the disruptive forces inherent in the nomadic life, and after this victory Aḥmad had to return to restore order in Somali territory which was to constitute his man-power reserve. After defeating various Somali chiefs he organized and trained this heterogeneous mass of tribes with remarkable skill into a powerful striking force, inflamed with fanatical zeal for the *jihād*[2] by the personality of the leader and greed for booty; though once the leader was killed and they experienced defeat the force of the invasion was spent.

[1] João de Barros, *Decada terceira da Asia* (Lisbon, 1628), f. 14.

[2] He had with him preachers of the *jihād*, chief of whom was the *walī*, Abū Bakr b. Naṣr ad-Dīn, surnamed Arshūta (*Futūḥ*, p. 38). Some of the Muslims were apprehensive of the result of a direct assault upon Abyssinia until Aḥmad showed them that a *jihād* must inevitably succeed. It is related that the inhabitants of Amājah in the Ankober region said to him shortly before the battle of Shemberā Kurē, ' "Neither your fathers, nor your ancestors, nor the amīrs ʿAlī and Maḥfūẓ, your father in law, nor Jarād Ibrāhīm and the former sultans of the Land of Saʿd ad-Dīn, dared attack the King of Abyssinia in his own homeland, but merely raided over the borders, took booty and returned, and if one of the infidels pursued them they fought to retain what they had taken. Yet you want to attack the King of Abyssinia in his own country. Take care you do not bring destruction upon the Muslims." To which the Imām replied, "Holy war in the way of God cannot cause disaster to Muslims". Then they said, "Our only desire is the holy war. Whoever of us is killed will attain Paradise and whoever lives will enjoy happiness".' *Futūḥ*, p. 42.

In 1529 Aḥmad won a decisive victory over the Abyssinians at Shemberā Kurē, but his nomads were still unreliable and difficult to control, and after the campaign, in spite of all his endeavours, many of them dispersed with their booty. At the same time he was faced with opposition at home in Harar from the conservative party. He set about eliminating these weaknesses by building up an army owing allegiance to himself alone and not to their tribal leaders, and two years later had so reconstructed his forces that he was able to begin the definite invasion and permanent occupation of Abyssinia. From then the story of the conquest is a succession of victories, spoilations, burnings, and massacres. In 1531 Dawāro and Shoa were occupied, the latter in the midst of the rainy season, and Amḥara and Lāstā in 1533. The former Muslim kingdoms of Bāli and Hadya, and the Sidāma and Gurāgē kingdoms were taken almost in his stride. The conquest was devastating in its destruction, irresistible in its ferocity, and appalling in its cruelties. In 1535 Aḥmad, in control of the south and centre of Abyssinia, for the first time invaded Tigrai where, though he encountered fierce opposition from the hardy mountain tribes and suffered some reverses, his advance was not stopped. His armies penetrated along the coast and lowlands and as far in the north-west as Tāka (Kasala) where they made contact with the Muslim Sultan of Mazagā, lower Walqāyt, a Nūba province probably under a Beja ruling class, which had formerly been tributary to Abyssinia. King Lebna Dengel became a hunted fugitive, harried from one mountain fastness to another; from Tigrai through Wagarā, Dambyā, Bēgamder, Gojām, and back again to Tigrai. Too late he realized the wisdom of Queen Helena, but in 1535 as a remote chance he had sent John Bermudez, a member of the former mission who had been detained in Abyssinia, to the King of Portugal to ask for assistance. The King of Portugal eventually sent ships with four hundred musketeers, but when they arrived in 1541 Lebna Dengel was dead and his son Galāwdēwos (1540–59) reigned in his stead.

The impression is given in the Muslim chronicle that almost all the Christian population of the highlands embraced Islam out of expediency. The following accounts are typical:

The people of Jān Zalaq had not embraced Islam, but had hidden themselves in the plains and mountains. The Imām, therefore, sent Khālid al-Warrādi with a force of cavalry to attack them. [He sent a messenger calling them to islamize and] they consulted together and said, 'If we disobey Khālid he will report to his master the Imām and the Imām will send against us an army from here and there. Most of the Abyssinians have islamized and the Muslims are scattered over all the land. If they hear that we have refused they will not let a single one of us escape alive. Our master Wasan Sajād has been killed, let us now join Islam.'[1]

The *wazīr* ʿAdlī received information that the Imām had encountered the king and that the Muslims had been routed and killed to the last man. This rumour was an absolute lie. Nothing of the sort had happened, but when the *wazīr* and the Muslims heard it they were cut to the heart, whilst those who had joined Islam from fear of death, rejoiced.[2]

The Ethiopian Chronicler asserts that 'hardly one in ten retained his religion'.[3] Some preferred to pay the *jizya*, but most were not given the choice, whilst those who resisted the Muslim arms were ruthlessly exterminated. Here is a typical account:

On the second day they arrived at Abbā Jarīma, which is two parasangs from Aksūm, and encamped there. Some of the inhabitants said to the Imām, 'The polytheists of Abbā Jarīma have fortified themselves in three strongholds, but they cannot resist you'. When the Imām received this information he encamped there and marched against them. The men of two of the castles agreed to his terms and he imposed upon them the *jizya*, but those of the third castle resisted, so he fought them and God routed them and exterminated them to the last man.[4]

Chiefs of Muslim districts such as Ifāt, Faṭajār, and Hadya which had been conquered by the Abyssinians, naturally favoured the invaders and made their people change over to Islam. The *Baṭrīq* of Ifāt, Awraʿī ʿUthmān, wrote to the Imām:

I was once a Muslim and the son of a Muslim, but the polytheists captured me and made me a Christian. Yet at heart I remained steadfast in the faith and now I seek the protection of God, His Prophet and yourself. If you accept my repentance and do not punish me for what I have done I will return to God, whilst these armies of the king which are under my command I will deceive so that they may come over to your side and embrace Islam.[5]

Some, however, preferred death to denying their faith:

They captured two *baṭrīqs* and returned to the Imām's encampment and presented them before him. He said, 'What is the matter with you that you haven't become Muslims when the whole country has islamized?' They replied, 'We don't want to become Muslims.' He said, 'Our judgment on you

[1] *Futūḥ*, ii. 176. [2] Ibid. 248.
[3] Conzelman, *Chroniques de Galāwdēwos* (1895), p. 123.
[4] *Futūḥ*, ii. 321; see also pp. 335, 337, 343.
[5] Ibid. 181–2.

is that your heads be cut off.' They said, 'Welcome.' The Imām was surprised at their reply and ordered them to be executed.[1]

The news of the arrival of the Portuguese at Maṣawwaʿ acted like a ferment throughout northern Abyssinia. Yesḥaq, the Bāḥr Nagāsh, who was still holding out in Tigrai, claimed assistance from the Portuguese in the name of Lebna Dengel's widow Sabla Wangēl. All Tigrai declared for the monarchy and Aḥmad's immediate efforts were concentrated upon hindering the junction of the 400 Portuguese, reinforced by Tigreans, with the troops of the king far away at Tegulet in Shoa.[2] The first encounter took place in 1542 at Anāṣā between Amba Alāgi and Lake Ashangi when Aḥmad was defeated and wounded, and in a battle which followed a few days later he only escaped capture because the Portuguese had no cavalry with which to pursue him. Some kind of demoralization must have overcome his nomad followers for Aḥmad then retired to the Zobul mountains overlooking the Dankali plain to reorganize, and sent a request to the Turkish Pasha of Zabīd for reinforcements of Arab, Turkish, and Albanian mercenaries to stabilize his troops. Nine hundred musketeers and ten cannon were obtained and Aḥmad again took the offensive and at an early encounter in the valley of Aflā (Wofla) the Portuguese leader Christovão da Gama was separated from his followers, captured, and beheaded. At this battle the Portuguese lost many of their leaders, 200 of their rank and file, and a large quantity of arms and ammunition. The Imām, thinking that his position was now unassailable, dismissed the Turkish contingent and returned to his earlier headquarters near Lake Ṭānā. But Aḥmad's military prestige had been weakened and in October 1542 Galāwdēwos was able to join up with the Portuguese and the northern army in Semēn. He did not hesitate to take the offensive and won a decisive victory at Waynā Dagā near Lake Ṭānā when the fate of Abyssinia was decided by the death of the Imām Aḥmad and the flight of his army. The force of the invasion collapsed like a house of cards. All the Abyssinians who had been cowed by the invaders returned to their former allegiance and the reconquest of the Christian territory proceeded without encountering any effective opposition.

*Effect of the Conquest on Christians and Muslims.* The immense toll that had been taken in human lives and material wealth was one of the least important consequences of the conquest. The rapid disruption of

[1] *Futūḥ*, ii. 180 (272).

[2] He was at Tegulet according to tradition; see Combes and Tamisier, *Voyage en Abyssinie . . . 1835–37* (Paris, 1839), iii. 217.

the old political organization showed that Zar'a Yā'qob and his successors had built up a great empire before all the Ethiopian Agao peoples had accepted a uniform allegiance to one king and one religion. The complete overthrow of the armies of warlike mountaineers by Aḥmad's forces cannot be explained solely by the genius of the Imām's leadership and his ability to organize and spur on nomad hordes to the *jihād*; we must also take into account the fact that these armies had been weakened by a profound relaxation of their moral fibre.

The moral consequences of the conquest upon the Ethiopian soul were profound. The people had joined Islam *en masse* and one cannot reject one's faith for another and return to it again and remain immune to the moral consequences. To cope with such a situation was beyond the powers of a Church which had too closely associated itself with the things of this world. The short fifteen years of Muslim rule also weakened the bonds of allegiance to the monarchy, against which conscription into the Muslim army had forced many to fight, and from henceforth the lives of the emperors were to be wasted in repressing feudal chieftains and provincial risings.

The monarchy and the Church, however, had never submitted to the invaders nor betrayed their faith and traditions; consequently these two emerged again as the dominating powers, but often in conflict with each other: the monarch for a time seeking to reconstruct the religious basis of the empire by adopting a progressive policy of co-operation with Western Christian powers, whilst the Church remained isolationist, conservative, and immobile.[1]

The effect of the war upon the Muslims was equally disastrous for it left the Islamic aggressor even more seriously enfeebled than his Christian victim. Far from having gained by devastating the Christian state the Muslim state was left impoverished and the ground cleared for its occupation by the Galla hordes. The Imām had gambled all the potentialities of the 'Afar and Somali nomadic regions in his great adventure. The gamble failed, as it would probably have done without the Portuguese intervention, for the high altitudes and inclement rainy seasons sapped the morale of his desert- and steppe-nurtured followers, whilst his levies left a social vacuum in the Muslim towns and nomad tribes, which, owing to the famine and pestilence which succeeded,

[1] The conquest had literary consequences since it led to the composition of the *Maṣḥafa Qēdar*, an Ethiopic ritual for the reception of apostates, and the *Anqaṣa Amin* (Gateway of the Faith), a manual of anti-Muslim polemics, written (*c.* 1550) by the *echagē* 'Embāqom (Habakuk), himself a Yemenite Muslim merchant converted to Christianity, who succeeded in becoming Abbot of Dabra Libānos.

could never be filled sufficiently to offer resistance to the Galla invaders.

## (*d*) *Partial Recovery*

Whilst Galāwdēwos was busy reorganizing his kingdom after the death of Aḥmad, the *wazīr* ʿAbbās attempted to form a state from the provinces of Dawāro, Faṭajār, and Bāli, but in 1545 Galāwdēwos settled the issue by a single battle and reoccupied the region.[1] Abyssinian control of these provinces, however, was destined to be but ephemeral, for about this time the advance-guard of a new nomadic horde, the Galla, arrived in Bāli, and made it their base for the incursions of succeeding waves.

A new sense of unity had grown up in Harar during the conquest, and its peoples, urged on by the Imām Aḥmad's widow, Bāti Del Wanbarā, were inspired with the desire to avenge him and again take up the conquest of the highlands which they still believed to be vulnerable. But the old spirit had vanished and the forces of Barakāt ibn ʿUmar Dīn and ʿAlī Jarād ibn al-Imām Aḥmad which invaded Dawāro were defeated by those of the governor of the province and its leaders captured. This catastrophe dismayed the Muslims, but Bāti Del Wanbarā succeeded in getting the leaders exchanged for Minās, brother of Galāwdēwos, who was a prisoner at Zabīd. The Abyssinians having completed the reoccupation of the territories beyond the Ḥawāsh turned to the conquest of pagan regions south of the Abāy.

Whilst the reconquest of Dāmot was going on, the kingdom of Harar made another attempt against the Christians, this time under a new leader, Nūr ibn al-wazīr Mujāhid, son of Aḥmad's sister, who became *amīr* in A.H. 959 (A.D. 1551/2). Nūr had been recognized by the people of Harar and the widow of Aḥmad as 'the leader of the new conquest' (*ṣāḥib al-fatḥ ath-thānī*) and she made him promise to devote himself to avenging Aḥmad before she agreed to marry him.[2] Nūr identified himself with the city of Harar in a new way, strengthening its defences by building the wall which still encircles the city, and became its national hero. His first ventures against the Abyssinians were unsuccessful and resulted in Harar territory being invaded and the city itself sacked in 1550. But the blow was not mortal and Harar soon recovered to take the offensive once more.

The situation was now complicated by the appearance in both the

[1] See W. E. Conzelman, *Chronique de Galāwdēwos* (Paris, 1895), pp. xxiii–xxv.

[2] *R. Sém.* ii. 267; C. Foti, 'La Cronaca Abbreviata dei Re d'Abissinia', *R.S.E.* i. 103–4.

north and south of new menaces to the Christian kingdom—the Turks and the Galla. In 1557 the Ottoman Turks took control of Maṣawwaʿ and Arkiko, moved up on to the Eritrean plateau, and established a fortress at Dabārwa. The Turkish Pasha Özdemür next led his soldiers into Agamē against Dabra Dāmo, massacred the monks, and profaned the church.[1] This act roused up the Tigreans and the chief of the northern provinces, Yesḥaq, the Bāḥr-Nagāsh, defeated Turkish troops sent to occupy the fertile Buri peninsula. Yesḥaq next moved against the independent tribes of Mazagā (the lower parts of Walqayt), who were united under a Muslim queen, Gaʿēwa, sister of Mukhtār, and continually raiding Abyssinian territory.[2] Gaʿēwa's forces were defeated and she fled to Debārwa where, to encourage Özdemür to make an expedition into her country, she stirred his cupidity by telling him where her treasures were hidden. Whilst he was in the west the Abyssinians seized Debārwa, and Özdemür, whose army had been weakened by campaigning in the hot climate of the Beja territory, was forced to fall back on Sawākin which, together with Maṣawwaʿ and Arkiko, was all that now remained under Ottoman rule.[3]

In the meantime Nūr had been named *amīr al-mu'minīn* by the people of Harar[4] and spurred on by Bāti Del Wanbarā had been carefully preparing to resume the offensive. He invaded Faṭajār in 1559. Galāwdēwos, who was in Gojām, sent his cousin Ḥamalmāl to invade Harar hoping to force the Muslims to turn back, but Nūr emulating Aḥmad's tactics held on, seeking to deal the Abyssinians a decisive blow in their own territory. Sultan Barakāt remained in Harar with a skeleton force, but the advance of the Abyssinian army forced him to abandon the city and he was shortly afterwards defeated and killed. In

[1] W. E. Conzelman, op. cit., pp. 74, 164. The Church of Dabra Dāmo (north-west of Adigrat) is one of the important monuments of the Axumite Empire. The monastery was founded according to tradition by *Abūna* Aragāwi, a disciple of St. Pachomius of the Thebaid, and was constructed between the sixth and eleventh centuries. It was one of the great diffusion-centres of the Axumite Christian culture southwards during the period of historical obscurity. The *amba* on which it is built is a natural fortress, which the Imām Aḥmad could not take, where the broken Lebna Dengel took refuge just before he died in 1540.

[2] She was probably chieftain of the Ḍubaina, once a powerful tribe which is listed (Dubanē) in a fifteenth-century British Museum MS. as living next to the Baria (*R.S.O.* ix. 453). Bruce also mentions the tribe in this district (*Travels*, IV. 30; III. 4). It was almost annihilated during the Mahdiyya.

[3] The Ethiopian and Portuguese accounts of these events differ considerably in details, but the general outlines are clear; cf. Conzelman, op. cit., pp. 77, 165–7; and Diogo da Couto, *Da Asia* (Lisbon, 1778), dec. vii, l. vii, chs. iv–v.

[4] The Walashmaʿ were still the nominal rulers of Adal. ʿUmar Dīn was succeeded by his son ʿAlī in 1553 and ʿAlī by his brother Barakāt b. ʿUmar Dīn in 1555. Barakāt being a soldier was active in helping Nūr to reorganize the army. After him the Walashmaʿ dynasty disappears.

the meantime, Galāwdēwos, who had only been able to collect a few troops, against everyone's advice advanced to attack Nūr instead of luring him farther into the country. Nūr chose to fight against the superstitious Abyssinians on the ominous day of Good Friday and Galāwdēwos was killed.

## (*e*) *The Galla Migrations*

At the time of Imām Aḥmad's invasion the Galla were a loosely knit confederation of tribes who occupied the valleys of the Wēbi and Jūba, reaching as far as the mountains to the east of Lake Abaya (or Margherita). Their original centre, according to tribal tradition, had been Walabu, part of the mountain chain east of Lake Abaya, when they were under a single Abba Bokku (Father of the Sceptre).[1] About A.D. 1500 social fermentation amongst the Somali which was contributory to the invasion of the Imām Aḥmad caused an expansion of the Isāq and Dārōd, and the Galla pressed by them from Ogadēn and Benadir, feeling the impulse of the nomad ferment and drawn by the social vacuum created by the Imām's armies, invaded Ethiopia. The invasion was not at first an emigration *en masse*. The Galla, like most nomadic invaders, began by launching raids and rapidly retreating. Their irruptions took two main directions: one from the south-west along the corridor between Mount Walabu and Lake Abaya, and another from the south ascending the Jūba and Wēbi river valleys.[2]

The first attack, which became legendary, was made by the Dawē, a subtribe of the Borāna, which threw itself on Bātēr Amorā and defeated an Abyssinian army. Shortly afterwards, under the *gada* Mēlbāḥ,[3] they invaded Bāli. Succeeding *gadas* invaded Dawāro (1545–7) and Faṭajār. This was the period when the fortunes of the Imām Aḥmad had declined and Galāwdēwos, having reasserted his rule over the territories conquered by the Muslims, had to face the new menace. He threw his best forces against them (1554/5) and inflicted severe defeats upon them, yet the advance of the horde was scarcely checked. They halted in the Bāli region, rich in pastures and water, to turn against the Muslim State of Harar (1567) which they laid waste in successive raids. The Arabic Chronicle of Harar records their devasta-

[1] Cf. Cerulli, *E.O.* ii. 169–70.

[2] An account of their invasion has been given by an Abyssinian monk of the sixteenth century named Baḥrey, which has been published by A. W. Schleicher, *Geschichte der Galla*, 1893; I. Guidi, *Historia Gentis Galla*, Paris, 1907; and summarized in E. A. W. Budge, *History of Ethiopia*, ii. 603–13.

[3] That is, the term of rule in which the Mēlbāḥ were in the *luba* grade, see below p. 191.

tions of 'the regions of Sīm, Shoa, Najab, Jidāya, Dakar and most of Harjāyā'.[1] At this time they began to form their famous cavalry by acquiring horses from the Somali. The invasion of Harar was followed by a three years' famine. The Amīr Nūr exerted every effort to help his people to recover, but after every respite the Galla would again descend like locusts and scourge the country, and Nūr himself died (975/1567–8) of the pestilence which spread during the famine.

The cycle of *gadas* which began with the *gada* Harmufu or Dulu (1562–70) carried the invasion into the very heart of the empire; after reaching the Ḥawāsh some columns turned north-west, whilst others travelled north-east by its valleys, and, at the end of the sixteenth and beginning of the seventeenth centuries, occupied fertile regions in the east of the plateau.[2] The invasion poured over the Province of Gāñ, then into Angot; whilst some even penetrated into Amḥara and Bēgamder, the heart of the empire.

Whilst this horde poured northwards from the Wēbi, another invasion current, consisting of the Gombichchu, Ada, and Macha tribes, flowed towards the sources of the River Gibē. Wallegga became their new homeland which they sanctified by making Walel their sacred mountain. From Walel the Macha swarmed over the Sidāma states into the provinces of Shoa. The forces of the Negus were quite unable to stem the flood. When Mināsdied (1563) a third of the empire had been invaded, and by the beginning of the seventeenth century the southern territories south of Shoa had been definitely lost and the borders of the empire carried back to the natural defences of the Abāy and Ḥawāsh, with Galla groups inserted on the eastern spurs of the plateau.

The normal effect of such a vast nomadic migration and encroachment upon an alien sedentary society might have been expected to superimpose the new race on the old leading to social assimilation, but until the last century the Galla remained distinct and impervious to Abyssinian cultural and social influence. This was due to the nature of the Galla political structure and the peculiar environmental conditions offered by Abyssinia. The pride of the Amharic ruling race caused the Christians to withdraw to more restricted territories, leaving the invaders inserted in intervening regions and, though living side by side for centuries, the peoples remained divided and at enmity one with another, each retaining its own identity comparatively unmodified.

1 E. Cerulli, 'Documenti arabi per la storia dell' Etiopia', *M.R.A.L.*, ser. vi, vol. iv (1931), p. 57.

2 Cf. F.-M. E. Pereira, *Chronica de Susenyos*, p. 60.

### (*f*) *Complete Elimination of the Muslim Threat*

When Minās, who had succeeded Galāwdēwos, died in 1563 the condition of the empire seemed desperate. The southern territories were in the hands of the Galla hordes, in the north turbulent feudal nobles like the Bāḥr Nagāsh were in revolt and in alliance with the Turks in Maṣawwaʿ who constituted an ever-present threat. But Minās was succeeded by his son Sarṣa Dengel (Malak Sagad) who turned out to be one of the greatest warrior kings who ever occupied the throne. His reign was chiefly occupied with wars. His conquests, however, were bought at the price of the impoverishment of the empire and proved ephemeral. He was only nineteen when he succeeded to the throne and had first to break up a formidable coalition of chieftains under a pretender to the throne, Ḥamalmāl, a descendant of Nā'od. He then tried to form a defensive organization in the south by retaking the Sidāma kingdoms to act as buffers against the Galla menace. The most formidable focus of rebellion, Yesḥaq the Bāḥr Nagāsh of Ḥamāsēn and Tigrai, who had remained faithful to his king throughout the whole period of the war with the Imām Aḥmad but had rebelled against Minās, was left until Sarṣa Dengel had fully established his rule within the country and taken measures against the Galla in the south. But the Bāḥr Nagāsh knew that his time would come and began negotiations with the Turks of Debārwa and the Muslims of Harar to try to form an offensive coalition against Sarṣa Dengel. The king learnt of his plans and decided to settle accounts with the weakest first.

*Fall of the Kingdom of Harar.* In the meantime the State of Harar, reduced to the last degree of weakness and decadence, was dying. Fratricidal strife had weakened its internal unity and its population, drained of its most virile elements by the Imām Aḥmad's armies, was in no state to resist the devastating Galla incursions, which also imperilled its commercial link with Zailaʿ and brought upon it a state of economic decline.

Nūr had been succeeded as *amīr* by one of his slaves, an Abyssinian convert called ʿUthmān, who had risen high in his service and whose detachment from the partisan strife made him for the moment acceptable to both the aristocratic and popular parties. But having succeeded to power he pandered to the aristocracy, authorizing wine-drinking and other abominations in the eyes of the zealots of the proletariat who were attached to fanatical rigorist shaikhs inspired by memories of the great Imām.

ʿUthmān negotiated a treaty with the Galla and induced them to attend the markets in Hararian territory. This was the first attempt made to weaken the nomadic warriors with the sublimate of civilization and bring them into contact with Islamic propaganda. He put Jibrīl, Nūr's son-in-law and an austere and fanatical adherent of the old school, in charge of one of these market centres. Jibrīl went to Zajrābar in Aussa where popular opposition centred around him and he was joined by many partisans. A trivial incident caused revolt to flare out. One of the stipulations in the agreement with the Galla had been that all refugees should be restored to them. A Muslima, daughter of a noble of Harar, who had been taken by the Galla, turned up at Aussa. Jibrīl refused the Galla demand for restoration, but ʿUthmān ordered her to be handed over. Revolt burst out, but ʿUthmān's general defeated and killed Jibrīl. Ṭalḥa, a son of the *wazīr* ʿAbbās, now became the centre of revolt and, whilst ʿUthmān was in Aussa, conquered the militia left in Harar and was elected sultan (1569), being the first of these *amīrs* to take that title. In 1571 Ṭalḥa was deposed since, says the Muslim chronicler, 'he did not during his reign go out to war or the *jihād*'.[1] The militaristic party brought the family of ʿUthmān back to power by electing his son Naṣīr as sultan and it was Naṣīr's son, Muḥammad IV, whom the Bāḥr Nagāsh invited in 1572/3 to join the coalition against the Negus.

The call to arms for a *jihād* against the Christians was immediately popular, for it was the last desperate attempt of the Hararian militaristic society to turn its weapons from the internecine strife, soon to annihilate its own social structure, to external conquest. Muḥammad took considerable pains over the reorganization of his army and went out to meet the Abyssinians in 1577. After a hard-fought battle on the River Wēbi he was defeated, captured, and executed together with the flower of the Hararian nobility, and Harar as a military power was extinguished for ever.[2]

Whilst the army was away the Galla took the opportunity to raid Hararian territory, destroying a hundred villages and even besieging Harar city. One, Manṣūr b. Muḥammad, organized new forces and was able to restore some semblance of order and regain the territory of Aussa. Manṣūr fell a prey to the usual internal partisan strife and was succeeded by Imām Muḥammad Jāsā, a member of Grāñ's family who, leaving his brother in charge of Harar with the title of *wazīr*,

[1] E. Cerulli, 'Documenti arabi', op. cit., text, p. 54.

[2] *Hist. Reg. Sarṣa Dengel, C.S.C.O.*, ser. ii, vol. iii (1907), pp. 57–59.

transferred the seat of the sultanate in 1577 to the oasis of Aussa in the middle of the scorching Dankali desert which he thought would be less accessible to Galla raids. Thus begins the miserable history of the Imāmate of Aussa. It did not prove to be secure from the Galla who raided it continually, and in 1583 the Warra Daya killed Muḥammad Jāsā. The struggle between the partisans continued and during the next five years there was a succession of eight sultans. Surrounding nomad tribes gave the State little respite and one Somali raid penetrated into and pillaged Zailaʿ which from 1630 became dependent upon the sharīfs of Mukhā. Aussa degenerated to a barbaric state controlled by the nomadic ʿAfar, and its dynasty finally disappeared sometime after 1672.[1] Nomadism had completely reclaimed the once powerful Muslim kingdom.

So ended the existence of the most powerful Muslim state of north-east Africa. Known first as Ifāt with its seat in eastern Shoa, it had passed into Adal with Zailaʿ as the chief centre, and finally Harar, whence it degenerated into nomadism in the Dankali desert. Behind the rather sterile accounts of the rise of adventurers, exhortation to the *jihād*, wars, turbulence, and partisan strife, we catch glimpses of the once brilliant civic life of Harar, the richly laden caravans from the coast, the crowded and well-stocked markets, the enthusiasm of the religious procession, the brilliance of the sultans' courts, and the encouragement of Islamic learning and the arts. We see more clearly the strength of the religious passions of the masses, their fervour for the *jihād*, unextinguished until the reversion to nomadism, and above all the formidable characters and military genius of the *amīrs*.

With the break up of the Harar State the vital force of the old Islam in north-east Africa ebbed. Islamic power at one time had seemed capable of expanding over all the provinces of Abyssinia and drawing its medley of peoples into its fold. Its political extinction, so complete and irretrievable, was due chiefly to its own internal weakness.

Harar itself continued to exist as a city-state which became independent of the Imāmate of Aussa in 1647 under ʿAlī b. Da'ūd. It no longer attempted to spread Islam by extending its political power, but through peaceful propaganda was to be the chief agency for its dissemination throughout southern Ethiopia during the ensuing centuries.

*Elimination of the Ottoman Threat.* Having destroyed the power of Harar, Sarṣa Dengel moved against Yesḥaq, the Bāḥr Nagāsh, who

[1] In 1672 *Imām* ʿUmar-Dīn b. Ādam ascended the throne (cf. Cerulli, 'Documenti arabi', op. cit., p. 86). Nothing is known of its final overthrow by the ʿAfar.

was in alliance with the Ottomans.[1] In 1578 he defeated their combined armies at ʿAddi Qorro in the Tigrai when both Yesḥaq and the Pasha were killed. The Negus then moved into the fortress of Debārwa, broke down its walls, and destroyed its mosque.

For some years the Negus was occupied in wars against Agao, Falāsha, Nilotic, and Sidāma tribes, and above all in repelling Galla invasions. Whilst he was in Sidāma Enārya, which he converted to Christianity, a minor chief of the Tigrai allied himself to the Turks and helped them to reoccupy Debārwa. The king returned and advanced against them, but the Turks retired into Arkiko and he decided to try and evict them once and for all from Abyssinia. He failed in this. The fortress was attacked but so strongly held that it could not be taken, and the Abyssinian army being without reinforcements had to retire to the mountains to eliminate the rebel Tigrean chief. After accomplishing this and returning to Debārwa the Negus found rich gifts awaiting him from the Pasha Kadāwert. He accepted these and made peace, and from that time (1589) the menace of Turkish conquest was lifted, for with the decline of Ottoman power, Arkiko and Maṣawwaʿ were handed over to a local Beja (Balaw) chieftain to act as *nāʾib* (deputy) of the Ottoman government.

The last years of Sarṣa Dengel were passed in comparative tranquillity, his conquests proved ephemeral, and after his death in 1597 the old troubles started again, for feudalism was becoming the real master of a country in which regional loyalties counted for more than loyalty to a state suffering continual disintegration through the strong Galla confederations moving ever deeper and deeper into the country.

## 4. PERIOD OF ISOLATION AND REGIONALISM

### (*a*) *Roman Propaganda and Nationalist Reaction*

After the defeat of Aḥmad Grāñ the remnants of the Portuguese had settled down and intermarried with Abyssinians and their numbers had been augmented by Jesuit priests sent to convert Abyssinia to Roman Catholicism. These received a fairly friendly reception and in 1622 Pedro Paëz, the most able and tactful of them, succeeded in persuading the Emperor Susenyos (1607–32) to join the Roman Church. Susenyos, however, guided by the bigoted and overbearing Alphonso Mendez who succeeded Paëz in 1626, tried to make the new faith the national one, but only succeeded in bitterly antagonizing both the

[1] For a detailed account of this campaign, see C. Conti Rossini, 'La Guerra turco-abissina del 1578', *O.M.* i. 634–6, 684–91; ii. 48–57.

priests and the mass of Abyssinian Christians. The reception of a Latin patriarch made Roman Catholic religious propaganda look like an attempt at foreign domination. He completely alienated the Abyssinians by suppressing their most sacred customs; they were rebaptized as though they were pagans, their priests were reordained and churches reconsecrated, graven images and the Latin rite and calendar were introduced; whilst deeply rooted customs, like circumcision and the observance of the Sabbath, were prohibited.

The revolts which broke out against this latinization of the Church were genuine popular insurrections.[1] So bitter was the feeling aroused that some chiefs declared that they would prefer a Muslim ruler rather than submit to a Portuguese domination. At length Susenyos, worn out by the strain, could endure the popular reaction no longer and issued this proclamation:

> Hark ye! Hark ye! We first gave you this faith believing that it was good. But innumerable people have been slain on account of it, Yolyos, Qeberyāl, Takla Giyorgis, Sarṣa Krestos, and now these peasants. For which reason we restore to you the faith of your forefathers. Let the former clergy return to the churches, let them put in their *tābots*, let them say their own liturgy; and do ye rejoice.[2]

He then abdicated in favour of his son Fāsiladas (1632–67) and soon afterwards died. Fāsiladas completely reversed his father's religious policy and Ethiopia returned to the old Church-State tradition upon which the Solomonid throne was based. The feelings which had been aroused were such that toleration of alien religious propaganda such as had been allowed by Galāwdēwos and Sarṣa Dengel was no longer possible. Fāsiladas expressed the popular feeling when he wrote to the Latin Patriarch:

> They detested nothing more, than the reiteration of Baptism, as if we had bin Heathens, before we had bin Baptiz'd by the Fathers. They re-ordain'd our Priests and Deacons, they burnt the wooden chests of our Altars, and consecrated some Altars of their own, as if ours had not bin consecrated before.... Those things (i.e. concessions) are offer'd now too late, which might have bin easily at first allow'd: For now there no returning to that, which all the whole Nation abhors and detests: for which reason, all further colloquies and disputes will be in vain.[3]

The Jesuits were expelled and Mendez, when he reached India, sent a petition to the King of Spain stating that the only means of converting

[1] This is made especially clear from the life of the woman saint Walatta Pēṭros; see the edition by C. Conti Rossini, *C.S.C.O.*, 1912.

[2] B. Tellez, *Travels of the Jesuites in Ethiopia* (Eng. trans. 1710), p. 242; Job Ludolphus, *A New History of Ethiopia* (Eng. trans. by J. P. Gent, 1684), p. 357.

[3] Job Ludolphus, op. cit., p. 364.

Abyssinia was a military occupation of the country.[1] All Abyssinians who did not return to the fold of their own Church were banished and their property confiscated. Further attempts on the part of Rome to send French Capuchins caused Fāsiladas to make an agreement in 1648 with the pashas of Sawākin and Maṣawwaʿ to execute all priests who tried to enter the country.

Abyssinian Christianity had suffered a profound spiritual crisis through the invasion of Imām Aḥmad when apostasy had been general, and succeeding rulers had dallied with the idea of adopting a gradual policy of reconstructing the religious basis of the empire if necessary with the help and stimulus of the Western Church. But the extent to which Susenyos went in this reconstruction made him seem a traitor to his sacred calling as head of the national Church and he was bitterly opposed, not only by the clergy, but by the feudal governors and the masses of the people.

Roman Catholicism was thus robbed of its prospective religious conquest of Abyssinia on both political and religious grounds. On the one hand, the policy of complacency shown by earlier kings towards the alien religious propaganda was turned into sharp and bitter persecution when the Abyssinians realized that it was being used to undermine their religious tradition and national independence. They believed that European missionaries and their converts were being adapted to an illegitimate use by Portugal in preparation for an attack upon Ethiopian independence; and it was in order to anticipate this supposed danger that Fāsiladas proceeded to stamp out Romanism so thoroughly and brutally.

But the chief reason for the failure of Roman propaganda was not political. It was above all rejected on religious grounds. The short-sighted Jesuit policy of latinizing the national Church evoked the spontaneous reaction of the people themselves. It was the refusal of the Jesuits to adopt a long-term policy of moulding their Western religious culture into Abyssinian forms which dealt Romanism its death blow, for only a long and patient process of cultural adaptation could have transformed it to suit the Abyssinian's own peculiar mentality.

### (*b*) *Atrophy of Abyssinian Christianity and Renewed Progress of Islam*

Fāsiladas's agreement with Muslims to secure Abyssinia against Western influence was a complete reversal of the former policy of

[1] Cf. C. Beccari, *R.A.S.O.*, vol. xiii (1913), letters nos. 13 and 23 to the King of Spain; Job Ludolphus, op. cit., p. 365.

reliance on the Portuguese to secure it from Muslim aggression through control of the Red Sea ports. All contacts with the Western world were broken, and it was the Muslims who now became the allies of the Abyssinians against what seemed to them the greater menace—the attempt of Europeans to undermine their national religion, the very embodiment of their national spirit. This isolation, besides causing religious regression and intensifying their characteristic national pride and xenophobia, aided the peaceful propagation of Islam.

During this time of internal religious troubles Islamic propaganda began to recover its equilibrium after the terrible shocks it had suffered, and was completely transformed. The whole attention of the Ethiopian Church had been concentrated upon the Roman Catholic danger to their national religious unity, and, when that had been averted, the Church had become involved in doctrinal disputes, a development which had been stimulated by controversies with the Jesuits. During this time Islam was progressing slowly but by peaceful means, especially amongst peoples only superficially influenced by Ethiopian expansion. Nor did its influence stop at the rapidly decreasing frontiers of the Christian kingdom; Manoel d'Almeïda, who lived in Ethiopia from 1624–33, says that in his time adherents of Islam were scattered throughout the whole of the empire and formed a third of the population.[1]

With the priests of the degenerate nationalistic Christianity of the wild highlanders involved in theological disputations, the simplicity and adaptiveness of Islam could not but appear attractive to the pagan peoples brought into contact with it. But Islam's force of expansion amongst pagans in Ethiopia was helped by the fact that it was the religion hostile to that of the Amharic race who lorded it over them. In its original expansion amongst the Agao Christianity had absorbed such of their own customs and religious patterns as did not conflict with the essence of Christianity, whilst at the same time it had transmitted to them a new vitalizing Semitic religious core. But Amharic Christianity was now fixed and sterile. The result was that as it had become more and more fossilized to embody the spirit and form of Ethiopian nationalism, it was regarded by pagan tribes as the tribal religion of their enemies. Islam, on the other hand, opening its arms to embrace all and sundry who cared to join its brotherhood by the repetition of a simple formula, and accommodating as it was to their indigenous

[1] R. P. Manoel d'Almeïda, *Histoire de la Haute Ethiopie*, in Thévenot, *Relations de divers voyages curieux* (Paris, 1696), ii. 7; *R.A.S.O.* v. 46.

practices, also gave new converts pride of membership of a universal religious system transcending all racial barriers, whilst their incorporation into the system opened up to them possibilities of deeper religious experience and greater control over the hostile world of spirits and demons.

Fāsiladas, after expelling the Jesuits, attempted to form closer links with neighbouring Muslim powers. He sent an envoy to the Imām al-Mu'ayyad bi'llāh of Yaman in 1642 asking him to banish or kill any Portuguese he came across; and another embassy in 1647 to his successor, al-Mutawakkil ʿalā'llāh, in charge of an Abyssinian Muslim, to inform the ruler of Yaman that not only did he desire friendly relationships with him, but he would not look unfavourably on the sending of Muslim missionaries to his dominions. A Muslim *ʿālim* was in fact sent in 1648, but he was greeted with so much opprobrium by the populace that Fāsiladas advised him to return and sent him away loaded with costly gifts.[1]

The son of Fāsiladas, Johannes I (1667–82), was alarmed by the progress of Islam and called a council at Gondar to decide what measures should be taken to resolve the religious confusion.[2] In 1668 this council promulgated an edict of religious discrimination, which decreed that the Franks (descendants of the Portuguese) must leave the country unless they joined the national Church, whilst Muslims, who could not be expelled because they were an essential part of the economic life of the country, were forbidden to live with Christians and must inhabit separate villages or separate quarters in the towns. Thus the Muslims in Gondar, the new capital founded by Fāsiladas far removed as he thought from the Galla threat, were compelled to leave the upper town and live in the lower quarter on the banks of the Qāḥa which they inhabit to this day.[3] The Falāsha were subject to the

[1] On the Yamanite mission see F. E. Peiser, *Der Gesandtschaftsbericht des Hasan ben Ahmad el Ḥaimī*, Berlin, 1894–8. See also letter no. 106 in Beccari, *R.A.S.O.*, vol. xiii (1913).

[2] I. Guidi, *Annales Iohannis I, Iyāsu I et Bakāffā*, *C.S.C.O.*, ser. ii, vol. v (1903), p. 8.

[3] Dr. Poncet, who visited Abyssinia 1698–1700 to treat Iyāsu I, who was afflicted with some form of leprosy, writes: 'Mahometans are tolerated at Gondar, but 'tis in the lower Part of the Town, and in a separate Quarter. They are called *Gebertis*, that is to say Slaves. The Æthiopians cannot endure to eat with them; they wou'd not eat even of Meat that is kill'd by a Mahometan, nor drink in a Cup they have made use of, unless a Religious Man shou'd bless it by reciting over it some Prayers and shou'd breath into it thrice, as it were to drive away the evil Spirit. When an Æthiopian meets a Mahometan in the Streets, he salutes him with his left Hand, which is a Mark of contempt' (Poncet, *A Voyage to Ethiopia*, 1709, p. 61). Poncet also mentions a town called Emfras, a day's journey from Gondar, which he says 'is the only town of Æthiopia, where the Mahometans have public exercise of their Religion and where their Houses are mix'd with those of the Christians' (op. cit., pp. 81–82). This may

same rules as Muslims. This law could not at first have been very effective because it was renewed again in 1678.[1]

The real effect of these decrees was only to aggravate the danger from Islam. The Jabarti Muslims of the highlands joined the ranks of penalized communities like the Jews, Armenians, and Parsees. Debarred from owning land and engaging in agriculture they became proficient in commerce and handicrafts and drew the trade of the region still more completely into their hands. Since they belonged to a universal church and therefore, in contrast to other penalized minorities, carried within themselves the missionary urge, their social ostracism brought them into close association with all the subjected peoples, Falāsha, Sidāma, Galla, and Shānqela, in their travels from market to market, and their Islam caused a slow social and religious fermentation amongst these peoples. Many of the Galla tribes accepted it as a social bulwark against Amharic nationalism when, had the Abyssinians sought to win them, they might by absorption have been drawn into the Abyssinian Church and nation.

A rather isolated incident from the reign of Iyāsu I (1682–1706), a great king who initiated many social and economic reforms and held up the disruption of the empire during his time, shows that the monarchy still had power to inspire respect from the petty Muslim coastal states. For centuries Abyssinia had employed Levantine merchants to export its produce and import foreign goods. In Iyāsu's time these trade connexions were flourishing. The negroid Funj domination over the nomad Arabs of the Sudan assured the caravans security between Gondar and Cairo.[2] The superintendent of this section was an

be the same town which the ambassadors of Ismāʿīl al-Mutawakkil, Imām of Ṣanʿā, found in 1648 near Gondar inhabited entirely by Muslims. When Bruce was in Gondar in 1770 there were 3,000 Muslim houses. The food prohibition only applied to flesh; Bruce writes: 'Flour, honey, and such-like food, Mahometans and Christians eat promiscuously, and so far I was well situated. As for flesh, although there was abundance of it, I could not touch a bit of it, being killed by Mahometans, as that communion would have been looked upon as equal to a renunciation of Christianity' (*Travels*, iv. 390).

[1] I. Guidi, *Annales Iohannis I*, pp. 36–37.

[2] At the beginning of the sixteenth century an Arabic-speaking black tribe of unknown origin called the Funj suddenly appeared on the Blue Nile, dominated the Negroid agriculturalists of the Jezīra and the Arab-Nubian nomads, brought the Christian kingdom of ʿAlwa to an end in 1504, and as the 'Black Sultanate' controlled the Nile valley from Dongola to the *sudd* region and from Kordofān to the Abyssinian frontier. The new orientation caused by settlement at Gondar as a fixed capital directed attention westwards and northwards instead of southwards, and frontier troubles and raids were continuous, especially in the reign of Susenyos, when the Tāka region was occupied. But on the whole the relations of the sultanate and Abyssinia were comparatively peaceful; neither regarded the other as a potential menace threatening their independence.

Egyptian called al-Ḥājj ʿAlī. The traffic between the Red Sea ports and the East was in the hands of a merchant of Armenian origin called Murād, whose operations extended to Egypt, Syria, and as far as India. The Turks had made the head of the Balaw, an important Beja family of the Samhar whose chief centre was Arkiko (or Dokono), their *nā'ib* or deputy. In 1692 the *nā'ib*, Mūsā b. ʿUmar b. ʿĀmir b. Kunnu, tried to extort a greatly increased import duty, and when Murād refused to pay he seized goods destined for the Negus which were waiting at Maṣawwaʿ. Iyāsu thereupon made an inland blockade of Maṣawwaʿ and made preparations to attack the *nā'ib*, who thereupon collected the confiscated goods, added costly gifts, and went himself to the emperor at Axum, where he was graciously received and pardoned.[1]

## (*c*) *The Triumph of Regionalism*

*Collapse of the Monarchy.* Since our chief concern is with the progress of Islam during this period we will content ourselves with a summary of the internal conditions in Christian Abyssinia as the background for our study of Islam.

The foundation of Gondar by Fāsiladas was disastrous for the unity of such a physically tortured region as Abyssinia. The activities of the State had always been limited, but formerly, when Abyssinia had not had a fixed capital, the emperor moved from place to place with his whole court and, since it is the *tābot* which gives sanctity to the building, with his church too. Since the central state authority was mobile his potential power extended to the farthest regions of his empire. Gondar, on the other hand, is in the heart of Amḥara, and though effective for the control of Bēgamder and to some extent Gojām and Dāmot, it was impossible for the king to make his authority felt in more distant provinces. A fixed capital enabled court intrigue to thrive more insidiously and *coups d'état* and the killing or imprisoning of monarchs became the rule. The kingdom of Gondar therefore slowly decayed, whilst Galla prisoners and mercenary troops drafted into the royal forces brought a further unstable element into the life of the Abyssinian capital, which soon came under their control.

Iyāsu II (1730–55) was the last Negus who had any semblance of authority, and even that was due to the influence of his mother and did not extend beyond the Amharic provinces and Gojām. He was nicknamed Iyāsu 'the Little' in contrast to his grandfather Iyāsu 'the Great'. He waged war with the Funj kingdom on the Blue Nile (1735 or

[1] I. Guidi, op. cit., pp. 171–2; cf. Bruce, *Travels*, iii. 476–7; iv. 203–4.

1744) and sustained a disastrous defeat before Sennār. In 1738 the *abūna* died and an embassy was sent to Cairo for a new one. The humiliation which it suffered is an indication of the depth to which the prestige of the monarchy had fallen in the eyes of the Muslim powers.[1] First the envoys were imprisoned by the *nā'ib* of Arkiko for six months, when, after being plundered of half the money destined for the authorities in Cairo, they were allowed to go. Their stay in Jidda was occupied with quarrels, and one of them joined Islam; whilst on the return journey the new *abūna* was held for ransom by the *nā'ib* of Arkiko. This affront was too outrageous to remain unnoticed and, since it could only have been carried out with the connivance of Mikā'ēl Sehul, the Rās of Tigrai, who dominated the *nā'ib*, Iyāsu came into conflict with the Rās. The prestige of the monarchy still counted for something and the Rās was defeated, but Iyāsu spared his life and indeed reinstated him with increased authority. After that the royal authority became purely formal and Mikā'ēl Sehul during the next forty years was the virtual controller of northern Abyssinia and its champion against Galla and Muslim influence.

Iyāsu's mother, in order to maintain her influence, had married him to Wabi, daughter of the Wallo Galla chief Amiṭo, who was baptized under the name of Bērzābēh.[2] The next Negus, Iyo'as I (1755–69), was Wabi's little son. Large numbers of Wallo came to Gondar and formed the royal praetorian guards. His Galla relatives were enriched, his uncles Lubo and Birallē, for instance, being made governors of provinces, and the Christian Amḥara chiefs entirely alienated. The Wallo became arbiters of the dynasty until they were replaced by the Yajju Galla. This introduction of a completely alien element into the social structure of highland society made the dismemberment of the empire inevitable. Rās Mikā'ēl became champion of the national forces and the Church, and in the ensuing years of struggle the provinces of Bēgamder, Tigrai, Lāsta, and Dāmot all participated with their armies as sovereign powers. From now on the history of Abyssinia is a history of separate kingdoms with the *negasti* still living in a state of tawdry magnificence at Gondar, but no more than puppet kings.

*Disintegration of the Empire and Galla Supremacy over the Throne.* The empire had never in its history been a truly homogeneous political unity, but rather a confederation of principalities, so that the emperors were rightly designated kings of the kings of Ethiopia. The unification

[1] On these events see I. Guidi, *Annales Regum Iyâsu II et Iyo'as*, *C.S.C.O.* (1912) pp. 88, 127–30.
[2] Ibid., p. 165.

of the State had been a slow process and never completely successful, though it was helped by the mobility of the central government and the need to concentrate effort against the menace of the Muslim powers. But the widespread apostasy during the invasion of the Imām Aḥmad Grāñ, the security from external threat following his defeat, and the internal wars of religion, had still further weakened the bonds between region and region. The strength of the Solomonid tradition had made the process of disintegration and separatism a long one, but gradually the distinctive peculiarities of each region had assumed predominance. Shoa, the very cradle of the Solomonid dynasty, is a good example. In Shoa, which was cut off from the rest of the empire by the Wallo Galla soon after the death of Iyāsu I, a small family grew from insignificant beginnings into the hereditary independent kingdom of Shoa, and it is from this local dynasty, through a later matrimonial alliance with a Solomonid, that the present Emperor is descended. Lāsta became independent during the time of Rās Mikā'ēl[1] under an Agao dynasty which traced itself back to the former Zāgwē royal house. Strangely enough Tigrai, though the most powerful of them all and quite independent under successive rulers, never succeeded in retaining an hereditary dynasty.

All this time the empire had been shrinking as the Galla advanced. They had surrounded and isolated many of the highly organized Sidāma kingdoms from whom they had encountered fierce opposition, they had ascended into the upper valley of the Abāy and spread over a large part of Shoa; whilst others had ascended the escarpment from the valley of the Ḥawāsh and penetrated into the highlands to form the Wallo, Yajju, and Rāya groups.

The Galla penetration of the highlands is important not only because of the part they played in the dismemberment of the empire by isolating provinces and providing the praetorian guards who dominated the monarchy, but also from the fact that they became Muslims. Cut off as they were from the main body of the Galla they were influenced by the Abyssinians amongst whom they settled or whom they pillaged, but yet they were not absorbed. They adopted a semi-nomadic or even a settled agricultural life, they absorbed many Abyssinian social and political institutions, they lost their former democratic structure, they became powerful warrior tribes independent and antagonistic to each other, whilst many were recruited into the armies of the Negus and local kings as praetorians, and did much to accentuate the barbarization

[1] Bruce, *Travels*, vii. 75.

of the Abyssinians. At the same time all these tribes (Wallo, Yajju, and Rāya) kept their Galla identity, and during the eighteenth century they reinforced their independence by the adoption of Islam.

But so disunited were these Galla tribes who penetrated and settled in the highlands that the monarchy was able to survive. Major Harris, who went on a mission to the King of Shoa in 1840, writes:

> Although not nominally tributory to Gondar, both Birroo and Adara Billé afford military aid whenever called upon, and the Wallo soldiery form the stoutest bulwark of the decayed empire. Were all these fanatic tribes of one accord, they could not fail to endanger the safety of Christian Abyssinia; but they are fortunately divided throughout by the same feuds and private animosities which sever the southern Pagans. Hating Christian and heathen with all the dire inveteracy enjoined by their creed, and slaying both without mercy on every opportunity, the Wallo preserve all the superstitions of the latter, below whom they are in many respects debased by Mohammedan bigotry; thus affording a melancholy proof of what the whole Galla nation must become, should it ever unfortunately happen that Abyssinia terminated her intestine struggles by falling under the grasp of a Moslem ruler. Intercourse with the northern states has imparted to the Wallo a higher degree of cultivation than is possessed by their countrymen in the south; and, passing nearly the whole of their time in the repetition of prayers, a proverb and general belief prevails, that their country can never be conquered by those who are not followers of the Prophet.[1]

During this period of regional sovereigns (called the period of the *masāfent*) from 1769 to 1855, the sacred character of the divinely ordained monarchy preserved the dynasty from actual extinction,[2] so that the Galla, however much power they wielded, did not aspire to the throne, though it was possible for a bandit chieftain like Rās Kāsa or the Shoan King Menelik to do so because they claimed Solomonid descent.

About 1840 political equilibrium seemed to have been reached and the new states to be fully born. The great protagonists had been reduced to four: Sāhla Sellāsē of Shoa, Wubē (pronounced Ubyē) of Semēn, Tigrai, and Lāsta,[3] Goshu of Gojām, and ʿAlī of the various Amḥara

[1] W. C. Harris, *The Highlands of Abyssinia* (2nd ed. 1844), ii. 354–5.

[2] Major Harris writes (op. cit. iii. 34), 'although torn by civil war from one extremity to the other, the bond of the ancient Æthiopic empire is still not entirely dissolved; and notwithstanding that the "King of Kings" has dwindled into the mere spectre of imperial dignity—is deposed and restored to the throne at the caprice of every predominant ruler—his name at least is deemed essential to render valid the title of Ras, and through the latter, of the governors of all the dependent provinces'.

[3] Ubyē, who was the sixth of the line of hereditary rulers of Lāsta, gained control of Tigrai after defeating Sab'agādis in 1831.

provinces (Dāmot, Bēgamder, Dambyā, and the capital, Gondar). The Church was the only national institution which constituted a bond between the four regions, but it had reached the lowest ebb in its history. Since the death of Abba Qērillos in 1830 it had been without an *abūna*, and when in 1840 Ubyē sent an embassy to Egypt to acquire a new one, one of his reasons was to get him to sponsor a war against Rās 'Alī on the ground of his being a secret unbeliever.[1] His arrival, write Ferret and Galinier, 'filled the Christian population with joy. . . . Only the Muslims could not rejoice at the triumph of the Christian Church; they alone, in depression for their religious concern, viewed the arrival of the head of the Church as a disastrous event to the interests of Abyssinia.'[2]

Some of these kings received envoys from Western powers, with whom they drew up their own political treaties, and it seemed as though the imperial tradition was broken for ever. But that tradition still survived and the renaissance of its power, which led to the weakening of regional rulers, the unification of the empire, and an unprecedented expansion over pagan and Muslim regions, began with the appearance on the horizon of a menace which was common to all Abyssinia and its Church. This was the rise in Egypt, the Sudan, and the Red Sea of a great Islamic power seeking to extend its dominion over the whole of north-east Africa from the Nile to the Red Sea. Faced with such a menace the imperial tradition re-established itself amongst the Abyssinians as the one force of cohesion which could preserve their national independence and faith from extinction by Islam, and the vital forces of the country reorientated themselves around the throne. In addition to this threat the menacing advance of European powers into Africa further helped to cement and consolidate national unity.

The change began in 1853 when the Muslim-Galla supremacy was brought to an end by Kāsa, the bandit nephew of the hereditary chief of Kwāra. He had gathered around himself a force bitterly hostile to 'Alī and Islamic influence, and by his victories over Goshu of Gojām, 'Alī of Bēgamder, Ubyē of Tigrai, and Ḫāyla Malakot of Shoa once more reunited Abyssinia, and, breaking with the Solomonid tradition, became King of Kings as Theodore III in 1855.

[1] Whatever 'Alī's real beliefs may have been, Ferret and Galinier write, 'even though he had always shown himself animated by a great tolerance towards the followers of the Prophet, yet he has never dreamt seriously of being converted to Islam, nor conceived the idea of raising himself against Christ' (*Voyage en Abyssinie*, 1847, ii. 79–80).

[2] Ferret and Galinier, op. cit., ii. 66–67.

## (*d*) *Progress of Islam during the Period of Regionalism*

Islam at the beginning of the nineteenth century was mouldering in a state of stagnant equilibrium. Similarly in this region it was decadent and rarely fanatical. Conversions were non-violent and for natural non-religious reasons. The zeal of the nomadic ʿAfar and Somali tribes, once so ardent, had abated, but, though they have no more than local history, they should not be forgotten since they are a factor in the spread of Islam in southern Ethiopia and amongst the Bantu of the Wēbi. The Galla of the eastern highlands (Wallo, Yajju, and Rāya), we have already shown, had accepted Islam as a bulwark against being swamped by Abyssinian nationalism.

The Galla of south-western Ethiopia who occupied Sidāma kingdoms, though only after two centuries of resistance, had mixed with the Sidāma and developed into the kingdoms of Jimma, Gēra, Gomma, Limmu Enārya, and Guma. This political change has been attributed[1] to the influence of Islam, but in fact it was the result of their taking over the system of the Sidāma states. The acquisition of Islam was but the casual effect of a deeper social cause. For many years Muslim traders from both the Sudan and south-eastern Ethiopia had been combining their trading operations with proselytization. They received a ready welcome at the courts of these rulers because they facilitated the prosperity of their country. Through them the kings were enabled to obtain a market for their products and import what they needed. They lived amongst the Galla-Sidāma, marrying Galla wives and in general making only one journey a year to the coast or into the Sudan. Thus they had ample opportunity to propagate their religion as well as their trade.[2] About the middle of the nineteenth century the chiefs of these five states joined Islam and were followed by most of their subjects.[3]

[1] For instance by Major W. C. Harris, op. cit. iii. 53.

[2] Cf. Massaia, *I miei trentacinque anni di missione nell' Alta Etiopia* (edn. 1922–30), iv. 78–79.

[3] Some of these Sidāma kingdoms had been converted to Christianity before the Galla occupied their countries. Their Christianity was in most cases very nominal, but not in all as we see from a letter of M. Antoine d'Abbadie dated 1843, which also shows how Christianity regressed in these outlying regions through the neglect of the Church during the period of regionalism. He writes, 'At Saka where the Muslim king of Enārya rules, many families in spite of vexations remained faithful to their Christian faith. In 1840 these Christians had not seen any priests for four generations. The touching perseverance of these unfortunate people is a veritable miracle! But that is not all. Near Enārya is Nonno where the Christians are very numerous. One of them was sufficiently informed to be able to calculate the date of Easter. We used to see him celebrate all the feasts of the Abyssinian Church together with his co-religionists; yet for more than a hundred years Nonno has had no priests and none of its Christians were baptized. Farther on, Mosha, a large and well-populated country, is full of churches and Christians. Every Sunday these unfortunate people, who had not a single minister

It was a natural change in a transitional society for it strengthened their independence, reinforced the authority of the rulers, and facilitated the slave-trade.

The Galla in the Harar region, many of whom were now semi-nomadic or settled, had accepted a nominal Islam through the propaganda of that city-state whose political influence, however, they rendered weak and precarious,[1] but the vast mass of the nomad Galla of the south and west (Arūsi, Borana, and Lēqa) were uninfluenced and retained their characteristic pagan institutions. Islam did not begin to spread amongst the Arūsi until the second half of the nineteenth century.

In Abyssinia proper Islam was spreading rapidly since more and more of the immigrant Galla tribes began to profess it. Out of the anarchy which followed the death of Rās Mikā'ēl, a chief of the Muslim Yajju (Warra Shaikh) Galla called ʿAlī (d. 1788) assumed control of central and north-western Abyssinia including the puppet emperor at Gondar and initiated a hereditary Galla dynasty of Bēgamder.[2] These chiefs had to become nominal members of the national

of God, used to lead the children and flocks around their churches crying at the top of their voices: "We invoke thee, O Mary!"' (*Annales de la prop. de la Foi*, xvii. 279).

The King of Enārya became a Christian in 1586 after an expedition by Sarṣa Dengel (*Hist. Reg. Sarṣa Dengel*, *C.S.C.O.*, *Scr. Aeth.*, ser. ii, vol. iii, pp. 137–43). For two centuries the kingdom resisted the Galla, but in the end its king took refuge in Kaffa and the Galla were left masters of its Sidāma inhabitants. Nonno was part of the kingdom of Enārya. It is extremely unlikely that the Mosha, as the Sidāma Sheka are called by the Galla, ever were Christians. They live in the extreme west of Sidāma territory next to the negroid Masongo and were pagan when conquered by Rās Tasamma in 1897.

[1] W. C. Harris, op. cit., i. 391.

[2] According to Guèbré Sellasié (*Chronique du Règne de Menelik II*, ed. M. de Coppet, 1930, i. 198) the family ancestor was ʿUmar Shaikh who came from overseas during the time of the Imām Aḥmad Grāñ and settled in Yajju. James Bruce gives us a vivid but exaggerated picture of Guangul, the first historical figure of this family, whom he met in 1770. His son ʿAlī was the first to become governor of Bēgamder with the title of *Rās*. Arnauld d'Abbadie, who travelled in Ethiopia 1838–41, wrote that ʿAlī 'voulut imposer l'Islamisme à ses sujets du Bégamdir, mais cette tentative faillit le perdre; il y renonça et . . . il mourut, recommandant à sa famille de respecter la foi de son peuple' (*Douze ans dans la Haute-Éthiopie*, 1868, p. 150). The following table shows the succession:

- Guangul (d. 1777/8)
  - (1) ʿAlī (d. 1788) (the Great)
  - (2) ʿAlī Gāz (d. 1803)
    - Goje
  - Kafay (daughter) m. Mersa Barento
    - (3) Gugsa (d. 1825)
      - (4) Imām (d. 1828)
      - (5) Māryē (d. 1831)
      - (6) Dori (d. 1831)
      - Alula
        - (7) ʿAlī (d. 1866)

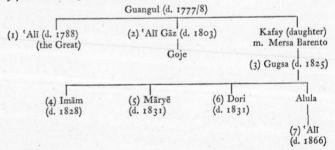

Church for political reasons,[1] but that did not modify their real sympathies. They favoured their co-religionists and some such as Rās Imām (d. 1828), son of Gugsa, openly supported Islam against Christianity. The last of the family, another ʿAlī (son of Alula son of Gugsa), although nominally a Christian, appointed his uncles, who were fanatical Muslims, governors of great provinces where they introduced Islamic customs and made proselytes by persuasion and by force. ʿAlī even tried to revive the cult of the Imām Aḥmad Grāñ by instituting pilgrimages to his tomb.[2] The chronicler Dabtara Zanab, who is naturally biased, writes: 'His relatives severely oppressed the poor; he was careless in rendering justice to all Abyssinians and in doing good. He feared not God and was Christian in name only, substituting magic (*asmāt*) for the Gospel of Jesus Christ'.[3] The result was that the discontented Abyssinian clergy were foremost in fomenting revolts against the Galla supremacy which was not ended until Kāsa defeated the last ʿAlī in 1853. It was during this period of anarchy, when the morale of the Abyssinian Church was at its lowest ebb, that conversions to Islam in the highlands were most numerous. An exaggerated claim has been made that during ʿAlī's rule one-third of the population of the central provinces joined Islam.[4] Although this could hardly be true even if it includes the Galla, it does show that there were numerous conversions.

[1] Cf. Ferret and Galinier, *Voyage en Abyssinie* (1847), ii. 324; G. Massaia, op. cit. xi. 98. A fundamental law of the Ethiopian State was that princes had to be Christians, therefore Muslims who aspired to the status of nobility had to change their religion. Such conversions were only nominal and when made governors of provinces they did all they could to favour Islam. Massaia writes: 'Ognuno comprende che movente di queste conversioni essendo la sete di regnare, nel fatto non si riducevano che ad una formalità esterna, restando poi i nuovi convertiti veri mussulmani nei cuori e nei costumi. E perciò accadeva che, elevati alla dignità di Râs, si cercondavano di mussulmani, dando ad essi la maggior parte di impieghi e colmandoli di titoli, ricchezze e favori: e così l'Abissinia cristiana invasa e popolata da questa pessima razza, passò coll' andar del tempo sotto il giogo dell' islamismo' (op. cit. ii. 162).

[2] Massaia, op. cit. ii. 162. Rās ʿAlī was by no means supreme among the Galla tribes. From the *Journals of Isenberg and Krapf* (1843, pp. 323–8) we learn that the Wallo Galla paid only nominal allegiance to him, that the seven Wallo tribes were always quarrelling together, that Imām Liban, son of Amadē, chief of the Warra Himāno was 'considered as the defender of the Mahomedan faith, and Head of the Mahomedan party; and this is the reason for the attachment which all these tribes entertain towards him. He is the representative of the Mahomedan power in Abyssinia. He is the Muhamedo, as they significantly call him' (ibid. p. 347).

[3] M. M. Moreno, 'La Cronaca di Re Teodoro', *R.S.E.* ii. 149. See also the account of Imām Liban's father, called Amadē (Aḥmad) of the Warra Himāno, who destroyed churches and converted Christians by force; H. Weld-Blundell, *The Royal Chronicle of Abyssinia, 1769–1840*, pp. 443 and 487–8; and C. Conti Rossini *La Cronaca Reale dell' Abissinia dell' anno 1800 all' anno 1840* (Rome 1917), §§ 1–2, 14.

[4] Reclus, *Nouvelle Géographie Universelle*, vol. x, pt. 1 (1885), p. 247; Massaia, op. cit. xi. 98.

Other travellers speak of large numbers of Christians of the plateau joining Islam.[1] On the other hand, it must be remembered that travellers passing along the recognized trade-routes and staying at places like ʿAdawa (Adua) where a quarter of the population were Muslim,[2] got an exaggerated impression of the number of Muslims; and such statements should be qualified by that of H. A. Stern who worked amongst the Falāsha about 1860, 'the followers of the Arabian prophet, though not numerous, except in Gondar, are still to be found in small bands all over the country.'[3]

It was during this period of troubles that the conversion of the Tigrē-speaking nomadic tribes in what is now called Eritrea began. These were Christian tribes and the two chief reasons for the change are those given by Plowden[4] for the conversion of the Ḥabāb about 1820; these were the anarchic condition of the country and the influence of Muslim traders and missionaries. The decadence and utter apathy of the hereditary priesthood allowed Islam to infiltrate unopposed. In many districts priests who had died had not been replaced, churches had been neglected and had fallen into disrepair. The loss of priests, and especially the *tābot*, for which Abyssinian Christians have a superstitious veneration, gave them a feeling of religious insecurity. Having lost the religious safeguards which had formerly guarded them through the crises of life they were ready to turn to another faith which could help them to regain their stability. Further, as Lejean writes:

> the fanatical nomads who surrounded them profited by their isolation to harass them and induce them by persuasion or by force to embrace Islam. These manœuvres took on a systematic character under the influence of the *nā'ibs*, whose fanaticism was here entangled with political machiavellism: the tribes having joined Islam could no longer refuse to pay them tribute, nor could they count on help from their co-religionists of Abyssinia.[5]

Traders were continually passing through their lands, setting up their markets at villages and traditional wayside centres and accustoming them to the simplicity and power of Islamic faith and practice. Then when the missionary urge reawoke in Islam at the beginning of the nineteenth century as a reaction to Western imperialism, through the influence of Wahhābism and the preaching of Sayyid Aḥmad ibn Idrīs

[1] See T. C. Beke, 'Routes in Abyssinia', *J.R.G.S.* xiv. (1844), 51–52; C. M. Isenberg, *Abessinien und die Evangelische Mission* (Bonn, 1844), p. 36.

[2] G. Sapeto, *Viaggio e Missione Cattolica fra i Mensa, i Bogos e gli Habab* (Rome, 1857), p. 140.

[3] H. A. Stern, op. cit., p. 109.

[4] Quoted below, see p. 160.

[5] G. Lejean, *Théodore II* (1865), p. 236.

al-Fāsī, in a revival which sent missionaries throughout the length and breadth of Islamic Africa, all the Tigrē-speaking nomadic tribes, whose ruling classes were certainly Christian, were claimed by Islam. The Banī ʿĀmir, who had been influenced earlier by the *fuqarā* of the Funj confederation of the Blue Nile into which they were at one time incorporated, were brought a more ardent Islam by Muḥammad ʿUthmān al-Mirghanī, a missionary sent out by Aḥmad ibn Idrīs in 1817. The Mārya and Bait Asgedē joined Islam about 1820 through the influence of traders and especially the Ād Shaikh family of missionaries; other Tigrē-speaking tribes were still nominally Christian but coming under Muslim influence, and after the Egyptian conquest they were all, together with the majority of the Bilēn, to find it politically expedient to adopt Islam.

Travellers have given as one reason for the success of Islam in Christian regions the moral superiority of the Muslims over the Christians, but it is extremely doubtful if this would have any effect upon these peoples. Rüppell says that the Muslim Jabarti were more active and energetic than the Christians. Most of their children learnt at least the elements of reading and writing, whilst Christian children rarely received any education at all unless they were destined for the priesthood or monastery. He also says that if a trustworthy person were needed to fill any post a Muslim was usually selected.[1]

The spread of Islam as elsewhere in Africa was facilitated above all by commerce. The Abyssinian is a warrior or a peasant and despises trade, consequently Muslims controlled all trade from the markets of the great towns to the smallest wayside market,[2] whilst all imperial trade connexions were with Muslim countries through the Muslim trading settlements along the coast.

During the time of internal troubles we should remember that Christian Abyssinia was faced by no direct menace from Islam such as would have served to unite all the Christians. The governors of Tigrai were arbiters of the *nāʾib* of Arkiko, the Sudanese Muslim confederation of Sennār was in a state of decadence and disruption, the petty oasis Sultanate of Aussa could hardly maintain its existence amongst the independent ʿAfar tribes surrounding it, whilst Harar was a commercial and religious city-state of little political importance; and the Somali to the south lacked all political cohesion. The Galla were the real menace. As we have seen, the empire was exhausted after the

[1] E. Rüppell, *Reise in Abyssinien* (Frankfurt, 1838), i. 327–8, 366.

[2] Cf. Ferret and Galinier, op. cit. ii. 411, G. Sapeto, op. cit., p. 140.

devastation caused by Grāñ's invasion, when they first began to swarm over the south like locusts so that it was said, 'that which the palmer-worm hath left hath the locust eaten' (Joel i. 4). Yet the Christians did not react against the Galla as a people who threatened their independence, for their lack of any real cohesion and the early victories of the emperors over them led the Ethiopians to underrate the menace to Ethiopian nationalism that they actually were. But the influence of the Galla through infiltration into the highlands was in fact deadly. If the Christians had only regarded their conversion as an auxiliary to their conquest, as the early Solomonids did with the Agao and Menelik at the end of the nineteenth century, and claimed these kindred tribes as brothers, the whole situation would have been altered. As it was the decadence of the Church and the Abyssinian pride of race which set up Christianity as a national possession did not allow this. So the Galla split up the highlands, joined Islam, and brought about the collapse of the monarchy and the temporary triumph of regional separatism.

The influence of Islam in Abyssinia at the end of this period was such that Cardinal Massaia, who spent thirty-five years in the country as a missionary, stated that were another Aḥmad Grāñ to come and unfurl the banner of the Prophet the whole of the country would become Muslim.[1] His statement certainly shows the extent of Islamic influence, but his conclusion is wrong, because it was in fact an external threat which once more led to the political unification of Abyssinia.

## 5. UNIFICATION OF THE ETHIOPIAN EMPIRE

### (*a*) *The Renaissance of Islam in the Nineteenth Century*

*The New Egypt and Abyssinia.* At the beginning of the nineteenth century new stirrings were evident in the life of African Islam which were to threaten the independence of Abyssinia and lead to its unification and an era of conquest. These stirrings showed themselves in two spheres, the political and religious. The first was the remarkable renaissance of Egyptian political power under Muḥammad ʿAlī and its expansion over the whole of the Nile valley and the Red Sea. The second was a process of religious fermentation amongst the peoples of the eastern Sudan, slow at first, but which was to burst out with devastating suddenness into a vast conflagration of Mahdist fanaticism.

Muḥammad ʿAlī's totalitarian rule brought to Egypt such wealth as it had not known since the days of the Fāṭimids. With this wealth

[1] Massaia, op. cit. xi. 98.

he was able to initiate and partially accomplish an ambitious programme of expansion. First he turned to the regions south of Aswān, and between 1820 and 1822 had brought under his rule without encountering any effective opposition all the little chieftaincies, remnants of the Funj confederation, along the Nile from Donqola to Sennār, together with the nomad tribes of the Buṭāna in the east and Kordofān in the west. In 1830 he founded the provincial capital of Khartoum at the juncture of the two Niles.

Muḥammad ʿAlī's conquests directly menaced Abyssinia. Naturally his cupidity was attracted by it. He had now established the political unity of the Nile valley for the first time in history, he was extending his rule towards its equatorial sources, and felt that the prosperity and security of Egypt should be fully assured by extending his conquests to those Ethiopian sources from which Egypt receives her great reserves of water.

The first hint of these ambitions came in 1818 when his son Ibrāhīm was appointed governor of the Ḥijāz and Abyssinia, which was included because the sultan had leased Maṣawwaʿ to Egypt. When Muḥammad ʿAlī undertook the Sudan expedition in 1820 he told Salt, then British Consul-General in Cairo, that he intended to invade Abyssinia after Sennār. Salt told him that the European powers would never tolerate an unprovoked attack on the only African power that had preserved its Christianity.[1] Sabdarāt in the Gash region was reached in 1823,[2] but Muḥammad ʿAlī did not follow up his conquests in Africa, because, like so many Egyptian rulers, he was diverted by the mirage of the conquest of Syria. When his Syrian adventure failed through coming up against Western powers and he realized that Egyptian expansion must be confined to Africa, he was in failing health and his finances were nearing exhaustion, yet he had sufficient energy in 1838 at the age of seventy to travel up the Blue Nile towards the Abyssinian frontier.

The Egyptians had three points from which Abyssinia could be harassed, Qalabāt and Tāka in the east, and Maṣawwaʿ in the west. In 1838 the first serious conflict took place when the Egyptians raided Abyssinian territory from Qalabāt and threw Gondar into a panic.[3]

[1] Sabry, *L'Empire Égyptien sous Mohamed-Ali* (1930), pp. 66–67; J. J. Halls, *The Life and Correspondence of Henry Salt*, ii. 68.

[2] 'Sennar Chronicle', see H. A. MacMichael, *History of the Arabs in the Sudan*, ii. 391.

[3] Gondar was not sacked as is often stated. This is confirmed from both Sudanese sources (cf. MacMichael, op. cit. ii. 398) and Abyssinian sources (Budge, *Hist. Eth.* ii. 482). See also F. Mengin, *Histoire sommaire de l'Égypte sous le gouvernement de Mohammed Aly* (Paris, 1839), iii. 97–98.

It was said, probably without foundation, that an agreement had been reached between Muslim Galla partisans of Rās ʿAlī and Egyptian emissaries who had penetrated there disguised as merchants to prepare the way for an Egyptian invasion. The raid caused much bitterness and accentuated religious hatred because so many churches were defiled by the Egyptians. Above all, it made an implacable enemy of Kāsā, nephew of Dajjach Kenfu, hereditary chief of Kwāra, Chalga, and other frontier districts bordering on Sennār, whose primary duty was frontier defence. Kāsā entered heart and soul into the border warfare against the Egyptians and the raid was avenged by Kenfu. Muḥammad ʿAlī intended to retaliate, but Rās Ubyē of the Tigrai complained to the French and British Governments about the infringement of Abyssinian territory, and they brought pressure to bear upon him to give up his ideas of conquest in Abyssinia.

After this, until the reign of Ismāʿīl Pāsha, Egypt abandoned any policy of direct conquest, though Egyptian influence consolidated itself on the border and began to penetrate the Eritrean lowlands where the Bani ʿĀmir accepted her suzerainty. Kasala was founded by Aḥmad Pāsha 'Abū Adhān' in 1840 as the capital of Tāka Province from whence raids were organized against the isolated Christian tribe of the Bilēn inhabiting the fertile valleys of the Keren region. Kūfit, forty miles from Kasala, was maintained as a frontier fort from 1852 to 1857, whence raids were made on the pagan Kunāma. In 1844 the Turks had tried to get a foothold on the Red Sea mainland by occupying Arkiko, only to be forced back on to the island, and in 1846 they leased Maṣawwaʿ to Muḥammad ʿAlī. The effect of foreign influence was to bring down bloody reprisals from Abyssinian chieftains upon the tribes in the Samhar plain and the valleys of the ʿAnsēba and Baraka who favoured the Egyptians, thus still further alienating them and opening the way to further Egyptian and Islamic influence.

*Islamic Awakening in the Sudan.* At the beginning of the nineteenth century there was a reawakening of Islamic propaganda which was most evident in the dervish orders. Most of the orders had fallen into a state of decadence and existed only as quasi-mystical schools, but through the teaching of Sayyid Aḥmad ibn Idrīs (d. 1837), a Maghrabī shaikh settled at Mecca, whose philosophy of life had been influenced by Wahhābī teaching, new militant orders like the Sanūsiyya or worldly ones like the Mirghaniyya were founded and the old orders were revivified.

For centuries Arabs from the Yaman, Ḥijāz, and Ḥaḍramawt had been infiltrating into the vast plains of the Sudan. Some had mixed with Nubian and Beja tribes between the main Nile and the Red Sea, producing mongrel Arabic-speaking Hamitic aristocracies like the Jaʿaliyyīn of Shendi. Others in the Jazīra, Kordofān, and Dārfūr had mixed with black tribes to form either sedentary agricultural groups with weak tribal ties or fully tribal nomadic cattle-breeding Baqqāra. All these tribes had come under Turko-Egyptian rule, and the work of propagandists was producing amongst them religious fermentation. At the same time the breaking up of pagan tribes through slave-raiding, recruitment into Egyptian regiments, and superficial islamization, brought new religious potentialities into an already dangerous field. At this stage amongst all these disquieted and mutually hostile groups began to spread the new words, *jihād* and Mahdī, words which had been virtually unknown to the placid Islam of the Funj kingdom, and kindled a slow fire which was to burst out into a conflagration of Mahdist revolt and sweep the hated foreign oppressors out of their land.

Both these movements, the expansion of Egypt and religious fermentation in the Egyptian Sudan, were premonitory signs of the reawakening of the Islamic threat to a divided and weakened Abyssinia.

## (*b*) *First Attempts at Unification*

The epic story of the rise to power of Kāsā is well known to all who are interested in Abyssinia.[1] He was a local chieftain who succeeded his uncle Kenfu in the command of the frontier province of Kwāra and built up a powerful army whose only allegiance was to himself. He came into conflict with Rāses Goshu of Gojām and ʿAlī of Gondar. By 1853 both had been defeated and he was ruler of Amḥara and Gojām, his only serious rivals being Ubyē of Tigrai and Ḫayla Malakot of Shoa. Two years later, after defeating the Rās of Tigrai, he was crowned emperor, taking the throne name of Theodore (Tēwōdrōs) because of an old prophecy that a king of that name would appear to destroy Islam and reconquer Jerusalem.[2]

[1] See W. C. Plowden, *Travels in Abyssinia*, 1868; H. Rassam, *Narrative of the British Mission to Theodore* (1869), pp. 278 ff.; C. Mondon-Vidailhet, *Chronique de Théodoros II*, 2 vol., Amharic text and trans., Paris 1905; J. M. Flad, *Zwölf Jahre in Abessinien, oder Geschichte des Königs Theodoros II*, 1869; Th. Nöldeke, 'Theodoros, König von Abessinien', in *Orientalische Skizzen* (Berlin, 1892), pp. 277–304; G. Lejean, *Théodore II*, Paris, 1865; M. M. Moreno, 'La Cronaca di Re Teodoro attribuita al Dabtara "Zaneb"', *R.S.E.* ii. 143–80.

[2] The first literary reference to this legend is in the *Fekkārē Iyasus* (Interpretation of Jesus) which belongs to the period of the early Solomonids. It would be indeed strange if some form of the Messianic hope had not awakened in a country like Abyssinia.

After breaking the power of the Wallo Galla who invaded Amḫara under their queen Warqitu, Theodore transferred the capital from Gondar to the natural fortress of Maqdala on the eastern edge of the highlands. Shoa capitulated in 1855 without a struggle when its king died on the eve of battle, and the young Menelik (b. 1844), son of Ḫayla Malakot, was taken and kept as a hostage. Having completed the unification of Ethiopia, Theodore had set himself three main aims: to break the power of the great feudal lords; to convert or destroy the Wallo and Yajju Galla; and to convert or expel all other Muslims. He also attempted to carry out moral reforms by prohibiting the slave-trade and the practice of polygamy. To him Christianity and Abyssinia were synonymous, but he tried to get religious unity in Abyssinia proper by compulsion alone, ordering that the Galla, Falāsha, Agao, and Wayṭo should be converted by force, and of course, failed[1]—in contrast to the policy of the early Solomonids with whom force was combined with the genuine missionary work of the monks.

Theodore's relations with the Coptic Church were gravely compromised by its Patriarch Q̱ērillos IV who agreed to the Khedive's proposal that he should personally conduct a political mission to Theodore with the object of establishing better relations between the two countries. Such a visit by a Coptic patriarch was without precedent in the history of Abyssinia. Theodore, who was unable to conceive how a Christian prelate could consent to act as the envoy of a Muslim power, received him very coldly in December 1856, and even imprisoned him for a few days, and he was not allowed to return until November 1857.[2]

Theodore's measures for consolidation and religious unity were

[1] His attempts to convert the Muslims having failed he issued a decree in 1864 proscribing Islam and declaring that all Muslims who would not become Christians were rebels. 'Cet acte', writes Lejean, who travelled in Eritrea 1860–4, 'était souverainement impolitique et injuste. Les musulmans étaient en Abyssinie dans la position fort subalterne qu'occupent les chrétiens d'Orient dans les États musulmans. Restés depuis les siècles étrangers au métier des armes, ils n'avaient jamais pris part aux troubles politiques de l'empire, et se contentaient de s'enrichir par le commerce, qu'ils avaient en partie monopolisé. Aussi, presque toutes les villes d'Abyssinie étaient musulmanes, soit en totalité comme Derita, Emfras, Alitiou-Amba, Haoussa, soit partiellement comme Gondar et Mahdera-Mariam. La moralité privée des musulmans était généralement supérieure à celle de la population chrétienne. On ne pouvait leur reprocher que l'abominable commerce des esclaves, qui est peut-être la base la plus nécessaire de l'islamisme: mais le négus avait le droit de frapper des coupables convaincus de traite, il n'avait pas celui de proscrire un culte tout entier. . . . La plupart se soumirent, comme à Gondar; d'autres (ceux de Derita par example) quittèrent leurs maisons et leurs petites fortunes péniblement acquises et se réfugièrent dans les bois' (G. Lejean, *Théodore II*, pp. 174–6).

[2] See G. Lejean, op. cit., pp. 83–85; W. C. Plowden, *Blue Book 1846–68*, pp. 175–6, 183; Stern, *Wanderings*, pp. 79–80; P. Dimothéos, *Deux ans de séjour en Abyssinie* (Jerusalem, 1871), ii. 105.

popular amongst a peasantry ravaged by long years of civil war, but his administrative reforms aroused the hostility of the feudal nobles. In the attempt to secure internal security he broke up the provinces into smaller units over which he placed his own governors. Naturally the feudal aristocracy reacted violently against this encroachment upon their power. Theodore realized that he had a difficult struggle before him and the rest of his reign was taken up with the attempt to crush both the nobles and the Galla. His unification having been carried out by force he had to rely on the prestige of his military might and fear of reprisals to maintain internal security. The rest of the story is well known. Revolts broke out continually and the rebels were pitilessly exterminated, his good qualities were submerged by the corruption of his nature in accordance with Acton's law and he degenerated into a cruel tyrant.

In 1862 Egypt made another abortive attempt to invade Abyssinia from the Sudan under Mūsā Pāsha Ḥamdī. Theodore and the Egyptian general avoided meeting each other[1] and an outbreak of smallpox forced the Egyptian army to withdraw to the Sudan. This was the year in which Theodore sent his famous letter to Queen Victoria, the ignoring of which by the Foreign Office led to Napier's campaign. In his ignorance of European politics he thought of England as a natural ally against Muslim powers, whereas in fact England had just been allied with the Turks against Russia. In this letter he wrote:

> My fathers, the Emperors, having forgotten the Creator, He handed their Kingdom over to the Gallas and the Turks. But God created me, lifted me out of the dust, and restored the Empire to my rule. He endowed me with power, and enabled me to stand in the place of my fathers. By this power I drove away the Gallas. But for the Turks I have told them to leave the land of my ancestors. They refuse, I am now going to wrestle with them.[2]

When no reply was received Theodore imprisoned the British Consul and other Europeans. In 1867 the British Government sent an expedition under Sir Robert Napier. Theodore, having alienated the whole of Abyssinia through his cruelties, was deserted and unable to offer any effective opposition and committed suicide when the amba of Maqdala was stormed. The success of the British expedition had considerable effect on Egyptian policy.

*Renewal of Egyptian Plans for Expansion.* The death of Theodore

[1] G. Lejean, op. cit., pp. 152–3.
[2] E. A. W. Budge, *History of Ethiopia*, ii. 492 ff.

marked the failure of the first attempt to reconstruct a unitary Ethiopian State, and when Napier withdrew the British force in 1868 the fate of Abyssinia was left to be fought over between Gobazē of Lāsta, Menelik of Shoa, and Besbes Kāsā of Tambien, with Egypt watching her opportunity in the north. Out of the struggle Kāsā arose triumphant and was crowned emperor as John IV (1872–89). Shoa, however, remained independent under Menelik who had escaped from Maqdala in 1865 and re-established himself on its throne. John had little opportunity for internal reform, for throughout most of his reign he was distracted by the encroachments of external powers, Egyptians, Mahdists, and Western nations, over all of whom he won a remarkable series of victories.

The opening of the Suez Canal in 1869 brought an end to the isolation of Abyssinia and when Egypt under Ismāʿīl Pāsha (1863–79) revived the idea of its conquest, the attempt was not planned to take place from the Sudan but from the Red Sea coast. The ease with which Theodore had been overthrown by Napier's force led Egypt to underestimate the task of conquering the country. In 1865 the lease of the ports of Sawākin and Maṣawwaʿ, which had lapsed after the death of Muḥammad ʿAlī, was renewed in favour of Ismāʿīl. Egyptian rule was more energetic than that of the Turks and was welcomed by the nomads who had been suffering severely during the anarchy of the last years of Theodore from the raids of the hill tribes. Soon some of these hill tribes themselves began to seek Egyptian protection and when Ismāʿīl appointed Münzinger, a Swiss adventurer, as governor of Maṣawwaʿ in 1871 he initiated the scheme of throwing a bridge across the Keren hills to link up the Egyptian possessions. He first reconstructed and fortified Maṣawwaʿ and then, making himself the 'protector' of the Bilēn tribes, he was able to occupy the Keren–Bilēn region in 1872. The Emperor John, although distracted by internal troubles, was near the point of declaring war on the Egyptians. At the same time the Egyptians were occupying the Somali coast from Zailaʿ (1870) to Cape Guardafui.

In the meantime Aḥmad ibn Abī Bakr, the Amīr of Harar who was visited by Richard Burton in 1855, had died (1866) and the throne had been usurped by Muḥammad ibn ʿAlī who was in league with the Galla and persecuted his own people, with the result that they appealed to the Khedive Ismāʿīl. The expedition under Ra'ūf Pāsha which had annexed Zailaʿ and Berbera crossed the desert to Harar and annexed it in 1875, without encountering any resistance except from some of the Galla tribes.[1] So ended the independence of the petty city-state of Harar after less than two centuries of existence.

Although the Egyptian occupation of the Harar region was but transitory, it had considerable effect upon the diffusion of Islam. The Galla of the region had tried to resist the invaders, but after various fights in which their primitive lances were of little avail against the firearms of the Egyptians they had to submit. The Egyptians managed to decoy their chiefs into Harar and threw them into prison, then forced them to dissolve their parliament, deliver up their Abba Bokku, cut off their *dufuras* or long hair, and submit to circumcision. A great number preferred to be killed rather than be thus humiliated, but after three or four years they were reduced to such misery that the majority submitted. Fekis were encouraged to travel in all directions to teach the social discipline of Islam, and the performance of the Islamic prayer was made obligatory under penalty of confiscation of property. That was the end of Galla supremacy in south-eastern Ethiopia.

In 1874 Egypt was left with a free hand by the Western powers to act as she pleased with regard to Abyssinia. Münzinger's plans and Ismāʿīl's only hope of success were based upon a disunited Abyssinia, but John, who had no intention of allowing the country to lapse into the anarchy of Theodore's later rule, had been consolidating his power. In 1875 three Egyptian expeditions set out, one from Zailaʿ which, we have seen, succeeded in occupying Harar; another diversionary one from Tajūra under Münzinger was annihilated by the Sultan of Aussa, who was in alliance with the Emperor,[2] on the shores of Lake Adobada on the Ḥawāsh; whilst the third and largest which set out from Maṣawwaʿ under ʿArāqīl Bey was also almost completely wiped out by John's Tigreans at Gundet near the Mareb.

Egypt, faced by this loss of prestige, prepared a new expedition in 1876. In response the Emperor John proclaimed a mass levy which took on the character of a crusade against the Muslims. It was in fact the first time for centuries that the Abyssinians as a whole responded to a call to protect their land and faith, and the clergy were the most potent instruments of propaganda. The popular movement was such that even Menelik, who the previous year had been intriguing with Münzinger, felt he ought to send his complement of troops.[3] The

[1] Cf. Naʿūm Shuqair, *Ta'rīkh as-Sūdān* (Cairo, 1904), iii. 90; L. Robecchi-Bricchetti, *Nell' Harar*, 2nd ed. (1896), pp. 118–20.

[2] Cf. G. Simon, *L'Éthiopie* (Paris, 1885), p. 117.

[3] According to Rohlfs, *Meine Mission nach Abessinien* (1883), p. 62.

Egyptians suffered a disastrous and ignominious defeat near Gura which sealed the fate of their imperialist pretensions. The peace which was arranged still left Egypt in control of the Keren area, but a few years later when the Mahdist revolt flared out in the Sudan, all her possessions in East Africa were abandoned.

*The Emperor John's attempt at Religious Unity.* The defeat of the Egyptians consolidated John's rule. In 1878 he settled relations with Menelik who was recognized as King of Shoa and Wallo but renounced his claim to the imperial throne. Although the unification appeared fairly complete John was faced with the eternal problem of creating a real unity which would endure after his death. He initiated reforms and endeavoured to revive the missionary impulse within the petrified state religion. He had seen the old fanaticism flame out against Egyptian aggression and felt that the only sound basis for his policy was religious sentiment, for this would make allies of the clergy and the people they could so easily inflame. Travellers have commented on his sincere but fanatical piety[1] and there are indications that he would have preferred a life of retirement. He had married a Muslim woman called Ḥalīma, after converting her to Christianity, and when she died in 1871 he vowed never to remarry or take any other woman. General Gordon wrote of him, 'Johannes, oddly enough, is like myself—a religious fanatic. He has a mission, and will fulfil it, and that mission is to christianize all Mussulmans.'[2]

In 1878 after his Shoan expedition he called a council of the Church at Borumieda (north of Dessié) to try to settle the doctrinal disputes which had agitated the Church for so long, and this Council also promulgated an edict which ordered the Dabra Libānos party to renounce their so-called heresy, whilst non-Ethiopian Christians, Muslims, Jews, Galla, Qamant, and pagans were ordered to join the national Church. Christians were given two years grace to submit, Muslims three years, and pagans five years. Shortly afterwards Muslims were ordered to build churches in the places where they lived and pay tithes to their parish priests. All officials of the State had either to accept baptism or resign their offices. The Imām Muḥammad 'Alī and Imām Abbā Watta, the two most powerful chiefs of the northern and southern Wallo Galla, were amongst those converted and took the names of Mikā'ēl and Hayla Māryām respectively. Some Muslims removed themselves into Galla country or Muslim lowlands or pagan areas

[1] See Rohlfs, op. cit., pp. 221–2; G. Simon, op. cit., p. 213.

[2] C. G. Gordon, *Letters to His Sister* (1902), p. 155.

where they formed new diffusion centres. Others conformed, but conformity meant very little for all that was required was the outward sign of baptism and payment of tithes. Cardinal Massaia saw some of them go straight from the church where they had been baptized to the mosque to have this enforced baptism wiped off by a Muslim holy man. Further, these conversions were confined to men only and, since the women are the preservers of tradition, they could have little real effect.[1] By 1880 some 50,000 Muslims, 20,000 pagans, and half a million Galla are said to have been baptized.[2] The result of such enforced conversions was merely to increase the hatred of Galla and Muslims for the Christians.[3] That such measures were contrary to the general tolerance of the Abyssinians is shown by Münzinger, who wrote in 1867: 'L'Abyssinie est généralement un pays de tolérance: chrétiens de toute confession, musulmans, juifs, païens vivent très paisiblement ensemble et font même des prosélytes sans que l'Église ou l'État s'en occupent.'[4] The attempt to impose a religion by political means always fails unless it is backed up by genuine religious feeling, and the Emperor John's attempt proved abortive because it was little more than a political expedient to get unity in the highlands masquerading under a religious guise. Full religious freedom was restored to the Muslims in 1889 after the death of the Emperor John.

*The Mahdiyya of the Sudan and Abyssinia.* The vast Sudan possessions of Egypt were at this time in a state of utter misery through misgovernment and the slave-trade, and the stage was all set for an outburst of fanaticism. The Dongolāwī slavers, of whom Zubair Pāsha was the chief, had organized the wild Baqqāra (cattle-breeding Arabs) for the purpose of the trade, but these had lately been somewhat repressed by the activities of General Gordon. When, therefore, a Dongolāwī feki, called Muḥammad Aḥmad, proclaimed himself the expected Mahdī in

[1] See Massaia, op. cit. xi. 60. He also writes of the important part which Muslim women played in diffusing Islam, op. cit. xi. 97–98.

[2] Rohlfs, *Meine Mission nach Abessinien* (1883), pp. 167–8; A. Oppel, 'Die religiösen Verhältnisse von Afrika', *Zeitschrift der Gesellschaft für Erdkunde zu Berlin*, xxii (1887), 307. The rite used for the baptism of a Muslim is described by H. Salt, *A Voyage to Abyssinia*, 1814.

[3] Massaia, op. cit. xi. 61–62. In John's treaty with Menelik, Art. VI stated that Menelik shall rule the Wallo Galla Muslims; Art. VII that Menelik must build Christian churches in the Wallo country and introduce Christianity there (Wylde, *Modern Abyssinia*, 1901, p. 471). Menelik did in fact baptize the Imām Abbā Watta of the Warra Ilu and other chiefs. Wylde writes, the 'wholesale baptism of the Galla tribes by the Abyssinians has not been nor is likely to be a success' (ibid., p. 8).

[4] Quoted by G. Douin, *Histoire du règne du Khédive Ismaïl*, iii, partie ii, p. 300. See also J.-B. Coulbeaux, *Histoire de l'Abyssinie*, i. 28.

1881, he was able, after he proved his divine mission by initial successes, to gain over both the more suppressed elements of the population who were easily fired to fanaticism by their misery, as well as the warlike Baqqāra seeking new outlets for their lust for plunder.

In 1883 the British, in control of Egypt since the revolt of ʿArabī Pāsha in the previous year, decided upon the abandonment of the Sudan. Qeḍāref on the Ethiopian frontier fell to the Mahdists in 1884, but the Egyptian garrison continued holding out in Kasala, fearing that its fall would leave the way open to the sea at Maṣawwaʿ. England sought, therefore, to gain the support of Ethiopia, and proposed that, in exchange for help in saving the garrison on the border, Egypt should cede the Keren-Bilēn territory back to Ethiopia. The garrisons of Qalabāt and other smaller places were relieved and Rās Alula was sent to relieve Kasala. Although he won a victory over ʿUthmān Diqna at Kūfit, the Kasala garrison failed to take advantage of it and the city was taken in 1885 soon after the fall of Khartoum. Berbera, Zailaʿ, and Maṣawwaʿ now all fell into the hands of European powers, whilst Harar, which had been evacuated by the Egyptians in 1885 and placed under one of its own chiefs, ʿAbd Allāh b. Muḥammad, was taken by Menelik in 1887.[1]

In 1887 the Abyssinians became more active and Negus Takla Hāymānot inflicted a defeat on the dervish *anṣār* under Wad Arbāb at Metemma. The Khalīfa regarded this town as an indispensable frontier fort and in June of the same year an immense army of dervishes under Abū ʿAnja and Zaki Ṭumal invaded Abyssinia and won a victory over Takla Hāymānot at Debra Sīna some thirty miles from Gondar. The victors entered Gondar, burnt buildings and churches, killed the priests and monks, and carried off the women and children. John ordered Menelik to march against them. He took his time and when he arrived the dervishes had retired. About this time a dervish expedition was sent into the Wallegga region in south-western Ethiopia. It made contact with Galla leaders, such as Jotē Abbā Iggu of the Lēqa Qēllem then engaged in resisting a Shoan invasion and penetrated as far as the Gibē of Nonno, but was defeated by Rās Gobana and forced to withdraw.[2]

In 1888 the Emperor sent a delegation to Omdurman nominally to pay his respects to the Khalīfa, but in reality to reconnoitre the land.

[1] Cf. Lord Cromer, *Modern Egypt* (edn. 1911), pp. 497–506.

[2] Cf. E. Cerulli, 'The Folk-literature of the Galla', *Harvard African Studies*, iii. 82–83; Guèbré Sellassié, op. cit. i. 253–4.

The report, showing him that all was not well within the Mahdist ranks, made him decide to discourage attacks on Abyssinia by an invasion of the Sudan. Metemma, his first objective, was held by 60,000 dervishes, but they were surrounded and completely overwhelmed. During the last stage of the battle, however, John was wounded and, through lack of adequate medical treatment, subsequently died. His army retired and the dervishes so harassed the retreat that the victory was turned into a rout. Yet at that point, when the dervish power was at its zenith, the Khalīfa turned his attention to the conquest of Egypt.

The reason why Mahdism made no serious attempt against Abyssinia, as might have been expected, was that the Khalīfa's eyes were all the time drawn by the mirage of the conquest of Egypt, and the four years of indecisive struggle with Abyssinia were but an unpleasant diversion from that attractive prospect. The Abyssinians, too, never regarded the Mahdists as a serious menace in comparison with the Western powers, and when in 1894 General Baratieri placed himself between two hostile forces by taking Kasala, John's son, Rās Mangasha of Tigrai, intrigued with the *anṣār* against him. Then followed the successive defeats of the Italians at Amba Alagi, Makalle, and 'Adawa (1896) which left their Kasala and other Eritrean garrisons isolated and open to attack by the dervishes. But the same year the British, who had been training a new Egyptian army, took the offensive and the reconquest of the Sudan was completed with the battle of Omdurman in 1898 and the death of the Khalīfa in the following year. Abyssinia had nothing further to fear from Islam in the Sudan.

### (*c*) *Menelik's Conquest of Muslim and Pagan Regions*

The three main features of Menelik's rule were the extension of the empire over the neighbouring Muslim and pagan countries in southern and south-western Ethiopia; the maintenance of Abyssinian independence (Italo-Abyssinian campaign of 1896) and the regularization of the question of frontiers (in particular the treaties of Addis Ababa of 15 May 1902, western frontier with Anglo-Egyptian Sudan, and southern frontier with British East Africa, 6 December 1907); and internal revolution and centralization by the progressive substitution of temporary governors for the rival kings who had divided the country among themselves. With the first of these only are we concerned, but a résumé of Menelik's conquests is important because they were to reincorporate in the Ethiopian Empire the Muslim and pagan regions in the east and south and west which had been lost since the Galla inva-

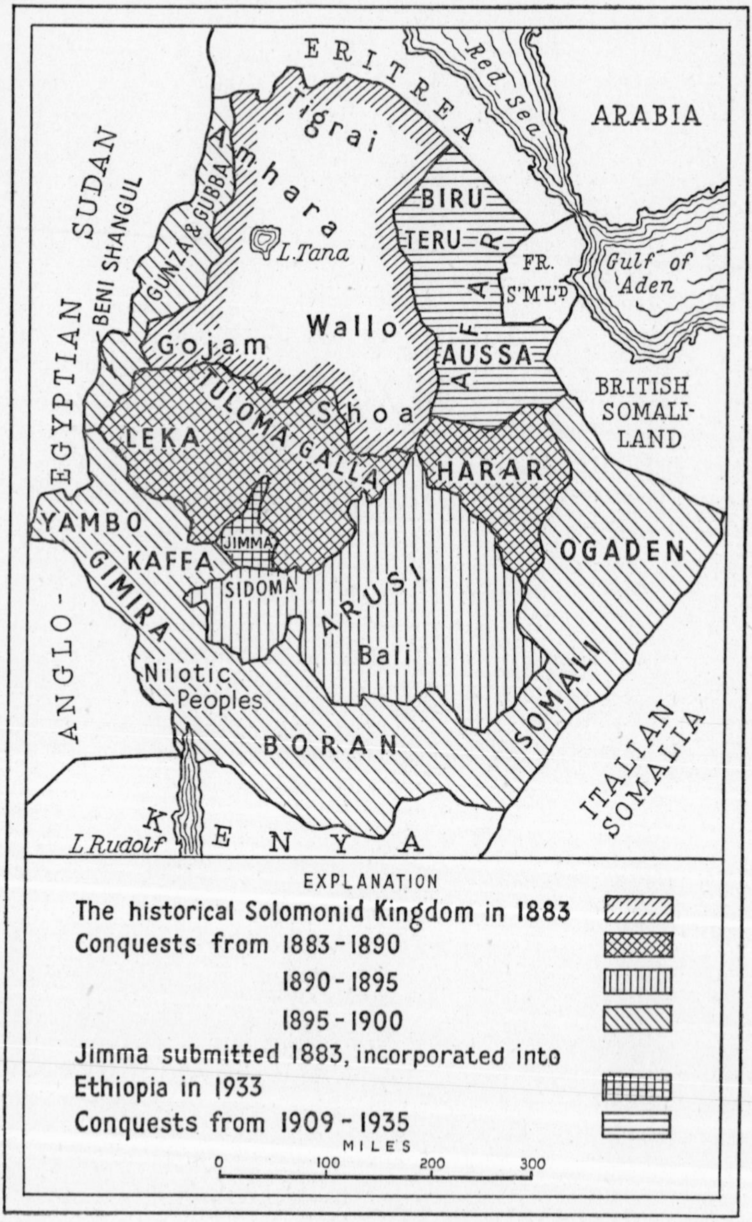


THE CONQUESTS OF MENELIK II

sions, control of which he believed to be essential to the consolidation of his power and the safety of the trade-routes.

Whilst Emperor John's struggle against Mahdism and Italian penetration was going on in the north, other far-reaching events were happening in the south. Menelik's predecessors had been gradually conquering the fertile region of the Wallo Galla and John had recognized his right to it when, after six years of campaigns (1871–6), Menelik had finally crushed all resistance. Menelik then turned his attention to the conquest of the rich regions south and west of Shoa. He began in 1881 by sending an expedition into the Arūsi region which was not very successful, but he soon turned towards the basin of the Gibē and Omo. The key to western Ethiopia was the powerful Sidāma kingdom of Kaffa which had fiercely defended its independence for centuries, but this he left until he had reduced all the surrounding countries. His first act was to save Kaffa from the attack of another king. The Negus of Gojām, Takla Hāymānot, instigated by John, had been making excursions into the Jimma and Kaffa regions to try and counteract Menelik's expansion. The first attack on Kaffa by Rās Diressa in 1880 provoked desperate resistance from the Kaffan king Gallitto and his son Kennito. This was followed by two more Gojāmite expeditions, and in 1882 Menelik, to save its becoming a prey to the Gojāmites, intervened by sending his Galla general, Rās Gobana, against them, and in a battle which took place on the territory of the Galla Gudru defeated the Gojāmite army and took its negus prisoner. The Emperor John, seeing his policy of equilibrium in danger, now intervened and was powerful enough to order Menelik to present himself with his prisoner. For fighting without his permission John took the Wallo Galla territory away from Menelik and Agao-Meder from Takla Hāymānot. The Wallo Galla now came under John who baptized its chief, Muḥammad ʿAlī, son of ʿAlī Libān, under the name of Mikā'ēl, and put half the Wallo country under him. But John, to avoid alienating Menelik too much, proposed a marriage between his own son and Menelik's daughter Zawdītu. In the agreement Menelik recognized John's son as successor to the imperial throne,[1] but received the title of Negus of Kaffa, together with approval of his plans for annexing the Harar, Galla, and Sidāma regions. Takla Hāymānot having lost much of his power, the succession was hardly in doubt when John's son died soon after his marriage; and when John himself

[1] Wylde, *'83 to '87 in the Soudan* (1888), i. 337; cf. Guèbré Sellassié, op. cit. i. 186 n. 3.

died in 1889, after the battle of Metemma, Menelik proclaimed himself king of kings.

During this time Menelik's generals were proceeding with the conquest of the Galla kingdoms between the Abāy and the Omo. In his conquest he evoked no national resistance from the Galla; on the contrary, those who were spared for the time being rejoiced in the subjection of inconvenient neighbours. The conquest was also facilitated by a great pestilence which decimated these regions in 1878 during which two-thirds of the population of Gomma are said to have been swept off. The Galla of Gudru were the first of these kingdoms to be conquered by Menelik's general, Rās Gobana, in 1882. Soon afterwards Sultan Abba Jifar of Jimma agreed to pay Menelik tribute and to facilitate the passage of Shoan troops through his territory. In successive years Menelik's troops occupied Guma, Gomma, Gēra, and the rich territories of the Gurāgē between the Ḥawāsh and Gibē. At the same time the numerous and mutually antagonistic Lēqa and Wallegga tribes of the south-west were subjected in various expeditions between 1887 and 1894, as well as the Sidāma territories of Hadiya, Kambāta, and Ṭambaro, east of the Gibē. Limmu, the last independent Galla kingdom of the west, fell in 1891 and the little Sidāma kingdom of Janjero (Yamma) in 1894. The same year Menelik himself personally directed a campaign against the Walamo. The heroic kingdom of Kaffa, of which Kennito (Gaki Sherocho) was now king, still survived, but Menelik was able to send a great expedition under Walda Giorgis and subject it in 1897. After this the remaining Sidāma kingdoms east of lakes Margharita and Chamo and the regions of negroid tribes, such as the Gimirra and Maji, in the south-west, were easily occupied. By 1899 the large southern Galla tribe of the Boran had been finally conquered.

Menelik's object was the permanent occupation of the conquered territories. When Galla principalities, such as the Jimma Abba Jifar and Lēqa Lakemti, yielded without resistance, he left them a measure of local autonomy and kept his promises of fair treatment; but when they opposed him his policy was one of ruthless extermination, as many districts which had been amongst the most fertile and flourishing in all Ethiopia bear witness. The population of Kaffa, for instance, is estimated to have been reduced by two-thirds.[1] Those who succeeded in escaping the slaughter were sold into slavery or reduced to the status of

[1] See Bieber, *Kaffa*, i. 168, 353 ff. for a description of the effect of the conquest. A more accessible account will be found in M. Perham, *The Government of Ethiopia*, pp. 318–22.

*gabar.*[1] Military colonies were established in all important centres and each soldier was given a number of *gabar*. Fields went out of cultivation and the forest began to encroach over cultivations and habitations. Christianity was re-established in these regions as the state religion and worship renewed in the churches that had fallen into ruin or been turned into mosques, and many new ones were founded. On the other hand, Islam was recognized in the south-western Muslim kingdoms which, with the exception of Jimma Abba Jifar, were organized as provinces. Muslims were not interfered with in the exercise of their religion, and Islamic courts were recognized as part of the judicial structure. In the case of Jimma, Menelik appears to have promised Abba Jifar that no churches should be built in his kingdom. After Abba Jifar's death, however, with increasing Abyssinian control, it became necessary to provide churches where the growing number of Abyssinian functionaries could worship.

The conquests of Menelik also brought into the empire many of the ʿAfar and Somali tribes of the eastern plains which had been islamized for centuries. When the Egyptians evacuated Harar in 1884–5 one ʿAbd Allāh b. Muḥammad b. ʿAlī ʿAbd ash-Shakūr was set on the throne by the Egyptian pasha and the British consul, but he did not long enjoy it. In 1886 he massacred an Italian expedition and the following year Menelik sent out a punitive expedition which defeated his small force at Challanqo and Rās Makonnen was appointed governor. Harar was the natural strong-point for control of all the neighbouring Galla and Somali tribes. The Arūsi Galla had already been subjugated, but the occupation of Harar brought the Abyssinians for the first time into direct contact with the warlike Somali peoples. Aussa, north of Harar, was invaded and annexed in 1896, and the following year Rās Makonnen began a series of expeditions which annexed the lands of the Somali ʿĪsa, Ogadēn, Merrēhān, and Awlihān, as far as the Jūba and Wēbi Shabeli. The Abyssinians did not find conquest easy in unknown, wooded, and unhealthy country against the fierce and mobile Somalis, and it was not completed until 1900. It was during this time that a Somali *wadād* of the Ḍūlbahanta tribe, called Muḥammad b. ʿAbd Allāh, initiated his *jihād* against the infidel Abyssinians of the north-west and the infidel British from across the sea.

*Lijj Iyāsu's attempt at a Muslim Revolution.* Although Menelik had

[1] The *gabar* system was a form of serfdom which was abolished after the restoration in 1491.

tried to destroy the old feudal system and put the organization of the empire on a new and firm basis, its stability depended upon his personal prestige and, once his firm hand was removed, the whole internal structure with the vast empire he had acquired was in danger of breaking into pieces. He had based his administration upon governors directly responsible to himself with limited personal authority, but no strong bureaucratic organization had been fostered, and the great regional barons were only awaiting the opportunity to regain their power.

Menelik had no direct heir and under the apparent calm of his later years the great feudatories, who were all related in some way to the emperor, were playing for power. One of the most powerful of them was Rās Mikā'ēl, chief of the Warrā-Himāno of the Wallo Galla, whom Menelik had married to his favourite daughter, Shoa-Aregash. Rās Mikā'ēl's ambition was to secure the succession of their son, Lijj Iyāsu. He had the support of the powerful Wallo tribes and aimed at a revival of Muslim-Galla predominance. In addition to his own tribes he gained control of the Yajju and began courting the Muslim tribes in the east who had been incorporated in Menelik's empire. For a time Ras Mikā'ēl's influence was counterbalanced by that of Menelik's first cousin Rās Makonnen of Harar, but that was removed when the latter died in 1906 leaving two sons, Hilma and Tafari, the future Emperor Hāyla Sellassē.

When Menelik became paralysed in 1907 he nominated Lijj Iyāsu (b. 1898) as his successor. This was officially proclaimed in 1909 and Rās Tasamma appointed tutor and regent. On Rās Tasamma's death in 1911 Lijj Iyāsu's father, Mīkā'ēl, became predominant, and the death of Menelik in 1913 gave him effective power. Lijj Iyāsu brought all eastern Abyssinia under his father's control by having him crowned Negus of Wallo and Tigrai in 1914, and the following year Bēgamder and Gojām were placed under his rule.

During the turbulent period just before Menelik's death Lijj Iyāsu had begun the process which was to lead to his open adoption of Islam. When the European war broke out in 1914 these inclinations were encouraged by German and Turkish diplomats. He made the *fuqahā* construct a genealogy deriving his ancestry on his father's side from the Prophet. He made prolonged stays in Harar where he adopted Muslim dress and customs. He put away his Christian wife, Romanē-Warq, and started a *ḥarīm* by marrying the daughters of ʿAfar and Galla chiefs, including a daughter and niece of Abba Jifar of Jimma. He built mosques at Dire Dawa and Jigjiga. In 1916 he officially placed Abyssinia in religious dependence upon Turkey, and sent the Turkish consul-general an Abyssinian flag embroidered with a cresent and the Islamic formula of faith. He sent similar flags to his own Muslim chiefs and promised to lead them to the *jihād*. He entered into negotiations with Muḥammad ibn ʿAbd Allāh, the Mahdī of the Ogadēn, and sent him rifles and ammunition. He then issued a summons to all Somalis, some of whom regarded him as the Mahdī, to follow him in a *jihād* against the Christians, and went to Jigjiga to collect an army.

To the Christians the accession of Lijj Iyāsu meant from the beginning the advent of a new Galla and thinly veiled Muslim dynasty. The Shoans were completely alienated by his policy and the Church, under the inspiration of Abūna Mattēwos, began a powerful agitation against the emperor and his father. When Lijj Iyāsu went to Jigjiga the Shoan chiefs revolted, massed their forces, and marched on Addis Ababa. From the *abūna* they sought a dispensation releasing them from their oath of allegiance to Lijj Iyāsu.[1] The *abūna* excommunicated him. 'Free us from our oath of allegiance, because we will never submit to Islam', the chiefs' message ran, 'we cannot deliver our country to the foreigner through the malice of Lijj Iyāsu, who is leading our kingdom to ruin.' He was deposed by public proclamation on 27 September 1917, and the *abūna* declared Menelik's daughter Zawdītū empress, with Rās Tafari, son of Rās Makonnen, as regent and heir to the throne.

These events took Negus Mīkā'ēl by surprise. He was at Ankober whilst Lijj Iyāsu was in Harar, so he marched on Addis Ababa at the head of his tribe of the Warrā Himāno, but was defeated and captured at the battle of Sagalē near Debra Brehān. Lijj Iyāsu fled to the ʿAfar country and no more was heard of him until 1921 when he reappeared in Tigrai, and was handed over to the Empress by a minor chief called Rās Gugsa Ar'aya.

### (*d*) *European Powers in the Region*

During the nineteenth century the history of the continent of Africa was revolutionized through the penetration of European powers, its secrets were being disclosed by intrepid explorers, and gradually its fortunes were being linked with an alien world. Abyssinia no more than the rest of Africa remained free from the extension of the threads of the web of world life, but its reactions were different. The complicated story of the interference of European powers in Abyssinia is outside the scope of this history, but we are concerned with European

[1] For a translation of the manifesto see *L'Afrique française* (1917), pp. 8–10.

control over the Muslim peoples of Eritrea and the Somalilands, the effects of which will be treated in a later section.[1]

The isolation which Abyssinia had imposed upon herself since the expulsion of the Jesuits was weakened during the period of regional separatism when many of the local kings received envoys from European powers and made separate treaties with them. It was finally broken by the British expedition to Maqdala in 1868. Abyssinia's danger seemed acute because as a result of the opening up of Africa it was once more exposed to foreign conquest, but the complete overthrow of the Egyptian expeditions in 1875 and 1876 by the Emperor John and above all the defeat of the Italians at Dogali by John (1887) and at ʿAdawa by Menelik (1896) preserved its political integrity until the Italian Fascist conquest of 1935–6.

The Muslim tribes of the surrounding lowlands having no cohesion suffered a different fate. Italy acquired the northern region now known as Eritrea, whilst the wide expanse occupied by the Somali tribes was partitioned by treaty between Great Britain, France, Italy, and Ethiopia. The first agreement between the British and Somali goes back to 1827 when a treaty was signed with the chief of the Habr Awal. The Government of India occupied Aden in 1839 and the next year made an agreement with the Sultan of Tajūra to acquire the islands of Musha and Al-Bāb, and another with the Governor of Zailaʿ to acquire the island of Awbad. The island of Perim was occupied in 1858 and Sokotra in 1876. Italy's first possession was Assab which she acquired in 1870. In 1874–5 the Khedive Ismāʿīl obtained from the Sublime Porte permission to extend his rule over the Dankali and Somali coast as far south as Cape Guardafui, but Egyptian rule only lasted ten years and when the Mahdī's revolt broke out in the Sudan her garrisons were withdrawn and Great Britain occupied Zailaʿ, Bulhar, and Berbera. Italy landed a military expedition at Maṣawwaʿ in 1885 and in 1889 signed the Treaty of Ucciali with Menelik which recognized Italian rule over the region north of the Mareb which they named Eritrea, a region they were able to retain even after their disastrous defeat at ʿAdawa. In 1889, by a convention with the Sultan of Obbia, Italy established a protectorate over his dominion. In 1901 a treaty with the Sultan of Mijurten extended the Italian protectorate up to Cape Guardafui and the Gulf of Aden. In 1902 the Sultan of Zanzibar recognized Italian rule over the ports of Banadir. Agreement with Ethiopia in 1908 gave Italy part of the basin of the Jūba, whilst

[1] See below, pp. 275–81.

in 1920 Great Britain ceded her the province of Jubaland with the port of Kisimayu.

During this time Britain had extended her 'protection' over various Somali tribes. At the same time France, which was contesting British expansion from south to north of Africa by a west to east expansion, occupied Obock in 1881 and extended her rule over Tajūra and Jibūti in 1885. The same year at the Conference of Berlin the Great Powers solemnly agreed upon the partition of Africa. In 1888 the British and French held a convention and defined their territories of influence, and England renounced possession of the islands in the Gulf of Tajūra. The confines of the British Protectorate in Somaliland were finally established by agreement with Italy in 1894 and with Ethiopia in 1897. The territory of the Somalis was now wholly partitioned by treaty between Great Britain, France, Italy, and Ethiopia. It was soon after this that the Somali *wadād*, Muḥammad ibn ʿAbd Allāh, began his long crusade against Abyssinian and British imperialism.

*The Mahdī of Somaliland.* The rising of Muḥammad ibn ʿAbd Allāh Ḥasan, called by the British 'the Mad Mullah' though he was neither mad nor a mullah, was an aspect of the anti-Western ferment which was running through African Islam during the last quarter of the nineteenth century, another aspect of which was the revolt of Muḥammad Aḥmad the Mahdī against Turko-Egyptian rule in the Eastern Sudan. Like the Mahdī of the Sudan the Mahdī of Somalia found favourable soil in the fanaticism of the congeries of nomad tribes.

The initiator of this movement, Muḥammad ibn ʿAbd Allāh, was born between 1860 and 1870 in the Ḍūlbahanta country. His father belonged to the Ogadēn Bah Gēri tribe. Muḥammad, like many other Somalis, travelled in his youth on ships in the Red Sea and this brought him into touch with Westernism. He made several pilgrimages to Mecca where he joined the *ṭarīqa* of Muḥammad Ṣāliḥ. On his return in 1895 he settled at Berbera, claiming to have been appointed *khalīfa* of the Ṣāliḥiyya in Somalia, with authority to propagate its doctrine, teach its ritual, and initiate new members. He did not adopt any of the characteristic features of the Mahdī, but began a vigorous propaganda calling the Somalis to a disciplinary religious life more in accordance with the precepts of Islam. His propaganda did not at first have much success amongst townspeople, in competition as it was with long-established *ṭarīqas* like the Qādiriyya whose adherents remained indifferent to his claims, and he soon transferred himself to Kerrit where he founded his first *jamāʿa*. From thence he moved to the Nogal valley amongst his mother's relations where he founded another *jamā'a* at Kob Faradod. His chief difficulty in gathering a following was due to tribal allegiance and inter-tribal feuds, and realizing the necessity of uniting the Somalis with a common aim in order to drive out Westernism he laid stress on the one thing the Somalis had in common, that is Islam, claiming that allegiance to his rule dissolved all tribal allegiances. His movement therefore involved the same kind of revolution in the conception of society as that of the Prophet Muḥammad and the Sudanese Mahdī. He refused to let his followers call themselves by the name of their tribes but adopted the unifying name of *darāwīsh*, with the outward distinction of white turbans. His forces therefore were not organized on a tribal basis and he gave new names to the corps he founded, such as the Ḥajattu 'the Scratchers'. But he was not completely successful in breaking the binding force of kinship, whilst his aims were too limited since they were confined to Somalis. He recruited too largely from the Dārōd, and after the decline of his religious prestige began in 1904, his position degenerated into that of the terrorist leader of a powerful faction of *darāwīsh*.

He ruled his followers with no light hand. D. Jardine writes, 'the Dervishes, collected originally from religious motives, subsequently by a political cry, more often by coercion, but chiefly by the opportunities for enrichment that the movement offered, were ruled by a terrible discipline'.[1] Immediate death was the penalty for the slightest offence or disobedience, whilst he went well beyond the precepts of Islam in his ruthless mutilations. He was extremely bloodthirsty, seizing upon any pretext to murder, on one occasion mutilating and massacring 300 Somali women who could not pray. At the same time he was a great leader and a man of indomitable courage, and it was these qualities and his knowledge of Somali character which enabled him to retain his hold over his followers. He was a master of eloquence and excelled in the art of composing the impromptu poems which so readily inspire and inflame the Somalis.

He came out into open rebellion against the British in 1899, proclaimed himself the Mahdī, and announced the *jihād* against all infidels, in which term he included, besides foreigners, all Somalis who retained their old allegiances and refused to join him. His first raid was significant for he wiped out the Qādiriyya *ṭarīqa*-settlement at Shaikh.[2]

[1] D. Jardine, *The Mad Mullah of Somaliland* (1923), p. 51.

[2] See the 'Lament on the Raids of the Mullah', quoted in J. W. C. Kirk, *A Grammar of the Somali Language* (1905), p. 180.

The British sent four expeditions against him between 1900 and 1904 but, though his forces were continually defeated, the rebellion could not be crushed. The struggle was long and wearisome without possibility of a decisive result against an extremely mobile enemy in a vast and sparsely populated country which could not be occupied. Shaikh Muḥammad Ṣāliḥ, in whose name he was propagating his doctrines, repudiated him, and in 1909 sent him a letter which was circulated throughout Somaliland excommunicating him because he had violated the rules of the Ṣāliḥiyya.[1]

The final expedition against him was in 1920, in which year, whilst still at large, he died of influenza. The effect of his rebellion upon all the northern Somali country had been disastrous and the restoration to normal conditions and resettlement of the Somali tribes in their old territories occupied the British and Italians for many years.

### (*e*) *The Reign of Hāyla Sellassē*

The State of Ethiopia, as we have seen, was formerly a hierarchy which preserved its constituent parts intact. Menelik converted what had been sovereign independent states to the hegemony of one over the rest. It was the work of Hāyla Sellassē to begin the process of consolidation into a unitary empire divided into standardized provinces.

He began with great disadvantages under the dual system of rule with Zawdītū, conservative and traditional, as empress, and himself, progressive and modern, as regent. At first their functions did not clash, for Zawdītū concerned herself primarily with internal affairs and Rās Tafari, as he was then, with external policy. He entirely dissipated the atmosphere of suspicion which had enveloped Ethiopia's external relations as a result of the designs of Lijj Iyāsu, and was able to achieve for his country full international status by gaining its admission into the League of Nations. But he soon turned to internal affairs, for his great aim was to eliminate the deeply rooted causes of disunity and insurrection and establish new standards of government and communal life. In 1926 he obtained the concession of the Wallo region as his fief in addition to that of Harar, he divided the army into autonomous bodies, relegated the old chiefs who were hostile to him and to his innovations to distant provinces, and as a result became arbiter of the great feudatories who had caused such internal instability. Filled with great ambitions for his country's progress he was yet wise enough to proceed cautiously. In 1928 by a *coup d'état* he assumed control and demanded

[1] The letter is translated in D. Jardine, op. cit., pp. 184–5.

and received the title of Negus. The Yajju Galla were discontented with the move and revolted in 1929. This rebellion linked with another of Rās Gugsa Woliē, but was crushed by March 1930. Zawdītū died two days after this revolt and Tafari ascended the throne as king of kings under the throne name of Hāyla Sellassē.

The following year the new Emperor promulgated a constitution for Ethiopia. This confirmed the unitary conception of the State, increased the powers of the emperor, and instituted a Senate and a House of Representatives whose members were nominated by him. This was a move which at the same time greatly increased his power and brought the feudal chiefs under his direct control in Addis Ababa.

With regard to the position of Muslims in Ethiopia religious liberty is freely allowed. After a short period under Emperors Theodore and John, when Islam was proscribed and all Muslims who did not abjure it declared rebels, the decree was abolished and the profession of Islam allowed. However, Muslims, whilst they could develop commercial activities, were excluded from public and magisterial posts and from any part in the political life of the country, and clearly divided from the ruling caste. Their position was that of simple tolerance, but has improved greatly under the present Emperor. It is worthy of note that the constitution promulgated in 1931 gives no hint of an official religion of the State and established equal rights for any native of Ethiopia to civil and military rank (Art. 19). Social prejudice, however, tended to make the position of Muslims under Ethiopian rule inferior to that of the Christians, for nationality and religion are inextricably bound up together. Muslims, however, under the present régime can acquire land in most parts; they hold important positions in all regions where Islam is the predominant religion, and official recognition is given to the important Islamic festivals. Muslim delegates were included in the Ethiopian delegation to the Peace Conference of 1946, and take part in important state functions.

After the First World War the democratic idea was trying to effect, through the League of Nations, the beginnings of a structure for world organization. The shallowness of such hopes was to be demonstrated through events in Abyssinia. In 1935 the Italians broke their pledges given under the Covenant of the League of Nations, the Briand–Kellogg Pact, and the Italo-Abyssinian Treaty of 1928, and waged war upon Ethiopia. The causes of this, the sacrifice of Ethiopia by the Western powers in an attempt to ensure the peace of Europe, and the course of the military operations, are too recent and well known to need retelling here. Addis Ababa was entered on 5 May 1936 and a Fascist empire proclaimed. That empire had a viceroy at its head and was divided into six provinces; Eritrea enlarged to include Tigrai, Amḥara, Shoa, Harar, Galla-Sidāma; and Somalia also enlarged to include the Ogadēn.

The Italian policy towards the Ethiopian Church was dictated by the way in which it was bound up with the Ethiopian nationalist spirit and aimed at weakening and undermining its influence rather than arousing resistance through overt persecution. Such massacres as that of the monks of Debra Libanos were confined to the early period of Fascist rule. This policy involved the active encouragement of Islam of which they constituted themselves protectors in a special sense. Mussolini's speech at Tripoli in 1937 set the tone:

> Fascist Italy intends to guarantee to the Muslim peoples of Libya and Ethiopia peace, justice, prosperity, respect for the laws of the Prophet, and wishes moreover to manifest its sympathy with Islam and the Muslims of the entire world.[1]

Orthodox Islam was given official recognition. The Muslims had formerly possessed no well-built mosques, but the Italians built them wherever there were Muslims, whether in the majority or in a minority. In places like Maṣawwaʿ and other coastal towns which had long been islamized old mosques were restored. In Abyssinia proper they built the great mosque at Addis Ababa and repaired those at Socota, Chelga, Dabarek, Islāmgē, and Dangela. They built others at Lake Ḥayq, Dessyē, Metamma, and Gondar. In the south mosques were built at Harar, Dire Dawa, Jigjiga, Miesso, Asba Littorio, Gobba, and many others in Galla and Sidāma regions. *Qāḍīs* were appointed over various districts to deal with matters coming under the *sharīʿa*. Although the least possible was done for Amharic, Arabic was introduced into all schools set up for Muslims and was also used in official decrees in the Jimma and Harar regions. In Jimma, which was planned as a great Islamic centre, a higher school (*dār al-ʿulūm al-islāmiyya*) was founded for teaching *fiqh* (jurisprudence).

Italy's dominion over Ethiopia was short-lived. She entered the war on 10 June 1940 and by April of the following year its East African phase was over. Italian Somaliland and Eritrea within their former boundaries came under British military occupation, the Tigrean addition being restored to Ethiopia. Hāyla Sellassē was restored to his

[1] A. Bertola, *Il Regime dei Culti nell' Africa Italiana* (Bologna, 1939), p. 162.

country as emperor. As a provisional measure until the end of the war the British forces held 'reserved areas' which were of strategic importance in Ethiopia itself, but the last section, that of Ogadēn inhabited by Somalis, was handed back in October 1948.

The outcome of the Second World War with its aftermath of revolutions and uncertainties has made it clear that basic changes are taking place in the civilization of the world. What place Ethiopia will have in the new Africa cannot be predicted. After the anarchic situation which prevailed in Ethiopia for so many centuries it is impossible for any truly democratic and constitutional government to materialize even in our time; nor could such a government hope to fulfil either the immediate or the deeper spiritual needs of its peoples. The overwhelming need of the country is primarily for social justice, for such constructive material achievement as will not upset social foundations, and for that unity which only an autocratic government could impose upon a land whose every characteristic leads to disunion. So only can habits of confidence in rulers, good-neighbourliness, and lawful behaviour be engendered which, without change from the organic to the organized type of life characteristic of Western society, might in time lead to a new form of political structure.

## 6. CHARACTERISTICS OF ISLAMIC PENETRATION

### (*a*) *The Expansion of Islam in North-East Africa*

Apart from the Meccan refugees of the first *hijra* who made no impression because Islam as a propagating agency was not then formed, the first Muslims who came to the East African coast were merchants, and the trading-stations where they settled as they stretched their trading relations inland became centres for the diffusion of Islam. In these stations they set up Qur'ān schools whose promising pupils were sent for further study to places like the Ḥaramain, Cairo, and Damascus, in each of which their numbers were sufficient to justify special *riwāqs* being set aside for them.[1] It was mainly through these coastal towns that the nomad tribes of the plains were influenced. The Beja tribes, most of whom are outside the area of our survey, were also influenced by the Islamic current coming from Egypt.

Until the great extension of Amḥaric rule under the early Solomonids in the fourteenth century the Christian kingdom was small in extent, and surrounded and interpenetrated by pagan tribes with whom it was continually at war. Islam therefore had full freedom of expansion

[1] See Ibn Baṭūṭa, i. 73; al-Jabarti (Fr. tr., Cairo, 1888), iii. 167.

for many centuries, yet, although it spread through the Sidāma kingdoms and into eastern Shoa, it never claimed the soul of the Sidāma. Some of the nomadic ʿAfar-Saho tribes became nominally Muslim during the fourteenth century, but to this day Islam has not revolutionized their lives. This seems to be chiefly due to the fact that although the Red Sea was so narrow Muslim Arab tribes have never migrated into this region. The process of islamization was not accompanied by a parallel process of arabization as in North Africa and the Eastern Sudan into which whole tribes migrated, chiefly from Egypt. The contrast therefore is remarkable between the Hamitic tribes arabized and islamized in the Sudan and those of this region who remained Hamitic in language and culture. The weakness of Islam in Ethiopia was at a later stage due to the strong cultural cohesion of the Christian State under its king of kings which dominated the plains, but for centuries there was nothing to stop Arab tribes from crossing the straits and spreading over the plains. One cause of their failure to do so was the unattractiveness of the Dankali plains, for, compared to the Sudan, very little of the Ethiopian plains is of a type to attract even nomadic Arab tribes. Also their natural migrational trends took them northwards and so eventually, like the Banī Hilāl, through Egypt to North Africa and the Sudan.

Arab traders, artisans, and adventurers were the chief medium of Islamic expansion; and coming as they did as individuals and not as tribes they naturally lived in close touch with the natives, adopted their language instead of imposing Arabic, and intermarried with them. Zailaʿ especially became a diffusion centre and trading relations were established with the highly developed Sidāma kingdoms of the vast and fertile regions of southern Ethiopia and resulted in a superficial islamizing of the ruling classes of the kingdoms as far west as Hadya around the River Gibē and northwards well into Shoa and along the eastern edge of the plateau. Farther south Maqdishū, Merca, and Brava became diffusion centres amongst the nomadic Somali.

During all this time Islamic penetration remained peaceful until the rise of the Abyssinian Muslim kingdom of Ifāt, whose desire for expansion was not fundamentally religious. It is true that Islam was used as a rallying cry, but there was no genuine fanatical religious fervour until the rise of the *amīrs* in the Zailaʿ region at the beginning of the sixteenth century, when it was adopted as the battle-cry of nomadic ʿAfar and Somali tribes seeking to burst out of their arid plains.

The wars of these Muslim Sidāma kingdoms with the Abyssinians, which lasted from the fourteenth century until the second half of the sixteenth century, prevented the founding of stable cities in the interior which could become cells of propaganda. Apart from coastal towns like Zailaʿ, Harar was the only inland city able to maintain itself as a Muslim centre and develop the Islamic arts and commerce. During this period it was the increasing political predominance of the Christian kingdom which prevented the spread of Islam. So superficial was the Islam of the Sidāma kingdoms that after the Galla invasion, which resulted in the absorption of many Sidāma into Galla tribes and the pushing back of others who fiercely defended their independence, scarcely a trace of the religion was left amongst them.

The conquest of the Imām Aḥmad Grāñ seems to have had little permanent effect upon the religious complexion of the highlands. Some colonies of Muslims were left behind and a few converted groups remained permanently islamized, but even before the conquest many groups of Abyssinian Muslims were inserted among the Christian Amḥara, especially in eastern Shoa. When Galla tribes flowed up into the highlands they were gradually influenced by these Abyssinian Muslims and joined Islam. These Muslims of the highlands, together with Wallo, Yajju, and Rāya Galla, were persecuted by the emperors Theodore and John as part of their policy for the unification of Abyssinia and were converted to a normal Christianity.[1]

Harar, however, continued as an independent city-state and a centre of commerce and of Islamic learning. Through its traders and propagandists Islam was spread amongst the surrounding Galla tribes. It also influenced more distant Galla, especially those who conquered Sidāma kingdoms in the Gibē region; Gomma being the first to be converted early in the nineteenth century. The fact that all these states followed the Shāfiʿite *madhhab* shows that they were influenced through Ethiopian Islam and not that of the Sudan which is Mālikite. Since Islam was introduced by merchants throughout southern Ethiopia the word *naggādi* 'merchant' is the universal term for 'Muslim'; for instance, the league of the 'Four Muslim' states of the south-west in

[1] The conversion of Muslims to Abyssinian Christianity was mainly by force during the reigns of Theodore and John, but there have been many peaceful conversions. The town of Tedrer (Saganiti district of Eritrea), which has a population of about 3,000, traces its descent to the *nā'ib* of the Balaw. They were formerly Muslim but were converted to Christianity by the founder of the monastery of Enda Johannes in this district. The people of Bait Meka (district of Takkale Agaba) were also Balaw who, as a result of mixing with immigrants from the Tigrai, became Christians. Again, the people of Dekki Aites in the Serāi were once Muslim pastoralists who arrived in this region ten generations ago, settled down as agriculturalists, and were converted to Christianity.

1882 was called *arfa naggādota*. The connexion of Harar with western Ethiopia is shown by the influence of the Qādiriyya *ṭarīqa* and by the veneration given to Shaikh Abādir of Harar by the Limmu Enārya. These western regions were also influenced from the Sudan during the Turko-Egyptian régime, especially through emissaries of the Tijāniyya and, to a lesser extent, the Sammāniyya *ṭarīqas*.

The gains of Islam were chiefly from paganism, except in Eritrea where a number of Christian tribes were islamized during the nineteenth century. Naturally, Islam first claimed the pagan nomadic tribes. The Bait Māla (Maʿāla), in northern Eritrea south of Sawākin, were converted by the middle of the fifteenth century, the Banī ʿĀmir, with other Beja, accepted a kind of nominal Islam when the Funj kingdom of the Blue Nile exacted a recognition of her suzerainty from them, whilst the Saho and ʿAfar tribes were influenced still earlier. The Egyptian domination of Eritrea in the nineteenth century, short though it was, exerted a powerful influence both from Kasala in the west and Maṣawwaʿ in the east; but far more important was the growth of 'holy' families like those of the Ād Shaikh and the Mirghanī. The founder of the former, Shaikh al-Amīn ibn Ḥamad who claimed a Quraishite origin, gained great influence through his alleged miracles and grouped around himself lone Muslims and Tigrē vassals fleeing from their masters. In this way a new and 'holy' tribe was formed which, growing rich and powerful, became an influential diffusion centre. Its influence spread through the Sāḥil and the valley of the ʿAnseba until it met the other Islamic current ascending the valley of the Baraka from Sawākin.

An important element in the spread of Islam in Africa has been Arab pride of race. The islamization of tribes throughout the whole region is linked up with legends of saints coming from Arabia who gave the leading families an aristocracy of Arab blood and thus exposed the whole tribe to the appeal of Islam; one individual in fact was sufficient to transform a Hamitic pagan tribe into a new Islamic community. This is shown in this region as elsewhere by the fact that the tribes of the coastal plains in their traditions make the beginning of their tribal history and their islamization coincident with the arrival of an Arab ancestor and tribal eponym. In most cases the authenticity of these genealogies is extremely dubious and none of these tribes have any conscious sense of Arab kinship like that felt by some of the nomad tribes of the Eastern Sudan, nor was Arabic superimposed on the former language. Undoubtedly Arabs were always coming over, especially from Yaman, but they were absorbed into the tribes. The Yamanite trading elements which spread about the country during the nineteenth century, on the other hand, have tended to keep themselves distinct from the people amongst whom they settled. In Jimma, for instance, although they married with Galla women, their progeny form a distinct element of the population. All the same these Yamanites have done effective work in spreading Islam in Galla regions. Another decisive factor in the social, economic, and religious diffusion of Islam in East Africa has been the slave-trade.[1] The Hamite turns Muslim with little dislocation to his own soul, whilst Islam and the acquired fiction of an Arab ancestry, give a cohesion to life and allow his raiding instincts full scope. The Hamite even more than the Arab has been the instrument of the slave-trade in Africa.

Another factor, about which we shall have more to say later, has been the way Islam has adapted itself to African mentality. As Cecchi, writing about the little Islamic kingdoms beyond the Gibē, observed, 'Islam for these peoples . . . is a religion which better than Christianity has adapted itself to their way of life'.[2]

Since the totalitarian conception of Islam has caused education to be essentially religious, Muslims, wherever their religion has spread, have always concentrated on education. Although teaching may be confined to little more than the recital of passages of the Qur'ān and the prayer formulae, this system of educational concentration upon religion is one of the factors which helped Islam so much to dominate the life of the peoples it has converted. But in this region, although so close to Arabia, Islam has been unusually weak in spreading its system of education. Al-ʿUmarī remarks that no schools existed in the Muslim Sidāma kingdoms, and we have noticed how completely their Islam was erased after the Abyssinian conquest. For long the Islamic educational system was confined to the coastal towns and Harar city, but during the nineteenth century north-east Africa was affected by the reactionary revival

[1] The history of slavery in the Empire of Ethiopia is such an unfortunate one that the writer has been careful to avoid overstressing the part played in it by the Muslims, who were its chief agents. Whilst the Church countenanced the institution of slavery, it should be pointed out that men were not wanting even in this barbaric Christian State who condemned slavery as contrary to the spirit of Christ's teaching by pointing out that 'in Christ is neither slave nor free'. The philosopher Zar'a Yāʿqob (*c.* A.D. 1600) reproaches Islam for destroying the equality and brotherhood of man by sanctioning the slave-trade since all mankind address God as 'Father' (*Philosophi abessini*, *C.S.C.O.*, *Scr. Aeth.*, ser. i, vol. xxxi, p. 11). Abyssinian Christianity therefore had the seeds of reform within it, whereas the tragedy of Islam is that, although the evils of the trade and the lot of slaves may be mitigated, the practice of slavery itself cannot be condemned because it is sanctioned by the Qur'ān, the very word of God.

[2] Cecchi, *Da Zaila alle frontiere del Caffa* (1886), ii. 342–3.

then taking place in Islam and Qur'ānic education spread widely. Teaching shaikhs of all kinds started schools in Muslim centres, especially in the kingdoms around the Gibē, in the Harar region, throughout Eritrea and Somalia, and in the Jabarti and Yamanite colonies. This side of Islamic culture has received a notable stimulus in those regions which have come under European rule.

### (*b*) *Abyssinian History and the Challenge of Islam*

Our study of the history of Islam in Ethiopia has been dominated throughout by the history of Christian Abyssinia. Nowhere has there been any escape from it. In fact, Islam in the region would have no history without Abyssinia. Now that we have approached the end of our historical study we may consider how it came about that this Monophysite Christian fortress was able to survive to become, as Professor A. J. Toynbee has put it, 'one of the social curiosities of a latter-day Great Society'. He instances as peculiarities of modern Abyssinia: 'the survival of her political independence in the midst of an Africa under European dominion; the survival of her Monophysite Christianity in the borderland between Islam and paganism; the survival of her Semitic language between the Hamitic and Nilotic language areas; and the stagnation of her culture at a level which is really not much higher than the level of the adjacent Tropical African Barbarism.'[1]

Some subtle factor in the consciousness of the people seems to determine the essence of what we call a national consciousness. Neither common blood, common culture, religion, language, nor political organization can in themselves make a nation. The Greeks, for instance, had a complicated ancestry, spoke different dialects, and clung to the autonomy of separate city-states, yet behind all these factors making for separatism they felt a sense of oneness against the rest of the world. So it has been with Abyssinia. The physical configuration of the country, two main languages—Amharic and Tigriña—the separate autonomy of regional rulers, all made for regional separatism, and yet the Abyssinians—Tigreans, Amḥara, Gojāmites, and Shoans—are a nation, as is shown by the national resistance evoked by any external threat from Muslims, Egyptians, and Western powers to their independence.

The controlling factor in her recognition of herself as a nation was Semitic blood and Semitic-Christian tradition. As far as physical

[1] A. J. Toynbee, *A Study of History*, ii. 365.

ancestry was concerned the Semitic factor was negligible. The Semitic invaders of northern Abyssinia were not numerous, they came as colonizers and settlers, and a process of assimilation with the Hamites took place. The victory of the Semite was not wholly won by force; it was the imposition of a new Semitic sentiment of unity of life upon an alien people. The controlling factor therefore in Abyssinian historical tradition is the Semitic tradition which includes, besides the linguistic and cultural element, the fictional tradition of Semitic blood. To the earlier Semite tradition was added subsequently the influence of Monophysite Christianity which became a state affair, the binding force of a very precarious political system.

In the highlands many forces helped the resistance against Islam. The Agao had been made essentially one people sustained by pride of race and an indigenized Christianity, which, as we have seen, is the method that Islam uses. On becoming Christians the Agao carried over into Christianity the same vigour by which they had defended their ancient pagan heritage, and at the same time they moulded the alien faith to suit that heritage, with the result that Islam when it presented itself was without the usual appeal that it has for Africans.[1] The Abyssinians had already acquired a super-tribal consciousness, an anti-foreign sentiment which made Islam appear inimical and dangerous to their own tradition and culture. The persecution of those whose faith differed from that of the ruler consolidated the community feeling, a common enemy being the only means of uniting the Abyssinians. In the conflict of Islam and Christianity it was less a matter of faith against faith than of one racial and cultural tradition against another. A most important factor in the maintenance of this racial tradition was the Solomonid legends and traditions, which gave a common foundation, not only consolidating the monarchy but giving a sense of racial superiority. The former institution of the matriarchate together with the cult of the Virgin Mother, reflecting as it did an Agao cult of a pagan goddess, gave the Abyssinians an attitude to women utterly opposed to that of Islam.

At the same time the Ethiopian pride of race was, after the Muslim conquest of the sixteenth century, to hinder the effective propagation of Christianity, until, with the formation of the great empire of

[1] Islam's conversion of pagan tribes into nations has been one of the most significant features of its conversion of Africans. C. K. Meek writes: 'It is largely due to Islam that numbers of tribes are now, before our eyes, forming themselves into nations' (*The Northern Tribes of Nigeria*, 1925, ii. 4, 10).

Menelik, we find the army once more imposing the religion of the dominant race upon conquered pagan populations.

Another important factor was the physical environment. As Professor Toynbee remarks, all the peculiarities of modern Abyssinia 'derive from the same cause: that is, from the virtual impregnability of the highland-fastness in which this Monophysite fossil is ensconced'.[1] It was this impregnability of the highlands which enabled Abyssinian Christianity to survive the successive dangers of an Islamic domination by nomadic tribes, the outpost tentacles of the Ottoman military power, the locust-like invasion of the Galla, the designs of the emergent totalitarian state of Egypt under Muḥammad ʿAlī and his successors for the unification of the Nile valley, the threat of the Baqqāra Arabs under Mahdism, and, finally, the menace of Western imperialism which was imposing itself over the whole of Africa.

The survival of Abyssinia was due to these two factors, the first of them the national spirit based upon the legendary foundation and the common faith, and the second physical impregnability. An external threat to Abyssinian independence has always been effective in evoking some form of national resistance which was able to make use of interior lines and the physical configuration of the country. The Islamic threat has been less serious than that of the Galla hordes and Western imperialism. Islam has gained little through actual conquest and in its peaceful penetration in the region its gains have been chiefly from paganism. The Galla invasion was so serious because many tribes settled in highland regions into which they had penetrated, but they ceased to be a real menace when they, too, succumbed to regional separatism and turned their hands against all men including their own brother Gallas. Their acceptance of Islam was a measure to enable them to retain their own identity, but most of those in the highlands have succumbed to the dominant Semitic language of the plateau[2] and in time will be absorbed into the Monophysite fold.

In our age the rise of Fascism in Italy led for a time to the domination of Abyssinia by a Western power in 1935–6, when the Italians waged war on the poorly armed Abyssinians with all the deadly weapons of the Machine Age. The Italians found in Ethiopia two opposing cultures:

[1] A. J. Toynbee, op. cit. ii. 365.

[2] It is because Amharic is a literary language that it must eventually dominate the empire. Hence the government's refusal to allow any other language than Geʿez and Amharic to be printed in the Ethiopic script. The Bible Society's version of the Scriptures in Galla in this script is proscribed. The schools of the missionary societies must teach Amharic primarily though they may use the vernacular in the early stages.

that of Abyssinian Christianity and that of Islam. By their recognition of Islam they hoped to secure the alliance of the Muslims against the resistance of the Amḥara. But the Italians could not complete the systematic 'pacification' of regional resistance because they entered into the imperialistic sphere in an age when other imperial nations, like the British, were evolving their policy from trusteeship, through partnership, to the eventual freedom of African peoples. Thus even in the modern world this 'social curiosity' still survives.

# 3

# Tribal Distribution of Islam

## I. INTRODUCTION

SINCE this is not a treatise on anthropology we shall only give a very general sketch of the mode of life and social structure of the Muslim tribes, together with an account of what is known of their conversion to Islam.

One of the dominant impressions which arises out of a study of the communities of the region is a realization of the profound power of culture—of the outlook on life—over the less profound influence of kinship and even environment. In physical type many of these peoples vary very little, yet one can easily distinguish between, for example, the Ethiopian Muslims (Jabarti) and the Ethiopian Christians of the great plateaux, although both are of the same physical type, speak the same language, and live in the same environment, by such things as their manners, facial gestures and expressions, by their very bearing and manner of speech. These differences are not derived from physical factors but are ways in which their different outlook on life expresses itself and constitute a distinct cleavage between people whose racial make-up, language, and environment may be the same. The depth of such cleavage varies. It is naturally not so definite between the Jabarti and their Christian neighbours as it is between tribes which in addition to religious culture also differ in their idea of kinship, social institutions, language, and environment. Again, it is less distinct amongst those tribes of Eritrea which were converted only during the last century from Christianity to Islam. The members of these tribes show no fanatical bias against transition from one religious system to another; whilst one will find Christians and Muslims within the same tribes, using the same social rites, and wearing both Islamic and Christian amulets.

The unity which many of the tribes of Ethiopia possess is not an underlying material unity of race or kinship. The general feeling of unity based upon the common factors of language, religion, and political organization is far more powerful than kinship, though normally some fiction of kinship is asserted; thus the 'tribal' group loses real consciousness of its diverse origins, though family tradition retains it in various forms. The traditional political system of the Kushites is based on the kinship group and not on the tribe,[1] consequently any larger organization than the kinship group is very unstable and this instability may lead to fresh organization. Members of larger groups also may be both within the group and outside it; for instance, although the Ād Shaikh sections of the Bani ʿĀmir belong politically to that federation, their deeper loyalty is to the Ād Shaikh of the Sāḥil with whom they have no political relationship. The cultural map of the peoples of north-east Africa has never been static and is in fact being redrawn all the time. The migrations of the Somali and Galla in particular have led to far-reaching social readjustments amongst the sedentary groups upon whom they overflowed and in their relationships to each other. Everywhere cultural boundaries overlap. Thus we have mixed Galla and Somali (e.g. Gerri, Nolē, &c.) associated in one tribe, still speaking their own languages so that it is not certain which language will triumph. Again, many Galla in the highlands associated with Amḥara have become, or are becoming, Amharic-speaking. The Galla of Soddo, through bordering on the Aymallel, no longer speak a pure Galla but a mixture of Galla and Gurāgē, their Christianization has brought in new elements, but their customs and mode of life are still Galla.

The cause of the great changes that have taken place in the constitution and organization of these peoples has more usually resulted from the impact of one society upon another. Such impact has three possible outcomes: it leads either to extermination, or assimilation, or to some form of the caste system. Examples of all three will be found in the history of the societies of this region. Complete extermination is virtually impossible, but a people may be so broken up and scattered or forced into slavery as to disappear completely as a distinct group. The Dobʿa is an example of a tribe that has completely disappeared.[2] Assimilation is the commonest. The Galla who occupied the Gibē region did not displace the former Sidāma population but absorbed them. At the same time the Galla themselves were not unaffected for they adopted many of the beliefs and institutions of the Sidāma whom they

[1] Brigadier Longrigg writes of Eritrean tribes: 'the use of the word "tribe" for these communities is more convenient than proper. If the tribes of the Arab world are taken as the norm, with their peculiar patriarchy among equals and singleness of loyalty based on tradition and the needs of life, then the "tribes" of Keren and the Sahil have no claim to the term. Their economics are tribeless, their traditions essentially those of the family and *enda*, their claimed origins geographical and diverse; and the serf-master relationship is farther still from the essential democracy of the Arab' (S. H. Longrigg, *A Short History of Eritrea*, 1945, p. 66).

[2] See above p. 81 n. 2.

assimilated. The same thing happened with the Somali migration into Bantu country in southern Somalia. Again, the indigenous population may be conquered by invaders who neither exterminate it nor coalesce with it, but retain it as a subject or depressed caste. Such are the primitive castes of hunters scattered about the region or the smith-caste of Tomāl amongst the Somali and Tumtu amongst the Galla, retained because the conquerors are afraid to learn the art and therefore despise it. The classes among the Tigrē-speaking tribes are another kind of discrimination; it is no rigid caste system, for with the passage of centuries the distinction between the classes weakened into the status of noble and plebian, and will eventually disappear. On the other hand, an indigenous people may admit whole tribal sections of peaceful immigrants seeking protection to live with them on sufferance as allied strangers, clients, or serfs. The dominant group reserves rank, position, and certain vocations, such as the bearing of arms, political authority, and ownership of land, as its exclusive preserve. In time this distinction too may weaken, as between the Asa Māra and ʿAdo Māra of the ʿAfar, and eventually, when all acquire the fiction of a blood-tie, will disappear altogether.

A study of the history of the conversion of pagan societies to Islam shows that they all follow the same prescribed pattern. We have as a rule only native traditions and they relate how a Muslim saint of noble Arab ancestry settles among a pagan tribe and is told by the Prophet in a dream that he is the chosen instrument of its conversion. Inspired by this vision he proves the power of his God through the miracles he performs and gains the recognition of chief and people. He marries the daughter of the chief and his son succeeds to the chieftainship of the tribe; thus by peaceful means or the *jihād* the whole tribe goes over to Islam.

These accounts are extremely untrustworthy and yet as an indication of the mode of conversion they are true. Apart from the chronology and the nobility of the exile this has always been the mode of conversion in Africa and continues to this day. Muslim pedlars or adventurers of diverse origins settle amongst a pagan tribe, marry into it and rear families, and quite naturally, whether pious Muslims or not, through confidence in their religious superiority, united with their ability to assimilate themselves into tribal life, first win over the chiefs and through them their subjects. The ease with which Islam, with its simple formulae, apparent lack of disruption of tribal life, and pagan sentiment, together with the acquisition of new power by the convert, can be accepted, make the change not so formidable and revolutionary a step as it might seem.

The reasons which caused the Christian tribes of Eritrea to join Islam were much more diverse and complex and almost all the following factors entered in. In the first place there is a general tendency for nomad tribes to accept Islam once it is presented to them because of the territorial freedom of its worship not tied to a fixed church building and priesthood, and because it makes so few demands for change in their habits and mode of life. Further, conditions in northern Abyssinia were extremely unsettled during the last two centuries. Christian tribes were cut off from their own main Christian tradition and neglected by their priesthood. Many also absorbed Muslim vassals into their social structure who soon came to outnumber the Christian master-class. But above all they were influenced by Muslim trading relations, by 'holy' families like the Ād Shaikh and Mirghanī, and later by Egyptian political influence. These tribes are especially interesting because, having been converted to Islam but recently, Islamic elements have been superimposed upon their former Christian system, whilst in their social life and superstitious background they retain elements which belong to their former pagan way of life and thought.

## 2. ABYSSINIAN MUSLIMS (JABARTI)

Other than the Muslim tribes, described in the sections which follow, there are families and villages of Muslims who live on the Abyssinian plateau and speak Amharic, Agao, or Tigriña as their native tongue. It is as a convenient term for these groups that the word Jabarti is used in this book. This, however, is neither the historical nor the modern usage of the word. It was first used as the name of a region for, as we have seen, the Muslim historians spoke of the territory of Zailaʿ as the land of Jabarta;[1] then the term was extended to all the Muslim kingdoms of southern Ethiopia, and, finally, to all Ethiopian Muslims.[2]

[1] See above p. 59. This is confirmed by Ibn Taghribird īwho, in giving the genealogy of Badlāy, one of the Adalite rulers, derives him from ʿUmar ibn Walasmaʿ al-Jabarti (*Nujūm*, ed. Popper, vii. 4). The Abyssinians derive the term from *gabr* (plur. *agbert*), 'servant (of God)'. On the meaning of the word see E. Cerulli, *O.M.* v (1925), 614 ff.

[2] When we read that there is a *riwāq* (loggia or portico) for the Jabarti at the Azhar in Cairo (*Khiṭaṭ Jadīda*, vi. 23; Al-Jabarti, iii. 167) the word is used for Ethiopian Muslim in general and it is so used in this broad sense in Abyssinia today, but they do sometimes use it in the narrow sense adopted in this book. *Eslām* (*eslāmāy*) (plur. *eslāmoč*) and *naggādē* are also used by Abyssinians as general terms for Muslims. The popular nickname is 'back-rinsers' (Amh. *qiṭ tāṭ ṭābi*, Galla *Islām huddu ḍiqattu*). The Ethiopian Chronicle uses the term *malasāy* (cf. Basset, *Études*, pp. 14, 15, 106), whilst the general Geʿez word was *tanbalāt*, *taneballa*, lit., 'to cry *nabīyu' llāh*', 'to pray', 'to preach', &c. (see Dillman, *Lexikon*, col. 562).

It must be clearly understood that in no sense is it the ethnic name of a people.

The Jabarti, in the sense of an Islamic *diaspora* to which we are restricting the term, consist of families or groups scattered amongst or mixed up with the Christian population of the highlands, from whom from the ethnical point of view they cannot be distinguished, although the cultural cleavage causes a distinct difference. They are Ethiopian Muslims who speak the language and preserve the general customs of the region in which they live, observing the *sharīʿa* only in matters connected with the religious cult, personal status, and family law.[1]

Such Muslim villages are scattered all over the highlands. They are strong in the northern territories of Ḥamasēn (5,900), Akelē-Guzāi (3,800), and the Serāi (9,200). The chief family of these Jabarti claim descent from ʿUthmān ibn ʿAffān, the third Khalīfa, and his wife Ruqayya, daughter of the Prophet, who were amongst the refugees to Abyssinia of the first *hijra*. They had a son who remained with his mother in Abyssinia. What seems to be genuine is the emigration from the Maghrib of a certain Shaikh Ādam al-Kinānī who propagated Islam and whose tomb at ʿAbī ʿAddī in the Tigrai is a Jabarti shrine. Naturally, with such claims to noble descent, his descendants, who live at ʿAdī Itāi in the Serāi, are held in great honour by the rest of the Jabarti.

Other Muslim villages are at ʿAdī Tegemes in Tigrai; Awasa in Semēn (Berok Waha group) near ʿAdī Arkai, many of whose people are traders whilst others engage in agriculture and cattle breeding; Darita in Bēgamder; many villages around Lake Ashangi; Ebbenat in the basin of the Reb near Dabra Tabor; the Ido district south of Dabra Tabor; Marawa near Aammista, and families in the Muggia (Agao) region. In Shoa the district of Ṭoṭosē just south of Dabra Berhān, whose inhabitants are Amharic-speaking, is Muslim; whilst farther to the south-east, on the borders of Gembi-bēt, groups of Muslims are numerous. Then there are groups in the chief towns such as Asmara and all other towns in Eritrea; Debarek, Dara, Islāmgē, Dangela, Dessyē, Addis Alem the Muslim suburb of Gondar, at Sokota, once the seat of the ruler of Lāsta, and at Addis Ababa, where

[1] In many such matters the Jabarti of Eritrea follow the customs of the Christians. 'Il diritto religioso così ammesso in Eritrea è diverso a seconda che si riferisca alle popolazioni cristiano-copte (abitanti l'altipiano abissino) o alle popolazioni musulmane del resto della colonia (*ad eccezione dei musulmani della zona abissina della colonia, detti giaberti e il cui statuto personale segue il costume e le norme dei copti*)' (A. Bertola, *Il regime dei culti nell' Africa Italiana*, 1939, p. 73).

out of a total native population of 86,468 in 1938, 5,324 were Muslims.[1] The strength of Islam in these towns is shown by the fact that the Italians built mosques in them all.

The conversion of some of these groups may well go back to an early period of Muslim propaganda when the sultanate of Shoa was flourishing. Some Jabarti derive their conversion from Aḥmad an-Najāsh, an Abyssinian disciple of the Prophet of the time of the first *hijra*, whose tomb in the Tigrai is still an important place of pilgrimage.[2] The presence of other groups, especially villages of agriculturalists, certainly goes back to the invasion of the Imām Aḥmad which left many Amḥara, Agao, and Tigreans permanently islamized. Others derive from families of Muslim traders who have settled in market centres and become abyssinized in language and customs, but not in religion. Some of those in the north (Ḥamasēn, Akelē-Guzāi, and Serāi) who all speak Tigriña, were founded by families of the Balaw.

In general, the Jabarti live on friendly terms with the Christian population who surround them, for they speak the same language and bonds of mutual interest link them together. Many of the chief families consequently have allied themselves by marriage and the wife has usually adopted the religion of her husband. On the other hand, they have sometimes come into conflict with the central government or local rulers, and, as a result of an outburst of anti-Muslim feeling caused by reaction against highland Galla or in consequence of an external threat from the Egyptians who were helped by the northern Jabarti, they have sometimes been persecuted and subjected to humiliating laws. Imperial decrees have deprived them of *resti*, which is the hereditary absolute land-right of an individual family within the *enda*. *Resti*-owners are known as *restenyatat* and form a kind of landed aristocracy: the Muslims could hold land only as tenants (*sedbi* in Akelē Guzāi)[3] or by right of purchase (*worki*). They have until

[1] *B.S.G.I.*, ser. vii, vol. v (1940), p. 170.

[2] The tomb of Aḥmad an-Najāsh is situated some 38 miles south of Adigrat. We know that it existed in the sixteenth century because it was visited by the Imām Aḥmad (*Futūḥ*, p. 317).

[3] The *sedbi* pacts are concluded for indefinite periods and are difficult to terminate. Dr. S. F. Nadel writes: 'The *sedbi* is said to have originated in the pacts which the Muhammadan immigrants on the plateau concluded with the land-owning Coptic groups. . . . One of the most dangerous features of the *sedbi* disputes is the religious antagonism which they may easily evoke. The Christian landowners, in demanding the termination of *sedbi*, are trying to oust the alien Muhammadans from the Christian-owned land. The Christians frankly admit their fear that this interminable lease might obscure the "sacred" rights and privileges of *resti*—rights and privileges from which all aliens must remain excluded. The Muhammadans, in turn, accuse the Christians of wishing to deprive them of the ancient rights acquired by their forefathers. Claims and counterclaims are both justified, and the disputes over land threaten

recently been excluded from positions of authority and rank, and for a short time, under the Emperor John IV, were not allowed to witness in court, as though they were slaves. But in general, although they were regarded as inferior in status, they were not badly treated and the land laws did not weigh on them much more heavily than they did upon many of their Christian neighbours.

The Jabarti are on a much higher level than most Muslims of north-east Africa. They are mainly artisans and merchants, for the Abyssinians, with their pride of birth and contempt of labour, left such occupations to them, but there are also a great many groups of cultivators. The Jabarti do not display the fanatical zeal often shown by nomads, because their prosperity is dependent upon stable rule and peaceful conditions. They are not very rigid in prayers and fasting and few, if any, go on pilgrimage. The headman of the village is called the shaikh and arbitrates on religious law, but many villages have someone they call the *qāḍī* who is usually the teacher at the Qur'ān school and *imām* of the mosque (*masjid*) which is a simple hut like their houses but kept in somewhat better repair. The *qāḍī* is maintained by gifts in money or more generally in kind given at the chief festivals or when a child reaches certain stages in the memorization of the Qur'ān. In *madhhab* they are divided between the Mālikiyya, Ḥanafiyya, and Shāfiʿiyya. The attitude of the Jabarti to women has been influenced by their environment. They generally have only one wife, their women are unveiled, held in great honour, and enjoy considerable liberty.

## 3. ĀD SHAIKH

The history of the formation and growth of the Ād Shaikh is recent enough to be known and, although not a large tribe, merits a special notice because it shows the way Islam can spread through the influence of a holy family and how it favours the growth of new political groupings under the cloak of religion. The tribe traces its descent from a Sharīf Ḥusain who emigrated from Arabia some sixteen generations ago. However this may be, and they do not claim to be *shurafā*, their history begins with the arrival in the Sāḥil of Shaikh al-Amīn (generally corrupted to Lamīn) ibn Ḥamad at the beginning of the nineteenth century. He gained a great reputation through his alleged miracles amongst the Muslim Tigrē-vassals of the Christian Bait Asgadē who came to seek his *baraka*. The Kantēbāi of the Bait Asgadē gave his

to turn into religious and racial feuds' ('Land Tenure on the Eritrean Plateau', *Africa*, xvi, 1946, 15–17).

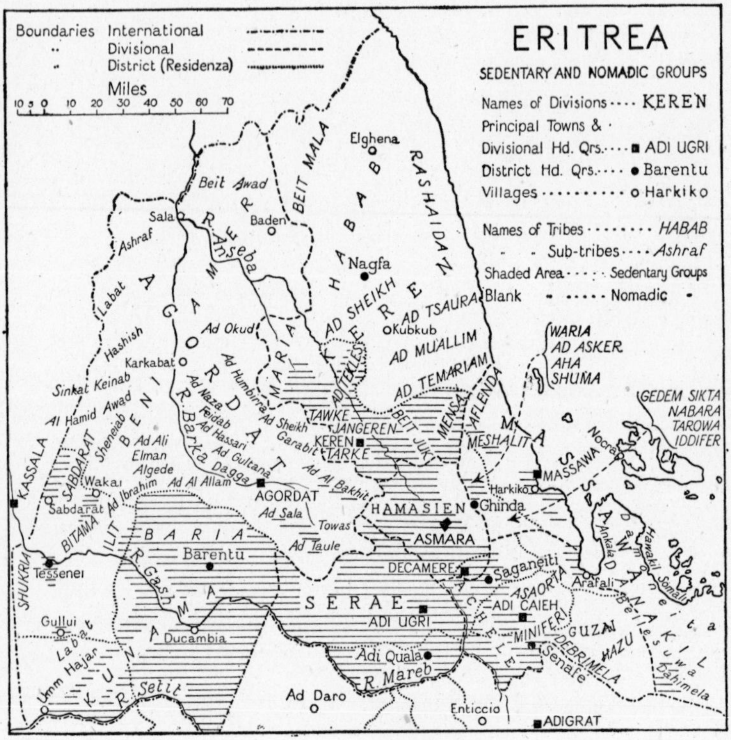


THE TRIBES OF ERITREA

from *A Short History of Eritrea* by S. H. Longrigg (Oxford, 1945)

daughter in marriage to Shaikh al-Amīn in order to secure his goodwill, and this process of obtaining wives from that tribe was continued by the Shaikh's very numerous family. They, on the contrary, never gave their daughters outside their own family on the ground that the Bait Asgadē were Christians, and when the Bait Asgadē eventually became Muslims through the influence of the Ād Shaikh the custom was still kept up. Thus, since they could have four wives and an unlimited number of concubines, the family increased very rapidly. In addition to this method of increase, the reputation that they gained as a 'holy' family drew within it whole families of Tigrē vassals and escaped slaves; consequently they adopted the same aristocratic system of masters and serfs as the other Sāḥil tribes from whom, whatever their origin may have been, they are now indistinguishable. Further, their animal wealth also grew rapidly through the gifts brought by people from all over the region to secure their intercession with God and man, whilst the Egyptians, during their rule, did not require them to pay tribute.[1] The family exploited its holy character by the usual means and they were accustomed to perform the *dhikr* of the Qādiriyya *ṭarīqa*. Shaikh al-Amīn became the centre of a special cult and the Sāḥil tribes invoke his name in the same way as the Mirghaniyya do that of Sayyid al-Ḥasan at all crises in life.

In time, as the tribe grew, sections split off from the main body in the Sāḥil and moved to Embēremi in the Samhar,[2] the ʿAnseba, and the Baraka where the Garabit (1,200) and the Faidāb (3,700) are now sections of the Banī ʿĀmir. In 1931 the main tribe in the Sāḥil numbered 7,115 amongst whom, of course, the true Ād Shaikh are in the minority. They are all pastoral herdsmen and have two permanent summer camps in the Sāḥil to which they return after following the winter pastures. Few of the family, except for those in Embēremi, now exploit their *baraka* and consequently the tribe has been displaced from its former pre-eminence in Eritrean Islam by the Mirghaniyya family.

## 4. BANĪ ʿĀMIR

The Beja are one of the great ethnic factors of the northern part of our region between the Nile and the Red Sea. During the first centuries of our era a powerful movement of expansion carried them west-

[1] W. Münzinger, *Ostafrikanische Studien* (1864), pp. 315–16.

[2] On the foundation of Embēremi by Shaikh Muḥammad b. ʿAlī b. al-Amīn who died in 1877, see G. Lejean, *Voyage aux deux Nils* (1865), p. 142.

wards into the kingdom of Meroë, northwards over the Egyptian frontier and southwards into the kingdom of Axum. With the decline of the kingdom of Axum they overran large tracts of its former territory, so that today many Abyssinian peoples speaking Tigriña claim a Beja origin (e.g. Tedrer in the Akelē-Guzāi and Dekk Itaïs in the Serāi).

The main body of the Beja who remained in their old territory between the Nile and the Red Sea came under Islamic influence through the infiltration of Arab traders and adventurers from the Rabīʿa and Juhaina who took Beja wives and settled amongst them. Such Arabs were soon absorbed but surrounding Islamic influences caused the Beja gradually to adopt a nominal Islam, along with which they acquired the usual fictitious Arab lineage and changed from a matriarchal to a patriarchal social structure. At the same time they preserved their racial characteristics and customs and most of them their language, so that they scarcely differ from the Beja described by Ibn Salīm a thousand years ago.[1] There are today four main groups which are federations rather than tribal units: the Bishārīn, Amar'ar, Hadendiwa, and Banī ʿĀmir. Of these, if we except the Balaw and the many odd groups mixed with other tribes in the plateau region, only the Banī ʿĀmir exist as a definite tribal federation in the region we are studying.

With the expansion of the Funj Confederation of Sennār in the sixteenth century the Beja tribes, roaming in the vast area between the Baraka and the Eritrean Sāḥil, came under its control, which however amounted to little more than the right to nominate the chiefs. The tribe now known as the Banī ʿĀmir was then forming. Racially it was a very mixed tribe because the valley of the Baraka has always formed a highway. It was a conglomerate comprising Tigrē sections from the hills assimilated to Beja groups in mode of life but retaining their Tigrē language, all of whom, Tigrē and Beja alike, were under a dominating class of Balaw,[2] who claimed as their ancestor an Arab called ʿĀmir ibn Kunnu from whom the tribe derives its name. In the seventeenth century, when they were incorporated into the Funj Confederation, the family of the Funj agent, who belonged to the Jaʿaliyyīn of Shendi district, constituted a new aristocracy, the *nabtāb*, whilst in the course of time all the vassal tribes, including the Balaw, came to be

[1] See Ibn Salīm's account in Maqrīzī, *Khiṭaṭ* (Cairo ed., A.H. 1324), i. 313–19.

[2] Münzinger says the Balaw gained supremacy 500 years ago: *Ostafrikanische Studien* (1864), p. 286.

known as *tigrē*.[1] The chief of the tribe, the *diglāl*, received from the Funj as symbol of his authority the three-horned cap which he wears to this day. Certain of the assimilated Balaw and other elements were once Christian,[2] whilst all the rest of the Beja were pagan. They were influenced sufficiently to adopt a nominal Islam by the *fuqarā* of the Funj kingdom, but the religion only got a real hold over them during the first half of the nineteenth century when Muḥammad ʿUthmān al-Mirghanī and his sons preached their *ṭarīqa* amongst them. During the Mahdiyya many of the Banī ʿĀmir sections, and notably the Bait Maʿāla, Sinkatkināb, Khasa, and Lebbat, fought against the dervishes, though most had subsequently to pay allegiance to avoid extermination.

The Banī ʿĀmir number roughly about 60,000 in Eritrea and 30,000 in the Sudan. They are a loosely knit federation of tribes under a paramount chief called the *diglāl*. The *diglāl* always has a deputy with the title of *shaikh al-mashā'ikh* chosen from a particular family, whose authority limits that of the *diglāl*. Some sections of the tribe speak the Semitic language, Tigrē, known locally as Khasa,[3] whilst others have retained their Hamitic language To-Beḍawe; others (e.g. the Gurashāb and Kokudu-āb) are bilingual. Their mixed origin is further shown by the fact that some sections are of Hadendiwa origin, others come from the Ād-Shaikh, from Tigriña families, from negroid groups, and from Arabian immigrants. The vast majority are nomadic pastoralists who travel far afield during the dry season in their search for grass. A few sections south-east of Agordat (Ād Sala, Ād ʿAlī Bakhīt, and Tawliyāb) have settled down to an agricultural life. The Tokar cotton cultivation scheme in Sudan territory relies for its pickers upon the seasonal migration of 12,000 Banī ʿĀmir and Ḥabāb from Eritrea.[4]

[1] According to Münzinger (op. cit., p. 288) the ancestor of the Nabtāb allied himself to the ruling family of the Balaw by marriage and his family grew in power until it gained full control. Their own confused traditions go back to a Jaʿalī of Shendi region of the Sudan, Abū' l-Qāsim (Shaikh Adanab al-Jamūʿī) whose son ʿAlī married a daughter of Chief Muḥammad Idrīs Adana of the Balaw. The tribe consisted of various units more or less related by marriage ties, and the *diglāl* family claim descent from ʿAkasha wad Nasa. ʿAkasha was a Jaʿalī and was assisted against the Balaw by a Funj army which drove out the Balaw from their stone-built towns so that they were enslaved and became Tigrē.

[2] A century ago the Ād ʿAlī Bakhīt and Bait Bijel (or Bidel), originally sections of the Deka Teshim of the Ḥamasēn who migrated to the Baraka two centuries ago and became *tigrē* of the Balaw, still preserved Christian customs in their propitiatory rites.

[3] Khasa is an ancient name (Egy. H̱'z'y) for the region from the Nile (3rd cat.) to the Red Sea. They are referred to in an inscription of ʿĒzānā (*D.A.E.* iv. 33, l. 9). A Beja tribe called al-Khasa, described as north of Saharta, between the Nile and the Samhar, was known to Ibn Saʿīd, *Géographie d'Aboulféda* (1848), ii. 210, 227; cf. Ad-Dimishqī, ed. Mehren, pp. 111, 151, 269.

[4] *Proceedings of the Northern Sudan Advisory Council*, 22 May 1947, p. 56.

The members of the ruling caste, the *nabtāb*, do not form separate communities but are distributed amongst the various sections, and as such have been the chief unifying factor within such a mixed tribe. The proportion of *nabtāb* to *tigrē* varies considerably; the Dagga clan, for instance, numbers about 4,000 of whom 400 are *nabtāb*, whilst the Ād Okud who number 6,500 have only 250 *nabtāb*. The 'commons' are known either as *tigrē*, or the Khasa, or 'the Arabs' which is a most confusing term, or the *ndessna* 'those who belong'. They were originally serfs in status, but the old distinctions have in general broken down, though the *tigrē* still have certain obligations to perform to the *nabtāb* and a *nabtāb* woman would never be given in marriage to a *tigrē*, nor may a *nabtāb* herd or milk his own animals. At the eighteenth tribal gathering held in 1947 an outstanding feature was the demand of the *tigrē* for emancipation from their *nabtāb* masters. The tribes are divided into a number of *badana* each under an *ʿumda*, which in turn are sub-divided into *ḥiṣṣa* or kinship-groups under a shaikh.[1]

Most of the Banī ʿĀmir now pay religious allegiance to the Mirghani family whose chief centres are at Kasala and Keren, but sections of the Ād Shaikh who joined the Banī ʿĀmir have also exerted a considerable religious influence. A recent religious figure who arose from the Ād Shaikh Fai-Faidāb was Sayyid Muṣṭafa wad Ḥasan (d. 1941) whose grave at Agordat is a well-known resort for people seeking his *baraka*. Another revered religious man is Shaikh ʿAmr of the Ād Shaikh Ḥāmid. The Ād Sharaf (1,600) who live amongst them are a distinct tribal group claiming an Arabian origin and exerting a strong religious influence.

The Bani ʿĀmir follow their own customary observances (*sawālif*, sing. *sālif*), which, in spite of the diverse origins of the tribe, have developed a general uniformity. Decisions taken by the tribal courts and by the tribal *qāḍīs* follow customary lines rather than the *sharīʿa*. They retain many magical rites, the Ajdūb clan (*tigrē*), for instance, being noted for their powers as rain-makers and rain-stayers.

### 5. BAIT ASGADE (ḤABĀB, ĀD TAKLĒS, AND ĀD TAMĀRYĀM)

These three Tigrē-speaking tribes of Eritrea, Ḥabāb (25,000), Ād Taklēs (10,000), and Ād Tamāryām (7,000), although they trace themselves back to a common ancestor Asgadē, who according to tribal

[1] On the structure of the Banī ʿĀmir society see S. F. Nadel, 'Notes on Beni Amer Society' *S.N.R.* xxvi (1945), 51–94.

tradition was a member of a family who had emigrated from Akelē Guzāi in the seventeenth century and settled in Rora Baqla (the Mule's Highland), are not now subtribes but are each autonomous with a tribal chieftain (*kantēbāi*). The relationship of the three tribes is as follows:[1]

- Asgadē
  - Be'emat
    - Gabra Kristos
      - Ḥabīb
        - Maflēs
          - Ḥebtēs (founder of the Ḥabāb)
          - Taklēs (founder of the Ād Taklēs)
        - Tamāryām (founder of the Ād Tamāryām)

The original arrivals in the Rora Baqla did not find their new homeland empty, and the nomadic tribes of Beja and Geʿez origin who were already there became in time subject to them, and so the distinction arose between noble and serf. Ḥebtēs placed his tribe under the authority of the Negus who invested him with the tribal drum (*nagārit*) and other symbols of authority, but in time, since the Negus was unable to exercise any real authority, such links ceased, the payment of tribute lapsed, and they remained virtually independent until they came under Italian rule.

The political organization of these tribes is tribal with a ruling caste and a serf caste similar to that of the Banī ʿĀmir. The serfs consist of two distinct groups, the Tigrē and Hadandoi. The Tigrē are the original population of the country (the Asfada, Almeda, and Haffara) upon whose labour the rulers lived like parasites. These Tigrē were nomadic pastoralists and had been converted to Islam before the arrival of the Bait Asgadē who were Christians. The Hadandoi were slaves whom the Bait Asgadē brought with them. Tradition relates that Asgadē had with him a priest and a slave called Hamdoi of Haso origin. The descendants of Hamdoi (called Ād Hamdoi, transposed to Hadandoi) are this other serf grouping and their obligations to the master class are not so onerous as those of the Tigrē who were treated as little superior to slaves.

The Ḥabāb and Ād Tamāryām are nomadic and pastoral, living in

[1] A. Pollera, *Le Popolazioni Indigene dell' Eritrea*, p. 194; C. Conti Rossini, 'Studi su popolazioni dell' Etiopia', *R.S.O.* vi. 370–1.

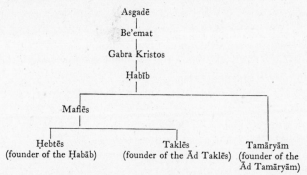

temporary encampments of roughly made huts or tents. Their winter migrations are wide in range and take them as far as to the low country of the Red Sea coast where a different rain system produces grazing during winter months. They have traditional camping sites where the old men and masters remain whilst the rest are with the flocks and herds. Some agriculture is carried on near the semi-permanent camping sites. The Ād Taklēs in the Keren district, however, have become agriculturalists and are sedentary. Their political organization is also changing from a tribal to a territorial basis and the distinction between noble and *tigrē* is breaking down.

The ruling caste of these tribes and the Hadandoi were originally Ethiopian Christians, whilst the *tigrē* vassals who formed the majority of the tribes were Muslims. The Christian origin of the ruling caste is obvious from their very names: Taklēs stands for *Taḳla Iyāsu* 'Plant of Jesus', Ḥebtēs for *Ḥabta Iyāsu* 'Gift of Jesus', and Tamāryām for *Ḥabta Māryām*, 'Gift of Mary'. But the rulers adopted first the Tigrē tongue of their subjects and afterwards, during the first half of the nineteenth century, their religion. G. Sapeto says that they were still Christian in name when he first entered the country in 1838,[1] but he found the process of islamization in full force amongst the Ād Taklēs, which had been accelerated by their becoming vassals of the *nā'ib*. Of the five or six thousand of the tribe at Dolqa a quarter had been baptized and the whole tribe in customs and way of life were more Christian than Muslim.[2] Working amongst them was a very intelligent shaikh from Gondar who had been trained at Ad-Dāmar in the Sudan and had performed the pilgrimage to Mecca.[3] Plowden, who was British Consul from 1844 to 1860, says that the change of religion was due to the troubled state of the country during the period of regional rule and the influence of Muslim traders and missionaries:

> The Ḥababs . . . have become Mahomedans within the last hundred years, and all, save the latest generation, bear Christian names, as do also the Abyssinians. They have changed their faith, through the constant influence of the Mahomedans with whom they trade, and through the gradual, and now entire, abandonment of the country by the Abyssinian chiefs, too much occupied in ceaseless wars with their neighbours.[4]

Münzinger, writing about conditions in 1860, gives further information:

> The three Ḥabāb became Muslims forty years ago. In proof that they were

[1] G. Sapeto, *Viaggio e Missione Cattolica fra i Mensa, i Bogos e gli Habab* (1857), p. 159.
[2] Ibid., p. 242.
[3] Ibid., pp. 232–4.
[4] W. C. Plowden, *Travels in Abyssinia and the Galla Country* (1868), p. 15.

once Christian, we have not only the names of the tribes, but also the ruins of churches in their lands, for example, at Hagara Nāgrām. In addition to this there are numerous Christian formulae and customs among them which also attest to their Christian faith. The account of their conversion is as follows. About 100 years ago Kantēbāy (i.e. chiefling) Ǧāweg of the Ḥabāb, accepted Islam, in the belief that this religion would bring him good luck and long life. He said to his priest: 'Destroy the *Tābot*!' But the priest said, 'I dare not destroy the *Tābot* of Mary.' Then Kantēbāy Ǧāweg took the *Tābot* with his own hands and broke it up with an axe. Following this the priests accepted Islam, and all their descendants are shaikhs of the tribe to this day.'[1]

Whilst conversion was due chiefly to political and economic reasons, the Ād Shaikh played a considerable part in the actual process for they had acquired great prestige amongst the *tigrē* vassals of the Bait Asgadē, many of whom split off and joined the Ād Shaikh tribe. The need to maintain friendly relationships with such a fervently Muslim tribe and with the Egyptians in control of Maṣawwaʿ and the Sudan whose emissaries, the Nā'ib family, were at work throughout the region, induced them to join Islam.[2] At first they kept up links by marriage with their kinsmen in the Ḥamasēn, but today religious and economic differences have caused such contacts to cease. With the decline in the religious prestige of the Ād Shaikh the majority of the Bait Asgadē joined the Mirghaniyya *ṭarīqa*.

[1] Quoted from E. Littmann, 'Bemerkungen über den Islam in Nordabessinien', *Der Islam*, i. 69–70.

[2] Another reason for the change of the religion which has been given is that it was adopted because of the natural necessity for a nomad tribe to use camels as domestic animals, since this was against Abyssinian customs. 'Our Workie told us this evening, that the people of the Habab, in the neighbourhood of Massowah, professed the Christian faith a short time ago; but that they turned Mahomedans on account of a monk, who forbid them to drink the milk of camels, and not being inclined to comply with this, they changed their religion' (*Journals of Isenberg and Krapf*, 1843, p. 91; cf. Münzinger, op. cit., p. 140). This seems scarcely credible since the Tigrē serfs, who alone dealt with animals, were Muslims before they attached themselves to Christian overlords, and there would never be any difficulty about their dealing with camels.

Rassam, who travelled in the region in 1864 to try and secure the release of the captives of Magdala, was told still another tale. He says that they had been left without priests, 'and an invitation to a sumptuous repast, prepared for them by their Muslim neighbours, sufficed to seal their abjuration of Christianity. It is a curious fact, that in these regions partaking by Christians of animal food slaughtered by Mussulmans is regarded by the latter as an outward and visible sign of conversion to their faith and *vice-versa*. The reason seems to be this, that when Christians slaughter an animal they repeat the words, "In the name of the Father, of the Son, and of the Holy Ghost", on putting the knife to the victim's throat; whereas Mohammedans simply repeat the formula, "In the name of Almighty God"' (H. Rassam, *Narrative of the British Mission to Theodore*, 1869, i. 88).

## 6. MANSA AND BAIT JUK

The Mansa are cultivators living in small permanent settlements east of the Bilēn some thirty miles north-west of Maṣawwaʿ.[1] They are divided into two groups, the Bait Abrehē or tribe of Abraham, whose chief centre is the village of Abna, and Bait Es͟hḥaqān or tribe of Isaac, whose centre is at Mehlāb. The ruling class is of Saho origin, hence their social organization is aristocratic with a ruling caste (*shemāgale*) and a serf-caste (*tigrē*). In each section a chief (*kantēbāi*) is elected. The Mansa were independent until the reign of Fāsiladas when they became more or less dependent upon the emperor, and the *kantēbāi* was invested with the symbolic golden bracelet, robe, cap, sword, and tribal drum. But with the decline of the monarchy they came more and more under the influence of local chieftains such as the *Nā'ib* of the Balaw of Arkiko and the Rās of Tigrai. In 1874 they came under Egyptian rule, and in 1889 under that of the Italians.

The Mansa ruling class were originally Christians and resisted Islam for a long time.[2] But during the nineteenth century, in consequence of the ruthless raids of Rās Ubyē of Tigrai, they became less resistant to the widely divergent missionary propaganda emanating from the two families of the *Nā'ib* and the Ād Shaikh, and later were subject to political pressure from the Egyptians. The chief reason for the change, however, seems to have been the loss of their *tābot* which was not only a religious but a tribal symbol. They did have churches[3] and one priestly family, but the priests were accustomed to travel with them during their tribal migrations to and from the plateau, and they carried the *tābot* about with them so that a church could be set up whereever they were.[4] During the troubles of the nineteenth century the *tābot*, which was a block of wood, had been hidden by the priest in a cave to save its falling into the hands of their enemies. When he was able to return to reclaim it he found it destroyed by white ants. The *tābot* has a most important symbolic value in the life of a Christian tribe and its loss meant that the Mansa ceased to carry out the rites of baptism and Holy Communion. The only Christian customs they

[1] On their traditions and customs see C. Conti Rossini, 'Tradizioni storiche dei Mensa', *G.S.A.I.* xiv (1901), 41–100, and K. G. Rodén, *Le Tribù dei Mensa*, 2 vols (Tigrē and Italian), Stockholm, 1913.

[2] W. Münzinger, in a letter dated 1865, refers to the Mansa and Bait Juk as still Christian; quoted by G. Douin, *Histoire du règne du Khédive Ismaïl*, III. i. 287.

[3] Sapeto was shown the sites of former churches; G. Sapeto, *Viaggio e Missione Cattolica fra i Mensa, i Bogos e gli Habab* (Rome, 1857), p. 151.

[4] On the significance of the *tābot* see above, pp. 26–27.

retained were the wearing of the *mateb*, which is the braid of blue silk worn around the neck by all Abyssinians, observance of the two sabbaths, the festivals and saints' days, refusal to eat the meat of an animal killed by Muslims, and the prohibition against eating camel or drinking its milk. These are still observed by those who have not joined Islam.

Left without their traditional safeguards the Mansa were open to propaganda by Islamic missionaries. Many of their *tigrē* were already Muslims, but the first of the ruling class to change was Jamīl of Ejāi who, travelling into the Baraka region in search of a kidnapped daughter, joined Islam at the missionary centre of Qaran in the Mogareh valley. The next was Dasit of Jagin, then Be'emat (d. 1907), the Kantēbāi of the Bait Abrehē. He had been imprisoned by Rās Makonnen in 1870 and, hoping to get aid in his internal tribal feuds, went to Shaikh Muḥammad ibn 'Alī b. al-Amīn of the Ād Shaikh at Embēremi and, professing himself 'disgusted with the Christians of Abyssinia', embraced Islam, together with his sons and some followers (1873/4). In 1884 a Muslim leader of the Bait Es͟hḥaqān, called Muḥammad of Hasama, became *Kantēbāi* of that tribe. Afterwards, through marriage ties or for material reasons, most of the tribe as groups or individuals joined Islam.

Islam has scarcely modified the social life of the Mansa who observe many Christian customs and keep Christian festivals. For instance, they still invoke the name of Mary in their rain-making ceremonies. Their distinguishing characteristics as Muslims are the use of Muslim names, the performance of *ṣalāt*, keeping the fast of Ramaḍān, and abstemption from eating the flesh of animals killed by Christians.

Since then both Swedish Evangelical and Roman Catholic missionaries have built up churches of converts to a large extent from Islam, for change of religion is no terrible crime amongst these tribes, which are now strong influences in the life of the tribes. In 1931 the religious distribution was as follows:[1]

| | *Aby. Church* | *Rom. Cath.* | *Protestant* | *Muslim* | *Total* |
|---|---|---|---|---|---|
| Bait Abrehē . | 90 | 30 | 430 | 3,300 | 3,850 |
| Bait Es͟hḥaqān . | 530 | 324 | 20 | 1,775 | 2,649 |
| Totals . . | 620 | 354 | 450 | 5,075 | 6,499 |

[1] These figures are not now accurate because the church built up by the Swedish Mission (Evangeliska Fosterlands-Stiftelsen) numbers about 1,000 adherents, whilst the Roman Catholics have also increased.

The *Bait Juk* may be mentioned here because they live in the valley of the ʿAnseba, between the Mansa and Bilēn. They also have nobles (*shemāgele*) and serfs (*seb medir* 'people of the land'), but the distinction between classes is not so clear-cut as it is with the Mansa. They are a Tigrē-speaking tribe of agriculturalists numbering about 4,000, living in eight permanent settlements, whose customs are similar to those of the Mansa. Sapeto found them 'Christians without faith', rapidly going over to Islam through the influence of Muslims from Maṣawwaʿ and commercial relations with the Ḥabāb.[1] In 1865, according to Münzinger, they were still nominally Christian, but today they are all Muslim.

## 7. BILĒN OR BOGOS

The high plateau north of the Mareb (Gash) is an appendage of Tigrai cut off from the main part of the province by the Mareb. The southern part of the plateau which drains into the Mareb is called Ḥamāsēn, the northern part which drains into the ʿAnseba, a tributary of the Baraka, is called Bogos. At some early date[2] Agao from Tigrai and Lāsta migrated into this tongue of high land and won it from the Baria and Tigrē tribes established there. The Baria were displaced and migrated to the region they now occupy.

These Agao are the Bilēn, sometimes called Bogos.[3] They were agriculturalists, organized only as kinship groups and not as a tribe. They absorbed some of the earlier Tigrē-speaking inhabitants as serfs, but contrary to the experience of other groups of immigrants they retained their own language and imposed it upon their serfs. The two chief waves probably gave rise to the two tribes of Taqwē and Gabrē

[1] G. Sapeto, op. cit., p. 223.

[2] The Bilēn were in this region by the beginning of the fourteenth century if the itinerary of St. Eustathius, a contemporary of ʿAmda Ṣyon I, through 'the land of the Baguas' on his journey to Alexandria can be relied on (cf. *Gadla Ewosṭātēwos*, *C.S.C.O. Scr. Aeth.*, ser. ii, vol. xxi, p. 37). It is, however, probable that Bogos was only the name of the country to which the Bilēn migrated at a later date. C. Conti Rossini conjectures that the first wave which carried them from Lāsta may have been due to the invasion of the Queen of the Hamūya at the end of the tenth century; other Agao migrations may have taken place during the civil wars leading to the fall of the Zagwē dynasty of Lāsta in A.D. 1270 (cf. C. Conti Rossini, 'Sovra una tradizione bilin', *G.S.A.I.* x, 1897, 153–6). Local traditions show that they were continually being joined by other Agao families escaping from local oppressors or the consequences of blood feuds.

[3] The Gabrē Tarkē claim descent from Boasgor ('sons of Boas') of which the word Bogos is said to be a corruption; others claim that it is derived from another ancestor called Bokustē or Bokusa.

Tarkē. In addition to these two tribes is a third small tribe, the Bāb Janjerēn, which though now speaking Bilēn, is not of Agao origin but grew up around a family of the Ād Sawra, a Sāḥil tribe. They live under the patronage of the Bait Taqwē and follow their system of customary law.

The Bilēn were formerly all Christian and were nominally under the Rās of Tigrai to whom they paid tribute, but in fact they had neither priests nor churches[1] and lived in their highland independent of any external authority, though often boys and girls tending their flocks were captured and sold as slaves. But when the Egyptians gained control of the Gash region their peril increased. In 1850 Ilyās Bey, Governor of Tāka (Kasala Province), reached an agreement with the Banī ʿĀmir and they made a joint raid on the Bilēn which failed. In 1854 Khusraw Bey made another better-planned raid which took the Bilēn by surprise. A large number were killed and nearly 400 women and children carried off into slavery. But Father Stella, a young Lazarist missionary working amongst them, took the matter up with Plowden, the British Consul at Maṣawwaʿ, who succeeded in getting the Egyptians to set the captives free and pay compensation for the cattle which had been carried off.[2]

In this state of things, having nothing to hope from the Abyssinians involved in their own internal troubles, the Bilēn began to change their religion in the hope that this would save them from the raids of the Egyptians and the Banī ʿĀmir. The first tribe to be converted to Islam was the Bait Taqwē who were more directly menaced.[3] On the other hand, many of the Bait Gabrē Tarkē joined Roman Catholicism in the hope that this would bring them the protection of Western powers.[4] The occupation of Keren district by Münzinger on behalf of the Egyptian Government considerably facilitated the movement to Islam within both tribes. After the Mahdist revolt the Egyptians abandoned the region and it was occupied by the Italians in 1888 who naturally encouraged the Roman Catholic mission, whilst the Swedish Evan-

[1] Plowden wrote (about 1848), 'Mugaira is, I think, the most northerly spot (in Bilēnland) where a church actually still exists, but I am pretty sure that there are now no priests' (W. C. Plowden, op. cit., p. 22); whilst the French Consul wrote, 'Les Bogos se disent chrétiens par tradition héréditaire, mais ils n'avaient ni prêtres ni églises vers 1854, lorsqu'un hasard providentiel amena chez eux un jeune missionnaire piémontais, le P. Giovanni Stella' (G. Lejean, *Voyage aux deux Nils*, 1865, p. 154).

[2] G. Lejean, op. cit., pp. 154–6.

[3] Münzinger, *Ostafrikanische Studien*, pp. 199–200; G. Douin, op. cit. III. i. 47.

[4] See letter of Münzinger to the Egyptian Minister for Foreign Affairs in 1865, quoted by Douin, op. cit. III. i. 279.

gelical mission has also converted a few. The actual religious distribution according to the census of 1931 was as follows:

| | *Bait Gabrē Tarkē* | *Bait Taqwē* | *Bāb Janjerēn* | *Total* |
|---|---|---|---|---|
| Muslim . . . | 4,500 | 11,370 | 1,078 | 16,948 |
| Roman Catholic . | 5,300 | 80 | 64 | 5,444 |
| Monophysite . . | 600 | .. | .. | 600 |
| Protestant . . | 50 | .. | .. | 50 |
| Totals . . . | 10,450 | 11,450 | 1,142 | 23,042 |

The custom of marriage relationships between the different clans has not been affected by their adherence to different religions or sects, the religious problem being solved by the wife's adoption of the religion of her husband.

The Bilēn are mainly agriculturalists living in small hamlets of from four to five houses. They have an aristocratic system with a ruling caste (*simager*), the original immigrants, and a serf caste (*mikeru*), who are the former inhabitants of the region, together with various groups who have voluntarily sought the protection of the Bilēn. These castes are hereditary and no matter how rich a serf may become he cannot change his status. He has no definite right even to change his lord, but changes do take place with the goodwill of the lord. He has obligations and dues to discharge to his master some of which if they are required of him may be onerous, but he enjoys freedom of movement and can live where he likes. He has definite legal rights within the tribe, he can inherit, witness in court, and contract marriage without the consent of his lord. The lord, too, has obligations of protection and assistance to render to his vassal. In general the land belongs to the vassals, which may show that the local inhabitants originally submitted willingly to the control of the Bilēn.[1]

Their social régime is patriarchal and the office of chief is hereditary, but the actual government is by a council of old men and chiefs of sections. They have a code of customary law (*Fatḥa Mogāreh*), but this has been greatly modified since their conversion to Islam and coming under Western rule. Their women, however, still do not inherit and their position seems little better than it was in the past.[2]

[1] On the relationship between master and serf see C. Conti Rossini, *Principi di diritto consuetudinario dell' Eritrea* (Rome, 1916), pp. 637 ff.

[2] 'La vertu des femmes est estimée très haut, et celui qui lui porte outrage est assimilé au meurtrier. Mais la femme, non respectée comme un être humain, l'est seulement comme propriété: personnellement elle est . . . assimilée à l'hyène, l'animal le plus méprisé de l'Éthiopie' (Reclus, *Nouvelle géographie universelle*, vol. x, pt. i, p. 233).

## 8. MĀRYA

The Mārya, some 25,000 in number, live north-west of the Bilēn, in the middle valley of the ʿAnsaba. They claim to be descendants of a Saho warrior who, with a group of soldiers, settled amongst Tigrē-speaking peoples during the second half of the fourteenth century and gradually, as the family increased through intermarriage, became a ruling caste and adopted the language of their serfs. The tribe is split into two sections, the Mārya Qayiḥ or 'Red Mārya' (8,440) and Mārya Ṣallīm or 'Black Mārya' (16,650).[1] These must represent two migrations, for the 'Black' are traditionally regarded as the 'first born', but both sections are noble and intermarry freely. The distinction is now entirely a territorial one, for the two groups live in strictly defined plateaux or *rore* divided by deep ravines whose physical features have affected the numbers and wealth of the tribe. That occupied by the Black is lower in altitude, hotter, with red soil and abundant water. They are able to keep camels and have vast numbers of goats which feed on the shrubs. The Red region is more elevated, colder, with black soil and little water. They have no camels but keep many sheep for which their pastoral conditions are suitable. Both tribes balance their pastoralism by cultivating the land around their semi-permanent encampments. They live in small groups of families of nobles and their *tigrē* who care for the animals and do the cultivation. Since their region also includes low valleys towards the Baraka they do not have to travel long distances and their encampments need only be broken up when they wish to leave the cultivable land fallow.

Their social organization is aristocratic like that of the Bilēn, but the chiefs of the tribes wield greater authority. Each tribe is entirely independent with its own hereditary chief (but only the chief of the Black is called *shum*) and there are a number of section-chiefs in each tribe. The descendants of their common ancestor Mārya constitute the nobles (*shumgalla* or *woled shum*) who, contrary to the custom among the Bilēn, can never lose their nobility by crimes against the tribe. The obligations of the *tigrē*-serfs to their masters are strictly regulated. They only can care for the animals and cultivation of the tribe. They have to supply their masters with butter, milk, and grain, make special offerings of animals at the marriages and deaths of nobles, and help them

[1] The distinction goes back to an early date because the 'two Māryā' are mentioned in the *Gadla Qeddus Ewosṭātēwos* (trans. by Turaiev, *C.S.C.O.*, *Scr. Aeth.*, ser. ii, vol. xxi (1906), pp. 37–38) and in a British Museum MS. dated A.D. 1455–6; see C. Conti Rossini, *R.S.O.* ix. 452–5.

to pay off blood money, which with the Mārya is very high, amounting to 800 cattle. Under Italian rule the more onerous duties of the *tigrē* have been considerably lightened, but the distinction between master and serf is still very strong.

The Mārya were once Abyssinian Christians and some of their clans (e.g. the Ād Tē-Mikā'ēl, a section of the Red) still bear Christian names, whilst ruins of churches are scattered about their land, as, for example, at Erota. For centuries they were isolated and quite independent of Abyssinian rule. In time their priests died and were not replaced, the agents of the Balaw family were carrying on commercial activities along with Islamic propaganda, and their *tigrē* mostly adopted Islam. Finally, between 1820 and 1835 the ruling class also thought it politically expedient to join the religion.[1] The adoption of Islam has considerably influenced the life of the tribe and has weakened many old customs; for instance, the right of the first-born son to inherit his father's estate to the exclusion of the daughters has been modified. On the other hand, it has scarcely begun to influence the rigid noble–serf relationship, though this will eventually change under the new ideas brought in by European rule.

## 9. MINOR GROUPS IN ERITREA

### (*a*) *Ād Sawra, Ād Muʿallim and Bait Māla*

These small groups are inhabitants of the Sāḥil along with the large Bait Asgadē groups who have already been described. The first two live along the Red Sea coast of the Eritrean Sāḥil and the third in the foothills in the north of Eritrea north-west of the Ḥabāb. All three claim an Arab origin. The Ād Muʿallim (1,000), as their name implies, grew up as a 'clan of teachers', and at one time were a thriving source for the supply of teachers for the Qur'ān schools of the region. They are now breeders of camels, sheep, and goats. The Bait Māla (Maʿāla), who are Beja pastoralists speaking Beḍawē, were converted to Islam as early as the middle of the fifteenth century.[2] They number about 2,700 and formerly formed part of the Banī ʿĀmir federation but are now independent. During recent years some groups have settled down to cultivation. The Ād Sawra, who speak Tigrē, differ from most of the other tribes of the Sāḥil in having a democratic organization. They have a council of chiefs, called *Abāy* or *Ojāl*, as their ruling body.

[1] Münzinger, op. cit., p. 228.

[2] Cf. C. Conti Rossini, 'Studi su Popolazioni dell' Etiopia', *R.S.O.* vi. 367.

### (*b*) *Tribes of the Samhar Plain*

The Samhar is the coastal region of Maṣawwaʿ extending inland to the foothills and some fifty miles north of Maṣawwaʿ. As is natural this region has acquired a mosaic of tribes who are uniform in religion since they are Muslim, but speak various languages, Tigrē, Tigriña, Saho, ʿAfar, Arabic, and Somali. Most of them are semi-nomadic and pastoral, who cultivate in the winter mainly along the banks of the few rivers and in the summer follow their flocks and herds. These groups have no caste system but follow the tribal system ruled by a council of elders who elect a shaikh.

For centuries the region was controlled by the *nā'ib* family of Balaw origin who lived in the towns of Arkiko and Maṣawwaʿ and the villages of Otumlo, Moncullo, Zaga, and Embēremi. The Balaw are of Beja origin and groups of Balaw are scatttered all over Eritrea mixed amongst other tribes.[1] They formed the ruling class of the Banī ʿĀmir during its formative years until they were supplanted by a Jaʿaliyyīn family from the Eastern Sudan. Since the sixteenth century their chief centre was at Arkiko (formerly known as Dogono or Dohona) where the Turks recognized their influence by appointing the chief as their *nā'ib* or deputy. Because of this position and their control of the Samhar the Balaw figure prominently in the history of the region. During the Egyptian occupation one of the *nā'ib* family was appointed Sirdar of the troops at Maṣawwaʿ. These Balaw of the Samhar were also a considerable influence in spreading Islam in Eritrea. Through their services to the Rās of Tigrai the family were given fiefs in the highlands which became centres for the spreading of Islam, their agents travelling widely in the Sāḥil and other parts collecting tribute and trade dues.

Other tribes of the Samhar are the Aflenda (2,500) who live to the north of the plain. They are semi-nomadic, of Beja origin, and speak Tigrē; one group, the Ād Egel Shaikh, have two distinct classes of nobles and plebs. The Meshalit (1,600) are a mixed group, now all speaking Tigrē, who live on the lower Wakiro and are cultivators and pastoralists. The Ād Hā, of Saho origin but speaking Tigrē, are pastoralists moving between the Ailet plain to the plateau of the Mansa. Other small unimportant groups are the Ād Shūma, Ād ʿAskar, Nabara, and Waria (Waira), all of whom speak Tigrē.

[1] The Muslims of Tigrai south of the Mareb are called Balaw in the *Futūḥ al-Ḥabasha* (p. 319), 'they belong to the tribe of the Balaw who inhabit Tigrai and are Muslims'. The author has undoubtedly confused the Balaw with all the Tigrean Muslims.

### (c) *Tribes on the Sudan Border*

These include the Sabdarāt (3,000) who are pastoralists but cultivate a good deal of millet and speak both Arabic and Tigrē. When the Turks occupied Kasala in 1842, they were under the protection of a family claiming descent from a *sharīf* of Mecca, but today the distinction has almost disappeared through intermarriage. Two tiny tribes are the negroid Elit (600) in the hills of Alkota with a language of their own, and the Bitima (150) now speaking Tigrē. The Ḥalanqa, who live in the Kasala region, migrated originally from the Serāi and were Tigrē-speaking until recently when they adopted To-Beḍawē from the Beja tribes around them. They were once a powerful tribe but continual wars reduced their numbers. Early in the nineteenth century they were divided in allegiance between the Funj resident and a feki of Ḥalanqa-Jamūʿiyya descent, then followed years of conflict with Hadendiwa, Abyssinians, and Mahdists. Under British rule they have been recovering in numbers and prosperity.

### (d) *Islands off the Red Sea Coast*

The largest group of islands in the Red Sea is the Dahlak archipelago to the east of the Gulf of Maṣawwaʿ. The chief inhabited islands are Dahlak which gives its name to the whole, Nokra, Nora, Dohol, Harat, Kubari, Daraka, and Dinifarikh. The people of Dahlak were the first East Africans to be converted to Islam in the eighth century A.D. and numerous gravestones in Kūfic and later forms of the script have been found there. For a time it was a semi-independent kingdom of considerable commercial importance with its own navy controlling the central Red Sea. Great cisterns for the storage of water are found carved out of the rock. The climate of Dahlak must have been as unpleasant then as it is now, for the poet Abū'l-Fatḥ Naṣr Allāh al-Iskandarī writes: 'the worst country is Dahlak, whoever lands there dies there: it is sufficient proof that it is a hell to say that its guardian is Mālik b. Shaddād.'[1] Today it has lost all commercial importance. Its inhabitants are Tigrē-speaking and so poor that they are unable to increase their diminishing stock by contracting marriages with families on the mainland. Amongst them live groups of Arabs, ex-slaves, Sudanese, and ʿAfar.[2] Apart from the goats, camels, and donkeys which

[1] Yāqūṭ, *Kitāb al-Buldān*, ii. 634.

[2] The figures of the 1931 census gave a total of 2,275 inhabitants of the archipelago, composed of Tigrē 1,475, Arabs 475, and ʿAfar 325.

the inhabitants possess, their only resource is fishing for pearls and mother-of-pearl, to buy which Banian and Persian merchants pay yearly visits to the market at Domolo village on Dahlak al-Kabīr.

South of this group is the island of Dessēt or Dessi, whose inhabitants (200) speak Tigrē and amongst whom are families of Asaorta, ʿAfar, and Arabs. The isles of Baca and Hawākil are inhabited by ʿAfar and Somali respectively.

All these little isolated groups are locally autonomous with a democratic régime and an elected chief. The Egyptian government during their occupation appointed a *shaikh al-mashāʾikh* over the various petty chiefs, but he had no real authority.

## 10. ʿAFAR OR DANĀKIL

The ʿAfar occupy a vast area stretching from the Jibuti–Diredawa railway in the south to the peninsula of Buri in the north, and from the shores of the Red Sea to the eastern spurs of the Abyssinian plateau. Their territory is most unpleasant, consisting of stony or sandy desert traversed by great lava streams.

The ʿAfar, who are called Dankali (plur. Danākil) by the Abyssinians and Arabs, are a Hamitic people of the same branch as the Somali. Their ancestors must have come across the Red Sea in the distant past but their history is unknown for, like that of all nomadic peoples, it is a tissue of migrations and super-impositions, of fractionings and regroupings. They are first mentioned by Ibn Saʿīd in the thirteenth century under the form Dankal.[1] They formed the nomadic part of the peoples of the kingdom of Adal and a substantial section of the Imām Aḥmad's armies. But the enthusiasm roused by the easy booty gained in the Imām's lightning conquest did not survive his death and the collapse of his armies. They were soon dispersed and back again in their miserable deserts, where in the one place where permanent settlement was possible the Sultanate of Aussa was formed. A deep hatred grew up between them and their former Somali allies, especially the ʿĪsa, whilst to that was added hatred of the peoples who occupied the eastern highlands, the Tigreans of Woggerāt and the Galla Rāya, Yajju, and Warra Babbo. The northern ʿAfar tribes such as the Dahrimela came under the hegemony of the rulers of Tigrai, but those in the centre and south, with whom the Shoan kings had to remain on good terms in order to ensure the safety of their caravans to the coast, always maintained a practical independence. In 1874 the

[1] Aboulféda, trans. St. Guyard, ii. 128, see above p. 60 n. 6.

Egyptians occupied the coastal towns, and the following year the Sultan of Aussa wiped out the Egyptian expedition under Münzinger. The Egyptian occupation of the coastal region lasted only ten years and left no traces. Aussa itself, being protected by deserts, was comparatively free from raids from the highlands and the Abyssinian power left it alone until the time of Menelik when, as a result of its sultan having formed treaties with the Italians, it was invaded in 1895 by a Shoan army and forced to pay tribute. But even so, no Abyssinian force dared to penetrate beyond the fringes and the ʿAfar were continually contending even for the possession of these.[1] A strip of land along the coast from Maṣawwaʿ to Asāb, about forty-five miles wide, separated from Abyssinian Danākil by a thin line of hills, became part of Eritrean territory and was garrisoned by the Italians. Lord Rennell mentions the good behaviour of the ʿAfar and the co-operation of the Sultan of Aussa with the British Military Administration.[2] After the region went back to Ethiopia things must have deteriorated, for in 1944 an Ethiopian expedition was sent against Aussa on the grounds of the insecurity of the trade-routes and its sultan captured and brought to Addis Ababa. He died whilst in captivity and one of his relations was made sultan. The position of Aussa remains as a semi-independent sultanate tributary to Ethiopia. The other tribes north of Aussa pursue their own free way.

The number of ʿAfar in Eritrea was estimated in 1931 at 19,270 (Asa Māra 5,045, ʿAdo Māra 14,225), in French Somaliland at 12,341, and about 60,000 inhabit Ethiopian territory. The ʿAfar are of medium height, lithe, slender, and well-proportioned. They have an oval face with fine regular features of the European type. Their eyes are fierce and penetrating, their noses narrow and straight or aquiline, their lips generally thin, their chin small and pointed, their skin deep coffee-coloured. Their hair is coarse and curly but never woolly and the men allow it to grow in a fuzzy mop. They are vivacious, bold, and courageous, but living in a country where life is so precarious has made them suspicious, treacherous, and bloodthirsty. 'No man may wear a coloured loin cloth, a comb or feather in his hair, nor decorate his knife with brass or silver until he has killed at least once.'[3] As Nesbitt says, 'The Danakils kill any stranger at sight. The taking of life has become

[1] L. M. Nesbitt, *Desert and Forest* (1934), pp. 68–69.

[2] Lord Rennell, *British Military Administration in Africa 1941–47* (1948), p. 147.

[3] W. Thesiger, 'The Awash River and the Aussa Sultanate', *Geog. Journ.* lxxxv (1935), p. 3.

a habit of their nature.'[1] But in the perpetual struggles that go on between clan and clan one must realize that it is not due to any natural blood-thristy nature, but a form of the perpetual struggle for existence in an appalling natural environment. They have a particularly bad reputation for attacking caravans and massacring expeditions, but no nomads living in such a land could possibly resist attacking or levying toll on caravans passing through their country from the coast to the highlands. Their women when young are pretty and graceful, but since they are treated as beasts of burden they age very rapidly. They wear long brown skirts, leave their breasts uncovered, and if married distinguish themselves with a piece of black cloth worn round their heads.

The ʿAfar are divided into two main groupings, the *Asa Māra* or 'red-men' and the *ʿAdo Māra* or 'white-men'. The 'reds' are regarded as the nobility whilst the 'whites' are thought of as an inferior stock. How the distinction arose is not clear. It has been claimed that the 'reds' are descendants of conquerors from the Abyssinian plateau. Tribal tradition, however, gives the south-east as their place of origin. They may be descendants of a more recent immigration from overseas,[2] but it is more probable that in the turmoil that followed the invasion of Aḥmad Grāñ many of his southern ʿAfar followers meeting the advancing Galla were forced to migrate into the Dankali desert where they imposed themselves upon the others and gave rise to the distinction. The distinction is scarcely that of two castes as amongst the Tigrē-speaking tribes, for the dispersion of the population in the grim fight for life would not allow of such a formation. Their relationship is rather that of noble and plebeian. Many of the ʿAdo Māra tribes, such as the Dahrimela and Belesuwa, are powerful and independent tribes, but the 'red' and 'white' distinctions do cut across one another in Asa Māra tribes such as the Damoheita. In such cases the authority of the nobles is political and economic since the chiefs and heads of kinship groups are naturally 'reds', and territorial rights are vested in them, though the 'whites' own herds and have rights of grazing on the 'reds' land.

The ʿAfar are divided into a large number of tribes and kinship groups, but no one has yet been able to get the distinctions clear because of their aversion to strangers. The chief tribes of the Asa Māra are the

[1] L. M. Nesbitt, op. cit., p. 79.

[2] Naturally their own traditions go back to the usual Arab immigrant; see R. Franchetti, *Nella Dancalia Etiopica* (1930, p. 226), for the Damoheita tradition.

Damoheita (10,000) which is the most important tribe in the north stretching from the Buri peninsula to Edd, sub-groups of which, under various names, live in Teru, Biru, the Rorom plain, and the valley of the Ala; the Alito and the Herto live in the plain of Sereba and valley of the Ererti (Eretro); the Filla Enda around Farar and on the Halhal mountains to the south-east of Aiuman, the Nassal and Hafara in Biru and at Beilul; the Burkeli to which the clan of the Sultan of Biru belongs; the Data Ḥasan, Asa ʿAli, and Assaho in Biru; the Modaito, the most important tribe in Teru, Aussa, and the south, to which the clan of the Sultan of Aussa belongs; the Airolasso between Mount Tajūra and Goda plateau; the Ād ʿAli between Rahaita and Tajūra to which the Sultan of Rahaita belongs; the Sohato between Ale Doli and Aussa; and the Adamta in Ala.

The chief ʿAdo Māra tribes are the Ankala of Asāb, Buri, and Beilul; the Belesuwa west and north of the Dogwa mountains in eastern Agamē; the Dahimela, a large independent tribe (over 10,000) scattered over a large area of the northern and central regions; the Ḥaḍārem who claim Ḥaḍramawt origin are divided into many small sections along the coast from Ras Shiaks to Ras Numeita and in the interior; the Dunna who assert that they came from Ḥodaida live on the Dimo mountains; the Aina Mela in the lower valley of the Golima and south of it; the ʿArabta between Mount Gurale and River Millē; the Duna on the Dimo mountains; the Doda between the town of Batiē and the valley of the Millē and in the coastal zone; the Gedimto dispersed in both Eritrean and Abyssinian territory around Lake Afrera (Guilietti), Data ʿAli mountains, and the plain of Illi Dabo; the Āsa Bakere south-west of Aussa, in the valley of the Ḥawāsh, with other scattered sections; the Maʿandita in the Imminu plain north of the Dobi; the Aisa Mela in the valley of the Ḥawāsh; the Devenak Māra of the high valleys between the River Ḥawāsh and the Obora, Ahmar, and Chercher mountains. The Ād Shaikha should be mentioned for it is a 'holy' tribe, living not as a single tribal unit but in family groups scattered amongst other tribes. They claim to be descendants of the Prophet and are held in great honour by other ʿAfar who make them periodical offerings in virtue of their alleged powers of control over the seasons. They are almost as ignorant of Islam as the others.

The traditional political system of the ʿAfar is based upon kinship groups (*ail* from Arab *ʿaila*) rather than tribal sections, and the heads of these kinship groups are the real holders of authority. They have become rather loosely grouped into tribes (*mehla* or *chidoh* or *gabīla*) mainly for the purposes of defence, whilst further modifications have taken place, especially along the coast where coastal ʿAfar grouped themselves into the sultanate of Rahaita and the minor shaikhdoms of Beilul, Meder, Edd, and Buri. In Ethiopian territory were formed the sultanate of Aussa whose sultan exercises a vague kind of authority over the southern regions; the minor sultanate of Biru, and the shaikhdom of Tajūra.

The chief of the tribe is called *dardar* and sub-chiefs *rās*. These offices may be hereditary or elected. In groupings such as the sultanates and shaikhdoms just mentioned, where leadership has become hereditary, two branches of the dynastic family hold office in turn. The *dardar* being from one branch and his deputy (*bulaita*) who succeeds him from the other; whilst the dead chief's son becomes *bulaita*, thus assuring his eventual succession to power. The authority of the chiefs of tribes is extremely vague and limited since all important decisions are made in the *kalām* or general assembly of the tribe. Some, such as the Ḥaḍārem, have no tribal chief at all. Amongst the nomads of the interior no true political organization exists, nomadic life has exaggerated the individualistic characteristics of the ʿAfar, and he respects no authority. But he is not self-conscious as an individual. He has no individual sense of crime. Crime is a collective responsibility of the group to which he belongs and the reaction is either a compensation from the kinship group or, if another tribe, a war of reprisal.

Nomadic life is static and the ʿAfar is an extreme example of this, so closely is he adapted to his environment. The equilibrium of the forces of man, animals, water, and grass in his life are so exact that all his energies are absorbed in the struggle for mere existence and he has no energy left for the arts or for the effort involved in uprooting and seeking a new life elsewhere. That is why he is such a fine 'specimen' if viewed in his life in his own deserts and a demoralized and useless individual if seen outside them.

What little sense of unity the ʿAfar possess as a people has nothing to do with kinship, for as we have seen they are not an ethnic unit. It is based on the factors they do possess in common, which are language, religion, and way of life. But even these have never enabled them to combine against a common enemy such as the Galla or Abyssinians, whilst they live in perpetual bloody struggles with one another.

The ʿAfar are essentially nomadic herdsmen. Living in an infertile country of desert, lava streams, volcanoes, and salt depressions, no other life was possible, and even that was precarious and did not allow large concentrations, so that there has been considerable infiltration northwards into more fertile regions, and this gave rise to the Saho groups. Their livestock consists chiefly of goats, some tribes rear camels, and a few in specially favoured areas have cattle. The majority with their goats and meagre camels migrate long distances in search of the scanty herbage, but the few cattle-owners of the Damoheita cannot move far from the richer grazing grounds of the Buri peninsula. The goats are tended chiefly by women and children whilst some of the men remain nearby on the watch. The majority stay in their village, though some are always on the look out for the approach of strangers. A few groups on the shores of the Red Sea are sailors and fishermen in the service of the merchants of the coastal towns. Some agriculture is done by the Modaito in the Aussa region where the Ḥawāsh forms a series of little lakes whose annual flooding irrigates the surrounding land and leaves a deposit of mud. The Dahimela also extract salt from the depressions in the torrid central regions which from earliest times they have traded with the Abyssinians in the hills.

Their huts, which are used chiefly for shade in the heat of the day and for the storage of their meagre food and possessions, are poorly built, hemispherical in shape, made of the interwoven ribs of palm leaves, and covered with a coarse matting. They are situated in open ground near wells and are the semi-permanent centres of their migrational movements. Some live in natural caves in parts where the soil is tufaceous or pumice. The diet of the ʿAfar consists chiefly of sour milk and sometimes a porridge made of *dura* flour. Only at festivals when an animal is killed do they get the opportunity of eating meat. They drink also an intoxicant which they extract from the *dōm* palm.

The ʿAfar do not hold God in any great awe. They think of Him, not as an omnipotent king, His powers are so obviously limited, but rather as a great shaikh worthy of following if He shows qualities of leadership and generosity. Since He shows little of either He is not taken into account very much. It is far more important to keep on the right side of one's tribal saint. The ʿAfar cannot be called fanatical Muslims; their hatred of strangers is due to other causes. They are extremely lax in the practice of their Islam and many remnants of their former paganism persist. They rarely pray, do not keep Ramaḍān strictly, and cannot read Arabic. The nomads keep strictly to themselves, mix little with other tribes, and never with non-ʿAfar if they can avoid it; they have no teachers so they have very little chance of learning anything of their religion. The Islam of those in the coastal towns has been more crystallized through mixing with others better versed in Islamic regulations.

## II. SAHO

These tribes are grouped together because they all speak the same language which is allied to ʿAfar, but they are of various origins and vary in organization, tribal law, and customs.[1] The majority live on the eastward mountain slopes of Akelē-Guzāi, Shimezana, and Agamē. They are mainly pastoralists, migrating in winter towards the coastal region, whilst in summer they travel across the Tigriña-speaking country far to the west across Akelē Guzāi and across the Mareb in the Hazamo plain to the Serāi. Such migrations in the past led to some groups settling on the plateau and changing their language to Tigriña or Tigrē (e.g. the ruling class of the Mansa and Mārya), whilst the contrary process sometimes took place, the Saho language being adopted by Tigrē- and ʿAfar-speaking sections (e.g. Teroʿa Bait Mosē). The westward movement and gradual settlement of these tribes is going on continually.[2]

The constitution of these tribes is democratic with an elected chief. They have no caste-system. They remained virtually independent of both the Tigreans and the *nāʾib* of Arkiko although they sometimes paid tribute to both. They appear in traveller's tales as wild and feared robbers dominating the Samhar and the eastward mountain slopes. Plowden says 'they are fanatical Mahomedans, without exception',[3] but now under Western control they have become peaceful nomads.

The largest tribe is the Asaorta (18,000) who migrate between the sea and Akelē-Guzāi and derive from an early wave of ʿAfar migration.[4] They dominated other peoples they found in the area and remained pagan for a long time. Mount Falūm was the centre of their ancient pagan rites where they still make a yearly sacrifice of a white cow.[5] They are now all Muslims through the influence of Arab immigrants, whose families became 'holy' sub-groups within the main tribe such as the Mē Embara, Bait Khalīfa, and Bait Shaikh Muḥammad. Many

[1] On the origins of the Saho tribes see C. Conti Rossini, 'Studi su popolazioni dell' Etiopia', *R.S.O.* iii. 852–3.

[2] See S. F. Nadel, 'Land Tenure on the Eritrean Plateau', *Africa*, xvi (1946), 3.

[3] W. C. Plowden, *Travels in Abyssinia* (1868), p. 23.

[4] The earliest reference to them (also to the Hazo and Taroʿa) is in a British Museum MS. dated A.D. 1455–6 as Asāwrtā when they occupied the same area they do now and must have been nominal Christians under Zar'a Yāʿqob (see C. Conti Rossini, *R.S.O.* ix. 452–5).

[5] Reinisch, *Die Saho-Sprache*, ii. 132.

of them joined the Mirghaniyya *ṭarīqa* during the nineteenth century.

The Asaorta are divided into five tribes, whence their name *kawn ʿarē*, 'the five houses', each of which has a separate chief. They are essentially mountain dwellers and are semi-nomadic in a state of transition to a sedentary life. Their migrations follow a regular pattern. They remain in the plain in winter for as short a time as possible when they do some cultivation, but they cultivate much more on the plateau where many sections are now sedentary, living in permanent houses of stone and thatch. The others only put up primitive tent-like shelters.

The Mini-Ferē, 'Sons of Mina', seem to be a fusion between Saho and an Abyssinian garrison placed in the country to bar the way to Saho migrations northwards. It is interesting to find that they now have two legends as to their tribal origins; one of which derives Mina from royal Abyssinian stock; whilst the other, invented after they became Muslims, traces his ancestry back to the Prophet.[1] The Mini-Ferē live between Senafē and Arafali and number about 11,000. Some of them were once Christian and agriculturalist sections who live on Mount Soira (especially the Asa Yofisha) still remain Christian, but the majority had adopted Islam by the beginning of the last century. They are divided into three sub-tribes, Faqā-t Harag, Rasamo, and Gāso. The first is a semi-religious tribe whose chief acts as *qāḍī* in appeal over the decisions of the other chiefs.

The Teroʿa (Torʿuwa)[2] who are the most northerly of the Saho, live between rivers Haddās and Algedē and migrate between the Ḥamāsēn and the coast. They were originally Tigrē-speaking but have changed to Saho. They are divided into two sections, Bait Sarāḥ (or Sarāḥ ʿArē) and Bait Mosē (or Mosē-t ʿArē), the latter being bilingual.

The Hazu or Haso (4,000) live east and south-east of the Mini-Ferē migrating between the Gulf of Zula and the River Endēli. They are fully nomadic and 'never cultivate, but live at feud with the Danakil and with their neighbours in Irob'.[3] They have a chief who has the title of *Ona* and every ten sections are under a *shun*.

The Debri-Mela, 'People of the Mountain', who number about 1,000, live south of Akelē-Guzāi on the mountain-chain of Mount Mola. They are divided into two sections: the Aladēs on Amba Debra who speak Saho and are nomadic pastoralists and Muslim; and the Lab

[1] Cf. C. Conti Rossini, 'Al- Rágali', *Boll. Soc. Ital. di Espl. Geog.* (1904), p. 22.
[2] Reinisch (op. cit. ii. 295) derives the name from *raʿaw*, 'to graze', cf. Ar. *tarʿiyya*.
[3] S. H. Longrigg, *A Short History of Eritrea*, p. 162.

Halē who are settled cultivators, bilingual, speaking both Tigriña and Saho, and have remained Ethiopian Christians.

Another large Christian Saho tribe are the Irōb (about 10,000) who live in Abyssinian territory in the eastern Agamē, south of the Debri-Mela and the Endeli river who migrate on to the plateau as far as the region of Debra Dāmo. They are gradually adopting the language and mode of life of the Abyssinians amongst whom they live. The family of Sab'agādis which played an important role in the history of Tigrai during the early nineteenth century belonged to the Irōb.

There are many other smaller Saho tribes, the Idda (1,200), Iddefēr (1,000), Baradotta (900), Assabat ʿArē, all of mixed origins, and other definitely ʿAfar tribes who now speak Saho such as the Reza Māra and Bellesuwa. Certain other small tribes which claim an Arab origin need mentioning because they are partly responsible for the conversion of the Saho to Islam. The Intilē Shaikh ʿArē, a branch of the Mē-Embera, are a 'holy' tribe, their centre is at Donagūb, but they have members scattered about all the tribes as Qur'ān teachers and mediators in disputes amongst the Saho. The Bait Khalīfa, Bait Qāḍī, and Bait Shaikh Maḥmūd are small groups of very mixed origin, lent a unity by common association; the Bait Khalīfa, for example, being composed of families of Sudanese, ʿAfar, Dassamo, and Asaorta. The Bait Qāḍī have the privilege of providing the *qāḍī* for the five Asaorta.

The constitution of the Saho tribes is democratic, they have no caste system and elect their chiefs, whose authority, however, once they are elected, is respected. They have their own system of tribal law which varies in each tribe. They are observant of religious practices and knowledge of the reading and writing of Arabic is fairly widespread, especially amongst the Asaorta. All alike will be found wearing amulets and telling their rosaries. They are very jealous of their women who live a most secluded life in their huts.

## 12. SIDĀMA

Before the Galla invasions the peoples, whom for convenience' sake[1] we call Sidāma, inhabited almost the whole of the southern part of Ethiopia. In the east they extended towards the Wēbi, in the west as far as the valleys of the Sobat and Diddessa, in the north they occupied

[1] 'Sidama' is the term used by the Galla for all non-Galla peoples, similar to the Somali usage of *gālo* for non-Muslim, and therefore means 'foreigner'. Amongst the natives of the region Sidāmo is the name of a single tribe. Europeans use the word as a convenient term for those peoples of Kushitic origin who belong to the linguistic family of which the Kafficho language is the most widespread and this has been its usage throughout this book.

much of Shoa, whilst in the north-west they crossed the Blue Nile and reached as far as western Agao-Meder. As the Abyssinians expanded they absorbed certain groups of northern Sidāma, whilst they placed military outposts in the centre of their region (e.g. the Gurāgē who are perhaps a fusion of the two peoples). As we have seen, the formation of Sidāma states, whose ruling classes accepted Islam, kept the Abyssinians back for a long while, until, after the consolidation of the Solomonid dynasty, they effected a military occupation of a large part of the Sidāma regions. Then came the Galla invasions which brought the Galla into northern, north-western, and eastern Sidāma territory, many were absorbed and Sidāma-land was reduced to little more than the Omo and great Rift Valley regions. The majority of Sidāma have retained their paganism through all these changes. The chiefs of Hadya and Bāli, we have seen, accepted Islam in the fourteenth and fifteenth centuries, but it was only a veneer and vanished. The Abyssinian conquests of the fifteenth century led to the conversion of some groups to Christianity, but the Galla invasion and the subsequent long period of isolation, which lasted until Shoan expansion under Menelik, resulted in the triumph of their paganism.[1] Since Menelik's conquest official Christianity has been adopted by many, whilst during the nineteenth century Islam made progress amongst the eastern tribes of Hadiya, Alaba, and Ṭambaro.

The incorporation of these Sidāma states into the Ethiopian Empire has had two effects. The chiefs of the pagan states had to accept a nominal Christianity, but those who claimed to be Muslims were left alone; secondly, it opened up direct contact between them and other Muslim centres which were being affected by the reawakening of Islam in southern Ethiopia during the second half of the nineteenth century and apparently caused further decadence of their paganism. But it is true that the Sidāma, like the Galla, easily adopt a foreign religion without in any way giving up the paganism of their ancestors. So far the two religious currents that have been contending for the souls of the Sidāma have failed.

Islam then is still rare amongst the Sidāma and is only professed by

[1] Enārya was converted to Christianity by Sarṣa Dengel in 1586. The invasions of the Galla caused Christian Sidāma to take refuge in Kaffa whose kings claimed to belong to it until 1854 (cf. Bieber, 'Die Geistige Kultur der Kaffitscho', *Rev. Ét. Ethn. et Soc.*, 1909, p. 45; *Kaffa* (Vienna, 1923), i. 173–4, ii. 419–44; Massaia, op. cit. v. 55–56). Major Harris reported many survivals of Christianity amongst the Sidāma (*The Highlands of Ethiopia*, 1844, iii. 76–79). The people of the islands of Zwāy seem to have been Christians from very early times and although they had no priests still preserved their churches and their ornaments until the conquest of Menelik (cf. Guèbré Sellassié *Chronique du règne de Ménélik II*, 1930, i. 335).

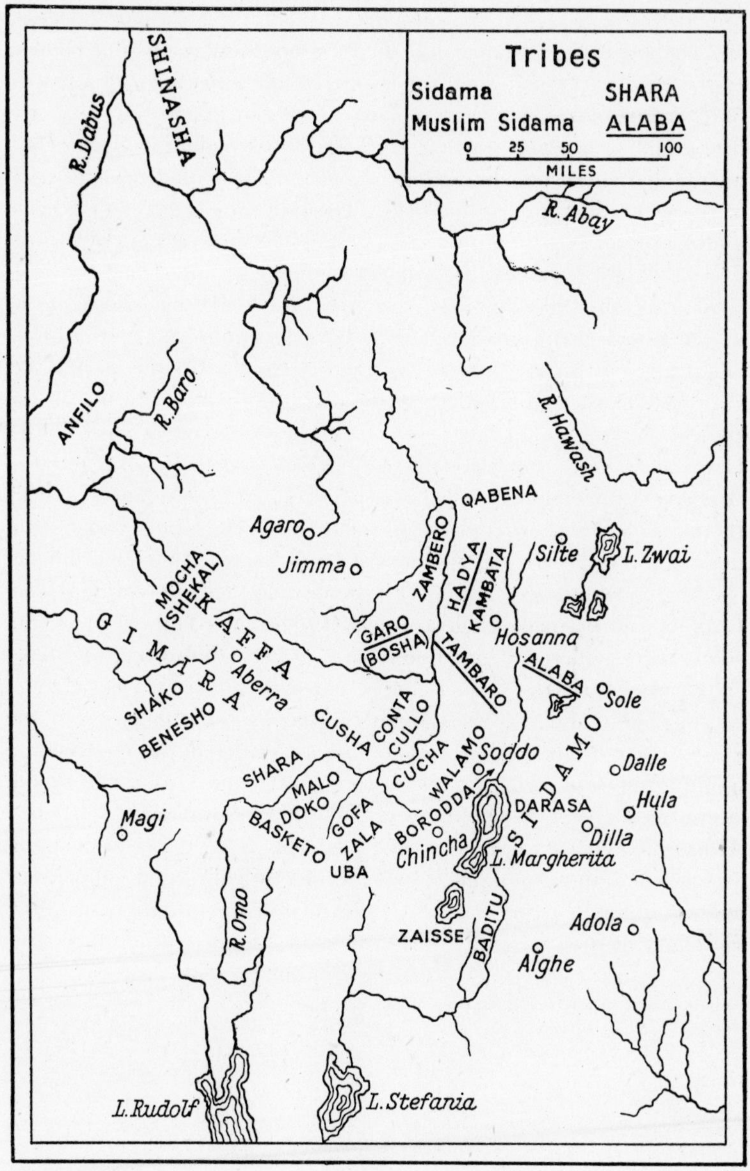


THE SIDĀMA REGION

four tribes of the eastern Sidāma, the Ṭambaro, Alaba, Gāro (Bosha), and Hadiya, though Islamic influence is strong in all the trading centres of the region. The Ṭambaro, who speak the same language as their northern neighbours the nominally Christian Kambāta, formerly formed the southern part of the large Muslim kingdom of Hadya conquered by the early Solomonid monarchs.[1] It was an independent state at the beginning of the Shoan conquest with an elected chief Negita who had been converted to Islam.

The Hadiya, who call themselves Gudēla,[2] are the remains of the ancient Muslim kingdom of Hadya who, as a result of the Galla invasion and subsequent isolation from other Islamic centres, reverted to a practical paganism.[3] They border on the Gurāgē in the north, the Gurāgē Ulbarag and Kambāta in the east, the Ṭambaro in the south, and the River Omo in the west. At the time of Cecchi's visit (1878) Hadiya was divided into two principalities. The northern, called Qabēna (Hadiya Wambē by the Galla), was an autonomous state under ʿUmar Baksa, an adventurer from Chaha who had made himself chief with the title of *Imām*. He became a Muslim, Cecchi says, to aid him in opening up commercial relationships with the kingdoms of Jimma and Limmu, and he made Hadiya into an important commercial centre, where were gathered together merchants, soldiers of fortune, deserters, and displaced persons. These people, when they were not engaged in war or slave-trading, 'amused themselves day and night in two or three huts bearing the pompous names of mosques, eating, drinking, sleeping, singing praises to Allāh or His Prophet, and, during our stay there, lacerating our ears with yelling and the sounds of timbrels and drums.[4] ʿUmar Baksa made his subjects send their sons at the age of six or seven to school in these mosques, where under the direction of various masters, amongst whom was an ʿAfar, they learnt to write and recite the whole of the Qur'ān by heart'.[5] It is as a result of this policy that

[1] Kambāta is first mentioned as an independent state by d'Almeïda, 'Narea pela parte de sudueste, Cambate pela do sul, Bally pela de sueste' (*R.A.S.O.* vi. 403) and Ṭambaro probably separated itself at the same time.

[2] See E. Cerulli, 'Note su alcune popolazioni Sidama dell' Abissinia meridionale', *R.S.O.* x. 599–610.

[3] Gudēla was formerly the name of the southern part of Hadiya, for a song in honour of Negus ʿAmda Ṣyōn speaks of him carrying his conquest throughout Hadiya as far as Gudēla; Guidi, 'Le canzioni geʿez amariñña in onore di Re Abissini', *R.R.A.L.* ser. ii, vol. v (1889), song ix.

[4] It is probable that they were performing the *dhikr* because they were adherents of the Qādiriyya *ṭarīqa*.

[5] A. Cecchi, *Da Zeila alle frontiere del Caffa* (1885–7), ii. 51–52; cf. also p. 57 on ʿUmar Baksa's propaganda amongst the pagans of his kingdom.

Hadiya became more or less islamized. He was succeeded in 1878 by Ḥasan ŋjāmo, son of one of ʿUmar's companions, who, allying himself with other Muslim chiefs in the south, put up a fierce struggle against the Shoan conquest. He was conquered by Fitawrāri Ḥabta Giyorgis and the country incorporated into the empire. The southern principality, lying between the River Omo and the Ṭambaro (called Hadiya Tufta by the Galla), submitted peacefully to Menelik's general and in consequence obtained much better treatment than the northern.

Whilst the Hadiya are Muslims in name they still practise their old pagan cult. Their sky-god is called *Wāʾa*, which is obviously equivalent to the Galla *Wāqa*. Their living cult is bound up with the various genii who live in trees and springs. Since the conquest of Menelik their Islam has been given new life through wider contacts with other Muslims.

The Alaba, who live between the River Billate and Lake Awasa and whose language belongs to the same group as the Kambāta, number about 40,000. They are agriculturalists and Colito (Gulitu) is their market centre where there is a mosque. They are mentioned (under the form Halaba) as part of the kingdom of Hadya in the Chronicle of Zar'a Yaʿqob (1434–68);[1] and by P. Antonio Fernandez, who travelled in this region in 1613, as a little state, tributary to Ethiopia, adjoining the Kambāta, governed by a Muslim who took Fernandez prisoner.[2] During the succeeding period of isolation their Islam died out, but it was again preached amongst them about 1830 by a Shaikh Kāna, who, like so many of the missionaries of this region, claimed to be a descendant of Shaikh Ḥusain. In consequence of the eastern influence they have adopted the Qādiriyya *ṭarīqa*.[3]

The Bosha, who are called Gāro by the Galla, are a Sidāma people, first mentioned in the songs in honour of the Negus Yesḥaq (A.D. 1419–29) as one of the countries paying a tribute of gold.[4] They were among the people converted to Christianity by Sarṣa Dengel during his expedition of 1586–7.[5] They were conquered by the Mecha Galla towards the end of the eighteenth century and their former wide area became restricted to the south-western region of the kingdom of Jimma, north of the Gojeb and west of the Omo, where they now live,

[1] J. Perruchon, *Chronique de Zar'a Yaʿeqob* (1893), pp. 16–22.

[2] D'Almeïda, *Historia Aethiopiae*, *R.A.S.O.* vi. 269–75.

[3] M. Moreno, 'Nuove Notizie sull' Alaba e sugli Alaba', *R.S.E.* i. 54–55.

[4] Guidi, loc. cit., *R.R.A.L.* vol. v (1889).

[5] Guidi, *Historia Gentis Galla* (1907), p. 203. They are also mentioned by d'Almeïda, *apud* Beccari, *R.A.S.O.* v. 23, 'O rio Zebee . . . nasce em huma terra á quem chamão Boxã no reino de Nareã, que he o mais austral deste imperio'.

which became a *koro* of Jimma when it was conquered by Abba Gomol, father of Abba Jifar II, during the first half of the nineteenth century. They escaped absorption and remain a Sidāma people speaking their own dialect of Kafficho, but also speak Galla. They have all become Muslim.[1]

Most Sidāma regions have some Muslim minorities[2] chiefly commercial. The rulers of the former kingdom of Kaffa placed very severe restrictions upon the entry of foreign merchants. Two markets only were open to them, that of Bonga for Christian merchants (*amaro*), and Kāya for Muslims (*neggādo*). Those Muslim merchants who wished to settle permanently in the country could not stay in Kāya but had to build huts at Tonkolla (15 km. to the east).[3] The last Kaffan king, Kennito, is said to have joined Islam in the hope of getting help from his Muslim neighbours, but even if this were true Islam did not gain any hold over his people. F. J. Bieber gives a few indications of the Islam professed in Kaffa. He says that the *neggādo* there are descendants of immigrant merchants from Darīṭa, Gondar, and Tigrai who settled down, married local women, and now speak Kafficho. They have a mosque at Tonkolla where prayer and Qur'ānic recitations are performed, but Islam is not professed by the true Kafficho.[4]

It was the policy of the Italians to strengthen Islam in southern Ethiopia, and the list of places where they constructed mosques in Sidāma-land at least shows the trading-centres where Muslims are concentrated, though these are not Sidāma:

> In some regions of Galla-Sidāma, as, for example, in the territory of the Omēto, the Muslims were regarded as pariahs; the hardest work and the most abject duties were reserved for them, their faith for years was the butt of insults and contempt on the part of all. They had almost no *qāḍīs* and the few they had enjoyed neither consideration nor authority. The Italian conquest has definitely given them dignity, independence, and tranquility: they have *qāḍīs* and mosques and complete liberty in the exercise of commerce and the practice of their religion. . . . In the Sidāmo territory, where the Muslims had only miserable mosques, the construction of a dignified mosque in Dallē has been made possible by a government contribution. Also in the residency of Hula the construction of a mosque has been started and another built at Cavallanca, an important Islamic colony. Enlargements have been made to

[1] Cerulli, *E.O.* i. 81, 102–4.

[2] There are Muslims, for example, amongst the Conta (cf. *Guida*, p. 531), and Sulu (Cerulli, *E.O.* i. 24).

[3] Cerulli, *E.O.* i. 187.

[4] F. J. Bieber, 'Die Geistige Kultur der Kaffitscho', *Rev. Ét. Ethn. et Soc.* (1909), 50–1; 'Das Land Kaffa', pp. 238–9; *Kaffa*, ii. 430–4. This account should be qualified by the remarks of E. Cerulli, *O.M.* v. 556.

the mosques of the Muslim centre of Calitú, and land has been granted in the Residency of Solē for the construction of a mosque. At Aberrà a Qur'ān-school functions and a mosque in wattle and daub following local usage is being constructed at Dilla. Others are projected for Alghē and Adola where the Muslim community has constructed a mosque. Also a little mosque has been erected in the village of Magi.[1]

Islam is not spreading amongst the pagan Sidāma tribes, but considerable movements to Christianity are taking place, notably amongst the Walamo. The Ethiopian State has encouraged the sending of priests and the building of churches in the chief centres, whilst the work of missions is being encouraged.

## 13. GURĀGĒ

The Gurāgē[2] inhabit the fertile mountainous district south of the Ḥawāsh, west of Lake Zwāy, north of the Hadiya and east of the River Omo. They are a Sidāma people but speak a Semitic language which has been deeply affected by Sidāma and other languages. It has been suggested that an Abyssinian military colony was originally placed in this region by the early Solomonids to guard the confines of their empire.[3] In the course of time the soldiers became completely amalgamated with the local tribes, but they left their language as their contribution to the cultural amalgam. On the other hand, the eastern tribes claim to be descendants of immigrants from Harar,[4] and it is not improbable that the invasion of Grāñ left behind pockets of his soldiers. The mountainous nature of their country, by isolating the Gurāgē groups, has given rise to a number of distinct dialects, notably Ulbaraj, Walanē, Gogot, Muher, and Chaha. Their civilization, however, is inferior to that of Sidāma tribes such as the Kafficho and Walamo.

From the religious point of view they show the greatest complexity. They were once christianized pagans during the days of Amḥaran expansion,[5] but most of them reverted to paganism when Amḥaran rule

[1] *Annali dell' Africa Italiana*, iii (1940), 710. Not all these places are in Sidāma territory. Maji (Mazi), which was formerly an important market for slaves, is the principal centre of the group of pagan tribes known as Gimira.

[2] The word *gurā-gē* means 'land of the left-hand'; Isenberg and Krapf, op. cit., p. 97.

[3] Cf. C. Conti Rossini, *Etiopia*, pp. 132–3, *Storia*, i. 283. The traditions of some tribes state that they are descended from soldiers of the Negus Zaraqo, i.e. Zar'a Yā'qob.

[4] L. Traversi, 'Viaggi nelli Arussi, Guraghe', *B.S.G.I.* (1888), pp. 123–4.

[5] See Alvarez, op. cit., pp. 293–4. João Bermudez, who travelled amongst them in 1549–50, gives an account of their paganism, *Breve relação da embaixada* (Lisbon, 1875), pp. 101–2.

was abandoned following the Galla invasions.[1] Shoan priests, however, continued to visit some parts of the country[2] and the kings of Shoa always laid claim to it. Sāhla Sellāssē (1813–47) conquered some of the tribes and took the title of Negus of Gurāgē.[3] Menelik sent his first expedition into their country in 1875 and seized five districts, but the conquest was not completed until 1889. He divided the country into fourteen provinces, eleven 'Christian' (since chiefs of all pagan tribes were required to be baptized) and three Muslim. The Shoan conquest, carrying with it a new influx of Abyssinians, brought Christianity back to the Gurāgē, many Christian groups now exist, the State religion is making continued progress and churches are being built all over the region. The Capuchin mission at Endaber has built up a Christian community. Islam has also been persistently infiltrating into the Gurāgē country through proximity to the Hadiya and through the influence of traders, for the whole of the commerce of the region is in the hands of Muslims, especially the Warjiḥē. The town of Silṭē (pop. 2,500), which lies at the foot of Mount Gurāgē, is the chief Muslim centre. The majority of the Gurāgē, however, remain pagan, but there seems little doubt that these will become Christians. Amongst the Chaha is a clan of sorcerors called Moet who are held in awe by all Gurāgē, Christian and Muslim alike. Azaïs and Chambard give the following table of religious distribution:[4]

| *District* | *Dominant religion* | *Other religions* |
|---|---|---|
| Chaha . . . | Pagan | Muslims and some Christians |
| Guieto (Gieta) . . | Pagan | Christians |
| Gadeba . . . | Christian | Pagans and some Muslims |
| Walanē . . . | Muslim | 1:3 Christian |
| Muher . . . | Christian | Pagans, no Muslims |
| Akelil-Kabena . . | Muslim | Some pagans and Christians |
| Eja (Eža) . . . | Pagan | Christians |
| Ennamor . . . | Pagan | 1:5 Muslims and some Christians |
| Gogot . . . | Muslim | Some pagans |
| Silṭē . . . | Muslim | Some Christians |
| Goumar (Gwemaro) . | Pagan | 1:2 Muslim |
| Masqan (Urib) . . | Christian | Some Muslims and no pagans |

[1] The Gomaro (Gwemaro) were converted by Sarṣa Dengel (Guidi, *Hist. Gentis Galla*, p. 203). On the survivals of this ancient Christianity amongst the Muher see Cecchi, op. cit. ii. 96. R. P. Azaïs shows how Christian elements are embedded in the paganism of the Gurāgē ('Le paganisme en pays Gouraghé', *Revue d'ethnographie*, 1926, pp. 21–27).

[2] Isenberg and Krapf (op. cit., pp. 178–81) report that priests of the Gurāgē were still numerous in the time of Sāhla Sellāssē.

[3] Isenberg and Krapf, op. cit., p. 250; W. C. Harris, *The Highlands of Ethiopia* (1844), iii. 77.

[4] Azaïs and Chambard, *Cinq années de recherches archéologiques en Éthiopie* (1931), p. 187.

Of the tribes not mentioned in this list the Gwera (Gura), Magar, Yacheret, Entagaña, and Ulbarag remain predominantly pagan; the Inor, Aymallel, Nuranna, and Dammo are Christian; and the Uriro are Muslim. There are some scattered Muslim groups such as those of Kwotar between the rivers Wabi and Walga, north-west of the Qabēna. They consist of elements of various tribes with a predominance of Eja. Many of them belong to the Qādiriyya *ṭarīqa*.[1] The commercial centre of Amaya in Nonno territory is a village of Muslim Gurāgē.

The Gurāgē are settled agriculturalists who also depend to a large extent upon their flocks and herds. They are intelligent and industrious workers, and in Addis Ababa the word Gurāgē is equivalent to 'porter', for many of them, as well as Sidāma like the Walamo, travel there for work when their cultivation allows them. They have fine regular features; the men dress like the Abyssinians, but the women still wear skin robes and ornament themselves with metal objects. The Abyssinians regard the Gurāgē as inferior, but often take wives from them for their women have a reputation for beauty.

## 14. OROMA OR GALLA

### (*a*) *Culture Contact and Change*

The name Galla is a nickname probably meaning 'emigrants' which is disliked by the people themselves.[2] Their own name is Oroma from *Ilm Orma* 'sons of Orma' after their eponymous ancestor.

We have seen how the Galla first marched into Bāli in the reign of Lebna Dengel and, taking advantage of the confusion and social vacuum left by the devastations of the Imām Aḥmad, broke like a tidal wave over Ethiopia. At this time they were a loosely knit confederation of tribes whose highly developed political organization represented a tribal symbol in which the soul of the people was incarnated. But as a result of their irruption into an historical region they escaped from the nomadic society's normal state of being a people without a history and exposed themselves to new forces of change and disintegration.

At the time of their migration they were nomadic herdsmen, ignor-

[1] Cerulli, *E.O.* i. 24.

[2] Reinisch suggested that Galla is probably derived from the Somali root *gāl*, 'stranger', and now especially 'non-Muslim' (*Somali Wörterbuch*, 1902, *gāl*). Arabic speakers are adept at producing derivations with an appropriate story attached and the tradition goes that when Wolab, the ancestor of the Ilm Orma, was summoned by the Prophet's envoy to embrace Islam, the Galla chief's refusal was reported to the Prophet in the words '*qāl la*' (he said 'No'). The Prophet, on hearing this, said, 'let this then be the denomination of the infidels in the future' (W. C. Harris, *The Highlands of Ethiopia*, iii. 45).

ant of the use of metals and the horse, but they acquired both these in Abyssinia and their cavalry armed with long lances and throwing spears became the terror of the peasantry armed only with swords and shields.[1] They scattered or subjugated many of the Sidāma tribes and pushed themselves into the western districts, some even settled between the higher courses of the Baro and Diddessa; they penetrated into Abyssinia proper, into the southern districts of Shoa, and even as far as Lake Ḥayq and the frontiers of Angot and cut off Shoa from Amḥara and Tigrai. They were enrolled as praetorian guards by the emperors and founded military colonies. Bruce thought that they could have conquered the whole country had they not met with smallpox during the reign of Iyāsu the Great.[2] But the real reason for their failure was that life in the highlands changed the Galla; it split up their tribes and because of their lack of cohesion they were not able to establish a Galla State before the Abyssinians, under Theodore, at last recovered their moral and responded to the challenge.

The Galla of the highlands who mingled with Sidāma and Abyssinians gave up the strictly nomadic life and gradually adopted many of their customs and cultural features, but without losing their own national characteristics and independence. During the second half of the eighteenth and first half of the nineteenth centuries shaikhdoms and principalities grew up with characteristics of their own. Among such powerful Galla groupings were the tribes in the Wallo and Yajju regions in the heart of the highlands between Lāsta and Shoa, amongst whom the Galla system suffered profound transformation for they took over the *gulti* and feudal structure of Amḥara society. Many became Amḥaric-speaking or bilingual. These Galla all adhered to Islam about the middle of the eighteenth century and religious fanaticism was added to racial antagonism. On the other hand, the many small Galla tribes who occupied a large part of the State of Shoa were converted to Christianity before the time of Menelik.[3] South-west of Shoa in the Gibē regions genuine principalities were founded upon former Sidāma kingdoms whose peoples also joined Islam early in the nineteenth century. Thus two Muslim blocks were formed, that of the Wallo, Yajju, and Rāya in the heart of Christian territory and the group in the Gibē valley in the centre of pagan societies. The Galla tribes surrounding Harar city were also gradually influenced to Islam. This movement

[1] The conquest of Adamawa by the Fulbe, whose success was due to their cavalry, early in the nineteenth century offers a similar parallel.

[2] Bruce, *Travels*, iii. 248–9.

[3] See Krapf, *Reisen in Ost-Afrika*, 1858, i. 101–2.

intensified during the short Egyptian occupation, but they were scarcely modified in their social structure until Abyssinian institutions were introduced after the conquest of Menelik in 1887.

The vast masses of Galla of the south were not subject to this process of social change. They remained nomadic herdsmen under their own republican form of government and because of this they remained pagan. The shock of the ruthless military conquests of the Abyssinians which broke up much of their tribal constitution and customary sanctions, opened the way to Islamic infiltration amongst the Arūsi tribes through emissaries dispersed from the missionary centre of Harar. The Boran, however, are still wholly pagan and have absorbed other tribes who fled before the Shoan conquests.

We can follow the evolution of many of the Galla tribes from the stage of pastoral nomadism to cultivation, with the parallel process in the political sphere of evolution from a democratic to an aristocratic system, and in the religious sphere from paganism to Islam or Christianity. These powerful conquerors, at first united by ties of blood and highly developed principles of social and political life, for nomadism demands a high standard of social behaviour and conformity, lost this solidarity; and as a result of their dispersion and social change this vast confederation of sister tribes became an agglomeration of enemy brothers. Once the Amḥara recovered their unity the Galla's lack of cohesion caused them to fall into a state of vassalage as the Amḥara's subject *fallāḥīn* or tribute-paying pastoralists, from which condition they are emerging during the present régime towards a state of greater equality with the ruling Amḥara.

## (*b*) *The People*

By reason of their dispersion over a vast territory and through intermarriage with indigenous peoples the Galla ethnical type was considerably modified. Some tribes still exhibit truly Hamitic physical characteristics especially since they mixed with other Hamitic tribes like the Sidāma, whilst others in the south-west are strongly negroid. The majority show every variation between these extremes.

In general, the Galla is intelligent, good-tempered, and now relatively peaceable, though he is very courageous when forced to fight. He has great powers of endurance in resisting fatigue and cold. The staple food of the agriculturalists is either grain or *musa ensete*. They drink beer and coffee and have learnt from the Abyssinians how to make hydromel. The plough is often used for cultivation, but in some parts all the work is done by hand. The nomadic Boran, who are essentially herders of cattle, lively mainly on cow's milk which they drink curdled. They also keep some goats, sheep, and a few loading camels. Their villages consist of a thorn *zarība* containing inner cattle-enclosures and semi-spherical grass huts for from ten to eighty families. Those near the perennial wells are permanent. During the rains they wander only to a distance of from two to three marches and make villages where they find water and grazing.

The Galla family is patriarchal and the father has the right of sale and life and death over his children. The eldest son has a superior position and takes two-thirds of the inheritance, the second two-thirds of the remainder, and so on. Adoption is common and the tie is such that the adopted son enjoys the rights of the first-born even if a son is born subsequently. Marriage is exogamous and by purchase, the price being generally paid in cows. It is indissoluble once the final sacrificial ceremony (*rạko-kako*) has been performed. The wife has few rights in Galla law, she may not inherit, but her social position is good, she goes about freely, has considerable influence, and travellers have contrasted her position with that of ʿAfar and Somali women. Monogamy is the general practice, but richer men who can maintain separate huts are sometimes polygamous. The levirate is maintained by most pagan tribes and a widow passes to her husband's brother together with her children.

Oromo or the Galla language is the most widely spoken language in Ethiopia. Considering the vast expanse of country over which it is spoken where the tribes are separated by formidable physical barriers and even other language areas, the language has remained remarkably uniform. The various dialects into which it is divided have not yet been thoroughly studied. They have been divided provisionally[1] into two main language groups: (1) southern, spoken by the Bararetta and Kofira-Galla who live on the banks of the Tana river in Kenya; (2) northern, which is divided into the dialects of:

Machcha, spoken by the Limmu, Guma, Gomma, Jimma, Gēra, Lēqa, Laqamti, and Nonno;

Tulama, spoken throughout Shoa;

Borana, spoken by the Warra Dāyā of Italian Somaliland, Borana, Jamjam, Arūsi, Ittu, and Karāyu. The dialect spoken by the Wallo seems to belong to this group.[2]

[1] Cf. M. M. Moreno, *Grammatica della Lingua Galla* (1939), p. 20.

[2] The following are the translations of the Scriptures into Galla: J. L. Krapf, *Mark* (1841) (southern dialect); Krapf, *Psalms* (1872) (Nonno dialect in Ethiopic characters); Onesimos

*Institutions of the Pagan Galla.* Some idea of the social, political, and religious structure of the pagan Galla is necessary in order to understand the Muslim tribes. The general pattern of their pagan institutions was originally much the same, for the Lēqa in the extreme west and the Boran in the extreme south even today have almost identical forms. But considerable changes have taken place in the islamized sedentary groups as a result of their contact with Sidāma and Muslim institutions and through the superimposition of Abyssinian political institutions. However, as we shall see, Islam could not completely abolish the tribe's ceremonial expression of its members' corporate emotions, and the characteristic institutions of Galla social life are not yet uprooted, for the *gada*-system which is central to it lingers on in all the former Muslim monarchies of the south-west, amongst the Muslim tribes of Harar and Arūsi and, of course, amongst the unmodified pagans such as the Boran and Lēqa, though with the imposition of Abyssinian political institutions it has lost actual political importance.

The political and social organization of the pagan Galla will be but briefly sketched since it is those forms which are more easily displaced, whilst the more purely religious, social, and personal elements will be referred to in a later section since many of these continue to exist in Galla Islam in some form or other, though of course with changes of emphasis, terminology, and means of expression, which have modified their inner significance in Galla life.

The Galla have a special social organization which must have had its origin in the 'age-groups' of the Hamitic Nilotes. Every Galla tribe is divided into groups called *gada* whose number varies from tribe to tribe.[1] East *gada* is made up of all the males of the tribe who are to be initiated at the same time. Membership of a *gada* does not depend on age but is hereditary. The periods of initiation are in general: (1) *dobbole* twenty-four years; (2) *qondola* eight years; (3) *luba*, subdivided into two four-year periods called *raba* and *gula*.

The *Abba Bokku* (holder of the sceptre) is the chief magistrate. He is elected from among the members of the *gada* in passing from the

Nesib, *The Holy Bible* (1899) (B.F.B.S. Ethiopic characters); Cahagne, *Matthew* (B.F.B.S., 1888, Ittu dialect); and the *Gospel of St. John* (in the Bararetta dialect).

[1] On the *gada*-system see E. Cerulli, *The Folk-Literature of the Galla of Southern Abyssinia* (1922), pp. 167–81; 'I riti della iniziazione nella tribù Galla', *R.S.O.* ix. 480–95, 'Ancora dell' ordinamento delle tribù Galla', *L'Africa Italiana*, v (1926), 25–31; 'Le popolazioni del bacino superiore dello Uabi', in Duca degli Abruzzi, *La Esplorazione dello Uábi-Uébi* (Milan, 1932), pp. 152–71; and D. Pecci, 'Note sul sistema della Gada e delle classi di età presso le popolazioni Borana', *R.S.E.* i. 305–21.

second to the third periods and remains in office until the end of the *gula*-period; *luba*, therefore, indicates the members of the *gada* whose *Abba Bokku* is in power. The *Abba Bokku* was assisted by a council which included all ex-officials and elders. Other magistrates were the *Moti* who executed the decrees of the assemblies, and the *Abba Dula* (father of war) who was only appointed to the office for a particular expedition. The *Abba Bia* are a new class of landed proprietors who grew up amongst the sedentary tribes with the decline of democratic rule; they are members of the council which advises the *Abba Bokku* and exercise minor functions.

These institutions still have significance in the social structure of many tribes, although under Abyssinian rule they have lost actual political importance.[1] The *Abba Bokku* is still elected and, though he can no longer enforce taxation, his people will contribute to his support voluntarily during his tenure of office. The tribes which have been most modified are those of the Abyssinian highlands (the Muslim Wallo, Yajju, and Rāya and the many Christian tribes of Shoa). The Wallo still elect an *Abba Dula* for a particular raiding expedition during which he has full authority over all the tribes involved, though a great chief like Negus Mīkā'ēl is the normal leader in a large tribal war. Amongst the Wallo and Rāya, whilst election to the office of *Abba Bokku* under the old republican form lapsed, the chief of the tribe was nominated by an assembly of notables, received the title of *bokku*, and was invested with a baton (*bokkich*) as symbol of office. After Menelik's conquest the chiefs were invested with Abyssinian titles, but are still known as *bokku*, whilst the village headmen are called *bokkicha*. Amongst the monarchal states of the Gibē it was the *Moti* who became king, and the Sultan of Jimma is still called by that title, whilst the institution of the *gada* has been profoundly modified.[2] Before the conquest of Menelik the Chercher territory (Harar Province), whose Galla population were settled Muslim agriculturalists, was divided into *bokku* over each of

[1] H. Weld Blundell wrote in 1905 of the chief of the Lēqa Naqamtē, 'the present chief who began life as "Gumsa", was baptized with most of his followers and soldiers, and blossomed out into Dejasmach Gabra Egsiabeher, or "servant of God". They still maintain, however, the system of an eight-year epoch or division of time, and the ceremonies of the *butta* (or eight-year period), still continue, though the power of the *luba*, within Abyssinian jurisdiction, has been merged into that of officials appointed by the King.' (H. Weld Blundell, 'Exploration of the Abai Basin', *Geog. Journ.* xxvii, 1906.) The *butta* referred to is really the sacrificial ceremony at the end of the second period of initiation by which the right is acquired to take part in the deliberations of the tribe (cf. Cerulli, *Folk-literature of the Galla*, p. 141).

[2] On the *gada* system practised today in Jimma Abba Jifar see Cerulli, *E.O.* i. 87 ff.

which was a hereditary *abba bokku*, but after the conquest Abyssinian institutions were introduced.

## (c) *Muslim Galla Groups*

### (α) *Galla of the Abyssinian Plateau*

The so-called Galla region in the highlands has been the scene of many encounters between races and religions and therefore exhibits considerable ethnical heterogeneity. It was once occupied by Christian Amḥara, as many ancient churches such as that of Dabra Egzi'a Beḥēr on the island of Lake Ḥayq bear witness, but Islamic influence was spreading even before the invasion of the Imām Aḥmad Grāñ for the Dobʿa of the eastern borderland were islamized pagans. Grāñ's invasion left ʿAfar-Saho groups in eastern Tigrai and Abyssinian clans in eastern Wallo and Shoa permanently islamized. A second wave of invasion which passed through the valleys and passes of the region was that of the Galla. Tribes travelling up the Ḥawāsh ascended into the highlands by the valleys which descend into the Dankali depression; those who ascended by the Borkenna eventually settled in the Wallo region, those who travelled by the Millē are the Yajju, and those by the Ala and Golima are the Rāya. The Wallo Galla occupying the region between Shoa, Amḥara, and Tigrai separated these countries and thus aided the dismemberment of the empire

The Galla, having arrived in a paradise of perennial pastures and abundant water, became permanent settlers and were profoundly affected by the new environment in which they found themselves. From the Abyssinians amongst whom they settled and with whom some intermarried, they added agriculture to their stock breeding, changed their language to Amharic, and took over the *gulti* and feudal organization of the society in which they found themselves, which completely modified their own democratic constitutions. From the Muslims of these regions all the Galla tribes adopted Islam during the period of regionalism as a measure to avoid the complete disintegration of their social body and maintain themselves over against Abyssinian imperialism. This religion was professed by the chiefs of the Wallo during the first half of the eighteenth century, but their subjects remained pagan and many of them were still pagan in the nineteenth century.[1] We have

[1] C. Conti Rossini, 'Ricordi storici dei Wallo', *Studi Etiopici* (1945), p. 91, n. 35. According to J. L. Krapf (*Reisen in Ost-Afrika*, 1858, i. 107) the Wallo were converted by an Arab called Debelo; but this is not an Arab name and tells us nothing. It is much more probable that they took over Islam from the Abyssinian Muslims who were already in the region.

already seen how these Galla tribes grouped themselves into two main federations, the Wallo and the Yajju and, occupying as they did key positions between the great Abyssinian regions, they were able to dominate the political scene from 1756 to 1853 and bring about the disintegration of the empire. Their influence caused a strong anti-Galla reaction under Theodore, which was continued under John and Menelik who completely destroyed the Muslim Galla political power. In spite of wholesale baptisms Islam still exerts a strong hold over the Wallo and Yajju, but in time the influence of Amharic and Christianity will lead to the disappearance of the Galla language and possibly their Islam.

The most northerly of these Galla are the Rāya who are also called Azēbo. These are not different tribes, they call themselves Rāya, but are called Azēbo by the Tigreans probably from the name of the country they occupied.[1] They inhabit the great plain in the east of the plateau which is watered by the Ala and Golima rivers. Ascending these rivers at the end of the sixteenth century they dispossessed the Dobʿa[2] and inherited their occupation of raiding the caravan routes between Tigrai and Shoa. They did not attain the same loose cohesion as the Wallo and Yajju and consequently did not play such a great part in the politics of central Abyssinia as the others. They were the allies of Rās Kāsa against the Emperor Theodore,[3] but when Kāsa became the Emperor John IV they were included in his campaign for religious unification; he sent expeditions against them and depopulated parts of their country, in which Tigreans settled and introduced agriculture. They started their raids again but were subjected by Menelik, and in the 1935–6 campaign they helped the Italians as irregulars.

They were pagans when visited by Pearce,[4] and were converted to Islam as recently as the first half of the nineteenth century. They are essentially pastoralists but do a good deal of cultivation, Corbetta being a typical example of a Galla village of agriculturalists. They still speak Galla, but many understand Tigriña through the settlement of Tigreans amongst them. Their political and social order has been greatly changed since they entered the highlands.[5] The *gada*-system of

[1] Cf. C. Conti Rossini, 'Uoggeràt, Raia Galla e Zobùl', *Boll. Soc. Afr. Ital.* lvi (1938), 90.

[2] Gerolama Lobo found Galla in the Azēbo region in 1626 (*Lettere dell' Etiopia dell' anno 1626 al marzo 1627*, Rome, 1629, p. 59); whilst Barradas (*R.A.S.O.* iv. 85) speaks of the Galla as established in the Dobʿa region in 1633.

[3] Markham, *A History of the Abyssinian Expedition* (1869), p. 87.

[4] Cf. H. Salt, *A Voyage to Abyssinia* (1814), p. 276.

[5] Islam no doubt helped the process because in the time of Pearce (*The Life and Adven-*

age-groups and most other characteristic Galla institutions have gone, though they still elect a war leader (*abbogas*, formerly the *abba dula*) whose term of office only endures during the particular raiding expedition for which he is chosen. All travellers who have visited them speak of their ferocity, a reputation which endures to this day.[1] They have always been the inveterate enemies both of the ʿAfar down in the plains and of the Abyssinians in the hills. They enjoyed complete independence until the time of the Emperor John IV, who devastated their country, but even after that they continued in their ways, were never completely subdued, and aided the Italians during the war of 1935–6.

The Yajju live south of the Rāya and north of the Wallo, having Aussa to the east, Amḥara to the west, and Lāsta to the north. Waldia is the chief town in their region, and others are Mokareet and Merta. They live in semi-tropical country of whose fertility Wylde writes:

> Ras Woly told me Yajju was entirely self-supporting, and required nothing from any other country but firearms and cartridges. That they grew their own cotton, dyed it, and manufactured it; they tanned the hides and skins that they required; they smelted their own iron for making spears, swords, knives, and agricultural instruments, they made their own pottery, and that they had every grain and oil seed that was required, and they had never suffered from starvation and they grew more food than they knew what to do with, and raised more cattle than required for local consumption, in fact that it is without exception the most fertile and happy country in Abyssinia, and one of the most healthy.[2]

The people of Yajju seem to be some type like the ʿAfar, who were probably Muslim before the Galla invasion, with whom the Galla intermarried and to whom they have transmitted their language. Like the ʿAfar and Somali they wear feathers in their hair after their first killing, and their graves are adorned with a stone for each man killed. Wylde thinks they are 'a cross between the agricultural original owners of the country and the pastoral peoples, as they seem to combine the agricultural and pastoral life, living by their flocks and by agriculture in which irrigation plays an important part'.[3] It is possible that the

*tures of Nathaniel Pearce*, ed. N. N. Halls, 1831, i. 94) the Rāya chiefs were elected and remained in office seven years, but the chief cause was the new social and political environment which gradually imposed new institutions on them.

[1] Bruce (*Travels*, iv. 134–5) writes of the savage people called Azeba. Markham calls them 'a cruel set of bloodthirsty robbers' (op. cit., p. 40; cf. also pp. 246, 379). See also *Journals of Isenberg and Krapf*, p. 428; A. Raffray, 'Voyage en Abyssinie et au pays des Gallas Raïas', *Bull. Soc. de Géographie*, vii série, vol. iii (1882), pp. 329–30; T. Lefebvre, *Voyage en Abyssinie* (Paris, 1845), ii. 66.

[2] Wylde, *Modern Abyssinia* (1901), p. 360.

[3] Ibid., pp. 359–60.

foundational element of the Yajju group were 'Afar-Saho peoples who had penetrated this region both before, as well as during, the great Muslim conquest, after which they were conquered by Galla. A process of mutual absorption took place, shown in hybrid tribal names like the Warra Shaikh; the Galla social and family life was profoundly modified and also their religion after they accepted Islam, but the Galla language and traditions predominated, whereby the Yajju continue to regard themselves as Galla. The Warra Shaikh family which produced Rāses Gugsa and 'Alī, whose control over central Abyssinia strangled the empire, was the chief branch of the Yajju. It has acquired the usual legend tracing its descent back to 'Umar Shaikh who came from across the sea.[1] When Hāyla Sellassē became King of Kings the Yajju were discontented with the move and rose against him towards the end of 1929, but the rebellion was crushed by Rās Mulugeta.

Wylde writes of the Yajju:

> The people are nearly all Mahomedans and the rule regarding drinking, made by their prophet, is not rigorously enforced, as they say, Mahomed did not forbid the use of liquor but the abuse of it, and if they get a trifle too much sometimes giving alms and being charitable will wipe away the offence.... My Somali servants, being strict Mahomedans and saying their prayers the orthodox number of times each day were horrified at the laxness of their co-religionists.[2]

Next comes the region of the Wallo Galla, defined by the Bachilo which separates it from Amḥara, by the Blue Nile from Gojām and by the Wanchīt and Jama from Shoa, in the north-east by the Millē and in the east by the Dankali plain. Galla, however, are not the only inhabitants of the Wallo region though it has become customary amongst travellers to call all its Muslim inhabitants Wallo Galla. Many Wallo do not belong to the Galla ethnical group at all. This is especially the case with the Wallo of the highest regions of the plateau in the east and south, the Amara-Saint region west of Dessiē, the massifs of Legambo and Legaida, and the Warra Ilu plateau. These, from the ethnical point of view, are Abyssinians, between whom and the genuine Galla the only common link is Islam. It seems that in these little-known mountainous regions the environment has tended by a process of mimetism to reduce and eliminate the contrast between the original inhabitants and the debris of invasions or migrations, so that the original type predominates.

[1] Guèbré Sellassié, *Chronique du règne de Ménélik II*, i. 198.

[2] Wylde, op. cit., pp. 357–8.

The Wallo Galla are first mentioned in 1581/2 in Dambya during the reign of Sarṣa Dengel,[1] in conflict with Aussa in the year 1590,[2] and as raiding Amḥara in 1622 in the reign of Susenyos.[3] We have seen how the Wallo became powerful in Gondar during the reign of Iyo'as (1756–69) whose mother was a Wallo princess.[4] As a result of their settlement in the highlands their own social life and political institutions were modified, their language changed from Galla to Amharic, and by a process of reaction against Abyssinian nationalism their chiefs began to adopt Islam during the first half of the eighteenth century. They were certainly all Muslim by 1840 when visited by the C.M.S. missionary Krapf, who was the first European to visit the Wallo.[5] About the same time French travellers wrote:

Moins féroces et meilleurs soldats, depuis longtemps les Wollo-Gallas ont renié les croyances de leurs pères. Convertis à l'Islamisme, ils reconnaissent pour chef de leur religion le jeune Imam-Liban, proche parent d'Ali, qui gouverne l'Amhara en qualité de Ras. Du reste, ils habitent un pays extrêmement fertile, labyrinthe naturel dessiné par des hautes montagnes, des défilés, des rivières qui coulent en sens inverse, et creusent vers l'Hawach ou vers le Nil leurs vallées pleines de verdure, de lacs et de moissons.[6]

There are seven Wallo tribes, called by the Amḥara *sabāt Wallo bēt*, 'the seven Wallo houses'; of these, 'the Warrā Himāno speak more Amharic than Galla; the Warrā Babbo and the Warrā Qallú speak Galla; the others Amharic mixed with Galla; and the tribes near Aussa, Galla mixed with Dankali'.[7]

The Wallo are now all agriculturalists attached to the soil with the tenacity of aboriginal inhabitants. The whole family takes part in the work of cultivation, and unlike the Amḥara the masters take their share in the work of the fields. Domestic slavery exists amongst them, their slaves being chiefly negroids from the west, but the institution scarcely influences their economic life. Wylde gives an unflattering description of the eastern Wallo:

The people are nearly all Mahomedans or profess to be of this religion, but they are all indescribably dirty with filthy clothes, it being too cold to wash and

1 F. Béguinot, *La Cronaca Abbreviata d'Abissinia*, p. 38.

2 'Aussa Chronicle', ed. Cerulli, *R.R.A.L.*, ser. vi, vol. iv (1931), 78.

3 'Nel 16° anno fece una spedizione in Amḥarā e in Anāzo e combattè contro i Gālla Wālo e Wačālē, li vince, ne uccise molti e fece preda di loro armenti e condusse in schiavitù lor donne' (F. Béguinot, op. cit., p. 45).

4 See above p. 105.

5 *Journals of Isenberg and Krapf* (1848), pp. 319–401.

6 Ferret and Galinier, *Voyage en Abyssinie* (1847), ii. 328–9.

7 E. Cerulli, 'The Folk Literature of the Galla of Southern Abyssinia', in *Harvard African Studies*, iii (1922), 13.

both soap or its substitute the shipti unknown. The men are a fine race, thick-set and large-limbed with plenty of hair about them, a great comparison to the northerners who have little hair either on their faces or bodies; the women are round, fat, ungraceful, broad-buttocked, large-sterned, coarse, ugly things, and about as unlovely as the female sex possibly could be, but at the same time good-tempered and always laughing. Their mouths being great gashes across their faces filled with wonderfully even white teeth, but their dirt and smell are simply unbearable; no beauty is to be looked for south of Yejju, except amongst the Amharans or true Abyssinians, and I cannot make out how the eastern and western Gallas belong to the same race, as the women of the western Gallas are slight, graceful little things with pretty hands and feet, and the eastern have large feet and hands of the most hideous shape, and their hair is also of a much coarser description.[1]

Christian islands, however, have been left behind in this predominantly Muslim region, and official influence since Menelik has caused the principle centres (Dessiē, Warra Ilu, and Akasta) to be inhabited chiefly by Christians, whilst Christian villages are scattered around the country except in the eastern part, where even the market town of Batiē is Muslim. The vast majority of the rural population of the magnificent valleys of the region are Muslim.

A hundred years ago Isenberg and Krapf, after describing the Wallo as bigoted and fanatical Muslims, continue:

The Wallo Gallas are much engaged in saying prayers and in blessing the country. They observe a custom I have never seen with other Mahomedans. They assemble early in the morning, say their prayers, take coffee, and Tohād (sort of tea), and smoke tobacco. This ceremony is called Wodācha. It lasts on Wednesday and Friday till after midday. They believe that they receive revelations from Allah on the Wodācha. On such occasions they particularly request from the Allah that he will give them cows, clothes, and whatever they want; that their Chief may find gold and silver; and that he may daily become stronger. I once heard them praying in this manner.[2]

What little can be learnt of their religion today shows that it is largely based upon superstitious practices. Illiteracy is general and even Qur'ān-schools are very rare. Although the majority of the Wallo are still attached to their Islam the assimilationist policy of the present government is seriously weakening its hold. The ruling families of the Wallo are the only Muslim Galla who have ever made any pretentions

[1] Wylde, op. cit., pp. 382–3.

[2] *Journals of Isenberg and Krapf*, pp. 323–4. The leader of prayer (Arab. *Imām*) is called *abba gār*. The adaptation of the pagan *wadāja* ceremony to Islam is mentioned later, see p. 262.

of Arab descent. They claim that their ancestor came from Persia and have pretended to the title of *sharīf*. From this family came the Negus Mīkā'ēl (Muḥammad 'Alī) who was baptized by Emperor John with whom he served against the dervishes. Subsequently he submitted to Menelik II and assisted in the defeat of the Italians at 'Adawa. The pro-Muslim Emperor Lijj Iyāsu was his son by a daughter of Menelik.

### (β) *Galla of the Upper Gibē*

The Galla who conquered regions like the Lēqa and Walleqqa where the conquered peoples were weak or which were sparsely inhabited, retained their old tribal system based on the *gada* unmodified, but those who came up against the Sidāma kingdoms of Enārya and Bosha (called Gāro by the Galla) of the upper Gibē were transformed both in social life and religion.

Their own tradition relates that this region was conquered around 1700[1] by six Macha tribes, detached from the mass of Galla migration south of the Abāy. This region is intersected by numerous rivers which formed the boundaries of a number of Sidāma kingdoms. Each of the conquering Galla tribes settled in one of these regions and their rule became territorial. Gradually as they settled to an agricultural economy the Galla fused with the subjected Sidāma and both became unified in the *gada* system, whilst the Galla adopted many of the religious conceptions and institutions of the Sidāma. During the second half of the eighteenth century and the beginning of nineteenth five monarchies emerged: Jimma, Gēra, Gomma, Limmu, and Guma: a form of government utterly foreign to the Galla. The religious life of these Sidāma-Galla peoples, now all speaking the Galla language, next acquired a new orientation, for between 1840 and 1870 these kingdoms adopted Islam through the agency of merchants coming from the Warjiḥe of Shoa, from Darīṭa in Bēgamder, and from the Egyptian Sudan. This change of religion was natural in that it helped to reinforce the independence of the states against both Sidāma and Amḥara, strengthened the authority of their rulers, and facilitated the growth of a thriving trade in slaves. Cerulli writes:

> The slight diffusion of Islamic culture and the survival of pagan beliefs in the Islamism practiced by these peoples, resulted in giving little evidence in those early times of a change of religion. But the Egyptian and Sudanese merchants aided . . . by Khedive Ismail began to form local centres of religious

[1] In 1703 Iyāsu I made an expedition against the Macha Galla who were ravaging the country of the Gibē and Enārya (R. Basset, *Études*, pp. 55, 165–6).

culture. The first among these centres was Jimma Abba Jifar. From these centres originated the first fanatics and the first attempts at rebellion.[1]

Shortly before the conquest of Menelik these states headed by Guma began to raid the pagan states of Lēqa Horda, Lēqa Billo, Nolē Kabba, and Hanna Gafarē, who leagued together as 'the Four Pagans' (*arfa Oromāta*) which caused the other coalition to distinguish itself by the title of 'the Four Muslims' (*arfa naggādōta*).

All these small Muslim and pagan kingdoms were conquered by Menelik between 1882 and 1897 and in consequence brought closer into touch with eastern Islamic centres such as Harar, which resulted in a considerable development of their Islam both in the direction of orthodoxy and in the influence of the dervish orders.

The first of these states to accept Islam was the little kingdom of Gomma, situated in the very centre of this group of states, whose capital was Haggaro. The reigning family was the Awallini, who claimed descent from a Somali shaikh called Nūr Ḥusain who emigrated from Maqdishu about 1780 and settled among them as their *qallichcha* or magician-priest,[2] whilst according to another account[3] the family was descended from a Muslim who came from Gojām. Major Harris wrote in 1841 'in Goma the Moslem faith is universal'.[4] At the time of Cecchi an *abba bokku* was on the throne assisted by the queen-mother.[5] This traveller found it the most civilized of these states, he wrote: 'The Galla of Gomma were the first (of these states) to embrace Islam. Both old and young always memorize the Qur'ān which is taught by migrant Muslims who put on the guise of learned men. In spite of all this they still preserve deeply implanted traces of their pagan superstitions'.[6] Gomma was conquered for Menelik by Besha Abuē in 1886. The country is very fertile, producing *ṭēf* (*eragrostis abessinica*), maize, coffee, and cotton; whilst its people have a reputation for intelligence.

Limmu Enārya was the next of these petty Galla states to be converted to Islam. It occupied part of the region of the old Sidāma State of Enārya and covered the mountainous territory between the valley of the Gibē of Enārya and the Diddessa, and had Sāka for its capital. The Sidāma kingdom of Enārya is included among the kingdoms con-

[1] E. Cerulli, 'The Folk-Literature of the Galla of Southern Abyssinia', *Harvard African Studies*, iii (1922), 22.
[2] Cecchi, *Da Zeila alle frontiere del Caffa* (1886–7), ii. 239.
[3] Guidi in *Mitteilungen des Seminars für Orientalische Sprachen*, vol. x, pt. 2, pp. 15–18.
[4] W. C. Harris, op. cit., iii. 60; cf. Massaia, op. cit., iv. 155.
[5] See Cecchi's account of this kingdom, op. cit., ii. 239 ff.
[6] Cecchi, op. cit. ii. 240.

quered by Yesḥāq between 1412 and 1428.[1] It was converted to Christianity by Sarṣa Dengel in 1586.[2] It defended itself vigorously against the Macha Galla invaders and Iyāsu I came to its aid in 1703.[3] It was conquered by them at the beginning of the eighteenth century. Tradition says that the conqueror was Teso, son of a Galla of Elikki, sister of a Muslim named Saʿīd. He was succeeded by Boko, who remained pagan, but his son Bofūn was converted to Islam by his uncle Mukhtār, the nephew of Elikki. In 1841, when Major Harris wrote,[4] the king was Ipsa, son of Abba Gomol, who resided at Garuka and reigned from 1825 to 1861.[5] He was generally known as Abba Bagibo after his war-horse. Cecchi says that he was a great magician, but in his declining years he lost his warlike spirit and along with that his magical powers weakened, whereupon Muslim merchants and adventurers who had been penetrating the country for some years previously succeeded in converting him to Islam.[6] When the Roman Catholics opened a mission in this region in 1846 Abba Bagibo said to them, 'had you come thirty years ago, not only I but all my countrymen might have embraced your religion, but now it was impossible'.[7] Cecchi also tells us that the only mosque in the country was a hut in the grounds of the royal enclosure where the king of his time, Abba Gomol, a fanatical Muslim, spent some hours each evening and much of Friday in prayer; but there were some shaikhs who had considerable spiritual authority, under whom were teachers of the Qur'ān known indiscriminately as *fuqarā'* or *qallichcha*.[8] Naturally the mosque of the people was then as it still is under a village tree at some spot hallowed by tradition. The people in general remained pagan or Christian for a long time,[9] but are now all Muslim. Dejjach Wolde Giorgis conquered the state for Menelik in 1891 and built the Church of St. Markos near the palace (*masera*) of which Massaia gives a description. The son of the last king was educated by Wolde Giorgis and converted to Christianity.[10]

The hilly region of Guma, lying to the west between Gēra, Gomma,

[1] I. Guidi, 'Le canzioni geʿez-amariñña,' *R.R.A.L.* ser. ii, vol. v (1889), hymn ii. v. 39, p. 56.

[2] Cf. R. Basset, *Études*, p. 120: C. Conti Rossini, 'Di un nuove codice' (1893), pp. 17, 21.

[3] Basset, op. cit. pp. 55, 165–6.

[4] W. C. Harris, *The Highlands of Ethiopia*, iii. 53–55.

[5] Cf. Paulitschke, *Ethnographie Nordost Afrikas*, ii. 242; Soleilet, *Voyages en Éthiopie*, pp. 221–30; Borelli, *Ethiopie méridionale*, 274–8.

[6] See Cecchi, op. cit. ii. 160.

[7] G. Massaia, *I Miei Trentacinque Anni in Missione nell' Alta Etiopia* (1923), iv. 79.

[8] Cecchi, op. cit. ii. 167.

[9] There were still some Christians left in 1840, see above, p 109 n. 3.

[10] Cerulli, *E.O.* i. 125.

Ilu Babor, Wallegga, and Limmu, was under the royal family of the Adami. The kings reserved for themselves the former elective title of Abba Dūla (Father of War), as well as the Sidāma royal title of *donacho*. Jawe Oncho (d. 1879), King of Guma, was converted to Islam between 1854–60 through merchants who came from Shoa and Darīṭa Māryām (in Bēgamder) and he imposed its profession upon his subjects. Guma became the most fanatical of these states. Islam was used as a pretext by Abba Jūbir, son of Jawe Oncho, in his war against the pagans of Kabba in 1882. Guma was conquered by Menelik in 1885, but Firrisa, the heir to the throne who had fled to the Ḥijāz, inspired by a Gomma shaikh of the Mirghaniyya called Shaikh ʿAbd ar-Raḥmān, returned in 1899, proclaimed a *jihād* against the Christian Amḥara, and maintained the war for two years. He was eventually caught and executed in Jimma, but all the Muslims of the region revere him as a *walī*.[1] The prevailing *ṭarīqa* in Guma is the Qādiriyya, but as a result of Shaikh ʿAbd ar-Raḥmān's preaching a group of Mirghaniyya has been formed.

Of the other former monarchies in this region, Gēra lies west of Jimma on the left slope of the Gogeb valley. It is a land rich in pastures and forests and produces coffee. Its former capital was Chāla or Cira. The kingdom enjoyed a period of prosperity under Abba Magāl (d. 1870) at whose court Massaia stayed in 1859 when he founded the missions of Chāla and Afallo. This king joined Islam as a result of the visit of Abba Jūbir, the son of the King of Guma, to his court in 1866. Abba Jūbir was the bearer of a circular letter from the guardian of the tomb of the Prophet in Al-Madīna.[2] The Galla rulers of Gēra had, it seems, absorbed Christianity from the former Sidāma population along with their system of government, for Cecchi records that Abba Magāl succeeded in converting his brother to Islam by inducing him to eat meat killed according to Islamic rite (which, as we have already mentioned, was for Christians and Muslims equivalent to apostasy, but was disregarded by pagans), 'in spite of the fact that his father, on his death-bed, had cursed those of his sons who had apostatized from Christianity'.[3] After his death his widow *gennē* Gumitti tyrannized over the country as regent for the last king, Abba Rago, who, with his mother, was made prisoner by Dejjach Besha Abuē in 1887 and died in captivity at Jimma.

The governors whom Menelik appointed over these four sub-pro-

[1] On Firrisa's rebellion see Cerulli, 'Folk-literature', op. cit., pp. 45–46.

[2] See Cecchi, op. cit. ii. 268–9, 309 n. 2, 342–3.

[3] Cecchi, op. cit. ii. 309 n. 2.

vinces had full powers and they and the Amharan soldiers lived off the land, though former Galla chiefs (*Abba Koro*) were given some degree of local authority.[1] The status of Jimma Abba Jifar, the last and most important of these monarchial Galla states,[2] was different, for, since it submitted to Menelik peacefully, it was allowed full local autonomy. Founded upon the old Sidāma kingdom of Bosha, it covers an area of some 25,000 sq. km. with about 300,000 inhabitants. It lies in the valley of the Gibē and is confined within the area formed by the course of the Omo to the east and south, by Mount Botor in the north-east, and the mountains of Limmu and Gomma to the north and west. It is plateau country, one of the most fertile and loveliest regions of Ethiopia, well populated, and cultivated for maize, vegetables, cotton, and coffee.

After the Galla conquest the Sidāma were assimilated into the Galla system and the Galla took over many of the institutions of the Sidāma including that of monarchy and a territorial system of rule. Authentic history does not begin until the reign of Muḥammad ibn Da'ūd (1861–1934), better known as Abba Jifar II,[3] who succeeded to the throne at the age of fifteen. The king had the Galla title of *moti* as well as the more recently adopted one of sultan, and the central part of his insignia was an armlet of gold. The heir to the throne (as in Gēra) bore the Sidāma title of *donacho*. Abba Jifar's accession coincided with the wars between Negus Takla Hāymānot of Gojām and Negus Menelik of Shoa. When Menelik extended his rule over Jimma in 1883 Abba Jifar was left on the throne because he submitted quietly and, except for one period in prison because he was suspected of helping Ḥasan Injamo of Hadiya, he was able to maintain good relations with Menelik. He also assisted his army to conquer and devastate the Sidāma kingdoms of Zinjaro, Koulo, and Kaffa. Abba Jifar was zealous in developing Jimma commercially, he lightened taxes and customs dues and especially facilitated the work of the *naggādis* or slave-merchants so that Jimma became the chief slave-market for south-western Ethiopia, where the light brown Galla girls who commanded such a high price in the slave-

[1] For an account of the system of Amharan rule over these regions see Cerulli, *E.O.*, vol. i, chap. ii.

[2] The other Jimma tribes (Rarē, Gobbo, Tibē, Argo, and Qadida), who live between the Gudru, Limmu, and Lēqa, are pagans or Monophysites.

[3] Abba Jifar 'lord of the dapple-grey horse' was the war-title of Tullu, King of Jimma. The first ruler is said to have been Abba Faro, who was followed by Magāl, Rago, Jifar I, Rebo, Boka, Gomol (or Gomo) who conquered Gāro and a part of Zinjaro. He was the father of Jifar II.

markets of Arabia could be purchased. The country was divided, following the Sidāma system, into seventy districts (*koro*), each governed by an *Abba Koro* and the whole area was surrounded by a thorn fence (*gudēma*), pierced by gates (*kēla*).[1] Abba Jifar tried to make Jimma a centre of Islamic studies, for he was regarded as a strict Muslim, and encouraged *fuqarā* to settle there and teach.

In his later years the old sultan retired from active rule and left the government in the hands of his grandson Abba Jawbir. In 1933 the Emperor appointed a governor to the Jimma region, all effective power was taken away from the sultan and the open conduct of the slave-trade suppressed. During the Italian occupation the sultan and chiefs welcomed the Italians who planned to make Jimma the great trading-centre for the south. They built the town now called Jimma (formerly Hirmata) and a great market centre some distance from the old Jiren where the miserable 'palace' (*masera*) of the sultan is situated. On the reoccupation in 1941 a governor-general of the Province of Kaffa-Jimma was appointed and the Sultan Abba Jawbir became a purely nominal figure.

A mixture of peoples live in the Jimma area though now all are Galla-speaking. In the middle of the eighteenth century the province was peopled by Sidāma, then followed the migrations of the Galla who kept the former inhabitants as a subject people and intermarried with them. The result of this intermingling is unattractive physically and morally. The Galla degenerated through the influence of the rich valley life and of Islam and they lost their characteristic Galla qualities. Their women are unveiled except for those of the chiefs with whom seclusion of women is a matter of social prestige. Parts of the region were occupied by immigrants from Shoa, Gojām, and Wallo, from the last of whom Abba Jifar drew his bodyguard. Tigreans are found at Gara, near Kullu, and at Adwas, south of Jimma. Abba Jifar encouraged Yamanī traders who flocked to his country to enjoy the profits of the slave-trade. There they married local women and their descendants, forming a distinct element of the population, comprise the trading element of Jimma. Probably 30 per cent. of the population of Jimma town are connected with trade. Jimma is still the chief trading-centre of the south-west and a great market (called *mandera* from Arab.-Pers. *bandar*) is held every Thursday when some 8,000 people congregate. Jimma is a great coffee-producing area and small trading-

[1] *Kēla* (Sidāma) also equivalent to customs houses (M. Cohen, *Études d'éthiopien méridional*, 1931, p. 396). This system of closed provinces was a characteristic of the Sidāma tribes of southern Ethiopia, from whom it was taken over by the Galla conquerors.

villages are scattered over the region. Other articles of trade are cotton, skins, and furs.

The conversion of the Jimma people to Islam was principally the work of merchants coming from the Egyptian Sudan by way of Metemma and Roseires. The Sultan Abbā Gomol, father of Abba Jifar, accepted Islam about the middle of the nineteenth century and forced his pagan subjects to a nominal profession. They keep many remnants of their former paganism, and the social life of some groups still gives the impression of a pagan community. In the town itself are four simply built hut-mosques, but rarely does one see anyone praying in the new mosque built by the Italians near the market. The writer visited one Qur'ān school in the Mandera which had thirty pupils under a Yamanī shaikh which did not differ from any similar school in Muslim Africa. Other shaikhs teach the Qur'ān in their houses and each group of villages is said to have someone who teaches the Qur'ān in return for help in the fields. Needless to say all the boys learn to recite mechanically without understanding the meaning of the Arabic. The prevailing *madhhab* is probably the Shāfiʿite, but many follow the Ḥanafite which was introduced from Gondar by one ʿAbd al-Ḥākim who is regarded as a *walī*.

Apart from these five former principalities many of the other Galla tribes north of them, such as the Nonno, have Muslim minorities. The Ḍaḍallē, who inhabit a region just north-west of the Hadiya, are all Muslim through the influence of that Sidāma tribe.[1]

### (γ) *The South-eastern Galla (Harar Province)*

We have already noticed when studying the history of Islam in Ethiopia that Harar was the only Muslim city in the interior which became a permanent centre from which Islamic propaganda radiated over southern Ethiopia. It was here that the Galla first made contact with Islam. In the early years of their conquest they proved a grave menace to the very existence of Harar, but it survived as a petty city-state with its own language and commercial and religious life, but with little political influence beyond the immediate environs of its walls, which it owed to the wisdom of Amīr Nūr who was awake to the seriousness of the Galla migrations. Its religious and cultural influence, however, was by no means restricted, and it has done more to spread Islam over southern Ethiopia than any other agency.

The political isolation into which Harar was driven by Galla and

[1] Cerulli, *E.O.* i. 24–25.

Somali tribes gave its inhabitants a strong impulse to religious fanaticism. No strangers were allowed to enter the city and consequently we know little of its life until its defences were first breached by Richard Burton in 1855 in the guise of a Muslim merchant. But we may take his description of it as a holy and commercial city, with its saints' tombs, schools of learning and well-stocked markets, a centre of pilgrimage and the slave-trade, a breeder of migrant *kulturträger* who were the missionaries of Islam as far as the kingdoms beyond the Gibē, as applicable to the previous two centuries.

Nearly half the inhabitants of the Province of Harar[1] are Galla, most of whom are now self-consciously Muslim. They all claim to belong to Barentu, the second great Galla group, and the relationship of the tribes is shown in the following table:

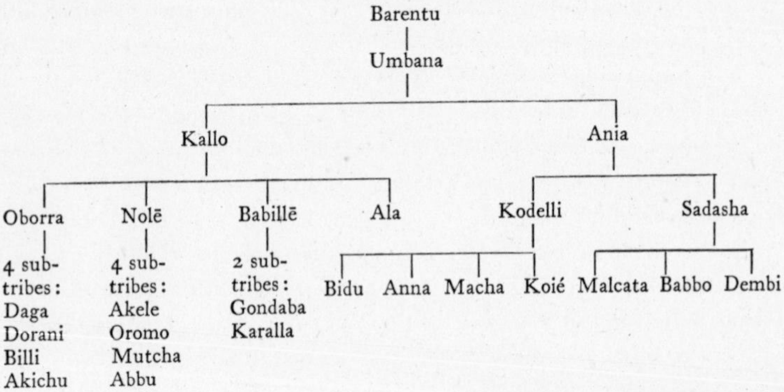


The Nolē and Ala are the largest of the Kallo group. The Nolē, who consist of Oroma and Somali mingled together, each speaking their own language, live between Belana to the north-west of Harar and the Dankali desert. Most of the Ala are south and south-west of Harar, another group who are pastoralist and agriculturalist live between Harar and Dire Dawa. The Oborra live west of Harar with Nolē to the east, Itu to the west, Nolē and Ania to the south, and ʿIsa to the north. The Babillē, who are mixed with Somali, live east of Harar in the mountainous massif of Gondudo and its valleys. The Ania group cover a wide extent of territory south-west of Harar, with Ala to the north, Itu to the west, Arūsi of the Wabi to the south, and Somali to the north.[2] The Chercher commissariat west of Harar where the Galla

[1] The population figures for the Province of Harar under the Italian administration were: Galla 46·8 per cent.; Somali (including Dankali) 31·2 per cent.; Amhara 20·1 per cent.; Arab 0·36 per cent.; cf. F. Santagata, *L'Harar*, p. 93.

[2] Azaïs and Chambard, op. cit., pp. 76–80.

number 217,309 out of a total population of 300,263 contains a mixture of tribes: the Itu who are still largely pagan, Ala, Jaso, Nomē, Kallu (or Deder), and Meta.

The Islamic culture of these tribes varies very considerably. Some are fervent Muslims, whilst others retain pagan rites which can in no way be reconciled with Islam. Azaïs and Chambard write of the Galla who live on the right back of the Chulul, near Mount Gorogarbi, that 'Islam is deeply implanted in this fertile plain and its teaching is widespread, because, whilst in many of the Abyssinian *Katama* (fortified settlements) there are no schools, here the smallest Muslim village has its own, with its *Kabīr* to gather the children in the precincts of the mosque and teach them to read the Qur'ān'.[1] On the other hand, most of the Itu and Ania are only partially converted to Islam, though they call themselves Muslims. They practice the *galma*, a definitely pagan rite, and the cult of Atēte, the goddess of fertility, which also cannot be islamized. These have disappeared amongst most of the other Galla of Harar Province. The *wadāja* is practised by all,[2] though with Islamic introductions since this is a ceremony which can be islamized.[3] All the Barentu regard two kinds of snakes, which are called *ilma* (son) and *akko* (grandmother), as tabu.

### (δ) *The Arsi or Arūsi*

The Arsi (called Arūsi in Amharic) are one of the great Galla groupings living in the vast region north of the Sidāmo and Borana and south of the great plain of Karayu through which the Ḥawāsh flows, between the Sidāma in the west and the valley of the Ramīs in the east. They derive themselves from the seventeen sons of Arsi, and consequently feel themselves to have a common ethnic origin, but they are much mixed, especially in the south, with the former Sidāma population. They are primarily a pastoral people. Certain mixed groups are agriculturalists and cattle-breeders living in permanent settlements from which at certain seasons the cattle are driven in search of pasture, but they become increasingly pastoral in the south where the country is less suitable for agriculture. They are a warlike people and have a reputation for savagery, and were only conquered by Menelik's generals after three arduous campaigns. In the region of Aselle and Huruta the *gabar* system was instituted after the occupation and proved a heavy burden on the population. They have, however, recovered under the rule of the present Emperor in numbers and prosperity. In

[1] Ibid., p. 75. [2] Ibid., p. 111. [3] See below, p. 262.

1925 the tribes were still organized under a *gada* system of five cycles of eight years each.[1] They are polygamous, and Azaïs and Chambard ascribe this, on doubtful grounds, to Islamic influence.[2] In the principal centres of their region are colonies of Abyssinian Christians, Arabs, and Somalis.

Major Harris wrote in 1841 that the Arūsi were all Muslims,[3] but that is impossible, for many have remained pagan to this day. Islam made great progress amongst the Arūsi tribes during the second half of the nineteenth century under a missionary of the Aḥmadiyya called Shaikh Nūr Ḥusain. When Menelik sent Rās Dārgē to conquer them in 1882 their resistance was organized by this shaikh who proclaimed a *jihād*.[4] A large proportion of the Arūsi are emphatic that their religion is Islam, but observance goes little beyond the observance of Ramaḍān in a faint way and avoidance of eating meat killed by a non-Muslim.

Dr. E. Cerulli gives the following religious distribution. In Arūsi Province,

> some few families living in the ʿAwāsh plain and some families living in centres where there are Abyssinian soldiers are Christian, naturally of the Monophysite belief. All the Arūsi tribes living east of the Cilalo between the ʿAwāsh and the source of the Wabi are pagan. All the tribes living west of the Cilalo and on the western watershed of the Galamo, that is to say the great majority of the population of the Arūsi Province, are Muslim. In the Province of Bāli, the peoples on the right bank of the Wēbi from its source to the height of Laggio are Christian. Those who live in the region south of Gobba as far as the curve of the Ganālē Doria are pagan. All the people living in the valley of the Wabi to the valley of Laggio, and those of the basin of the Web are Muslim: therefore the majority of the people of the Province. . . . It is worthy of note that the Muslim Galla designate the pagans in this region by the name of 'Awama', a word which is of uncertain origin. In reality, however, traces of paganism and pagan rites are also plainly visible in the Christianity and Islam of these peoples.[5]

Characteristic features of the paganism in their Islam are the pil-

[1] Azaïs and Chambard, op. cit., p. 209.

[2] 'Ils prennent des femmes en proportion de leur richesse. . . . Sans doute faut-il voir là une influence musulmane et aussi la nécessité d'avoir beaucoup d'enfants pour garder les troupeaux, car, en général, les Oromo ne pratiquent pas la polygamie, sauf quand ils sont musulmans' (Azaïs and Chambard, op. cit., p. 212).

[3] W. C. Harris, *The Highlands of Ethiopia*, iii. 258.

[4] E. Cerulli, in *Harvard African Studies*, iii. 88.

[5] E. Cerulli, 'Le popolazioni del Bacino Superiore dello Uabi', in the Duca degli Abruzzi *La Esplorazione dello Uábi-Uébi Scebéli* (1932), p. 141.

grimages to sacred mountains like those the pagans make to the Abba Muda of the Dallo, veneration of the sacred enclosures (*hujūba*) around springs, and their retention of magical beliefs and practices.

## 15. THE SOMALI

In the northern part of the area of our survey we have given a brief description of a number of tribes who because of the conditions imposed by the nature of the land they inhabit show great linguistic, ethnical, and cultural diversity. On the other hand, its southern part offers much more uniform conditions of life and the Somali tribes who form its chief inhabitants are a distinct type, speaking a single language.

The Somali are a very large ethnical block whose habitat today includes a strip of territory in French Somaliland, the whole of British and Italian Somalilands, the Ethiopian Province of Ogadēn with parts of Bāli, Harar, and Arūsi, and part of north-western Kenya. The northern Somaliland which declines towards the Gulf of Aden begins with an arid and barren coastal strip between the sea and the maritime hills. The foothills which follow are equally unpleasant. Next comes true nomad country, undulating plains covered with coarse grass and intersected with broad sand streams. This is followed by the main mountain range and the plateau which slopes southwards through a vast expanse of very different and much pleasanter country to the rivers Wēbi Shabēli and Jūba which flow throughout the year.

*Historical Outline.* The Somali[1] for long occupied only the African coast of the Gulf of Aden in what is now British Somaliland, whilst the southern part of their present homeland was occupied by Bantu tribes (the *Zanj* of the Arab geographers), some of whom were displaced by Galla. By the beginning of the sixteenth century the Somali had all adopted Islam through the settlement of Yamanite and other Arabs in the coastal commercial centres; and during that century a great movement of expansion took place among all the eastern Hamites, whose members were continually increasing. Since new religious influences have so often precipitated the irruption of nomads, the conversion of

[1] In classical times the Somali were known collectively as *βάρβαροι* and are so called by the Arabic geographers of the Middle Ages, who also mention individual tribes by name (e.g. the Hawiyya by Abū'l-Fidā, ii. 232 and Ad-Dimishqī, ed. Mehren, pp. 111, 151). The name still survives in the town of Berbera in British Somaliland. The word *Sūmālē*, which is of unknown origin, first appears in an Ethiopic hymn eulogizing Negus Yesḥāq's (1414–29) victories (see Guidi, 'Le canzioni geʿez-amariñña in onore di Re Abissini', *R.R.A.L.*, vol. v (1889), hymn ii. v. 70) and is used frequently in the *Futūḥ al-Ḥabasha* which was written about 1540/50. The *Futūḥ* also names separate tribes who joined the Imām Aḥmad.

the ʿAfar and Somali to Islam and their irruption over the highlands and the Somali expansion into the country of the Galla and Bantu may well be related, because the two processes did coincide. Under the Imām Aḥmad the ʿAfar and some of the Somali tried to overwhelm the fertile highlands of the semitized Agao. The ʿAfar movement failed, but the Somali were more successful. Spreading out of their limited and arid region they moved westwards and occupied all the steppes of the Ogadēn and the first buttresses of the central massif as far as Harar. In the south they swarmed over the Banādir and the valleys of the Wēbi Shabēli and Jūba, from whence they repelled the Galla who were pushed north-west towards the valleys of the upper tributaries of the Jūba where the Boran now live. This Somali movement is said to have started in the fourteenth century when the Hawiyya (Ajurān) migrated to the region between the lower courses of the Wēbi and Jūba, but the movement did not become strong until the sixteenth century when the Galla were really set on the move. At that time the Somali consisted of fairly small groups, but ever since they have been increasing, especially during the last three generations, under the relatively peaceful conditions of European rule. At the same time their flocks have expanded beyond the limited feeding capacities of their ranges, and their continual infiltration into neighbouring territories has occasioned political difficulties. Even today the southward movement has not stopped.[1] In this process of expansion some of the Somali mixed with Galla and Bantu thereby giving rise to hybrid Somali tribes such as the Raḥanwēn who are Dijil in origin mixed with Galla, whilst some of the Ajurān have mixed with both Bantu and Galla. The northernmost tribe, the ʿĪsa (Dir in origin), who live in French and Ethiopian territory, have been much influenced by their greatest enemies, the ʿAfar, so much so that, apart from the language, they seem in customs and mode of life to be more ʿAfar than Somali.

*The Tribes and their Social Organization.* The Somali[2] are grouped into three great divisions; the Northern (Heggi), Hawiyya, and Sab. The Northern includes the great groups of Dir, Isāq, and Dārōd who

[1] The Somali first crossed the River Jūba between 1842 and 1848 (cf. *Handbook of Kenya Colony*, 1920, p. 234), and in 1909 the ʿAbd Wak and ʿAbdallah reached the Tana country in the Northern Frontier District of Kenya where the movement was checked and they are now obliged to keep to prescribed grazing areas.

[2] Little reliance can be placed upon any of the population figures. The Italian census of 1931 gave 922,814 for the whole population of Italian Somalia, but Professor C. A. Nallino thought it should be reduced by half (*Raccolta di Scritti*, ii. 7). In Harar Province, Somali and ʿAfar were estimated at 475,003 (Santagata, *Harar*, p. 92). The French estimate (1936) for their region was 23,728 Somalis and the British 344,700 (1932).

live in French and British territory, in Ethiopian Ogadēn and the northern parts of Italian Somalia. The Hawiyya (Ajurān, Gaggunḍabe, and Gurgate) occupy the whole of the Shabēli valley, and the Sab (Raḥanwēn, Dijil, and Tunni) live in the south-west (Banādir) between the Hawiyya and the Jūba river [1] Amongst the northern Somali live three tribes of outcastes, the last remnants of pre-Hamitic aboriginal peoples.[2] In central and southern Somali regions are remnants of the pre-existing Bantu inhabitants, having the status of serfs, who have assimilated the language of their conquerors and with whom they are now federated (e.g. the Shīdla in the middle valley of the Shabēli with the Mobilēn Somali; and the Shabēli in the middle Wēbi under the Ajurān). Poverty at home has forced large numbers of Somalis to seek work abroad, and they will be found along the Arabian coast and the Persian Gulf, in ports of India, Marseilles, Liverpool, Cardiff, and elsewhere.

The large northern groups of pure Somali origin ascribe their nobility, not to purer racial origins, but to an Arab origin. Now whilst it is true that many Somali tribes have absorbed some Arab blood this has in no way affected their peculiar characteristics. They are extremely proud of being Somali and though they may delight in the fiction that they are descendants of the Prophet or his companions and have constructed elaborate genealogies, they do not consider themselves Arabs, and inter-marriage with Arabs today is almost unknown. Many tribes have intermarried very considerably with Bantu and Galla since large numbers of the peoples conquered in their expansion remained as serfs, were absorbed by the conquerors and gave rise to Sab groups; but in spite of all this the Somali form a very definite ethnical and cultural type and are extremely proud of their race.

The foundation of society amongst the true Somali is the *rēr* (or *hēr*) or large kinship-group, which is self-contained and consists of a group of families, the offspring of a common ancestor by whose name (Habr A, Habr B, &c.) the *rēr* is known. When the *rēr* grows large it tends to split up into several *rēr* with new names, whilst the whole group constitutes a new tribe.[3] The individual's loyalty is not confined

[1] The dialectal grouping of the Somali language, according to Cerulli (*R.S.O.* viii. 693 ff.), corresponds to that of the main Somali divisions: Dārōd, spoken by about 45 per cent., including the large groups of Mijurtini, Ogadēn, Warsangālī, and Dūlbohānta; Hawiyya by about 30 per cent., especially in the valley of the Wēbi Shabēli; the Isāq by the 'Isa, Habr Yūnis, H. Awal, and H. Jalo; and the Sab by the Raḥanwēn and similar tribes.

[2] On these outcaste tribes see below, p. 224.

[3] The use here of the term 'tribe' is very largely arbitrary, for the political structure is not

to his own *rēr* but extended to the whole tribe to which he belongs by birth, whose privileges he can claim and to which he has obligations to perform. In such a system primogeniture plays a special part, and this assures a privileged position to the *rēr* descending from the eldest son of the common ancestor, which generally provides the chief of the tribe. If another Somali tribe or a group of non-Somali origin joins the tribe, they are regarded as 'clients' and remain in a position of inferiority. Economic and political necessities may force a *rēr* to migrate to other regions where it is autonomous, but the sentiment of common descent persists and forms a definite link with other members of the same tribal family.

On the other hand, the southern Sab (e.g. Raḥanwēn and Dijil) which consist of mixed somalized negroid-Galla agricultural groups, have a different system. Various causes, their mixed origin, security, historical or environmental reasons such as possession of cultivable land, pastures and watering places, have caused groups of varied origins to federate. Such a federation, not having a common ancestor, will often adopt the name of the locality they inhabit. Examples are the *Shān Dafēt*, 'the Five Dafēt', Dafēt being the name of the place and not the ancestor; *Seddīda rēr Egēn*, 'the three tribes of the red-land' (Tunni) in the region between the Wēbi and the Bravan coast. Along the Somali coast were also various small sultanates (Majērtēn, Hobya, Maqdishu, Brāva, Kismāyu), whose sultans once had the powers of constitutional monarchs; but these are outside the normal organization of Somali society and under European rule have lost all political importance.

In the true Somali organization each *rēr* (*hēr*) has a chief chosen by the elders. He is assisted in governing by a *shir* or committee of elders which deals with communal matters such as migration, grazing, and watering. The tribal chief's title varies considerably (*bogr* or *bohr*, *jarād*, *damīn* (Ar. *ḍamīn*, guarantee), *imām*, *malāq*, *ūgās*, *wobar*), his effective power is very small, depending upon his personality, prowess as a leader, liberality and family prestige, in other words, it depends upon tribal public opinion. It is generally weak because it is the *rēr* and not the large tribe as such which is the foundation of the social system, whilst the nomadic life develops the independent and individualistic spirit of the tribesmen who consider themselves the chief's equals.

stable. A tribe is called *ṭol* amongst the Hawiyya, sometimes the Arabic *qabīla* is used, but the terminology varies considerably, and a *rēr* may be a larger or smaller tribal unit.

The tribe as such has hardly any legal function since the patriarchal group is the outstanding feature. The elders' court (*sagale*) settles civil and criminal cases as well as social problems according to tribal custom. The acceptance of Islam has led to an accommodation of tribal custom to the *sharīʿa* in certain spheres, but the two often clash. The northern tribes, for instance, still retain the levirate. According to the *sharīʿa* a widow is free to marry whom she pleases, but tribal custom decrees that she shall not marry outside the family of her deceased husband. She is usually expected to marry one of her husband's brothers, but has some right of choice. This custom is called *dumal.*[1] In regions where there is a *sharīʿa* judge (*wadād* or *qāḍī*) the council will often send matters concerning personal status to him or seek his advice. In towns and settlements customary law cases come before a committee of elders (also called *shir*) which has power to decide criminal and civil cases. European control has meant a strengthening of the *sharīʿa* because the government has given executive power to the *qāḍī* as a recognized official of the established legal system. Feuds between tribes are a normal part of life. Actual clashes are not now so frequent amongst the tribes under European rule, but they are kept alive by disputes over blood-money,[2] which of course are *rēr* and not individual matters.

*Mode of Life.* The Somali may be divided into two categories whose ways of life and Islamic outlook are utterly different. The majority group are the nomadic herdsmen of the forest and steppe regions; and the minority group are the agriculturalists and townsmen who live in urban centres or in settlements and villages along the rivers. The townsmen were the first Somali to be islamized and for centuries have been in touch with Muslim culture. They are organized into communities bound together, not by tribal ties, but by bonds of citizenship. The townsmen play an important part in the life of the nomads whose representatives travel regularly to the towns to barter their sheep, goats, and oxen, and other produce such as hides and butter to satisfy requirements they cannot produce for themselves, such as rice, dates, and cloth. The community centres of the townsmen are the mosques and coffee-houses. In these they conduct all their affairs from marriages to business transactions. The organized Islamic life of this group is much more intense in contrast to the religious indifference of the nomad. We have already

[1] See R. E. Drake-Brockman, *British Somaliland* (1912), p. 146; N. Puccioni, *Antropologia e Etnografia delle gente della Somalia* (1931–6), iii. 102.

[2] The Arab term *diya* and the Somali *mag* are used for the compensation for murder or manslaughter; whilst the Somali *hagh* is used for injury or assault.

mentioned the village group organization of the agriculturalists, whilst another most important recent development, that of religious community collective-farms, will be mentioned later.[1]

The nomads of the *rēr* live a communal life with their flocks and herds continually moving within their respective grazing grounds in search of herbage and water-holes. The men, assisted by the children, care for the herds, milking the cows and camels, taking them to pasture, and returning them to the cattle enclosure (*zarība*) at night. Their animal husbandry displays considerable knowledge, they watch where their best beasts graze, care for them when they are ill, and remove ticks and other pests. The watering-places are their communal centres where they discuss the affairs of the *rēr* in the shade of the trees. The women attend to domestic duties, food preparation, wood collection, and butter making. It is also their duty to pull down and re-erect the hut[2] during their periodical removals, but the men erect and repair the thorn *zarība* in which the cattle are kept.

*Religion.* The South Arabians have naturally had continual trading relations with the east coast of Africa. The kingdom of Saba' possessed commercial establishments along the coast of Banādir especially for the incense trade and the *Periplus of the Erythræan Sea* shows that these ports were in the hands of Arabs in the first century A.D. Islam, as we have seen, was carried to the Somali coast at an early date through these Arab trading relations.[3] Coastal towns such as Zaila' and Maqdishu were developed through Arab and not Somali commercial enterprise. These centres had varying lengths of independence, and in time the Arab immigrants lost their racial characteristics and became completely Somalized though strongly Muslim. Ad-Dimishqī (1256–1327) wrote: 'the island of Berbera is inhabited by black Muslims who follow the

[1] See below, pp. 238–9.

[2] The commonest type of nomadic hut is the *gūri*, a temporary hut of sticks bent to make an arch and covered with matting. In the coastal towns the huts (called *'arīsh*) are made of wattle and daub, matting or grass.

[3] The Somali have a tradition (see G. Révoil, *La Vallée du Darror*, 1882, pp. 315–16) that one Jabarti b. Ismā'īl was shipwrecked in A.H. 75 on the coast and lived in the grotto of Gōd-Baroro near Cape Guardafui. Acquiring renown through his powers of discovering hidden treasures he was able to marry Dubarra, a relation of the King of Dur. He had a son named Harti (Dārōd) who was the ancestor of the Dūlbahanta, Dechichi, Majērtēni, and Warsangāli tribes. Tradition also relates that in the fifteenth century a Sharīf Isḥāq b. Aḥmad left the Ḥaḍramawt with forty-four saints and landed at Makhan on the windward coast. He settled down at the town of Met near Burnt Island, where his tomb still exists, and became the father of noble families claiming Arab ancestry through the children of Magadle, producing the Ba Habr Magadle tribes, and through an Abyssinian woman whose sons founded the Ba Habr Habushed tribes; L. Robecchi Bricchetti, *Nel Paese degli Aromi* (Milan, 1903), pp. 114–17.

Zaidite and Shāfiʿite rites'.[1] Maqdishu, which was at first almost entirely composed of Arab immigrants, resisted the process longest. It remained independent throughout the period of the Ottoman-Portuguese struggle and was only occupied by Saif I of ʿOmān in 1698 for a short period. By this time it was completely somalized, even the ruling clans changing their name, the Muqrī clan, for instance, which has always provided Maqdishu with its *qāḍī*, becoming the Rēr Faqīh.

From these centres the coastal tribes were first influenced, but the islamization of the tribes of the interior was a very slow process, in which Islam had to contend against a virile paganism and especially a body of customary law which is still even in our day resisting the encroachment of the *sharīʿa*. Gradually these tribes accepted a nominal Islam, but they remained independent and mutually antagonistic tribes until the nineteenth century when France and Britain in 1884, Ethiopia in 1886, and Italy in 1889 occupied the whole of Somali territory.

In religious knowledge and practice a vast difference will be distinguished between the nomads, on the one hand, and the townspeople and villagers on the other. Orthodox Islam is naturally strongest in the coastal towns which have long been in touch with the wider Islamic world. In these towns schools of learning developed and scholars went abroad to study in other centres. In the interior the only Islamic centres are the collective farm *ṭarīqa* settlements.

The nomadic Somali is by nature neither fervently nor fanatically religious. The rising of Muḥammad ibn ʿAbd Allāh at the beginning of this century did not grow and gain impetus on religious grounds, and the call to the *jihād* as such did not awaken response in either townsman or peasant or nomad. As in the Sudan so in Somalia it is the Hamite-Negroid mixture which is more stirred by religion. The true Somali has tended to accept the exterior forms of Islam whilst remaining comparatively unchanged in his inner life. Islam satisfies him just because it does not attempt to revolutionize his inner life. He rarely prays, few seem even to know any prayers other than the *fātiḥa*, but he is prepared to perform certain formal duties of Islam provided that they are easy to carry out and affect neither his social customs nor his real interests. If he does pray he prefers to pray communally or in the open if he is seeking a reputation for piety. What he enjoys is anything belonging to the social side of religion such as the *mūlid* celebrations of his favourite saint. He loves to take part in his own imperfectly islamized

[1] Ad-Dimishqī, ed. Mehren (Leipzig, 1923), p. 162.

pagan rites and ceremonies, which he feels to be really necessary, as formal prayer is not, to keep him on the right side of potent influences in the unseen world.[1]

The priests of the nomad are the *wadāds* who are itinerant friars; but even these, with the exception of some few who may have studied at *ṭarīqa* settlements, are invariably ignorant. Little real study goes on even in the *ṭarīqa* settlements where the day is spent on the cultivation. Most members never even learn to read or write, for they know by heart the hymns and *awrād* they have to sing or recite after prayers or at the *dhikr*. Sir Richard Burton writes of one of his companions:

> This worthy never prays, and can neither read nor write; but he knows a chapter or two of the Koran, recites audibly a long *Rātib* or task, morning and evening, whence, together with his store of hashed Ḥadīth (tradition), he derives the title of *Widād* or hedge-priest.[2]

This is as true now as it was then. The majority of the *wadāds* cannot write a letter in intelligible Arabic, but they have mastered sufficient sections of the Qur'ān for use in impressing and for prophylactic purposes, for their chief business in life is to treat illness and devise amulets (*herzi*, Arabic *ḥirz*) which will guard the wearer against the evil eye, or help him to acquire a woman or wealth or children. Dr. Drake-Brockman writes of the *wadāds*:

> These people, who are easily distinguished by their headgear, which consists of a small grass-woven skull cap round which is rolled a turban, and the usual cloth trousers worn by most Mohammedans, are, as a rule, a quiet, well-behaved, and unoffending class, who either live in small colonies known as 'tarikas', or wander from village to village throughout the year, entirely dependent on charity for the necessaries of life. . . . These itinerant priests must not be confounded with the self-seeking products of the coast towns, who only preach the Word as a means to an end.[3]

## 16. MUSLIM NEGROID TRIBES

### (*a*) *Baria and Kunama*

In the Barentu area of south-west Eritrea are two negroid tribes, the Kunāma[4] who number about 15,000 and inhabit the inhospitable

[1] On the state of Islamic knowledge and practice amongst the ʿIsa see L. Robecchi Bricchetti, *Nell' Harar* (Milan, 2nd edn., 1896), pp. 68–70.

[2] R. F. Burton, *First Footsteps* (mem. ed.), i. 17.

[3] R. E. Drake-Brockman, op. cit., pp. 108–10.

[4] The Kunāma are called Badēn or Bazēn by the Abyssinians and Bāza by the Sudanese. They are mentioned by Arabic authors, Al-Yaʿqūbī (*Hist.* i. 218), Ibn Ḥawqal (ed. H. Kramers, i. 55, 57), and Maqrīzī (*Khiṭaṭ*, i. 310, 315).

region between the Gash and Setit, and the Baria (9,500) who live north of the Gash. They are remnants of tribes which were at one time much more widespread in the lowlands extending as far as the River Atbara[1] and have been gradually pushed into their present habitat by Beja pressure. These two pagan peoples were regarded as legitimate prey by all the surrounding tribes. They have been raided regularly by the Banī ʿĀmir and other Beja tribes from the north and west and by Abyssinians from Tigrai and Amḥara country. Organized raids by the Abyssinian royal forces are recorded in 1585 by Sarṣa Dengel and in 1692 by Iyāsu I.

Both tribes are sedentary agriculturalists living in large permanent villages. Their languages, so far as our present knowledge goes, are unrelated to any other languages in Africa and to each other. The Baria are entirely Muslim but most of the Kunāma are still pagan, their rites being similar to those of some Nūba groups of southern Kordofan.[2] Although many were converted to a nominal Islam during the last century they can scarcely be called self-consciously Muslim. Others have been influenced by Roman Catholic and Swedish Protestant missions, both of which have formed churches.[3]

The Baria are divided into two main sections, the Nerē of the Hajar (Mogolo) district and the Mogarēb, so called from the district of that name. Before the Egyptian occupation they were independent tribes though they paid some tribute to the Banī ʿĀmir, but after the foundation of Kasala when the Egyptians became dominant in the region they paid them tribute.

Lejean, who travelled in Eritrea 1860–64, writes:

> Vers 1856, les Égyptiens étaient venus à Koufit pour prêcher l'islamisme à coups de fusil aux Barea: ils avaient razzié quelques villages, emmené force captifs, et les avaient remis en liberté sur leur promesse de se faire musulmans. C'est pour cela que le village frontière de Mogollo et un autre voisin ont, seuls parmi les Barea, embrassé l'islamisme.[4]

From this time Islam made considerable progress amongst the Nerē,

[1] Eratosthenes (276–194 B.C.) and other Greek writers mention the Μεγάβαροι and the Blemyes between Meroë and the Red Sea. Their name for the River Atbara Ἀσταβόρας probably meant 'river of the Baria'. They appear under the form Bāryā in the inscriptions of the Axumite kings ʿĒzānā (*D.A.E.* iv. 33) and Ḥaṣāni Dān'ēl (ibid. 43). They are mentioned by many Arabic authors, ʿAbd Allāh b. Aḥmad al-Aswānī (Maqrīzī, *Khiṭaṭ*, ed. Weit. iii. 258–9); Ibn Ḥawqal (ed. H. Kramers, i. 55); Maqrīzī (*Ilmām*, p. 2); and Qalqashandī (*Ṣubḥ*, v. 303). The word Bāryā has become the equivalent of 'slave' amongst the Abyssinians.

[2] On their paganism see A. Pollera, *I Baria e I Cunama* (Rome, 1913), pp. 78–97.

[3] In 1931 the religious distribution of the Kunāma was 5,160 Christians, 7,000 Muslims, and 3,140 pagans.

[4] G. Lejean, *Voyage aux deux Nils*, p. 145.

especially at Bisha and in the villages of Shilko and Hebredda, whose inhabitants in any land dispute put their cases either before the *qāḍī* of the Banī ʿĀmir or the *qāḍī* at Kasala. In 1861 the Baria were raided by the Abyssinians of ʿAdi-ʿAbo who burnt Mogolo. In consequence the unfortunate people had to pay tribute to both Abyssinians and Egyptians. Abyssinian pressure also caused a temporary set-back in the movement to Islam,[1] but later when Egyptian rule strengthened the movement to Islam became stronger until it affected the whole tribe. Under Italian rule it was able to recover in numbers and prosperity.

The Baria are divided into clans like the Kunāma, but during the Egyptian régime in the Sudan they acquired a paramount chief who was given the official title of *nāẓir*. Their language seems to have been subjected to Hamitic influence in its grammatical forms, though its vocabulary remains pure. Islamic conceptions have overlaid many of the original features of their pagan culture. More especially it has caused radical change in the structure of family life, for this is the first thing to be affected by Islam. Marriage customs and relationships have been changed and observers report that the former freedom and equality of women has been replaced by complete subjugation. Descent is now counted in the paternal line in contrast to the Kunāma who retain the matrilinear system. At the same time their social life is bound up with a deep substratum of animistic beliefs and practices. They pay great attention to talismans, curses, and incantations, their rain-makers (*atfai*) still exist, elaborate death ceremonials are observed, and their clans retain their magic powers.

### (*b*) *Bani Shangūl Region*

The term Bani Shangūl is applied to the tribes occupying that part of Abyssinia which lies between the Blue Nile and the Sudan border. These peoples border upon the Como and the Lēqa Sibu Galla on the south and east, and with kindred tribes of Berta in the Sudan Fazogli region on the west; in the north the Blue Nile divides them from negroid tribes living west of Agaomeder. They speak various dialects kindred to those spoken by the Berta of the Sudan, and many are quite clearly an islamized section of the Berta. The Abyssinians call all negroes Shānqēla, and the Arabic-speaking Sudanese came to call this particular group the Bani Shangūl.[2] These Berta are a confedera-

[1] Cf. G. Douin, *Histoire du Règne du Khédive Ismaïl*, vol. iii, pt. 1, p. 44.

[2] Chataway has suggested that *Banu* is not Arabic but is a corruption of *bela*, the Berta word for 'hill', *S.N.R.* xvii. 112.

tion of mixed blood, but regard themselves as belonging to a single stock.

Islamic influence first penetrated into the region through the Funj kingdom of Sennār which claimed a vague overlordship of its people, but, as in neighbouring regions like Guba which are still pagan though under a Muslim governor, Dejazmach Abū Shōk, it had little effect upon the religious complexion of the country. The rulers of both Fazogli and Bani Shangūl were a branch of the Hamaj rulers of Keili; and a sister of Dawra Maias, second king of Keili, founded the Bani Shangūl line about 1720.[1]

These various negroid groups were converted to Islam by fekis from the Eastern Sudan who married the daughters of the chiefs and whose descendants constituted an aristocracy of masters, the rest of the people having the status of slaves. These aristocratic groups are known as *Waṭāwīṭ* (literally 'bats'), and constitute about ten per cent. of the population of the Bani Shangūl region. In the Anglo-Egyptian Sudan, of course, the Berta subjects are no longer slaves.

This area was visited in 1835 by J. Russegger, an Austrian sent by Muḥammad ʿAlī to report on the gold resources of his dominions. He wrote that this whole region was called by the Arabs *dār al-Berta*, that among the natives of the Dul range and neighbouring countries are many Donqolāwī *jallāba* (traders) who carried on the gold trade in particular. These Danāqla were much looked up to by the negroes, and propagated a knowledge of Arabic, protecting all travellers other than white men.[2] When Beltrame, an Italian missionary, visited the Bani Shangūl region in 1855 he found there two chiefs, Shaikh al-Faḍlī, a Jaʿalī refugee who had taken part in the burning of Ismāʿīl Pasha at Shendi in 1821, whilst the other was a Berta. Beltrame's description[3] shows that the people were Berta with a ruling aristocracy of Jaʿaliyyīn and that Islam was gaining ground. A Donqolāwī (Rikābiyya) slave-trader, Shaikh Khōjalī, later became the most powerful chief in the area, and another Italian traveller, Matteucci, speaks of meeting him in 1878. After the conquest of Menelik in 1898 Shaikh Khōjalī succeeded in preserving its autonomy subject to the payment of a tribute of alluvial gold. Later the whole region was unified into one province under Khōjalī. The Italians formed a Bani Shangūl Com-

[1] Cf. Chataway, *S.N.R.* xiii. 255.

[2] See J. Russegger, *Reise in Ägypten, Nubien, und Ost-Sudan* (Stuttgart, 1844), II. ii. 576.

[3] Quoted in *S.N.R.* xvii. 218–23.

missariat comprising the region inhabited by Berta, Gamosha, and Waṭāwīṭ.[1]

The chief of these political groups, living along both sides of the Khor Dabus (or Yabus) is the Khōjalī tribe whom the Galla call Shōgale. The ruling class pretend an Arab origin though as we have seen they are Donqolāwī mixed with negroid Berta. Their Berta subjects are arabized to the extent of calling themselves Muslim, though the majority of their customs are frankly pagan. They are bilingual, speaking Sudan Arabic as a lingua franca as well as their own dialects. Cerulli writes:

> Their Arabic is, naturally, that of the Sudan; and, as always happens in Muslim countries, the foreign domination, in this case Abyssinian, has necessarily led to the favouring of Arabic to the detriment of the local Berta dialects, either for immediate practical reasons or indirectly, provoking by reaction a major feeling of Muslim solidarity.[2]

The chief activities of these people, apart from their basic agriculture, are the caravan trade with the Sudan, which includes the slave-trade,[3] and gold-washing during the rains. They are Shāfiʿite in *madhhab* and the *ṭarīqas* of the Eastern Sudan have many followers amongst them, the prevailing one being the Tijāniyya.

## (*c*) *Bantu and Somalized Bantu Groups*

In southern Somaliland, especially along the banks of the Jūba and

[1] The Italians divided this Commissariat into two residencies whose chiefs and population were:

| | *District* | *Chief* | *Population* |
|---|---|---|---|
| Residenza di Asosa: | | | |
| | Asosa | Shaikh al-Khōjalī | 8,000 |
| | Belfodio | At-Tōm Muḥammad | 5,500 |
| | Corcalifa | Amīr Rabbu | 3,500 |
| | Bashīr | Shaikh Nāṣir ʿAlī | 9,000 |
| | Dul | Shaikh Maḥmūd Ḥāmid | 7,000 |
| Residenza di Becca: | | | |
| | Becca | Shaikh ʿAbd al-Khair | 35,000 |
| | Cacogula | Muḥammad al-Amīn | 7,000 |

[2] E. Cerulli, *E.O.* ii. 112.

[3] M. Perham writes: 'Every year slaves found refuge and took out freedom papers across the border. In 1933, for example, 255 slaves from Beni-Shangul and Guba gained their freedom in this way in the Sudan; and a whole village of 126 people fled and were settled near Roseires. Indeed, the Watawit and even the governor himself, were for years a great problem to the Sudan Government because of their encouragement of poaching and slaving expeditions. In 1929 Khogali's wife was sentenced by a Sudan court to ten years' imprisonment for her share in a great slave kidnapping conspiracy extending into the Sudan (*The Government of Ethiopia*, p. 327).

Shabēli, live various groups of negroid agriculturalists belonging to the Bantu group, some of whom have adopted the language of their Somali overlords, whilst others speak Ki-Swahili and other Bantu languages. These negroes are the remnants of the original inhabitants of the fluvial region of Somaliland who were overwhelmed by the wave of Somali conquest.[1] Though they were freed by the Italians from actual slave status some of them continued to regard themselves as morally subject to Somali tribes (e.g. the Shīdla to the Mobilēn), whilst others formed themselves into autonomous villages or federations of villages, such as the Elāy of Baiḍoa and the Shabēli.

These Bantu groups comprise the Wa Gosha, Gobawein, Wa Boni, and Ribi in the Jūba region; and the Shīdla, Shabeli, Dube,[2] Makane, Rēr 'Isa, Kawole, and Giddu in the Shabeli region. Most of these groups adopted Islam from the Somali[3] and, whilst it may rest very lightly upon some of them whose social life remains distinctively pagan, others have been deeply influenced, for Islam was able to give them the spiritual stability which they had lost when their tribes were broken up.

## 17. MINOR GROUPS

### (*a*) *Arabs*

Arab immigrants are found all over the region, in the coastal towns from Maṣawwaʿ to Maqdishu and in all the chief commercial centres in the interior.[4] Coming mainly from the Yaman and Ḥaḍramawt they have been impelled through poverty at home to seek their fortunes abroad. The social handicap which they suffered in their new environment through having to contend against the instinctive prejudices of the natives amongst whom they settled compelled them to take whatever opportunities were open to them. Since the Abyssinian is essentially either a warrior or a land-hungry peasant, the immigrants became traders or artisans of various kinds, especially bricklayers and carpenters. A large number of them are temporary immigrants and do not bring

[1] On these groups see E. Cerulli, 'Gruppi etnici negri nella Somalia', *A.A.E.* lxiv (1934), 177–84.

[2] The Dube and Shabeli are often referred to as the Adone (correctly *Addōn*), but this is merely the Somali Dārōd word for 'slave' and is their designation for these northern groups; cf. L. Robecchi Bricchetti, *Somalia e Benadir* (Milan, 1899), pp. 417–21.

[3] Some have remained pagan, e.g. the Wa Boni who are not Bantu, cf. *Guida*, p. 580.

[4] In Maṣawwaʿ, for example, the Arabs numbered 2,700 out of a total population of 9,300 in 1931; in Harar Province (pop. 1,517,833) they number 5,543 of whom about 1,000 live in Harar city; in the Jibuti administrative area of French Somaliland there are 4,083 Arabs out of a total population of 12,986, most of whom live in the town of Jibuti.

their families, but make temporary unions (*mut'a*) with local women.[1] In Jimma a large settlement of Yamanites grew up during the last century, whose descendants by Galla women, although permanently settled, continue to keep themselves as a distinct element from the rest of the population.

In the Empire, following an exchange of letters between the Imām Yaḥyā and the Emperor Hāyla Sellassē, it was agreed that the Yamanites should be placed under the Ethiopian Government from the administrative point of view, but the Arabs from Aden and the Ḥaḍramawt are under British protection. All these immigrants are usually united in an association or trade-guild under an elected shaikh who looks after their interests and settles disputes.

In 1846 a whole nomad tribe, the Rashā'ida, migrated across the Red Sea into the Eritrean Sāḥil.[2] They can still scarcely be distinguished from an Arabian tribe and keep themselves distinct from other tribes. They are the only group of permanent immigrants who have preserved their own dialect, culture, and occupation intact. The main body lives in the Kasala area and a smaller group near Tessanai.

In addition to these, as we have seen, other Arab families and large numbers of odd individuals have been completely assimilated into local tribes to whom they have given a fiction of Arab aristocracy.

### (*b*) *West African Sudanese*

In certain regions of Eritrea immigrants from the Western Sudan known as Takrūr are found. The greater part are a fluctuating population of pilgrims to Mecca who work at various centres whilst in transit, but others have settled down permanently to agriculture. At Qalabāt (formerly Metemma) is a colony of Takrūr who were already esta-

[1] The disproportionate number of men to women is shown in Addis Ababa where in 1938 there were 1,563 Arabs of whom 934 were men, 244 women, and the rest children; *B.S.G.I.*, ser. vii, vol. v (1940), p. 170.

[2] The Rashā'ida came first to the region between Sawākin and 'Aqīq, but the Mahdiyya outburst caused the tribe to move more to the south along the coast of the Sāḥil whence part returned later to Anglo-Egyptian territory. They are chiefly breeders of camels and goats, but are also good cultivators in contrast to the other pastoral tribes of the Sāḥil. They number about 1,000 of whom about 250 have moved to Tessanai as cultivators. They are divided into three main kinship groups, Zinenu, Barasa, and Baratik; a fourth group of fishermen, Jāhidīn, who occupied the barren islands of Dohol and Harāt in the north of the Dahlak archipelego, found them too inhospitable and returned to Arabia. The Rashā'ida live scattered about in small family groups with their goats and camels. In dress and customs they remain an Arab tribe. The women wear the voluminous clothes of the *badawiyyāt* and veil their faces completely, the girls half veil; the men in addition to the white cotton *jubba* wear an '*abāya* of woven camel hair, with *kufiyya* and '*aqāl* on their head.

blished there in the time of Burckhardt (1814). Other colonies are found at Tessanai, Nogara, Agordat, Keren, Asmara, and Maṣawwaʿ. In Asmara there is a large settlement of Sudanese from the Anglo-Egyptian Sudan. The 1931 census for Eritrea put the total of westerners at 3,700 whilst the British after their occupation estimated them at about 8,000. Takrūr are also found in the Ethiopian provinces of Wālqayt and ʿAdi ʿAbo. These westerners are robust and intelligent workers, but are despised by the local tribes.

### (*c*) *The Argobba*

The people known under this name consist of two isolated groups speaking the same Semitic language, about whom little is known. The Argobba North, who number about 2,000 to 2,500, are first mentioned in the *Futūḥ*.[1] They live in the region of the Borkenna, a tributary of the Ḥawāsh, which is part of the former kingdom of Ifāt. Their chief still retains the title of Walasmaʿ and Major Harris refers to a Walasmaʿ Abagāz as the hereditary governor of Argobba subject to Shoa, whose job it was to maintain good relations with the ʿAfar in order to facilitate the caravan traffic to Harar and the coast.[2] The Argobba South (300–400) live on the hills south of Harar between the Besidimo and Gobelli valleys amongst the Ala Galla. Their tradition relates that they were led to this region by a Shaikh ʿUmar two hundred years ago.[3] O. Neumann says they 'are strict, even fanatical Mohammedans'.[4]

### (*d*) *Outcaste Peoples*

Scattered about north-east Africa are various pariah castes. They are remnants of former aboriginal negroid peoples who have not been absorbed and live amongst the peoples who subjected them as primitive hunters or performing despised and feared occupations such as smithery or magic.

The Wayṭo are a hunting caste, who live on the banks of the Abāy and the southern and western shores of Lake Ṭāna and ply the rafts made of bundles of papyrus (called *tānkwā* in Amharic). They are Muslims but are despised by their co-religionists.[5] R. E. Cheesman writes of them:

> Waitos are now converted to Muhammedanism and speak Amharic. Their

[1] *Futūḥ*, p. 175.

[2] W. C. Harris, op. cit. i. 324–5; ii. 346.

[3] M. Cohen, *Études d'Éthiopien Méridional* (Paris, 1931), p. 360, n. 1.

[4] O. Neumann, 'From the Somali Coast through Southern Ethiopia', *Geog. Journ.* xx (1902), 374.

[5] H. Rassam, *British Mission to King Theodore* (1869), i. 314.

original language and the rites and ceremonies of their old beliefs are forgotten. The cult of the hippopotamus is one of the few survivals of ancient custom; they eat the flesh and no man can marry until he has killed one.[1]

Others say that they are still practising pagans. Mittwoch says that they are unacquainted with the Qur'ān, but use such Arabic phrases as *al-ḥamdu li'llāh* and celebrate the feast of *'Arafa* on the 10th *Dhū'l-ḥijja*.[2] Their Islam is purely superficial and they have merely absorbed a few oddments from Islamic culture. They do not circumcise and eat flesh such as the hippopotamus which is impure to Muslims.

Amongst the Somali live various tribes of outcastes. The chief of these are the Mijān, a serf-caste who are hunters or trappers and also act as hewers of wood and drawers of water for the Somali tribes, amongst whom they are scattered; the Yibir, a sorcerer-caste who exist on the fees they are paid for charms and amulets; and the Tomal who are a smith-caste. About these outcastes Kirk remarks, 'they profess to be Mohammedans like pure Somalis, but the Midgans are very lax in their religion, being unclean in the matter of the meat they eat'.[3] These castes, by an Islamic rationalization, are regarded as being in a perpetual state of ritual impurity (*najāsa*). They do not form separate groups but live amongst the various Somali tribes.

[1] R. E. Cheesman, 'Lake Tana and Its Islands', *Geog. Journ.* lxxxv (1935), 491.

[2] Mittwoch, 'Proben aus dem amarischen Volksmunde', *Mitt. d. Sem. f. Orient. Sprachen zu Berlin*, vol. x, pt. 2, pp. 214–15.

[3] J. W. C. Kirk, *A Grammar of the Somali Language* (1905), p. 184.

# 4

# Special Characteristics of Islam in the Region

In our study of the religious life of the Muslims of this region we shall need to distinguish between various layers. The topmost layer is that of traditional orthodox Islam. Although Arabian centres are so close, this influence has yet been very weak, probably because no permanent Muslim Kushitic kingdoms were able to develop as cultural nuclei from which Islam could radiate. Apart from the coastal towns where orthodox Islam is strongest, only the city-state of Harar has been able to maintain a continuous influence throughout the centuries.

Then there is the influence of an esoteric Islam which has been creeping in, especially during the last century, through the emissaries of the dervish orders. Consequently the performance of the *dhikr* and practices connected with saint-worship are becoming more and more the focal centre of their Islam than formerly and are bringing a fervour and devotion into the religion of the people which could never be evoked by orthodox Islam.

But stronger perhaps than either orthodox or esoteric Islam in its influence upon their actual religious life is the pre-Islamic sediment. As in the rest of Muslim Africa there has been a symbiosis between this sediment and Islam. Although they feel themselves to be true and loyal Muslims superstition and magic pervade their Islam and reveal the influence of their former Kushite paganism. The various peoples of the region are at all possible stages of the Islamic path, but everywhere can be seen the process by which Islam assimilates those inerradicable rites and beliefs which it is powerless to abolish by attaching to them orthodox interpretations and explanatory Muslim legends.

## I. THE ORTHODOX SYSTEM

### (*a*) *Orthodox Observance*

The aim of orthodox Islam is the maintaining of Muslim solidarity by the formation of a collective mentality. It seeks to canalize and direct religious feelings so that they become conventional. This is the primary aim of Muslim education, but in addition to the formal education as the means of preserving the Islamic cultural tradition, there is the educational influence of the whole milieu into which the individual is born, for this determines his life and ensures social and cultural continuity. The numerous events of social and family life, circumcision, marriage, and death, each have their prescribed usage. Again there is conformity in manners, dress, bearing, mode of speech, and the expressions employed. All these religious and communal relationships are directed by the *sharīʿa*, the great fossil-bearing strata of the Islamic structure, because this is the primary means of unifying the group. Outward observance is the important thing, and the community is limited to this and not to interference with the inner life which is a matter between the individual and God. The genius of Islam is the preservation of individualism through all these means of maintaining the religious-social unity. The very means for the formation of a collective mentality, such as prayer, fasting, and the pilgrimage, are truly individual acts, and each Muslim keeps his own individuality and learns to respect that of others within prescribed Islamic limits. This preservation of a measure of individualism has not normally led to schism for two reasons: because of the tremendous force of Islamic collectivism, and also because Islam allowed for other formations, within the religious body, yet outside that ruled by the *sharīʿa*, formations which catered for pressing needs of the spiritual life unsatisfied by the formal means of worship. The religious fraternities are the outstanding example of such formations; though of course the leaders of these fraternities, in order not to have the religious authorities against them, must affirm first of all their spiritual descent through orthodox Ṣūfi doctors. Orthodox Islam, therefore, is of paramount importance in the life of the Muslim community, whilst its influence upon the deeper life of the spirit is correspondingly weak.

Although Islam does not in principle recognize tribal and national differences and loyalties, in fact the various peoples put racial prejudices before the religious feeling of fraternity. Antagonism and hatred often exist between peoples and tribes and this may be carried over into places where they are obliged to live together. Throughout the towns of this region, as in most urban centres of African Islam, adherence to Islam does not lead to unity of leadership and worship amongst different cultural groups. Although they are all Muslims and may be closely associated in other ways, the various peoples have not mixed and each lives its own distinct communal life. This also includes racial discrimination in religion, each group having its own saints, religious leaders, and places of worship. Harar city is a good example; its population, apart from two thousand Christians, consists of twelve thousand

Hararīs proper who speak the unique city language, ten to fifteen thousand Galla, a thousand Arabs, and a thousand or more Somalis. Within the city's ancient walls these various peoples have not intermingled. Although Islam is common to all they do not practice it in common. When they pray they congregate in their own places under their own *imām*. They have distinct Qur'ān-schools, and, since the introduction of the Ḥanafiyya *madhhab*, they are often distinguished in rite.

The effect of Islam upon the position of women varies according to the depth of the islamization. In general, the greater the hold of orthodox institutions the lower becomes the status of women. There are, however, notable exceptions. The position of women amongst many of the Jabarti and in Hararian society is much higher than amongst most Muslims. The comments of Muḥammad Mukhtār, an officer who was in Harar during the Egyptian occupation, could be applied to the women of Harar of today:

> Chose remarquable . . . la femme est très respectée, au moins autant que chez les nations chrétiennes. Elle a beaucoup d'influence sur son mari qui est aux petits soins pour elle; ce que la femme veut, le Harrari le veut et son moindre désir est obéi comme un ordre et sur-le-champ. . . . Elles sont les premières à aider leurs maris à gagner le pain journalier et dans ses travaux manuels.[1]

He also says that the Hararīs, with the exception of the *amīr*, had only one wife, whilst divorce was practically unknown. As a natural consequence, he adds, they are virtuous and chaste [2]

The influence of orthodox Islam is exercised by official religious representatives such as *qāḍīs* and mosque functionaries; by students who have studied in Harar, Jimma, the coastal towns, and abroad, who on their return set up Qur'ān-schools wherever there are any Muslims; by 'holy' families claiming Arab descent who have been a great factor in spreading and consolidating Islam; and by Yamanite and other trading-colonies which usually have a shaikh teaching the recitation of the Qur'ān.

The towns are the chief centres of organized Islamic life. Mosques are found only in cities and towns. Villages generally have a space under a tree consecrated by usage for congregational prayer. In southern Ethiopia the men, if not working in the fields, gather together at midday in these places, perform the *ṣalāt* and continue sitting in a

[1] Mohammed Moktar, 'Notes sur le pays de Harrar', *Bulletin de la Société Khédivale de Géographie*, i. 365.

[2] Ibid. 366–7.

circle, chewing *kāt*[1] and mumbling prayers. On Friday nights the so-called learned and pious often pass the whole night under a tree or in a mosque chewing and murmuring their prayers. The Friday prayer is naturally the best attended and some love to leave the dust on their forehead as a sign of their piety.

How strictly Ramaḍān is kept it is difficult to say. In towns and amongst families like the Ād Shaikh who have a reputation for piety to keep up it is universally observed, but some of the nomad tribes are very lax in keeping it. The Galla have a practice of purging themselves during the days preceding the fast in order to expel, not only the impure food and forbidden drink they have consumed throughout the year, but also the pagan practices in which they have indulged. As elsewhere overeating is the rule during Ramaḍān and the food bill of the towns-people doubles itself. Each region or group has its own Ramaḍān speciality. In the south it is *kori* and *fettfett* (meat soup and crumbled

[1] *Catha edulis* or *celastrus edulis*. The word is pronounced *qāt* in Arabic, *kāt* by Muslim Ethiopians, *chāt* by Christians, and *gofa* by Galla. Maqrīzī (*Ilmām*, p. 7), who speaks of its usage amongst the peoples of Ifāt, especially by scholars to keep them awake over the dreary tomes of Muslim law, calls it *jāt*. The district of Harar is the chief centre of its cultivation. Chewed in small doses it causes a pleasant insomnia, in larger doses a slight intoxication. In flavour it is slightly bitter and astringent.

*Kāt* is first mentioned in the 'Wars of ʿAmda Ṣyōn' (Perruchon, p. 331), when Ṣabr ad-Dīn, boasting of what he will do when he conquers the Christian kingdom, says ' "I will take up my residence at Marʿadi, the capital of his kingdom, and I will plant *chāt* there", because the Muslims love this plant'. Al-ʿUmarī (op. cit., pp. 11–13) gives an interesting account of its usage in Ifāt. According to tradition, Shaikh Ibrāhīm Abū Zaḥarbūi introduced *kāt* into Yaman from Abyssinia. Ibrāhīm Abū Zaḥarbūi, 'was one of the forty-four Hasrami saints who landed at Berberah, sat in solemn conclave upon Auliya Kumbo or Holy Hill, and thence dispersed far and wide for the purpose of propagandism. He travelled to Harar about 1430, converted many to Al-Islam, and left there an honoured memory. His name is immortalized in Al-Yaman by the introduction of *Al-Qāt*' (R. F. Burton, *First Footsteps*, i. 54). This account is purely legendary because Al-ʿUmarī (loc. cit.) writing about 1345, gives another account of its introduction into Yaman in the reign of Al-Mu'ayyad Dā'ūd who personally found good reason for rejecting it. The Muslims of Harar have a legend that two saints who used to pass the night in prayer often found themselves dropping off to sleep, so they prayed God to give them something to keep them awake. Whereupon an angel appeared and revealed the shrub to them.

*Kāt* usage is spread over South Arabia and the Muslim regions of Abyssinia (except amongst the ʿAfar). It is not used by Christians, but plays a great part in the social life of the Muslims, and great chewings take place at the festivals of birth, circumcision, and marriage, and at tomb vigils. It is the first thing offered to a guest. Many Muslims have become weak-minded from excessive indulgence. It is not chewed by many women except witches and wise women. Muḥammad Mukhtār (loc. cit., pp. 368–9) describes a *kāt*-party he attended in Harar, which lasted from nine to eleven in the morning, during which chapters of the Qur'ān and praises of the Prophet were chanted. Many of the Muslims of the south, when they wish to cultivate their fields, call the people of the neighbourhood together and then drink the infusion made from coffee rind called *hoja* and chew *kāt* from six in the morning until ten. Then stimulated by the *kāt* they can work until evening without stopping.

bread); they drink *hoja* (an infusion made from coffee rind), tea, and milk, and pass as much time as possible during the day in sleeping.

In spite of the proximity of the holy places very few perform the pilgrimage to Mecca,[1] but those who hold religious and teaching offices try to go because it enhances their prestige amongst their ignorant and superstitious co-religionists.

The usual festival celebrations are observed throughout the region. Nothing very unusual has been noted about the practice of the highland Muslims and coastal townees. For *al-ʿId al-kabīr* or *ʿArafa* (the last word is extended to the whole month of *Dhūʾl-ḥijja* in southern Ethiopia and Somalia) and *al-ʿId aṣ-ṣaghīr* they first perform the *ṣalāt* in the open air outside the town and listen to the *imām* preach a *khuṭba*, then return in procession to slaughter their victim (*ḍaḥīya*) of whose flesh some is eaten by the household and some given to the poor. During the festivals they put on new clothes, make social calls, visit saints' tombs and family graves and, if connected with a *ṭarīqa*, perform the *dhikr*. In Addis Ababa they organize horsemanship displays in the city itself and on the plain of Fel-Woha for three days.[2]

Teaching shaikhs of various kinds run Qur'ān-schools in all Muslim centres. The terminology employed over such a wide area varies considerably. *Shaikh* (pl. *shuyūkh*) and *faqīr* (pl. *fuqarā*) are universal in the north, where also the Northern Sudan *faki* (pl. *fuqarā*, not *fuqahā* except in the specialized sense of 'juris-consult') will be heard. *Wadād* (pl. *wadādīn*) is universal amongst the Somali; *kabīr* (Ar. 'the exalted') in Harar and amongst the Galla of southern Ethiopia.[3] The Hararīs also use *mumie* for grade of teacher inferior to the *kabīr*.[4] Wherever a settled Islamic community exists there is someone who has memorized the Qur'ān and runs a school. He owns a plot of ground, cultivates with the help of his pupils, and leads the prayers at the traditional place under the village sacred tree. Often he is the local witch-doctor, he dispenses amulets, cures diseases, and invokes saints and spirits alike. He is the very centre of village life, he keeps alive the spirit of Islam and helps to maintain the villager's pride in being a Muslim. The teaching given is very meagre. Except in the towns no one learns the whole of the Qur'ān and many of the teachers only know certain sections. The boys

[1] The number of pilgrims from the whole of Italian East Africa in 1937 was 1,779 (total pilgrimage 33,830), in 1938, 1,110 (63,716), and in 1939, 696 (57,543).

[2] A description of the celebrations in Addis Ababa is given in the Constantinople journal *Iqdam* (3 July 1923), translated in *O.M.* iii. 78–79.

[3] See Azaïs and Chambard, op. cit., p. 34.

[4] See E. Cerulli, *Studi Etiopici*, i. 41.

normally learn small portions by heart without knowing the meaning, together with the ritual prayers and ablutions.

### (*b*) *Islamic Law and Customary Codes*

As elsewhere in Islamic Africa the effective operation of the *sharīʿa*, the canon law of Islam, is very limited and is always subordinate to the code of the rulers whoever they may be, whether European or Muslim. Sir Richard Burton writing of Zailaʿ under Muslim rule in 1854 says:

> The Kazi has the administration of the Shariat or religious law: he cannot, however, pronounce sentence without the Governor's permission; and generally his powers are confined to questions of divorce, alimony, manumission, the wound mulct, and similar cases which come within Koranic jurisdiction. Thus the religious code is ancillary and often opposed to '*Al-Jabr*'—'the tyranny'—the popular designation of what we call Civil Law. Yet is *Al-Jabr*, despite its name, generally preferred by the worldly wise.[1]

A further limitation of the *sharīʿa* derives from the fact that it is subordinate to the local custom of many of these tribes, though gradually, especially in the towns, amongst the detribalized and in mixed settlements, it gains greater hold. When Muslim regions came under the rule of Western powers they introduced a new judicial system, but recognized both the *sharīʿa* and customary law in civil matters and both *qāḍīs* and tribal courts were allowed to function. European rule, however, has tended to strengthen the *sharīʿa* to the detriment of tribal custom. Similarly in Ethiopia a separate system is provided to deal with matters of Muslim civil law.

The Kadis' and Naibas' Councils proclamation (No. 62 of 1944) repealing an earlier, but almost exactly similar, law, provided for Muslims by setting up *Kadis*' and *Naibas*' councils with jurisdiction over questions regarding Mohammedan marriage, divorce, guardianship, succession and *Wakf* gifts. Appeal was to lie from the *Naibas*' to the *Kadis*' council and thence to a court of *Shariat*, consisting of not less than three judges nominated by the Minister of Justice. The decision of this court was final. Thus in matters of Muslim civil law there was a self-contained system which was not under the High

[1] R. F. Burton, *First Footsteps*, pp. 88–89. Cf. also Muḥammad Mukhtār, writing of Harar under the amīrs before the short Egyptian occupation, 'Les habitants de Harrar sont tous musulmans imbus des principes religieux les plus sévères, les plus austères, tirés entièrement de la voie de *Chafe*. C'est dire que les *Kadis* jugent tous les procès et que leur pouvoir est absolu; seulement, comme leurs jugements devaient avant tout plaire à l'Émir qui avait la manie de s'occuper de tout, politique, justice, etc., il s'ensuivait que la plupart du temps, pour être agréable à leur maître, ils rendaient des arrêts tout à fait injustes' (*Bull. Soc. Khédivale de Géographie*, i. 364).

Court. It is interesting to note that in his speech at the re-opening of parliament in 1942 the Emperor said: 'When we established *Kadis'* Courts by law we did it in order to achieve national unity.'[1]

Although Islam in practice accommodates itself to a great many indigenous customs, particularly in the purely religious sphere, it does insist upon such reform in family life as will bring it into conformity with the *sharīʿa.* This may take a long time to achieve, especially amongst nomads like the Somalis, but continual pressure is always being exerted to get *sharīʿa* practice recognized in this sphere. All the pagan Galla and Somali tribes were once exogamous, but this practice has, through a process of centuries, been discontinued by the Somali. The Muslim Galla, being still fairly recent converts, are in process of change; some, such as the northern Rāya, retaining exogamy, whilst others allow marriage within the clan. The chief of the Rāya Galla in the Arūsi region[2] who are Muslim, told Dr. Cerulli that the practice of exogamy had now fallen into disuse through the influence of Islamic law, but that the grey-beards much regretted the change.[3] Yet the same tribe still retains the levirate which Islam has not yet displaced, though undoubtedly this will be accomplished in time, for the bond of the levirate only holds if the Galla marriage rites have been completed. According to Galla custom a woman whose husband has died must marry his brother or one of his cousins within the seventh generation. Her only way of escaping the obligation is to flee to her own people, and if she is successful the family of her former husband can only claim the refund of the dowry. If, however, the marriage has only been contracted before a Muslim shaikh without the Galla rites (the *rako*) the bond of the levirate is not established.[4] Consequently Muslim law is weakening the hold of Galla law to the degree that such contracts are allowed by the Galla family. Similarly the northern Somali, though they have been islamized for centuries, still retain the levirate, whilst women are excluded from inheriting real estate.

Three of the four recognized legal systems are followed in north-east Africa and their distribution was affected by the centres from which Islamic influence first came and through political events. The Shāfiʿite is the most widely diffused *madhhab* since most of the Somali and Galla

[1] M. Perham, *The Government of Ethiopia* (1948), p. 156.

[2] These are not to be confused with the Northern Rāya (see above, p. 194), but are a branch of the Boran living east of Shaikh Ḥusain in the region between lakes Hida and Sauena.

[3] E. Cerulli, 'Le popolazioni del Bacino Superiore dello Uabi', op. cit., p. 176.

[4] Cf. E. Cerulli, loc. cit., pp. 174–5.

belong to it. It is weakest in Eritrea.[1] Its wide diffusion is due to the region having been most influenced by the Islamic current coming from Arabia. Eritrean tribes like the Banī ʿĀmir which have been converted by emissaries from the Eastern Sudan belong to the Mālikite rite.

During their brief occupation of Eritrea, coastal settlements on the Red Sea, and the Harar region, the Egyptians introduced their official Ḥanafite code and the Italians thought it simplest to keep it on. This is, therefore, strongest in these towns and in Eritrea. In Addis Ababa there are two Ḥanafite mosques, and after the short Egyptian occupation it gained a foothold in the predominantly Shāfiʿite Harar. A few ʿIbāḍīs will be found amongst Somali immigrants in Eritrea and amongst Ḥaḍramawtīs, whilst there are Zaidites amongst the immigrants from Yaman, though most of these have either changed or pretend to be Sunnī.

The distribution of the *madhāhib* is as follows:

*Shāfiʿite*

The ʿAfar (Danākil) of Asāb, Rahaita, Edd, and Beilul.

Immigrants from Yaman; Somali immigrants in Eritrea.

Sections of Ḥaḍārem (i.e. those Ḥaḍramawtīs who are not ʿIbāḍites), Ād Sawra, Ād Muʿallim, and certain Jabartīs.

Northern Galla (Wallo, Yajju, and Rāya).

Harar city and the surrounding Galla tribes.

Galla in south-west Ethiopia (Guma, Gēra, Gomma, Jimma, Limmu, Ḍaḍallē) and the Arūsi.

Gurāgē.

Sidāma (Ṭambaro, Alaba, Hadiya, and Gāro).

Banī Shanqūl.

Somali in general, with few exceptions.

*Ḥanafite*

Maṣawwaʿ, Arkiko, Monkullo, Otumlo, Zula, Ailat, Asus, Gumhot, Asāb, and other coastal towns; Islands of Dahlak; Arab immigrants from Ḥijāz; Indian Muslims.

Saho tribes (Teroʿa, Asaorta, Mini-Ferē, and Haso).

Ād Tamāryām, sections of the Ḥabāb, Ād Muʿallim, Ād Sawra, and Ād Taklēs.

Mansa and Bait Juk.

The ʿAfar of Buri.

Jabarti of Bēgamder. Certain Galla of Jimma.

A quarter of Harar city.

[1] The Italian census of 1931 gives the following proportions between the *madhāhib* in Eritrea: Mālikites, 205,043, 65 per cent.; Ḥanafites, 78,477, 26 per cent.; Shāfiʿites, 28,442, 9 per cent.

*Mālikite*

Ād Shaikh of the Sāḥil, Baraka, and Embēremi.
Banī ʿĀmir.
Sections of the Ḥabāb.
Baria and Kunāma.
Algedēn, Sabdarāt, Ḥalanqa, and Aflenda.
West and East Sudan immigrants.
Wayṭo of Lake Ṭāna.

The institution of *waqf* (pious endowment) is weak compared to most Islamic countries. In Harar city and all the coastal towns which have been most in contact with Arabia mosques and established Qur'ān schools will normally possess a *waqf* of books and some supporting property. The land belonging to a *ṭarīqa*-settlement is *waqf* for all practical purposes and passes from *khalīfa* to *khalīfa* by virtue of his office.

## 2. THE DERVISH ORDERS

### (*a*) *Propagation of the Orders*

The basis of the religious orders (*ṭuruq*, sing., *ṭarīqa*, 'path') in Islam is the belief that the believer who desires to attain communion with God needs the guidance of one who is experienced in the 'path' thereto, one who has been blessed by God on earth by special virtue (*baraka*), and who can act as an intermediary between the disciple and God. The founders of the *ṭarīqas* were such guides and their spiritual descendants inherit their *baraka* and continue their functions to this day.

The religious orders based their doctrine on medieval Ṣūfism to which they contributed nothing in the way of original doctrinal elements, although they gave new stresses and emphasis to particular elements of Ṣūfism. On the other hand, they considerably developed certain Ṣūfī practices and modes of devotion and evolved new methods and forms; whilst, as they spread into Africa and were absorbed by peoples with a primitive cultural heritage, their spirit and aims underwent a further transformation.

The method of following the Ṣūfī 'path' (*ṭarīqa*) has always depended upon the peculiar tendencies of the shaikh, thus in north-east Africa, as in other parts of the continent, the original mysticism of the orders was vulgarized to suit the mentality of primitive peoples, thaumaturgy was exalted at the expense of theosophy, whilst mystical exercises degenerated into orgiastic dances. No real apprenticeship was required before initiation. All that was demanded was the learning of the liturgy of the order, whilst initiation was simplified to the taking of a solemn oath of allegiance to the shaikh. Nor did they demand much discipline from the neophytes in the way of retreat, prayer-tasks, and fasting. On the other hand, mass performance of the regular services with the *dhikr* song and dance was exercised immoderately in the attempt to produce psycho-physical effects; whilst the local shaikh of the order was venerated to a degree little short of deification.

The orders are a late importation into the religious life of East African Islam. Al-ʿUmarī, who collected his facts about A.D. 1332–8, says that in none of the seven Muslim kingdoms of southern Ethiopia was there a single *madrasa*, *khānaqāh*, *ribāṭ*, or *zāwiya*.[1] The Qādiriyya was the first order to be introduced by Yamanite and Ḥaḍramawt immigrants into training centres such as Maṣawwaʿ, Zailaʿ, and Maqdishu, and thoroughly established itself in the coastal regions. One Sharīf Abū Bakr ibn ʿAbd Allāh al-ʿAydarūs who died at Aden in A.H. 909 (A.D. 1503) is said to have introduced it into Harar. As a result of this early diffusion and through becoming the semi-official *ṭarīqa* of Harar it is the most widely diffused order in this region.

No other orders were introduced until the nineteenth century, but when at the beginning of that century, as part of the reactionary movement then taking place in Islam, new orders were founded and the old ones revivified, this region was also subjected to new propaganda, though it was rather attentuated compared to that taking place in other African regions. The re-awakening of the propaganda force of the orders goes back mainly to a remarkable man, Sayyid Aḥmad ibn Idrīs al-Fāsī (1760–1837), who acquired great fame in Mecca and became the teacher of a number of men who branched out into new orders. The ideals and aspirations of these leaders diverged considerably, but they were all inspired to ardent missionary zeal and pushed their orders into Muslim and pagan Africa. The most famous of his pupils, Muḥammad ibn ʿAlī as-Sanūsī (1787–1859), scarcely influenced this region, chiefly because his order was not well established in the Arabian homeland and he made Cyrenaica his main centre.[2] Those orders, however, which rooted themselves in Arabia itself soon began to spread into East Africa.

The spirit of these new orders was different. The old ones like the

[1] Al-ʿUmarī, *Masālik al-Abṣār*, trans. Gaudefroy-Demombynes, p. 3.

[2] Paulitschke, it is true, speaks of widespread Senūsī activity in this region (*Ethnographie Nordost-Afrikas*, p. 72; see also H. Duveyrier, *La Confrérie musulmane de Sîdi Mohammed ben ʿAlî es-Senoûsî*, Paris, 1886, p. 50), but it seems clear, especially since he speaks of 'the Senūsī-establishments of the Qādiriyya', that he has confused the Senūsiyya with other orders.

Qādiriyya had no centralized organization but were esoteric schools working chiefly in Muslim regions, filling the void which orthodox Islam with its rigid legalistic attitude to life left in the hearts of the African Muslims. These new orders, however, were full of propagandist zeal, their spirit had changed, less stress was placed on teaching, rather the aim of each order was to increase its power by augmenting the number of its adherents and canalizing all authority in the hands of the shaikh. Thus certain orders tended to acquire political power; the Sanūsiyya, for instance, became an independent organization in Cyrenaica and Wadā'i not subject to any other authority, whilst the Mirghaniyya in the Anglo-Egyptian Sudan maintained a powerful hold over adherents under the rule of a foreign governing body and is today of great political importance.

Sayyid Aḥmad ibn Idrīs himself did not found a *ṭarīqa* and the one which appeared under his name has had a relatively minor influence. It was spread in Somaliland chiefly by Shaikh ʿAlī Maye Durogba of Merca (d. 1917) and has developed a number of agricultural settlements. It has also a centre in southern Ethiopia amongst the Arūsi Galla through having assumed guardianship of the sanctuary of Shaikh Ḥusain, but has scarcely affected the Arūsi although an unsuccessful attempt was made by a Somali, al-Ḥājj ʿAbd Allāh ʿIsā, to establish settlements amongst them.

Sayyid Muḥammad ʿUthmān al-Mirghanī (1793–1853) was sent by Aḥmad ibn Idrīs into the Egyptian Sudan at the beginning of the nineteenth century and preached amongst the Banī ʿĀmir in Eritrea in the name of his master. After the latter's death he set up as an independent shaikh of his own order, the Mirghaniyya or Khatmiyya. But his son al-Ḥasan (d. 1869) is chiefly responsible for its present influence amongst the Sudan tribes, the Banī ʿĀmir, and other Eritrean tribes, and founded the township of al-Khatmiyya, part of Kasala, as the seat of the order in East Africa.

Another of Aḥmad's pupils, Ibrāhīm ar-Rashīd (d. 1874), founder of the Rashīdiyya, who claimed to transmit the authentic Aḥmadiyya, did not himself acquire much influence in this region, though there is a *khalīfa* at Maṣawwaʿ who fills the post of *imām* at the mosque of one of their holy men; but Ibrāhīm's pupil, Muḥammad ibn Ṣāliḥ, in 1887 branched out into a derivative *ṭarīqa*, the Ṣāliḥiyya, with its seat at Mecca, which became very influential in Somalia through the preaching of a Somali, Muḥammad Gūlēd (d. 1918), and the widespread formation of collective farms, generally known as *ṭarīqa* settlements, along the banks of the rivers. The movement of the Somali Mahdī, Muḥammad ibn ʿAbd Allāh al-Ḥasan, had its origin amongst the Ṣāliḥiyya.

The founder of the Raḥmāniyya, a branch of the Darqawiyya (Shādhiliyya), Muḥammad b. M. b. Masʿūd b. ʿAbd ar-Raḥmān al-Fāsī (d. 1878), built a *zāwiya* at Mecca in 1857 and afterwards preached along the coast of the Red Sea from Sawākin to Maṣawwaʿ, where his *khalīfa*, Aḥmad al-Hajūnī al-Ghafrūnī, made himself independent. This branch order (Ghafrūniyya) seems to have disappeared during the Mahdiyya.

The Sammāniyya was introduced amongst the Jabarti on the Eritrean plateau by a Maghrabī shaikh, Ādam al-Kinānī, who is buried in the Serāi near ʿAbi ʿAddi. A shaikh from the Egyptian Sudan also propagated it amongst the Galla of Jimma Abba Jifar and Limmu Enārya, but it has not acquired much influence in south-western Abyssinia.

The Tijāniyya is the most influential order amongst the Galla of Jimma Abba Jifar and Gomma, where it was imported by a Sudanese shaikh. It is also active in the Bani Shangūl area and in Guma, though in the last its influence is secondary to that of the Qādiriyya.

Other orders of minor importance are: the *Shādhiliyya* (a mystical school rather than a definite order) which has *zāwiyas* in Maṣawwaʿ and Asmara; the *Rifāʿiyya* amongst the Arabs of Somalia, especially Maqdishu and Merca, whilst a few other followers are to be found in the Gibē valley region. Some of the Ād Shaikh and Arab immigrants in Eritrea belong to the *Ḥaddādiyya* which was imported from the Ḥaḍramawt.

### (*b*) *Organization of the Orders*

Since none of these orders originated in this region the shaikh resides elsewhere, but authority is delegated to *khalīfas* to act as his deputies in teaching and initiating new members. These regional *khalīfas* normally acquire such authority and prestige that they eclipse the actual shaikh in the eyes of their local followers. The *khalīfa* names his successor before he dies, or if he fails to do this an omen taken on his grave settles it. The successor is never chosen by the actual shaikh of the mother order, though if the link has not been broken his approval is usually sought. Although the hereditary principle is not necessary or invariable the *khalīfa* will normally be succeeded by one of his sons since he is supposed to have his father's *baraka* dormant in him which, once the *khalīfa* has chosen him, whether in the flesh or from the tomb, and he is formally installed, becomes active.

The authority of each regional *khalīfa* (generally referred to as the shaikh) is founded upon a chain of tradition which has two divisions: *silsilat al-baraka* (chain of benediction) which connects him with the founder of the order and *silsilat al-wird* (chain of initiation) which connects the founder with the Prophet. It is the practice of some of the orders to recite these chains as part of their spiritual exercises.

The *ṭarīqa* is given by the khalīfa to others by a formal initiation (*ʿahd*, covenant) which is usually accompanied by a *dhikr*-recital and followed by a feast.[1] Before the assemblage of affiliates the khalīfa holds the novice by the hand under his cloak, and, repeating the formula after him sentence by sentence, the novice swears to perform the duties incumbent upon a good Muslim, to accept the khalīfa as his spiritual leader and guide by the *baraka* of Shaikh so-and-so, the founder of the order. The khalīfa in accepting him as a novice assures him of the protection of the Prophet and of the founder, then he leads him aside and repeats in his ears in a low voice the sacramental formula (*lā ilāha illāʾllāh* (there is no god but Allāh) three times, and adjures him to repeat it one hundred times after each of the ritual prayers together with the phrase *astaghfir Allāh*, 'I ask God's forgiveness'. These 'prayer-tasks' are called *awrād* (sing. *wird*), *aḥzāb* (sing. *ḥizb*) or *rawātib* (sing. *rātib*) and consist of such short formulae or litanies or prayers composed by the founder and other eminent Ṣūfīs. As the initiate advances along the 'path' his shaikh gives him longer tasks to perform and new prayers to recite; whilst at the same time he is instructed in his duties towards God, his shaikh, fellow members, and the community of Islam. At the initiation the novice is often given a *sijjāda*, which is a piece of skin for use as a prayer-mat which he carries about over his shoulder, a vessel made of bark and fibre containing water for his ablutions, and a hundred-bead *tasbīḥ* or rosary to enable him to perform his prayer-tasks.

A member who has been formally initiated and received into the *ṭarīqa* is known as a *murīd* or 'aspirant', but this word is only used on formal occasions such as the *ʿahd*. Members of the *ṭarīqa* settlements are always known as *ikhwān* (brethren). Dr. Cerulli says[2] that three grades of initiation higher than that of *murīd* are known amongst the

[1] A brief description of an initiation ceremony is given by Robecchi Bricchetti, *Somalia e Benadir*, pp. 422–3.

[2] E. Cerulli, 'Note sul movimento musulmano nella Somalia', *R.S.O.* x (1923), 19.

initiates in Somalia. The first of these is that of the *quṭb*, which, of course, is not the exalted *quṭb* (Axis) of literary Ṣūfism, but merely a superior grade of mystical attainment. The next degree is attainment to the state of *al-wāṣil* (one who has attained union (*wuṣl*) with God); whilst the third and highest, which is only accorded to local founders of orders such as Muḥammad Gūlēd, is that of *al-maddād*, which seems to be equivalent to *al-quṭb ar-rabbānī*. Women, who are generally old, are often affiliated to an order and take part in its exercises. They are called by the Somali term *abbayāl* (sing. *abbaya*) which means 'eldest sister'.

Apart from members actually initiated by the taking of the *ʿahd*, many others (known by the initiates as *muntasibīn*) are loosely attached to the orders. They know little or nothing of the tenets or ritual of the order, they do not live in settlements or *jamāʿāt*, and carry on their ordinary occupations, but they regard the *khalīfa* as their special shaikh or *wadād*; they bring him offerings, seek his *baraka*, attend and take part in the performance of the collective *dhikr* and special anniversaries of the order.

The mode of development, social organization, and spheres of influence of the orders vary considerably and the organization of some is of special interest.

The Qādiriyya was the first *ṭarīqa* carried to these regions. This order is strongest along the coast and especially in urban centres where definite schools of study have been founded. It has remained essentially a teaching order, whose members seek primarily the *dhikr*-ecstasy. It has no centralized organization and only a few agricultural settlements. The shaikhs of the order attract around themselves groups of students which often break up at their death, when the students attach themselves to other leaders or to the most outstanding of their pupils.

The Tijāniyya, which was introduced into the Muslim kingdoms of the valley of the Gibē early in this century, was given official protection by the Sultan Abba Jifar of Jimma, who, however, restricted its influence to teaching and the practice of the cult. Groups were not allowed to acquire communal land and they have no settlements. The order, however, has been a most effective force in strengthening the Islam of these settled Galla agriculturalists.[1]

In Somalia the missionaries of the Ṣāliḥiyya and the Aḥmadiyya have during the last thirty years settled in the 'black land' (*ʿarra madō*), the

[1] On the importance of the dervish orders in Galla regions of south-west Abyssinia see Cerulli, *E.O.* i. 96–97, 129; ii. 189–93.

fertile land mainly along the rivers especially suitable for agriculture which is shunned by the nomadic Somali because it is malarial and infested with the tsetse fly. In these settlements (called *jamāʿa* 'community', corrupted to *jamāha* by the Somalis) they collected around them groups of followers who were chiefly somalized Bantu together with outlawed members of Somali tribes. The Italian government encouraged this process of settlement since they introduced a stable element into a predominantly nomadic environment whose influence would be in the interests of law and order and against rebellions like that of Muḥammad ibn ʿAbd Allāh. The land is owned by the whole community as a kind of collective farm and each of the *ikhwān* is assigned his specific duties of work on the land and care of livestock. The shaikh of the *jamāʿa* has full powers conferred on him by the regional *khalīfa* and allots the work. Sometimes he allots a specific portion of the land to a particular 'brother' to cultivate, but more generally the fields are divided into six groups in each of which each member has to work one day a week.

These settlements are centres of propaganda and teaching and have attracted somalized Bantu and dispossessed racial elements who are prepared to settle to agriculture. They have also offered a new home to the Somali who is outlawed from his tribe. Normally such exclusion, due to crime within the tribe, offers little hope of survival (compare the critical situation of the Prophet Muḥammad until he was invited to Yathrib), but the religious community, if he can stick the life, offers him reintegration in a new society. The *jamāʿas* have taken advantage of tribal disputes to extend their holdings and have often been a cause of friction with nomadic tribes who originally roamed their land over questions of watering, boundaries, and tribal allegiance.

### (*c*) *Qādiriyya*

The Qādiriyya is the oldest self-perpetuating order in Islam and there are few parts of the Islamic world where it is not active and none where the name of its founder, ʿAbd al-Qādir al-Jīlānī (A.D. 1077–1166), is not revered. It was the first order to be introduced into north-east Africa and consequently is more widespread than the more recent orders. It entered through the commercial and maritime relations that existed between the coastal towns and other Islamic countries. It is strong in the Harar region and became very widespread in Eritrea, chiefly through the activities of the Ād Shaikh.

The people of Maṣawwaʿ believe that ʿAbd al-Qādir al-Jīlānī himself died on the peninsula where there is a mosque in his name and his anniversary (*ziyārat al-Jīlānī*) is celebrated on the 11th Rabīʿa' l-Awwal. The order is said to have been brought to Harar by a *sharīf* Abū Bakr ibn ʿAbd Allāh al-ʿĪdarūs (or ʿAydarūs), called *al-Quṭb ar-Rabbānī* (*the Divine Axis*), who died at Aden in A.H. 909 (A.D. 1503).[1] It is the predominant *ṭarīqa* in all the coastal towns and in Harar whose *amīrs* gave it official recognition. It has *jamāʿas* ('congregations', equivalent here to *zāwiyas*, but not landowning settlements) scattered throughout the territory of the former amirate as far as the Ḥawāsh in most of which the leaders seem to be Somalis, for the true Hararīs will not live outside their walled city. The order has no centralized organization, but most *jamāʿās*, including those in south-west Ethiopia,[2] are affiliated to mother-*zāwiyas* in the Harar region. One of the chief centres is that of Shabeli, east of Harar, at the head of which was a Somali shaikh, ʿAbd Allāh b. Muʿallim Yūsif, author of a collection of treatises (*rasā'il*) attacking the Ṣāliḥiyya entitled *al-majmūʿat al-mubāraka*. The Hararīs are not prohibited from using *awrād* (liturgies) belonging to other *ṭarīqas* and told the writer that they recite the *wird at-Tijānī* morning and evening and *awrād* from a Tijānī manual.[3]

The order has spread amongst the Muslim Galla of the Arūsi region from the Web and Wabi, and ʿAbd ash-Shakūr, *amīr* of Harar (1783–94), had a mosque built on the holy site of Shaikh Ḥusain and dedicated to ʿAbd al-Qādir al-Jīlānī.[4]

The Qādiriyya was introduced into south-west Ethiopia by a Somali shaikh and has acquired a considerable number of adherents. In Jimma and Gomma, where the Tijāniyya is the dominant *ṭarīqa*, it is not very strong, but in Guma it is predominant. It has also spread amongst the Limmu Enārya, the Gurāgē, and the Alaba, Ṭambaro, and Hadiya (Sidāma).

Whilst the order had been long established along the Somali coast it does not seem to have spread inland until 1819 when Shaikh Ibrāhīm Ḥasan Jebro acquired lands and established a centre which grew into the town now called Bārdēra on the Jūba, whence the whole settlement came to be called the *jamāha* (the Arabic *jamāʿa*) by the Somalis. This

[1] He is mentioned in the *Futūḥ al-Ḥabasha* (text, p. 13). He is still venerated in Aden and the Ḥaḍramawt as well as in Harar and was the author of a book on the wearing of the *khirqa* (habit) called *al-juz'u 'l-laṭīf fī kaifiyyat libs al-khirqat aṣ-Ṣūfiyya*.

[2] Cf. Cerulli, *E.O.* ii. 192.

[3] *Qaṣd as-sabīl fī 't-ṭarīqat at-Tijāniyya*, by M. al-Hafīẓ b. ʿAbd al-Laṭīf, Zaqāzīq, 1929/30.

[4] Cerulli, *Studi Etiopici*, i. 44.

was the origin of the *ṭarīqa* settlements which we have already mentioned, a form however which was taken up and developed by other orders. In 1840 Shaikh Ibrāhīm conquered and destroyed Brāva because its inhabitants would not accept his religious views, but three years later the Tunni besieged and destroyed Bārdēra, dispersing its inhabitants, and it was not reinhabited for some twenty years. Today it is little more than a large village. During the last fifty years or so the order has spread very widely in southern Somalia from *zāwiya*-centres at Brāva (*khalīfa*: Sharīf Hāshim), and Maqdishu, owing its attraction amongst certain groups to a reputation for a sound and orthodox Islam. A Shaikh Uwais ibn Muḥammad al-Barāwī, a freedman of the Tunni tribe born in Brāva, did much to spread the order in the interior. He established a *jāmiʿ* and *zāwiya* near Tijēglo and worked principally amongst the Raḥanwēn. He was bitterly opposed to the pretensions of the 'Mad Mullah' and wrote a Somali poem against his followers,[1] by whom he was assassinated in 1909. His tomb at Biollei near Tijēglo is the scene of a great yearly *mūlid* which lasts for three days. Other prominent shaikhs were ʿAbd ar-Raḥmān ibn ʿAbd Allāh ash-Shāshī (d. 1913), popularly known as Shaikh Ṣūfī, founder of a *zāwiya* at Maqdishu[2] where his tomb-mosque is situated. He concentrated on teaching rather than propaganda. Shaikh ʿAbd Allāh ibn Yūsif al-Qalanqūlī was the propagator of the order amongst the Mijurtini. He wrote various pamphlets on Ṣūfism collected in *al-majmūʿat al-mubāraka*, amongst which is a violent attack on the Ṣāliḥiyya.[3] New pressures in the social order and the need to take account of new social necessities have resulted in the establishment of a few *ṭarīqa* settlements, the largest being that of Belet Amin near Afgoi.

The Qādiriyya has groups of followers in Eritrea at Maṣawwaʿ, Asmara, and most of the larger towns. It is strong amongst the tribes of the Sāḥil and many other Eritrean nomads regard ʿAbd al-Qādir al-Jīlānī as their patron saint, but they can scarcely be said to practice the cult. The order was introduced amongst the wild Rāya (Azēbo) Galla between Tigrai and Amḥara about eighty years ago by Shaikh Muḥammad al-Annī. His successor *khalīfas* were Muḥammad ad-Dānī (d. 1924) of Dāna village in Yajju who initiated some of the Jimma Galla, followed by Shaikh Imām and Shaikh Misbāḥ (d. 1942).

[1] The poem is included in the collection *majmūʿat al-qaṣāʾid* by Sh. Qāsim b. Muḥyīʾd-Dīn of Brāva.

[2] Author of *shajarat al-yakīn* (The Tree of Truth) included in the collection of lives of contemporary Somali Qādiriyya shaikhs, called *al-majmūʿat al-mubāraka*, Cairo, A.H. 1338.

[3] On these Somali shaikhs see Cerulli, *R.S.O.* x. 12–14.

During the same period the order acquired followers amongst the Wallo and a *zāwiya* exists at Dessié.

## (*d*) *Aḥmadiyya*

Sayyid Aḥmad ibn Idrīs al-Fāsī (1760–1837), founder of this order, played an important part in the reactionary movement in Islam at the beginning of the nineteenth century. A reformer, as well as a mystic, he aimed at Islamic unity and was in sympathy with the Wahhābīs. He therefore tried to reform the more extravagant practices and doctrines of the Ṣūfī orders and laid great stress on a sound knowledge of the Qur'ān and the *sharī'a* as the essential basis to all seeking to enter the mystical path. His biographer writes:

> When he was certain that his teachings had taken root in the souls of his companions and had circulated in their blood he sent them to different countries as missionaries of conciliation and propagandists of unity and peace, for the uniting of Muslims and the revival of religion. He achieved complete success through their propaganda in Islamic countries. He chose each one for the particular region in which he thought he would be most successful. This wise selection made his mission a brilliant success so that you could hardly find any place where he did not have either a disciple or a novice.[1]

Aḥmad's success incurred the violent opposition of the *'ulamā* of Mecca and he had to retire to Ṣabyā in 'Asīr where he died in 1837.

The order was brought to East Africa about 1870 by a Somali shaikh, 'Alī Maye Durogba, who was admitted whilst in Mecca on pilgrimage. After his return to his homeland he devoted himself fanatically to spreading its doctrines and organizing a *jamā'a*. He acquired great fame through his visions and the miracles he performed and obtained many proselytes especially from the tribes of the middle Shabeli region. His propaganda was specially adapted to the mentality of the Somali, little more being required of them than ability to recite the *shahāda*, perform the ritual prayer and certain *awrād*, pay the required dues, and, since his death, go on *ziyāra* to his tomb. He died at Merca in 1917 and the anniversary of his death (5th Safar) is a great festal occasion. Thousands go on *ziyāra* to his tomb at Merca from all parts of Somalia. The festival lasts fifteen days and culminates in a great *dhikr* on the actual night of 5th Safar, when they form an immense circle and, to the accompaniment of singing, recite their formulae in raucous sawlike voices accompanied by rhythmical swaying of their

[1] Short biography by Shams ad-Dīn b. M. 'Abd al-Muta'āl appended to the edition of Aḥmad's *Kanzu 's-sa'ādati wa 'r-rashād* (Khartoum, 1939), p. 17.

bodies until daybreak. Once they have got well worked up large numbers fall foaming to the ground in induced epileptic convulsions. Somehow or other adherents of this order have assumed guardianship of the tomb of Shaikh Ḥusain in Bāli where they have a *zāwiya*.

The adherents of the Aḥmadiyya are not as numerous as those of the Ṣāliḥiyya and Qādiriyya, but like the former the order has acquired lands and founded agricultural settlements. Its leaders take a somewhat greater interest in teaching than do the Ṣāliḥiyya.

### (*e*) *Ṣāliḥiyya* (*Rashīdiyya*)

When Aḥmad ibn Idrīs died in Ṣabyā, Ibrāhīm ar-Rashīd (d. 1874), one of his pupils, claimed to have been appointed his successor and the dispenser of the true Aḥmadiyya, whilst other pupils such as Muḥammad ibn ʿAlī as-Sanūsī and Muḥammad ʿUthmān al-Mirghanī claimed to have received permission from their master and the Prophet to found new *ṭarīqas*.

It is possible that the Aḥmadiyya-Rashīdiyya was first introduced into Somalia by one of Ibrāhīm's sons or pupils because Robecchi-Bricchetti, referring to the important settlement of Hen in the centre of the Ogaden, says that it was founded by Saʿīd (ibn?) Ibrāhīm ar-Rashīd about 1850.[1] Ibrāhīm was succeeded by his nephew Muḥammad ibn Ṣāliḥ (d. 1919) and it is through a Somali pupil of his that the order achieved its present wide diffusion in Somalia where it is known as the Ṣāliḥiyya. This pupil was Shaikh Muḥammad Gūlēd ar-Rashīdī (d. 1918) who was appointed regional *khalīfa* by Muḥammad ibn Ṣāliḥ. He settled amongst the Shīdla in the middle of the valley of the Shabeli, obtained land, and founded a *zāwiya*-settlement. Subsequently he founded another amongst the Ajurān, but later returned to the Shīdla region and founded the *zāwiya miṣra* where his son and successor, ʿAbd al-Wāḥid, continues to function. Another active missionary was ʿAlī Nairobī[2] (d. 1920) whose centre was at Bandar Salām, on the Jūba river south of Bārdēra. The order is active, too, in British Somaliland where it has a number of settlements centred round the tomb of the dead founder-shaikh,[3] but has not spread outside the Somali region.

[1] L. Robecchi Bricchetti, *Somalia e Benadir* (Milan, 1899), p. 426.

[2] He was so called because he belonged to a Ḍūlbohanta section which had migrated into north-west Kenya.

[3] The chief *ṭarīqas* in British Somaliland (some of which are Qādiriyya) are at Berbera, Hargeisa (founded by a Shaikh Mattar from Harar), Zailaʿ, Shaikh, Berato, Hahi, and Au Barkhadla.

The theoretical rules of the Ṣāliḥiyya are: renunciation of all earthly vanities and aspirations (thus they are sometimes seen with shaved heads because the Somali is extremely proud of his hair); solitude and isolation as far as possible from all non-adepts; avoidance of coffee, tea, and tobacco (this prohibition is strictly observed); the social drill of congregational prayer; and the recital of litanies (*adhkār* and *awrād*) at specific times of the day in solitude and in congregation. These rules were not very suitable to the Somali temperament and the order spread more rapidly amongst the somalized Bantu and slaves than amongst the true Somali. Soon agricultural groups of freed slaves began to form and attract Somalis outlawed from their tribes. In this way its political influence spread through the life of the land and it was used as an instrument to stimulate fanaticism in national uprisings such as the rebellion of the 'Mad Mullah' and that of the Sayyid Muḥammad Yūsif in the valley of the Web against Abyssinia in 1917. The 'Mad Mullah' claimed to have been appointed *khalīfa* by Muḥammad ibn Ṣāliḥ and derived sufficient prestige from this to initiate his propaganda amongst the Somali, to suit whom he modified certain precepts of the order. He had undoubtedly been initiated by the Shaikh during one of his pilgrimages, but Muḥammad ibn Ṣāliḥ repudiated his claims in 1904. Since his death the process of building up settlements has been proceeding steadily. Apart from de-tribalized people of the settlements, the Ogadēn and Ḍūlbahanta sections of the nomadic Somali belong to the order.

### (*f*) *Mirghaniyya or Khatmiyya*[1]

The founder of this order, Muḥammad 'Uthmān al-Mirghanī (1793–1852), was sent by his master Aḥmad ibn Idrīs into Egypt and the Sudan as a propaganda agent and preached amongst the Banī 'Āmir in 1817. After the death of his master he set up as an independent shaikh, completely modified the rule of Aḥmad, developing his theory of the Khatmiyya as the seal (*khatm*) of all *ṭarīqas*, and sent out his sons to proselytize in other regions. Al-Ḥasan was sent to Sawākin, from whence he travelled into the Sudan where he was conspicuously successful. Amongst the Beja tribes of Eritrea he won over the Banī 'Āmir, the Ḥalanqa and Ḥabāb, all of whom had been first influenced by his father. He settled amongst the Beja at Kasala where he founded the township of the Khatmiyya which he made the African see of the order.

[1] For a more detailed account of the history and practices of this order see J. S. Trimingham, *Islam in the Sudan* (1949), pp. 210, 215–17, 231–5.

He died there in 1869 and today is more revered throughout the Sudan and Eritrea than the founder himself, an oath taken on his tomb, for instance, being far more binding than one taken on the Qur'ān. When the revolt of the Mahdī broke out the Mirghaniyya family, with everything to lose, supported the Government and headed the Banī ʿĀmir and Shukriyya against the dervishes. After the reoccupation two of the leaders, ʿAlī and Aḥmad, returned to Kasala, restored the tomb of al-Ḥasan, and succeeded in completely re-establishing the influence of the order.

At the present time the order is very strong in the Eastern Sudan and in Eritrea where the Banī ʿAmir, Ḥabāb, Ād Taklēs, Ād Tamāryām, and Asaorta belong to it. Apart from Kasala on the border, their chief centre in Eritrea is at Keren where the local *shaikh as-sijjāda*, Sayyid Jaʿfar b. Abū Bakr b. Jaʿfar b. M. ʿUthmān, lives.

The Mirghaniyya was established in the Maṣawwaʿ district by Sayyid Hāshim al-Mirghanī who first came there in 1860 when it was under Ottoman rule. He died in 1899 and is buried at Otumlo near Maṣawwaʿ, where his *ḥōliyya* (anniversary festival) is celebrated every year. He was succeeded by his daughter Sharīfa ʿAlawiyya (d. 1940) who lived at Keren, whilst another daughter, Sharīfa Maryam, succeeded to the Red Sea hills and lives at Sinkāt.[1]

Some Mirghaniyya influence penetrated into south-western Abyssinia towards the end of the nineteenth century and there are many *zāwiyas* in Guma where the Qādiriyya is the prevailing *ṭarīqa*. These were established by Shaikh ʿAbd ar-Raḥmān, a native of Gomma, who was initiated whilst on pilgrimage, at the time of the revolt in Guma against Abyssinian rule.[2] There is also a small group of followers in Addis Ababa.

[1] The relationships of the Eritrean groups are shown by the following table:

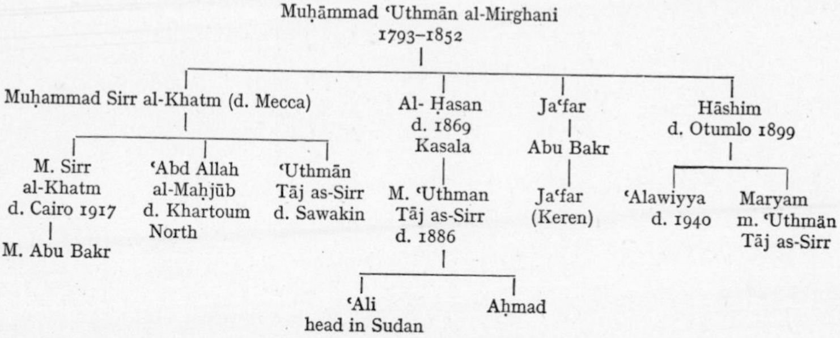


[2] Cf. E. Cerulli, *Folk Literature of the Galla*, p. 50.

### (g) *Tijāniyya*

The Tijāniyya was founded in 1781 by Aḥmad b. M. b. al-Mukhtār at-Tijānī. He was very active in the Maghrib spreading his order and his emissaries acquired a great following in the Western Sudan.

Al-Ḥājj Yūsif of Jimma, who was initiated whilst on pilgrimage in Mecca by the West African khalīfa, Alfa Hāshim,[1] introduced this order into the Jimma Abba Jifar kingdom early in the present century. He seems to have been mainly responsible for its present influence. He gave the order to Sultan Abba Dula, father of the present Sultan Abba Jawbir. Abba Jawbir himself was originally initiated into the Qādiriyya, but afforded official protection to the Tijāniyya, although the Qādiriyya strongly opposed its influence. Yūsif's son, Aḥmad Nūr, is the present khalīfa. The order has also spread into Gomma, Gēra, and Guma.

E. Cerulli writes: 'It may appear remarkable to find establishments of the Tijāniyya of southern Oran (Algeria) at Jimma, but it was brought here by a shaikh coming from the Sudan and received a most favourable reception, so much so that today it has become the most authoritative'.[2] Whilst West African Tijānī influence from Dambidollo (Sayo) undoubtedly came into Jimma before the present century, the writer's own inquiries lead him to believe that the chief reason for its rapid spread was the work of al-Ḥājj Yūsif and official recognition by the sultans. Emissaries from the Sudan have carried the *ṭarīqa* amongst the Bani Shanqūl where it is the prevailing *ṭarīqa*.

In the Jimma area the Tijānīs hold their assembly (*ḥaḍra*) every Friday night (our Thursday evening) between *ṣalāt al-ʿaṣr* and *ṣalāt al-maghrib*. The normal performance is first the *dhikr*, then the feasting, followed by the recitation of the Prophet's birth story (*mawlid an-nabī*). Each member in turn sacrifices a sheep and the performance is usually beside his hut. The *mawlid* for some unknown reason is only sung during four months (Rabīʿ I and II, Jūmādā I and II). The birthday of at-Tijānī is celebrated yearly when special *madīḥ* and the *mawlid an-nabī* which he wrote are sung. The daily litany (*dhikr al-awqāt*) is supposed to be recited by members every morning and evening and is often recited after one of the afternoon prayers. It consists of *al-istighfār*, *ṣalāt ʿalā'n-nabī*, and *at-tahlīl*; each recited one hundred times.

[1] Alfa Hāshim, a *muqaddam* of the Tijāniyya, was a political refugee from Nigeria who settled at al-Medīna in 1903. He died in 1934 and was succeeded by his son Ibrāhīm.

[2] E. Cerulli, *E.O.* i. 96.

### (*h*) *Sammāniyya*

This order, which is an offshoot of the Khalwatiyya, was founded by Muḥammad ibn ʿAbd al-Karīm as-Sammānī (1718–75). It was introduced into the Egyptian Sudan by Shaikh Aḥmad aṭ-Ṭayyib ibn al-Bashīr (d. 1823) and from there it was brought to the Jabarti on the Eritrean plateau by Shaikh Ādam al-Kinānī who is buried in the Serāi near ʿAbi ʿAddi. It has also some followers in south-western Ethiopia where it was introduced by a trader descendant of Shaikh Aḥmad aṭ-Ṭayyib called Sharīf Ḥusain as late as 1920. He died at Gondar where his tomb is visited. His son Muḥammad is now *khalīfa* in Jimma but he has not a strong following. The order also numbers some adherents among the Limmu Enārya.

## 3. SAINT WORSHIP

### (*a*) *Saints and their Tombs*

Although the Muslim offers God *ṣalāt*, the formal ritual prayer, because it is His due, the homage of the slave to his master, yet his innermost aspirations and yearnings are directed to his saint or to the Prophet, whilst his devotional life is expressed through the practices in visiting the shrines (*ziyāra*), through the *dhikr* of the religious confraternities and in islamized indigenous rites.

The saints are men believed to have been specially favoured by God during their earthly life, who continue after their death to provide a link between Him and the material world. They are believed still to inhabit the places where they died and also to visit other places where they have signified their presence by appearing to the believer in a dream.

Whilst the orthodox, in their concern for the preservation of the unique deity of God and avoidance of *shirk* (the association of others with God), deny that there can be any cult of saints other than paying them honour and seeking their intercession with God, the vast majority regard the saint as an actual object of worship and the source of the blessing they seek.

As elsewhere the Muslims of this region are inveterate devotees of saints. The saints whose tombs are scattered all over the Islamic regions were rarely, and in the case of nomads never, born amongst the people in whose territory their shrines are situated. They are men who came from outside, claiming in many cases to be descendants of the Prophet, wearing an aspect of piety, asceticism or learning, and ready to prove possession of thaumaturgic powers. These claims impressed the uncultivated people amongst whom they settled in the villages and plains, in town, country, and desert. They performed their prayers scrupulously, they taught the children, they worked cures, they brought down rain. All alike, nomad or villager, were credulous of their learning and respected their *baraka* or wonder-working powers. Sometimes they were the first propagators of Islam in that part, more commonly they brought new life into the Islam of the people; but, however ignorant they actually were, they were a symbol of the wider Islamic culture amongst illiterate peasants or nomads. They deserved to be honoured when they died. When dead they became more fully charged with supernatural power, and the local centres of that power were their tombs.

Their descendants often formed holy families which lived under the shadow of their saintly ancestor, inheriting his *baraka*, and exploiting it. Some remained small families attached to the shrine and thrived on the gifts of the pilgrims, others in nomad areas formed the nuclei of new social groupings, some (e.g. Ād Shaikh) actually developed into tribal groups taking the form of the society they grew up in, whilst others were scattered amongst the tribes as clans of teachers (e.g. Ād Muʿallim) or *qāḍīs* and religious functionaries or wonder-workers.

The more famous of the dead saints received from their devotees well-built tombs whose whitewashed cupolas shine in the sun across the wide plains or from the summit of a mountain. Inside such a tomb is the actual grave, usually a plain cement or mud mound, sometimes more elaborately got up. Passages from the Qur'ān are inscribed on the walls and on the covering of the grave. In them are other relics of the saint, his shoes and cloak perhaps, his Qur'ān or book of *awrād*, also offerings which are of no use to the tomb guardians and property which has been deposited for safe keeping whilst the owner is travelling, for which a premium is paid to the saint when the property is reclaimed. These are the more famous tombs. Often all the tomb consists of is an enclosure surrounded by a simple wall of stones or mud with the grave marked by head and foot stones, and, if no convenient tree is available, with a long stick sticking out on which bits of rag from the visitor's garment are tied to keep the saint mindful of the devotee and his requests. Often cemeteries grow up around the tombs. The more famous tombs become cult centres, whether or not the saint was connected with a *ṭarīqa*, and pilgrimages are made to them on the anniversary of the saint's birth or death. These tombs are an integral part of the life of the people amongst whom they are situated.

The practices involved in *ziyāra* to these shrines, although each has its own unique local usages, follows normal Islamic practice. Worship at the shrines takes two forms: visits in honour of the saint and visits to secure his aid. The word *ziyāra* is especially attached to the annual pilgrimage, whose practices involve the procession round the tomb, visit inside, with the appropriate prayers, eulogies chanted in his honour (sometimes performance of *mūlid* with a *dhikr* and recitation of Qur'ān), sacrifices and communal festival meal. Visits to seek the saint's help, in obtaining a child or healing and the like, involve making a conditional vow and when the petition is fulfilled votive offerings must be made otherwise the blessing will recoil on the votary as a curse. The shaikh in charge and his family direct the worshippers in the circumambulation, the appropriate prayers of praise and thanksgiving, and the form of making a vow; he supervises the offering of votive sacrifices and receives a portion on behalf of the saint.

Tombs and shrines are most numerous in the coastal towns and Harar region where Islam has been long established, but tombs are scattered about in every Muslim region. Not only have actual persons been canonized, but sometimes legends have grown up around some name or an unknown grave for which there is no authentic claim, whilst others are survivals of former pagan cult shrines. Foreign saints who are universally revered by Muslims are not very popular; ʿAbd al-Qādir al-Jīlānī being the only really popular one owing to the widespread influence of the Qādiriyya, for the practice of the orders and the veneration of saints are both aspects of one phenomenon. Sometimes a local saint of the same name, ʿAbd al-Qādir, has been confused with him. At Maṣawwaʿ they claim that he died at the place of the mosque dedicated in his name, and his anniversary (*ziyārat al-Jīlānī*) is celebrated by pilgrimages and the accompanying ceremonies on 11th Rabīʿ al-awwal. Jibūti has a *maqām* dedicated to him which is the only place of pilgrimage to which the wild ʿĪsa Somali are admitted.[1]

The most revered saints of Harar are the Amīr Nūr ibn al-Mujāhid, the saviour of the city after the collapse of the Imām Aḥmad's armies,[2] who is regarded as its patron saint, and Shaikh ʿUmar Abādir.[3] The Amīr Nūr is venerated by the Hararīs so much because of the way in

[1] *R.M.M.* iv. 140. A *maqām* (lit. 'place of standing') is a place which a dead saint visits, usually indicated to a worshipper in a dream.

[2] See above pp. 91–3; E. Cerulli, *Studi Etiopici*, i. 46–48; R. F. Burton, *First Footsteps*, ii. 12.

[3] The names of seven other saints buried near the various gates of Harar are given in R. P. Azaïs and R. Chambard, *Cinq années de recherches archéologiques en Éthiopie* (1931), p. 7.

which he identified himself and the fortunes of Islam with Harar city. His tomb is situated between the Fanḍāla gate (Bāb al-Futūḥ), the French hospital, and the house of Amīr ʿAbd Allāh. Its construction is similar to that of the tomb of Shaikh Ḥusain. It is under the guardianship of the *ʿulamā* of Harar who have the duty of regulating the pilgrimages and ceremonies performed there. The anniversary of the *amīr's* death is celebrated in Rabīʿ al-awwal (which month is called in Hararī *nadi mawlūd*).

Nothing certain is known about Shaikh ʿUmar Abādir al-Bakrī,[1] whose tomb is in the southern quarter of the city near the Bisidimo gate (Bāb as-Salām).[2] Tradition says that coming originally from Jidda he was one of the first propagators of Islam in the region.[3] From Harar his cult has spread into Limmu Enārya.[4]

Another early missionary was Shaikh Ibrāhīm Abū Zaḥarbūi who went to Harar in A.D. 1430, converted many to Islam and was buried at Zailaʿ where his tomb close to the Ashurbura gate is still a goal of pilgrimage by many ʿAfar.[5] He was traditionally one of the forty-four saints of the Ḥaḍramawt who, after a solemn meeting at Awliyā Kumbo, so called in commemoration of the gathering, dispersed to preach Islam. In Harar he became a *kāt*-adict and they attribute to him its introduction into the Yaman. He performed numerous miracles, amongst others that of being transported in the air to Mount Ḥākim near Harar where Shaikh Ḥusain's son is supposed to be buried.

Another famous saint of Zailaʿ is Saʿd ad-Dīn, the martyr king of Adal. His tomb used to lie on the island and Sir Richard Burton described it as 'a mound of rough stones surrounding an upright pole. It is still popularly venerated, as is proved by the remains of votive banquets, broken bones, dried garbage, and stones blackened by the fire.' The tomb has now been completely washed away by the encroaching sea, but there are many other shrines dedicated to him scattered about the

[1] On this saint see E. Cerulli, *Studi Etiopici*, i. 48–50, and L. Robecchi-Bricchetti, *Nell' Harar* (1896), p. 133.

[2] R. F. Burton, op. cit. ii. 14. A photograph of the tomb is given in L. Robecchi-Bricchetti, op. cit., p. 135.

[3] P. Paulitschke, *Harar, Forschungsreise nach den Somâl- und Galla-Ländern Ost-Afrikas* (Leipzig, 1888), p. 215.

[4] Cf. Cerulli, *E.O.* i. 129–30.

[5] R. F. Burton, op. cit. i. 54. The inscription dated A.H. 1155 (A.D. 1741/2) which Burton read on the wall of his mosque has disappeared (see Paulitschke, *Harar*, p. 65). The tomb of Sh. al-Ḥākim on the hill of that name, south-east of Harar, is said to be that of the son of Sh. Ḥusain. It is mentioned by Cecchi (*Da Zaila alla frontiere del Caffa*, ii. 619) and Mohammed Mukhtar ('Notes sur le pays de Harrar', *Bull. Soc. Khédivale de Géographie*, i. 360) both of whom call him Shaikh Ibrāhīm al-Ḥākim.

town. Other tombs in Zailaʿ are those of Shaikhs Ibrāhīm ibn al-Ḥākim,[1] ʿAbd al-Qādir, and Shaikh Dīni, son of Saʿd ad-Dīn.

Somaliland has large numbers of saint-celebrations since each local *ṭarīqa*-group celebrates its own founder. Such practices are very popular amongst the mixed groups of somalized negroids who are more easily carried away by the enthusiasm of mass *ziyāra* gatherings and by the *dhikr* practices than are the true Somali. Two widely popular saints are Shaikh Uwēs and Shaikh Ṣūfī who have been mentioned as propagators of the Qādiriyya amongst all these mixed agriculturalist groups. But according to Cerulli, 'the most popular saint of Somalia is Au Ḥiltir whose veneration perhaps carries traces of former pagan beliefs'. Au Ḥiltir, according to the Hawiyya legend related by Cerulli,[2] was born among the Raḥanwēn and became celebrated for his piety. When they were carrying his body to bury him his corpse took to flight and, after some adventures during which it was rejected by the people of Galada, it alighted amongst the Shīdla who received it with honour and offered sacrifices. In return for their recognition Au Ḥiltir gave them the priceless gift of the River Shabeli. Such tales of saints seeking their own final resting-places though usually by other means than flight are common amongst the Somali. A saint who is venerated by the Isāq and Habr Awwal is Au Barkhadla,[3] who Dr. Cerulli has suggested may be identified with Yūsuf Barkatla, ancestor of ʿUmar Walashmaʿ, founder of the Ifāt dynasty.[4] Local tradition, however, says that he died early in the sixteenth century.[5]

Others who are venerated as saints because they were the introducers of Islam and the symbol of tribal solidarity are the ancestors of the various tribes. At Mait (or Mahet) is a tomb to Shaikh Isḥāq, ancestor of the Ba Habr Magadle tribes.[6] At Būr Hakkaba is the tomb and *zāwiya* of Shaikh Mu'min who was a notable missionary and became the ancestor of the Rēr Shaikh Mu'min which provided the ruling dynasty to the Elai (a tribe of the Raḥanwēn).[7] Another tomb in the Arora valley is that of Aḥmad Fuqarā, founder of the Fogorotto (*fuqarā'*), a sub-tribe of the Asaorta. The association of a former pagan

[1] Robecchi-Bricchetti, *Nell' Harrar*, 2nd ed. (1896), p. 99.

[2] *R.S.O.* x. 30–31.

[3] J. W. C. Kirk, *A Grammar of the Somali Language* (1905), p. 198; L. Robecchi-Bricchetti, *Somalia e Benadir* (Milan, 1899), pp. 428–9.

[4] E. Cerulli, *R.R.A.L.* ser. vi, vol. iv (1931), p. 67.

[5] R. E. Drake-Brockman, *British Somaliland*, p. 219.

[6] Drake-Brockman, op. cit., p. 54.

[7] E. Cerulli, 'Gruppi etnici negri nella Somalia', *A.A.E.* lxiv (1934), 182; Robecchi-Bricchetti, op. cit., p. 428.

holy place with a Muslim saint is seen at the tomb of Shaikh ʿAbd Allāh at Follōha, a locality in the region of the Dasamo, a sub-tribe of the Mini-Ferē, where they sacrifice a white cow yearly in honour of their special *jinni.*[1] The Raḥanwēn pilgrimage to Būr Éibi, which is not far from Būr Hakkaba, is not associated with a particular saint:

> This hill is the goal of a picturesque pilgrimage by the Raḥanwēn on the Day of ʿArafa. Each rock, each opening, each path, has a name and meaning; there is the Grotto of Fāṭma, the rock of Sīdī Aḥmad ibn Idrīs, the cave of Sh. Ḥusain Banyālē, the Grotto of Shaikh ʿAbd al-Qādir al-Jīlānī, the Mosque of Abū'l-Qāsim. The pilgrims ascend in the evening by an easy path, stopping every moment, praying and whining the whole night, with their foreheads covered with earth which they keep on until time rids them of all traces.[2]

All the Eritrean tribes and towns have their saints either connected with the orders, such as Muḥammad Hāshim al-Mirghanī whose *ḥōliyya* (anniversary of death) is celebrated in Jumādā'l-Ākhira; or with holy families, such as the tombs of the Ād Shaikh family of which that of Shaikh al-Amīn is the centre of a special cult. The tomb of another of the family, Muḥammad ibn ʿAlī (d. 1877) at Embēremi near Maṣawwaʿ almost rivals it as a place of pilgrimage. A famous shrine honoured by the Jabarti and Saho is that of Aḥmad an-Najāsh in Agamē.[3] This tomb is visited by the women of the Asaorta who wish to obtain children. First a goat or a kid is sacrificed and the woman remains some four or five days praying for the saint's help; after which she leaves the cemetery, strips herself, and rubs earth taken from the tomb over her body.[4] Another shrine much revered by the Eritrean Jabarti is that of Ādam al-Kinānī at ʿAbi ʿAddi.[5]

Tombs are also scattered about the enclave of the five Muslim principalities of the Gibē region.[6] One of these is that of Shaikh ʿAlī Derār on the hill of that name near Kumbe. Cerulli remarks that hills of this formation were generally the seat of a pagan cult, so that it is legitimate to suppose that the tradition is another instance of the taking over into the local Islam of a former high place venerated by the inhabitants.

Places of manifestation (Ar. *bayān* or *maqām*) where saints have appeared to people in dreams are common in all these coastal cities. Dr. Drake-Brockman writes of Zailaʿ:

> The Zeylayi are very superstitious, and as scarcely a month goes by without someone seeing the apparition of a Sheikh, whereupon a shrine is at once set up

[1] L. Reinisch, *Die Saho-Sprache* (Vienna, 1890), ii. 131–2.
[2] *Guida*, p. 592.
[3] See above p. 152.
[4] L. Loria, 'Usi matrimoniali Assaortini', *A.A.E.* lxvi (1936), 22.
[5] See above pp. 151, 236.
[6] See Cerulli, *E.O.* i. 24–25, 63; ii. 10.

by himself or by his friends on the spot, it can be imagined how common these structures are all over the town; sometimes they may be seen right in the middle of the thoroughfare, but more commonly they are within the precincts of some enclosure. I have heard on good authority that there are three hundred and forty-four of these shrines in the town.[1]

The Somali Hawiyya have united this form of manifestation with a pre-Islamic cult of spirits called *gashin*. They are heaps of stones now venerated as the alighting-places of saints and it is usual for passers-by to add their contribution to the heap. Such a *gashin* dedicated to a Somali saint Au Mād[2] is found in the territory of Bādi ʿAddo at the place where, when the time of prayer arrived, the camel carrying his corpse stopped and refused to move until the attendants had performed the prayer.

### (*b*) *Pilgrimage to the Sanctuary of Shaikh Ḥusain*

The sanctuary of Shaikh Ḥusain in the plain of Goba merits a longer notice since it is one of the most interesting religious phenomenon in north-east Africa. The foundation of the original sanctuary goes back to the old Muslim Sidāma kingdom of Bāli and today local Hararī tradition claims him as the first missionary to the country.[3] When the Galla conquered Bāli in the sixteenth century they took over the cult of the shaikh as it had been developed by the islamized Sidāma and into it they assimilated many of their own beliefs and practices. The result is a strange amalgam of Islamic saint-cult and Mecca pilgrimage ceremonies with Kushitic pagan-cult and Galla Abba Muda pilgrimage ceremonies. The sanctuary has been visited by a number of travellers,[4] but the ceremonies have only been fully described by Dr. E. Cerulli from whose invaluable account most of the material which follows is drawn.[5]

The main pilgrimage takes place in February of each year, the anniversary of the saint's death, and bands of pilgrims will be found arriving from all over the region. The sacred sites are grouped in two distinct

[1] R. E. Drake-Brockman, op. cit., p. 29.

[2] See E. Cerulli, *R.S.O.* x. 6, 32. Mād and Maḥād are Somali corruptions of the name Muḥammad.

[3] Azaïs and Chambard, op. cit., p. 18.

[4] See A. Donaldson Smith, *Through Unknown African Countries* (1897), pp. 52–61, and O. Neumann, 'From the Somali Coast through Southern Ethiopia', *Geog. Journ.* xx (1902), 376–8.

[5] See E. Cerulli, 'Le popolazioni del Bacino Superiore dello Uabi' in Duca degli Abruzzi, *La Esplorazione dello Uábi-Uébi Scebéli*, pp. 72–76, 146–52; *Guida dell' Africa Orientale Italiana*, pp. 468–9.

sections: the village which contains the tomb and the valley of Kachamsarē. The entrance to the sacred zone is marked by two trees of the species called *hallo* by the Galla, where the pilgrim gets his first view of the sanctuary and recites the *Fātiḥa*. Then the way opens out into the arid plain of Shaikh Ḥusain with, on the horizon, a view of the hill of Dodola which, the Galla say, the saint caused to be miraculously transported from Gedeb. Near the pool of Dinkiro, fed from a miraculous spring, is the mosque of the shaikh,

> a huge square stone building, forty feet across, the walls being projected above the roof at the four corners so as to form parapets, while from the centre rose a handsome dome thirty feet high. The tomb was surrounded by a high stone wall, and this again, together with two other stone buildings, was within a square a hundred and fifty feet across, surrounded by a wall ten feet high, and having a large, handsome gateway.[1]

The remains of the saint are in a crypt surrounded by four stone columns. Within the area is also the *qubba* of the father of the shaikh, a mosque said to have been partly constructed by the saint which has a phallic monolith in its courtyard, and a mosque dedicated to ʿAbd al-Qādir al-Jīlānī which was constructed by Amīr ʿAbd ash-Shakūr of Harar (reg. 1783–94) and is in charge of a Somali shaikh.

A path, which is flanked by various venerated symbols (the footprints of the dove and mule, and the tree of Abū'l-Qāsim), leads to the valley of Kachamsarē where the pilgrim visits the grotto of the snake, so called from a formation due to the action of water on the rock, before entering which he burns incense. Other objects in the grotto petrified by the shaikh according to tradition are a nude woman in the act of combing her hair and a group of horsemen, regarded variously as Amḥara horsemen or Ittu Galla who tried to invade the region. Other places to be visited are the grotto of the sinners, from which the pilgrim collects pebbles and earth called *jawara*; the valley of the sinners into which he throws the pebbles, after which he is in a state of ritual purity; a wishing-cave from which the pilgrim collects grass and utters his wish; the skull for contemplation; the honey grotto where water, symbolical of the honey made for the saint by his bees, trickles out of a black rock; and a precipice which opened up to engulf a sacrilegious person who had dared to spy upon the Shaikh conversing with the Prophet.

The custodianship of the tomb is the hereditary charge of a Somali family who have joined the Aḥmadiyya *ṭarīqa*. They hold the various

[1] A Donaldson Smith, op. cit., p. 52.

offices, one is the *Imām* (called Imām Shāfi'i) who is the head of the whole sanctuary; another al-Ḥājj Maḥmūd, teaches Islamic law in the school attached to the chief mosque; whilst the third, Shaikh 'Abd al-Qādir, is the *qāḍī* of the sanctuary. Donaldson Smith gives an account of what appears to be a *dhikr*, but which from the description recalls the Qādiriyya rite rather than the Aḥmadiyya, unless, as is quite likely, the Aḥmadiyya rites have degenerated through contact with the Qādiriyya in this remote place:

Led by an old man with long grey hair, they went through such contortions as I never believed human beings capable of. All were provided with long sticks in lieu of spears, which they crossed with one another, making a deafening sound, at the same time singing and shouting to the accompanyment of a huge bass drum. They clapped their hands, danced, and twisted themselves into all manner of mad shapes.'[1]

The *Abba Muda* was formerly the supreme religious authority of the Galla and pilgrimages to him were a prominent feature of Galla religion. Some Abba Mudas are peculiar to certain tribes, others common to all the tribes. The most celebrated is that to the Abba Muda of Dallo on the left bank of the Ganāle Doria, which is visited by the southern Rāya Galla after circumcision.[2] The islamized tribes of Arūsi and Bāli each have their own *muda* on the summit of a mountain or near a spring. Pilgrimages are made to these *muda* by members of the tribe, though not for instruction, but only to seek his intercession to enable them to obtain their desires as with a Muslim *walī*. Considerable modification has taken place through the islamization of the old Galla pagan cult. It is probable that the localization of the *muda* is due to the influence of the original Sidāma inhabitants of the region who were assimilated by the Galla. Many of these mountains now have Muslim names like Abū'l-Qāsim,[3] 'Abdoi, Amīn Nūr, and Lāzim al-Baḥrī.[4] In such a sphere of religious confusion it remains doubtful, as Cerulli observes, 'whether in reality the assimilation of ancient pagan

[1] Donaldson Smith, op. cit., pp. 55–56.

[2] An account of this pilgrimage is given by E. Cerulli, loc. cit., pp. 142–5.

[3] Mount Abū'l-Qāsim is the *muda* of the Guri tribe, but owing to its association with the cult of Shaikh Ḥusain it is visited by all the pilgrims. Neumann says there are in it a dozen or so caverns which are inhabited by pilgrims during the pilgrimage season, whilst not far off is the grave of Abū'l-Qāsim, a descendant of Shaikh Ḥusain, 'made in an artificial bower situated in a wonderful tropical forest full of lianas and palms. The grave is covered with glass beads and ornaments of copper and brass. Similar ornaments are to be seen on some trees in the forest, and no visitor would dare touch these holy objects' (Neumann, loc. cit., pp. 377–8).

[4] Lāzim al-Baḥrī, an obvious slave name, is said to have been the slave of Ḥusain. It is the *muda* of the Rāya.

rites into the local Islam had already taken place at a relatively ancient epoch in the Kingdom of Bāli itself, or whether the Galla immigrants after adopting Islam have in their turn adhered to the local cults of the Muslim Sidāma, absorbing them into the system of their own tribes'.[1] For more distant Galla regions the pilgrimage to Shaikh Ḥusain seems to be actually confounded with pilgrimage to *Abba Muda* because of the proximity of the old *Abba Muda* centre to the tomb of Shaikh Ḥusain, for Cerulli was told in west Ethiopia that Shaikh Ḥusain is the *Abba Muda* of the Muslims.[2] This belief has helped enormously to increase pilgrimage to the tomb, for it is regarded as holy land by Galla as far west as Wallegga and by Somali as far south as Banādir.

It is difficult to disentangle Islamic elements from the cult, for though such elements as the pool of Dinkero fed by a miraculous spring and the throwing of pebbles may be connected with *zamzam* and the stoning at Minā', these too were themselves originally elements of the pagan Arab cult. Such ceremonies are merely parallel to the *ḥajj* ceremonies and not intrinsic, the Islamic elements being mechanically juxtaposed alongside the original fully integrated elements of earlier Sidāma and Galla cultures.

## 4. THE PRE-ISLAMIC SEDIMENT

The Kushite peoples of this region who were converted to Judaism, Christianity, and Islam were formerly pagans and much of their former religion was not displaced by the monotheistic religions which claimed their allegiance

In Islam we have already shown that whilst the *sharī'a* is strong and in time will triumph over many aspects of customary law, yet the spiritual elements are weak; therefore such purely religious pagan elements as can by the Islamic process of syncretism be in some way reconciled with the sovereignty of Allah are retained in the new religion. The unity of God must be preserved at all costs but since that is achieved by the remoteness and awfulness of Allah His very distance involves the necessity for intermediaries and a subsidiary realm of spirits. In regions where Islam has been long established, God's gifts are not dispensed directly but through the mediation of saints, whilst

[1] E. Cerulli, loc. cit., p. 145.

[2] E. Cerulli, *E.O.* i. 98. E. Cerulli mentions three works published in Cairo on the life and miracles of Shaikh Ḥusain: *Kitāb rabī' al-qulūb fī dhikr manāqib wa faḍā'il sayyidinā 'sh-shaikh Nūr Ḥusain*; *Kitāb nuzhat al-asrār wa ṭahārat al-aqḍār*; and *Nisbat ash-sharīf* (cf. E. Cerulli, 'Publicazioni recenti dei Musulmani e dei Cristiani dell' Etiopia', *O.M.* viii (1928), 429–32.

in those parts which have only been Muslim for 100 or 200 years they are dispensed chiefly by means of a spirit-world retained from their former paganism.

The forms of pagan political and social organization are gradually displaced through Islamic contact, but the more purely religious, social, and personal elements continue to exist in Kushitic Islam without exception, though of course with changes of emphasis, terminology, and means of expression, yet with their inner significance in people's lives scarcely modified. The peoples hold, for instance, the universal belief that the soul survives death, but local colour decides what particular form or embodiment their belief takes. Further, all these peoples continue to make a definite distinction between the group in its everyday life and its 'sacred' state when ceremonies are being performed collectively and various taboos are in force. We have shown that the laws governing family life are always modified in time and changed into conformity with the *sharīʿa*, but at the same time the pagan transitional rites (Van Gennep's *rites de passage*) at birth, marriage, circumcision, and so on, are retained, but so linked up with Islamic festivals as to make the latter hardly seem Islamic at all. Circumcision, for instance, because of the accompanying ceremonial, resembles a pagan initiation ceremony and it is often the custom, as amongst the ʿAfar[1] and Beja[2], for all the boys of the age-group to undergo the operation on the same day.

The religion, then, of many of these peoples, such as the islamized Galla, is in a most peculiar state of transition. Myth and legend, with their idealization of both nature and tribal history, are not easily displaced and continue to exercise a powerful emotional influence upon the life of the tribe; some of these elements are in a process of despiritualization, whilst others are being reorientated by the new Islamic influence.

### (*a*) *The Concept of the Supernatural*

The supreme deity of the pagan Kushites of the plateau regions was the sky-god whose name amongst the Agao was *zār*. This word still survives amongst the Bilēn (*jār*), Gonga (*dāro*), and the Kafficho (*yero*). It survives also as an evil spirit in the Amharic *zār*, Somali *sār*, and the Hadiya *jāra*. The Galla call their sky-god *wāqa*, the Gurāgē *wuqābē*, the Hadiya *wāʾa*, the Somali in general *ebba*, and the Hawiyya Somali *wāq*. The titles *yero*, *wāq*, and *ebba* were transferred to Allah

[1] See W. Thesiger, 'The Awash River and the Aussa Sultanate', *Geog. Journ.* lxxxv. 6.
[2] G. W. Murray, 'The Northern Beja', *J.R.A.I.* lvii (1927), 43–44.

when they became Muslims. The word for 'sacrifice' amongst the Hawiyya Somali is *wāq-daʿil*, 'offering to the sky-god'. It was a simple process to change their conception of the sky-god to Allah because He is a remote conception to begin with, and popular Islam in its accommodation with animism, whilst avoiding the sin of *shirk* (polytheism), was ready to accept all the subsidiary realm of spirits as well. In so far as Islam offered something akin to animism the new religion could easily become the spiritual possession of the animistic Muslim. Once it has been accepted the new doctrine has the opportunity to gain greater hold and gradually influence the inner life. On the other hand, the former god may degenerate into an evil spirit,[1] like the *zār* of the Abyssinians and the *sār* of the Somali, whilst patron spirits or patron saints may take the place of the former patron god of the group in their communal religious life.

The Agao *zār* rite is found throughout the highlands and therefore has been absorbed by the Muslim Galla. Through Abyssinian slaves it has spread into other Muslim lands, the Ḥijāz,[2] Egypt,[3] and the Anglo-Egyptian Sudan.[4] E. Cerulli writes:

> These beliefs about evil genii (*zār*) are widespread among the Christian Abyssinians, and certainly from very early times. From Abyssinia the slaves who have been carried away into slavery in Arab countries have also spread the *zār* superstition amongst the Muslims of Egypt and Arabia. If the idea of a genius which invades human beings is common to peoples of diverse origins, the Abyssinian belief that the *zār* can be forced to go out of the body of the possessed through the performance of special rites is, in Christian Abyssinia, of Kushitic origin.[5]

The *zār* ceremony has inherent powers of syncretism. The Galla have introduced into it both pagan and Muslim elements. The drinking of the blood of the sacrificial victim may be a Galla element,[6] whilst the girding of the head with its peritoneum is most certainly Galla.[7] The *zār* ceremony is called *wadāja*, the Galla name for communal prayer,[8]

[1] Similarly the prophet Muḥammad classed the ancient gods of the pagan Arabs among the *jinn*, see Qur'ān, xxxvii. 158.

[2] Cf. Snouck Hurgronje, *Mekka* (1889), ii. 124–8.

[3] Cf. P. Kahle, 'Zâr-Beschwörungen in Egypten', *Der Islam*, iii (1912), 1–41, 189–90.

[4] Cf. J. S. Trimingham, *Islam in the Sudan* (1949), pp. 174–7.

[5] E. Cerulli, *E.O.* ii. 35.

[6] Cf. M. Leiris, *L'Afrique fantôme* (Paris, 1934), pp. 367, 381; also an article by the same writer, 'La croyance aux génies "zar" en Éthiopie du Nord', in *Journ. de psychologie normale et pathologique* (1938), pp. 108–25.

[7] Cf. Leiris, op. cit., pp. 367, 381, 395.

[8] Ibid., pp. 336–7, 440.

*kāt* is chewed during the performance,[1] and some of the *zār* spirits called up, not only by Muslim Galla but by Christians, are Muslim.[2] Shaikh Muḥammad Zaid, who died in Tambien in 1932,[3] was a famous master of *zār* ceremonies. The Arabs and Swahilis of the East African coastal region south of Somali territory practise a performance similar to the *zār* called *Ngoma ya Pepo*; Pepo being the equivalent of the *zār*-spirit and *fundi* or *mganga* is the title of the officiant.[4]

The *sār* ceremony amongst the Somali differs from the *zār* and is probably the survival of a pagan sacred dance.[5] Besides rites of exorcism it seems to include others seeking the actual incarnation of the spirit. The ʿAfar Asa Māra, who unlike the Somali do not have a wide range of dances, perform an oracle dance called the *jenile*. The *jenile*, who may be a man or a woman, is an ordinary member of the community who is able to fall into a trance and deliver oracles. For its performance the men form a close circle and chant and clap their hands until the *jenile*, who is seated nearby covered with a *shamma*, enters the circle, then the dancers, without moving their feet, bend forward chanting faster and faster until the *jenile* in a trance answers their questions.[6]

Along with the cult of the sky-god the Kushites believe in the existence of a whole realm of subsidiary spirits who are localized in certain trees, streams, and hills. *Atēte*, the Galla goddess of fertility,[7] is a kind of minor deity and the cult survives amongst the Muslim and Christian Galla alike.[8] She is invoked as the Mother Creatress (*yà ayo úmtu*) and also Marēm or Mārām, a fusion with the cult of the Virgin Mary professed by the imperfectly christianized Sidāma whom they assimilated. A male goat is sacrificed to her in September, the Galla new year. The Omēti reverence *Ṭalahē*, the spirit of the River Omo. The southern ʿAfar localize a spirit on Mount Ayelu, an isolated volcano in the south of ʿAfar-land dominating Badhu. On its summit is a rectangular walled enclosure which they visit on pilgrimage after the rains, sacrifice sheep, and pray for the fertility of their animals and success in war.[9] Another mountain sacred to the ʿAfar is Gurʿali, north-west of Aussa, to which pilgrimages are made. The ʿAskarē-Asaorta, who are fervent

[1] Ibid., pp. 391, 426. [2] Ibid., pp. 387, 414. [3] Ibid., p. 440.

[4] See R. Skene, 'Arab and Swahili Dances and Ceremonies', *J.R.A.I.* (1917), pp. 420–34; Velten, *Desturi za Waswahili*, pp. 149–67.

[5] See E. Cerulli, *R.S.O.* x (1923), 5–6; *Ency. Is.* iv. 487.

[6] W. Thesiger, 'The Awash River and the Aussa Sultanate', *Geog. Journ.* lxxxv (1935), 8.

[7] It is unlikely that *Atēte* has any connexion with the masculine god ʿ*Athtar* of the Sabaeans, but may well have with Amharic *atēt* 'fortune'.

[8] Cf. E. Cerulli, 'Folk Literature', pp. 127, 130; *E.O.* i. 58–59, 97.

[9] W. Thesiger, 'The Awash River and the Aussa Sultanate', *Geog. Journ.* lxxxv (1935), 8.

Muslims, have a *jinnī* on Mount Falūm to whom they make an annual sacrifice of a white cow.[1] Tribes composed of both Christians and Muslims combine in those rites on 'high places' which are retained from their former paganism. The Mine-Ferē, for instance, join together on Mount Ḍagarri ʿAlī at the season when the migration of the coastal pastoralists into the mountains begins, on which occasion a member of the Aḥmad Gāsha section sacrifices two goats and an ox. In the winter months they sacrifice a white cow on Mount Baranlo.[2]

The term *jinn*, which corresponds approximately to the Ethiopic *jānēn*, has spread through the Qur'ānic sanction for their existence[3] to include all local spirits with a vague and generally impersonal individuality. They partake of both human and animal qualities. The term is extended in every islamized region to include whatever manifestation appears to have no natural cause and of course anything thought to have an unknown supernatural origin. If a man is killed by a spear the cause of death is obvious, but if a man falls off a rock he may well have stumbled over a *jinn*, or if a woman gives birth to a monster it is clear that she has had relations with a *jinn*. Springs especially are regarded as inhabited by spirits and are usually the centre of cults whose object is to keep them placated, for they are not necessarily hostile to mankind; the water may even have creative or healing properties, the spirit of the spring will become a saint and be accepted as orthodox.

A feature of Galla religion assimilated from the Sidāma is the *hujūba*, or sacred grove, in places where a spirit has localized itself. These have their special custodians and are centres of pilgrimage where sacrifices of cattle are made. The Arūsi Galla and Sidāma venerate the spirit of the source of the Wēbi Shebeli which is surrounded by a *hujūba* of junipers where the spirit of the spring is worshipped. It is gradually being islamized and is now under the care of a Muslim of the Adamoñe, a sub-tribe of the Farasa (Arsi). Sycamore trees especially are venerated by all Kushitic peoples. The ʿAfar, Galla, Sidāma, and Somali all make offerings to them. The Galla regard them as the abode of nature spirits (*ayana*). The trees are adorned with offerings such as food, clothes, and honey. Isenberg and Krapf write of the Yajju Galla:

I also observed another extravagant superstition, which we could scarcely expect from Mahomedans. They pay great respect to certain trees. There was

[1] L. Reinisch, *Die Saho-Sprache*, ii. 131–2.

[2] C. Conti Rossini, 'Al Rágali', *Boll. Soc. Ital. Espl. Geog.* (1903), p. 243.

[3] For example: 'He created Man from clay like pottery: and He created the Jinn from a flame of fire' (lv. 13–14), and the whole of *Sūrat al-Jinn* (lxxii).

a tree in Mersa which they particularly hold in great reverence. My people, desiring to sit down under its shadow, were immediately driven away, lest the Adbar[1] should be angry. Adbar means keeper or watchman. They grease this tree, and perform religious ceremonies under it. Nobody dare touch or damage the tree without risking a severe punishment.[2]

Every household of the Galla has also its own tutelary genius. Amongst some Somali *Arawailo* is a spirit consulted by women before matrimony. She is said to have been a former black queen of the Habr Toljala tribe. Her spirit dwells in certain mounds of stones (an important one is a Murihi) upon which the men throw stones and where women place a rag from their skirt.[3] Similar cairns amongst the Hawiyya are the *gashin*, formerly connected with a pagan cult, now the places where a Muslim saint alighted when he visited their country. It is customary to add a stone when passing the spot. The Somali word *gūl* (Galla *qollo*, Kafficho *qolo*, Amharic *qollē*, genius loci), which today means 'fortune', is also the name of a former spirit. No contradiction exists in the mind of the believer as to the compatability of their beliefs in spirits with the sovereignty of Allah. If you ask an animistic Muslim Galla what is the relationship between Atēte and Allah his bewilderment shows that such a question had never before entered his head.

Mixed up with these beliefs in spirits are remnants of former fetish beliefs which must have been assimilated by Kushites from other peoples. Certain animals or trees are the special home of certain spirits. The crocodile is regarded as an incarnation of Ṭalahē by the Omēti, the lion is sacred and cannot be killed by certain Galla, whilst the snake-cult is widespread amongst the Galla. These beliefs go underground when they are converted to Islam, but linger on in other forms such as food-taboos and special sacrifices. The Mantān (Somali), for example, sacrifice a camel, ox, sheep, and lamb at festivals, but each animal must be offered by a special clan.[4]

Belief in the *buda* (wer-wolf; Tigriña *ṭabīb*, Ar. *ṭabīb*, physician), a malignant man who transforms himself by night into some animal and

[1] *Adbār* is the plural of *dabr*, normally 'convent', but which J. B. Baeteman (*Dictionnaire Amarigna–Français*, Diredawa, 1929) gives the meaning of 'protection', and then especially in Shoa, 'arbres consacrés aux génies et sous lesquels, deux fois par an, on tue des moutons en leur honneur'. Certain divinatory writings are called *haṣāba adbār*. These Galla must have adopted the belief in *adbār* from the Abyssinians.

[2] *Journals of Isenberg and Krapf* (1843), pp. 439–40.

[3] Drake-Brockman, *British Somaliland* (1912), pp. 168–72.

[4] E. Cerulli, *R.S.O.* x. 7.

goes about seeking victims, is common all over the region. Such a *buda* has powers of the evil eye, belief in which is universal. Amongst the Somali the chief of the tribe is often credited with the 'hot-eye' (*kulul*).

### (*b*) *Forms of Religious Behaviour*

The priest amongst the pagan Kushites was either the head of the family in family ceremonies or the chief of the clan in corporate functions. Considerable modifications have taken place, but the peculiar functions of the patriarch or chief have survived in some form or other. Such practices did not require any accommodation to Islam for the Islamic sacrificial acts which acquire significance amongst the imperfectly islamized, are performed by the head of the family. All the hereditary chiefs of the Somali tribes are accredited with magical powers. The silver baton of the Sultan of Aussa is regarded as a magical object in which something of the chief himself is enshrined which is confided to envoys on special missions.

The chief religious act amongst the Galla is the *wadāja*,[1] the family or communal prayer-gathering which is accompanied by a feast of bread or roasted corn and coffee, beer or hydromel, a portion of which is offered to *Wāqa* (deity or numen). It may also include the sacrifice of a sheep. Such a ceremony was linked with Islamic festivals without any far-reaching social readjustment. Prayer amongst the Muslim Galla continues to be a communal affair and the word *wadāja* is normally used by the Wallo and Rāya Galla for the Islamic evening prayer. But the word has also degenerated for it is used of an assembly of *zār*-worshippers or sorcerers. Zervos writes:

> The Muslim sorcerers have their own 'society'. If anyone wishes to obtain a favour or draw down a curse upon his enemies, he invites several old men of the village, buys them *kāt* and passes the whole night with them singing, praying and cursing if it is an enemy or blessing if it is a question of a benediction. This is called making *wadāja*. The interested party seats himself in the middle of the *kabīras* who spit *kāt* on his head crying 'yaklūm' (may it be fulfilled). In general, the *wadāja* lasts the whole night.[2]

As pagan groups became more complex through contact with other

[1] On the *wadāja* as practised in Harar Province, see Azaïs and Chambard, op. cit., pp. 109–12.

[2] A. Zervos, *L'Empire d'Ethiopie* (1935), p. 93. The Chronicle of King Theodore (*R.S.E.* ii. 161) records how a Muslim *qāllichchā* of the Warra Himano called Shaikh Yāsīn held a *wadājā* to fortify the people against Theodore.

peoples special classes differentiated themselves which took the place of the group functioning as a whole. Religious and secular leadership split and magician-priests, living under rules which separated them from the rest of the group, became special clans. The Galla have a wide range, for they were peculiarly ready to import magical practices from others such as the Sidāma with whom they were in contact. Normally, except in the case of Islam, such adoption of foreign religious elements did not involve any wide social readjustment.

When these pagan peoples adopted Islam the Muslim shaikh took the place of the magician-priest as the holder of this store of magical lore, but he was often called by the same name. The Yajju and Rāya Galla still call their shaikh or *qāḍī* by the title of *qallicha* which is the former name for their heathen magician. Similar is the Somali usage of the word *wadād*. In the same way the Muslim Galla have transferred the name for the house of a sorcerer (*darasa*, lit. (sacred) enclosure) to the *zāwiya* of a shaikh. The transference of the name was natural since there would at first seem to be little difference in their functions, for both were the repositories of religious knowledge among an ignorant and superstitious people. Gradually Islam has transformed the basis of their knowledge by introducing Islamic magical arts and in the course of time elements of Islamic law, such as the correct mode of slaughtering animals. It is these men who provide the amulets which all wear to guard against or conciliate unseen powers. To them they have recourse if illness or misfortune befalls them. They discover the agency and, by means of exorcism, with sacrifice and offerings, effect a cure. Amulets[1] are worn by everybody from the Beja in the north to the somalized Bantu in the south. The principle employed is that of assimilation of the sacred force by contact. They are thought of as emanations of the divine power and consequently the more powerful the *baraka* of the person who provides them the more effective will be the protection and therefore the greater the cost. Thesiger writes that the ʿAfar youths and children in Badhu, 'wear a piece of skin round their necks, wrists and ankles. This they are given by the witch doctor of the tribe to bring them luck in killing.[2] The Galla who imposed themselves upon Sidāma regions incorporated into their social structure Sidāma castes of

[1] In Eritrea and Abyssinia amulets are generally called *ḥijāb*; in Somalia *gertās* (Ar. *qirṭās*) 'neck amulet', *gadon* 'arm amulet'; ʿAfar *waraqa*; Galla *birzi* (Ar. *ḥirz*). The Somali also use *herzi*, *kudomo*, and *makram* for the whole amulet-pouch containing bones, roots, or claws in addition to the written charm.

[2] W. Thesiger, 'The Awash River and the Sultanate of Aussa', *Geog. Journ.* lxxxv (1935), 5.

healer-magicians.[1] These are no less respected than the Muslim *fuqarā* whose reputation is to a large extent based upon their reputed magical powers. They profess to cure all illnesses, which are regarded as the effect of evil spirits, by means of their evocation, exorcism, and the use of remedies extracted from herbs.

The islamized magicians know sufficient of the Qur'ān to be able to recite sections for their ritual purposes or to use it in making amulets, but follow traditional rites in other magical practices such as foretelling the future. As in all Islamic countries the practice of *khaira* or *istikhāra*, 'divination' or control by fore-knowledge, is universal. The days of the week, the date of the month, and the months of the year are all auspicious or inauspicious for certain acts and a *qallicha* or *wadād* or shaikh is always consulted before the date for travelling, contracting a marriage or the like, is fixed. Divination from the entrails is practised by Muslim Galla. Sir Richard Burton writes of the Somali:

> The *fal* (reading fortunes in the rosary) acts a prominent part in Somali life. Some men are celebrated for accuracy of prediction; and in times of danger, when the human mind is ever open to the 'fooleries of faith', perpetual reference is made to their art.[2]
>
> They have traditionary seers called Tawuli . . . who, by inspecting the fat and bones of slaughtered cattle, 'do medicine', predict rains, battles and diseases of animals. This class is of both sexes: they never pray nor bathe, and are therefore considered always impure; thus, being feared, they are greatly respected by the vulgar. Their predictions are delivered in a rude rhyme, often put for importance into the mouth of some deceased seer. During the three months called Ragalo the Koran is not read over graves, and no marriage ever takes place.[3] The reason of this peculiarity is stated to be in imitation of their ancestor Ishak, who happened not to contract a matrimonial alliance at such epoch: it is, however, a manifest remnant of the pagan's auspicious and inauspicious months. Thus they sacrifice she-camels in the month Sabuh, and keep holy with feasts and bonfires the *Dubshid* or New Year's Day.[4]

In their funerary rites certain outward accommodations are made to

[1] Cf. Cecchi, op. cit. ii. 240–1, who calls them *maliki* which is really the name for the spirits which are conjured up.

[2] R. F. Burton, *First Footsteps*, i. 40.

[3] Dr. Drake-Brockman writes: 'The Somalis in the interior will usually marry at any time of the year, but those at the coast who have been more in touch with Arabs, refuse to marry during the three months collectively known as "Rajalo" ' (which correspond to the months Rabīʿ al-Ākhir, Jumādā' l-Ūlā, and Jumādā' l-Ākhira). 'The Somalis who adhere to this custom have no other reason for doing so than that they consider it the correct thing to do, if they are to be recognized as good Mohammedans' (op. cit., p. 144).

[4] R. F. Burton, op. cit., pp. 80–81.

Islamic prejudices. The religious ceremony is confined to men, though women often follow the corpse to the grave, the Fātiḥa is recited and Qur'ānic portions read, whilst the orientation of the grave follows the Islamic custom; but their beliefs connected with the life after death go very much farther than Islamic beliefs as is shown by their practices. The Somali believe that it is necessary to provide food and clothes for the dead by sacrifices and distribution to the poor, and it is the practice to ensure regular sacrifices by making testamentary provision in the will. 'At certain unlucky periods when the moon is in ill-omened asterisms those who die are placed in bundles of matting upon a tree, the idea being that if buried a loss would result to the tribe.'[1] The nomadic 'Afar have not adopted the Muslim recessed grave, but build *waidellas*, which are platforms of stones upon which the corpse is laid and then walled up. The coastal tribes, except for famous warriors and in thinly populated areas where there is no one to dig a grave, have adopted the Muslim grave (*kabarē*, Ar. *qabr*). They also frequently commemorate the dead by a special memorial called *das*.

The influence of pre-Islamic practices is especially evident amongst all agriculturalists in the cycle of seed-time and harvest: in the ceremonies of inauguration, death and rebirth of the land, first day of labour, first day of harvest, rites to protect crops against the evil eye, rites to ensure good rains and a fruitful harvest; all of which are associated with pagan supernatural sanctions controlling the process of fertility. Islam is yet too superficial in the lives of many of these peoples to have absorbed these ceremonies or re-set them as allowed rites such as *istisqā'* (prayer for rain).

Most of these people believe that rains can be obtained or stayed by magicians. Rain-making (*rōb-dōn*) amongst the Somali is performed by making a sacrifice in sacred places hallowed by tradition which are probably the ancient centres of pagan rites. They have a great rain-making ceremony called *lak* which is performed at the beginning of the season of the great rains. It is undertaken by the whole group, each *rēr* making its own contribution of animals for the feasting, and consists of a great communal prayer, Qur'ānic recitations by *wadāds*, prayers for rain and sacrifices. The whole festival lasts ten days and is a great occasion for the gathering of families and *rēr*-chiefs to discuss communal affairs.[2] The Galla rain ceremony (*raya*) is universal amongst Muslims as well as pagans. It consists of a solemn procession of women and children who go about chanting prayers in search of a special grass

[1] Ibid., p. 81.

[2] C. Zoli, *L'Africa Orientale* (Bologna, 1935), p. 382.

from which they weave wreathes. Magic is often associated with particular clans or families. Amongst the Hadiya (Muslim Sidāma) the rain-makers (*anjāncho*, pl. *anjām*) constitute a clan who enjoy special privileges and rights but are subject to certain taboos such as prohibition from cultivating, shaving, buttering the hair, and having relations with women other than their own wives.[1] The Ajdūb clan (Tigrē) of the Banī ʿĀmir are noted for their rain-making powers. Amongst the ʿAfar the chief of the tribe is the rain-maker, as is shown by Thesiger's description of the installation of the Shaikh of Badhu:

> The Shaikh of Badhu is always the eldest male of the two ruling families of the Asboura and Badogalet, sub-tribes of the Madima. On being invested with his office he changes his name, and is believed to receive the power of controlling the rain. The Dankali are fully convinced that it always rains on this day, even from a clear sky.
>
> The Shaikh is clad in a red and white cloth. He is smeared with *ghee* and may not now put his feet upon the ground. He is carried in a special chair some 200 yards towards the rising sun and back.... On his return the chair is placed upon a bed outside his hut. Then earth from the summit of Mount Ayelu, the sacred mountain, is rubbed upon his hands, earth from beneath a large *shola* tree upon his feet, and clay from the bottom of the Awash River on his forehead. The Shaikh is next saturated with *ghee*, and the crowd fight to touch him. For a week he will not drink water nor take a bath. They bring a red and a white goat and two bulls, one red and the other white. The Mesara then lift up the red bull, and holding it over the Shaikh they cut its throat so that the blood flows down upon him. The Asoda then kill the red goat in like fashion. The Shaikh's son or nearest male relative kills the white bull and the white goat and his tribe smear themselves with the blood. More *ghee* is poured over the Shaikh, first by the men, next by the women, and finally by the children. When the ceremony is over every one indulges in an orgy of feasting.[2]

Many Hamitic cattle-rearing tribes (Banī ʿĀmir, Ḥabāb and Galla) have a milk ritual.[3] Milk possesses virtue which is not only lost if the customary observances are not carried out but may have harmful consequences to the drinker.

A very popular festival which goes back to paganism among the

[1] E. Cerulli, 'Note su alcune popolazioni Sidama dell' Abissinia Meridionale', *R.S.O.* x. 605.

[2] W. Thesiger, 'The Awash River and the Aussa Sultanate', *Geog. Journ.* lxxxv. 7–8.

[3] It has been suggested that the cow was originally the totemic ancestor of the clan. Agatharchides (K. Müller, *Geographi graeci minores*, Paris, 1855, i. 153 f.) in describing the troglodyte polyandrous nomads of East Africa whose subsistence was based upon their flocks and herds, says: 'they give the name of parent to no human being, but only to the ox and cow, the ram and ewe, from whom they derive their nourishment'.

Somali is the celebration of the *dab-shid* (lit. kindling fire) or New Year's Day. Popular tradition shows its pre-Islamic origin by calling it *'īd fara'ūn*, 'the Pharaonic festival'. It is also called *istūn.* Amongst the islamized Bantu population at Afgoi it is called 'the feast of beating' because of the thrashing matches which take place, presumably to expel evil influences. The purpose of the *dab-shid* is to remove or ward off evil influences. It begins with the kindling of a fire outside each hut and across this the head of the house must jump or cast his spear.[1] It is an extremely popular and widespread observance; the *'ulamā* have never dared to risk popular resentment by frowning on it and it has been assimilated by proclaiming that its performance is an expiatory act for sin. During the ceremony divine protection is sought for good crops, abundant pastures, and fertility of animals and women.

Pre-Islamic practices show themselves in the methods used for taking oaths because this is done upon what is really holy and to be feared. Just as a pagan will swear falsely by the high god, but not by his spirits, so the imperfectly islamized Muslim will swear falsely by Allah on the Qur'ān, but not by a pagan symbol or on the tomb of his saint. In each case this distinction is due to the nearness of the spirit or saint and the remoteness of God. Sir Richard Burton writes that the oath on stone is regarded by the 'Īsa and Gudabirsi badawin as even more binding than the popular religious adjurations. When a suspected person denies his guilt, the judge places a stone before him saying 'Tabo!' (feel!); the liar will seldom dare to touch it. Sometimes a Somali will take up a stone and say 'Dagáhá' (it is a stone), he may then generally be believed.'[2]

Ordeal by fire is resorted to in grave matters by the 'Afar and Somali to prove the truth of a witness. The 'Afar method is to place a red-hot iron axe between the hands of the suspected person and make him hold it for a time decided by the judge who bases judgement upon the state of his hands.[3] R. F. Burton writes:

> The Somal, as usual among the heterogeneous mass amalgamated by Al-Islam, have a diversity of superstitions attesting their pagan origin. Such for instance are their oaths by stones, their reverence of cairns and holy trees, and their ordeals of fire and water. . . . A man accused of murder or theft walks down a trench full of live charcoal and about a spear's length, or he draws out

[1] The Berbers of north-west Africa have a similar fire ceremony on the *'āshūra*, the 10th Muḥarram, equivalent to the Muslim New Year's Day. See E. Westermarck, *Ritual and Belief in Morocco* (1926), ii. 65–69. [2] R. F. Burton, *First Footsteps*, i. 145 n. 1.

[3] A. Pollera, *Le Popolazioni Indigene dell' Eritrea*, pp. 258–9. The Imām Aḥmad used this method during the sack of Lālibela; cf. Basset, *Futūḥ*, text, p. 314.

of the flames a smith's anvil heated to redness: some prefer picking four or five cowries from a large pot full of boiling water. The member used is at once rolled up in the intestines of a sheep and not inspected for a whole day.[1]

The somalized Bantu of central and southern Somaliland have kept many of their former pagan customs. The people of Balguri, ʿEl Qode, and Sigale (near Merka) have a fertility ceremony called the *jimado* which remains completely pagan.[2] Both the Sigale and Balguri people keep the image of a cow roughly carved in wood and about the size of a calf in a hut which is placed in charge of the oldest inhabitant. They celebrate the *jimado* at Sigale six days after the *dab-shid* (New Year) with the participation of the people of Balguri, then a week later at Balguri when the Sigale and ʿEl Qode assist. The ceremony begins with the recital of the *fātiḥa* (the sole Islamic introduction) before the hut where the fetish is kept, after which a cow is slaughtered and eaten and prayers offered that their flocks and women may be fruitful. Then the guardian opens the hut and pulls out the cow, around which they perform dances and sing songs in its honour. The festival lasts from Sunday to Wednesday morning when the *fātiḥa* is recited again and the cow taken from Sigale to ʿEl Qode with singing and dancing along the way. Afterwards it is returned to Sigale and again locked up. The only other occasion when the fetish is brought out is during the rains of the *dir* season when it is carried to the bank of the Wēbi and left there alone for an hour.

Certain imperfectly islamized Somali have through living in the same communal environment as the Galla been re-paganized. Many years after the Boran occupation of Dirri there was a migration of islamized Somali from the east into the eastern Boran territory. These at first drove the Boran back, but those who penetrated farthest came under Boran influence and were reduced to the status of a subject tribe. These are the Gubbra Migo who are camel-owners like most Somali tribes (*gubbra* in Boran means 'slave'). Their relationship to the Boran is peculiar. They are divided up amongst the different Boran tribes, live in the same settlements and call themselves Boran, but cannot intermarry with them. They have their own peculiar customs but practically all trace of Islam has gone.

Other tribes of Somali origin in eastern Bāli who have lost their Somali characteristics through mixture with other peoples are the Carrara on the right bank of the Wēbi between Dare and Daro, the

[1] R. F. Burton, op. cit., p. 79.

[2] See F. Barile, *Colonizzazione Fascista nella Somalia Meridionale*, pp. 113–14.

Sarar on the left bank of the Wēbi Gestro, and the Gurra (Garre or Gurre) between the Wēbi Gestro and Dumale;[1] other Gurra inhabit the El-Wak oasis in the Northern Frontier District of Kenya.[2] The process of paganization amongst the Gurra has not gone so far as to eliminate all trace of Islam. They are a pastoral people owning camels, cattle, and sheep and have maintained their independence; those east of Muddo speak Somali, those around Muddo speak both Somali and Boran, whilst those farther west speak Boran only. Similarly Islam grows weaker and weaker as one goes west, until among the most westerly tribes only a few chiefs pretend to pray. They still call themselves Muslims, but the only traces left are that they use a corruption of the Muslim salutation instead of the Boran *gari*, eat what is *ḥalāl* and keep their women's heads covered.[3]

## 5. THE ASSIMILATION OF ISLAM BY PAGANS

We are now in a position to consider the impact of Islam upon indigenous cultures and their reaction to it. In our study so far we have had to take into account two cultures: that of the impinging culture of Islam and the African culture which received the impact. We have had to bear in mind also the modifications wrought on the recipient culture by the aggressive culture, and also the reverse process—the modifications brought about in Islam through its need to adapt itself to the mentality and mode of life of its new adherents. The problem is complicated both because the Islam presented to pagans was already paganized or, if that is too strong a word, at any rate peculiarly adapted to Africa; and also because of the growth of such mixed populations as the culture amalgam represented by the mixed Galla-speaking peoples of the Jimma Islamic enclave.

The Islamic civilization as presented to the pagans of the region is anything but uniform. First, the most casual traveller can hardly fail

[1] B. Francolini, *Annali dell' Africa Orientale* (1938), p. 1130.

[2] *Handbook of Kenya Colony* (1920), pp. 234, 255.

[3] C. W. Gwynne writes that the numerous tribes of the Garre, 'occupy El Wak and along the Daua as far east as Malka Re. Although of pure Somali origin, and nominally Mohammedan, they have to a large extent adopted the language and many of the superstitions of the pagan Boran Gallas. To the west of the Garre, who do not extend beyond the east end of the Goro escarpment, are several minor tribes of Somali origin, who have even to a greater extent than the Garre lost their original religion and language. The chief of these are the Rendile and Gabra' ('A Journey in Southern Abyssinia', *Geog. Journ.* xxxviii, 1911, 124; cf. A. Donaldson Smith, op. cit., p. 160). The Rendile, who are camel nomads (Northern Frontier District of Kenya), are probably of mixed origin, possibly Masai, but they have come under Somali influence at some stage of their wanderings. All trace of Islam, if it ever influenced them, has gone.

to realize that there are two main cultural levels in the Islamic society of Africa: that of the nomadic herdsmen and that of the villages and towns. The Islamic culture of the majority of the nomads is in its most primitive form; they are in fact the most primitive people of the whole region. Amongst them the distinctive features of Islam—ritual prayer and fasting, the observance of the *sharīʿa*, and social customs such as the segregation of women are unknown. They never pray, neglect their religious duties, and follow their own customary law. Their chief Islamic characteristics are the keeping of Ramaḍān, profound respect for holy men and their shrines, and enthusiasm for the *jihād* when preached to them by the right man. The nomads, traditional enemies of cultivators, have practically no Islamic influence upon pagans unless they erupt out of their desert and steppe homeland and obtain political domination over settled societies, when, with the change in their own life, comes emphatic change in their Islam and its imposition upon conquered peoples. As Nöldeke points out, 'Bedāwīn, who are lukewarm about religion, no sooner adopt a settled mode of life than they become transformed into bigoted Muhammadans'.[1] In this region the nomadic outburst under the Imām Aḥmad Grāñ failed, in contrast to the Fulbe outburst from the western Sahara over the Western Sudan which resulted in the setting up of new Islamic states. As we have already shown the nomads' part in the islamization of north-east Africa has been largely passive and unconscious, either through the absorption of pagan peoples into a Muslim tribe's own social structure or through their expansion over settled regions.

From the beginning Islam has been based upon the city as is shown by the Qur'ānic legislation which is primarily urban. It is urban Islam which preserves and transmits Islam in its most distinctive sense. In Africa this transmission is through actual contact at the markets in the towns and by the wayside, through itinerant merchants and hedge priests, and through Qur'ān schools set up in villages.

The rapid conversion of pagans to Islam during the last century is not difficult to understand. Islam is disseminated by people possessing a form of world outlook who are at a higher cultural stage than the pagan, people who are or have become Africans and are therefore not so distant or distinct as Europeans. Islam has the overwhelming advantage of rarely finding itself in direct contact with pagans whose cultural level is so far below, or at any rate so different, as to preclude a friendly understanding. It is true that a world of difference exists

[1] *E.R.E.* i. 659.

between fully developed urban Islam and primitive Islam in Africa, but there is a series of gradations in the Islam of Africa which act as insulators absorbing Islamic radiation and passing it on, diminuendo, to pagan societies. The psychological shock involved in the change of religion is thus reduced to the minimum. Islam does no violent uprooting but shades off into a long series of gradations and the Islam which actually touches the pagan is often little removed from paganism. Since, however, Islam is a universal religion its ultimate effect upon tribal cultures is a gradual disintegration and gradual transformation of the whole society upon which it impinges, but the process is such that the disintegration and reintegration seem natural since they are but the reverse and obverse of one process. The new culture gives immediate values without displacing the old. It is like tribal life on a wider pattern without territorial and linguistic barriers.

The problem of defining limits in certain of these societies passing through a transitional stage is almost impossible. Yet, although at no single point in the process can anyone draw a definite line and set up a boundary stone inscribed, 'Here paganism ends and Islam begins', there is a stage where one can say, 'This man is a Muslim, not a pagan'.

Three stages in the assimilation of Islamic culture may be observed in pagan societies subject to Islamic radiation. First of all, the stage by which the pagan merely adopts superficially certain elements of the material culture of Muslims, none of which elements are specifically Islamic. Such things are the adoption of the Muslim form of dress, ornaments, and food habits such as tea, coffee, or *qāt*-usage.

The second stage involves the assimilation of actual religious elements of Islamic culture. This assimilation is facilitated by the pagan's belief in impersonal power resident in and working through persons and things (the phase of religion known under the term of Dynamism). This makes him ready to test and make use of any new technique of supernatural control which comes into his experience. Consequently it is concerned primarily with the pagan elements in Islam. The itinerant Islamic magician (*faki*, *wadād* or shaikh) finds the pagan only too ready to believe in his alleged powers and to buy his charms, protective amulets, and fortune-giving talismans. He treats illness or averts disaster by the established Islamic methods of incantation, an integral part of which is the use of incomprehensible Arabic formulae as magical charms. The pagan appreciates such methods and readily employs them because they work with the automatic precision which he associates with his own traditional magical rites. So far this assimilation has nothing to do with Islam as a distinctive higher religion, and the adoption of such elements of the Islamic religious culture means nothing in itself until the pagan loses faith in his own religious customary safeguards. Where there is any conscious adoption of Islam it is limited to the adoption of Muslim names, participation in the Ramaḍān feast but not the fast, and is the merest veneer. It does, however, open the way to the next stage.

The third stage of assimilation, which has an infinite number of gradations, is characterized by a genuine belief in the efficacy of Islamic sanctions, and involves actual change in custom and habitual conduct. Such things are the marking out of a sacred prayer-place, the occasional performance of ritual prayer, the observance of the fast of Ramaḍān, the orientation of the grave towards Mecca, and the taboo on animal food containing blood. The part played throughout this stage by the saint-cult can hardly be overestimated. It is this above all which has served to bind more firmly in the Islamic faith those who become votaries. Along with these new acquisitions goes the gradual disuse of pagan social customs such as the practice of the levirate, exogamy, and initiation ceremonies, and the adoption of Islamic social practice in their stead. This is generally a fairly late stage, unless the process is accelerated by external causes such as the encouragement of a Muslim or European government, and it marks the definite transition from a pagan to an islamized society. It is at this third level that the education of children to prepare in them a collective mentality and introduction to the worship technique of the dervish orders begin to play a part in providing the Muslim neophyte with a spiritual home. He thus gains a wider outlook, a new self-assurance, and a feeling of religious and social solidarity, with which comes a readiness to distinguish between insiders and outsiders (*dār al-Islām* and *dār al-ḥarb*) and the feeling of belonging to the favoured, the *umma* of God. At the same time no more of the old is given up than is absolutely necessary, whilst the new that is accepted is coloured by the background of the past. The old beliefs do not lose all their validity to the African Muslim's life; on the contrary, certain beliefs gain a renewed vitality by acquiring an Islamic orientation. Although ancestor-worship, for example, decays because it is too completely bound up with the old life, belief in nature-spirits, charms, and witchcraft (which are more individualistic, are not bound up with the old corporate life, and whose correct use can give the individual a feeling of security in a changing world) acquires a new vitality. Entrenching themselves behind the new conception of God, they coalesce with Muslim ideas and colour Muslim institutions by giving them a magical or materialistic interpretation. Naturally such syncretism weakens genuine religious life for the elements which have been assimilated in turn assimilate Islam to their own standards.

Thus it will be understood that although, as we have shown in the previous section, such an immense disparity exists between the religious and social life of many of these peoples and the doctrine and law of Islam we are not thereby to conclude that they are pagans and not Muslims. It has been pointed out that whereas St. Paul says, 'he is not a Jew who is one outwardly' (Rom. ii. 28), the Prophet's doctrine was, 'he is a Muslim who is one outwardly', in other words who pronounces a fixed formula and observes a fixed rite. Thus it is that we often find fierce loyalty to Islam combined with utter ignorance of its teaching and complete laxity in the performance of even primary religious duties. They may not know how to pray but they divide mankind into believers (*mu'minīn*) and unbelievers (*kāfirīn*). We may find it difficult to distinguish between their customs and manner of life and those of pagans if we examine them in isolation, yet if we look at their life as a whole we shall find that it is Muslim. We have to see it dynamically in terms of the process of modification of the old culture, of the persistence of many old institutions (methods of oath-taking and rain-making), ideas and sentiments (reverence for high places, springs, the sycamore), and the gradual evolution of a new Islamic culture interwoven with elements of both cultures. The test is a psychic one. Some subtle factor in their outlook on life has changed. Many naïve and primitive ideas of life have gone. Pagan life-sanctions have been transformed into Islamic sanctions. Although they may believe in a vast realm of spirits they now believe in only one God. The only possible criterion is to know whether they themselves claim to be Muslims because that is the only way of knowing in what they ultimately place their trust. Within they have done with paganism though they have not outwardly broken with it. They have no knowledge of Islamic law, they may never pray, their customs and superstitious beliefs betray their animistic heritage, but if they pay reverence to the Law and to those who do claim to know the Law they are certainly Muslims.

In order to understand what happens when Islam claims the souls of pagans it must be realized that Islam does in time re-create the entire life of the new believer. His life has a new basis and that must lead to entire renewal. This does not necessarily happen quickly and indeed it may take centuries to change the life-basis of a whole pagan people.

Now the method by which this is done is both through the acceptance of a new inner re-creative principle whereby the new religious symbols give a new context and driving points to religious life; and, secondly, through the encroaching demands of Islamic law. Typical of the operation of the first in the pagan-community-become-Muslim is the bifurcation of the social-religious cult. The actual pagan ceremony (e.g. the Galla *wadāja*) may be retained, but the pagan prayers are changed to Muslim prayers and the whole purpose of the ceremony therefore acquires a new orientation. The second, however, is much more profound in the long run. Gradually the convert acquires a number of legal ordinances which in time lead to the complete transformation of his whole social and family life. Since an institution like the family has its roots in all aspects of life, the change from a matrilineal to a patriarchal family, to choose an extreme example, must affect the whole basis of social life. For the individual it is much more the attempt to fulfil the Muslim's religious and social duty which entangles him more and more deeply in the net of Islam.

Islamic law therefore clashes with customary law, but it may be centuries before it assumes predominance. What Islam requires primarily is reverence for the Law even though it is not observed. What Islam does in the first place is to accept customary law, just as on the spiritual plane it accommodates itself to certain forms of animistic belief. But this accommodation to customary law is less deep than its accommodation to animism for there has been from the beginning an inner connexion between Islam and animism, whilst the link between Islamic law and customary law is much weaker. Expediency comes first. Orthodox Islam insists as soon as it can on certain minimum requirements chiefly connected with family life, and then customary law and the law of the ruler, since they cannot be got rid of, are allowed to exist alongside Islamic law. The greater the hold that orthodox Muslim institutions gain over the people the greater the influence of Islamic law. European control of Muslim Africa during the last century has helped this process very considerably. The Western rulers with their reverence for a code were ready to seize upon the structure of the *sharīʿa* to regulate the social and family life of peoples who up till then had been nominal Muslims, and by their recognition of Muslim education and enforcement of the *sharīʿa* they turned sedentary groups into more orthodox Muslims. This is what happened under British and French control of Eastern and Western Sudan. In north-east Africa, too, Islam has been considerably strengthened in the regions that are under European rule—the Anglo-Egyptian Sudan, the Somalilands, and Eritrea.

## 6. THE INFLUENCE OF WESTERNISM

European control has considerably influenced the periphery of the life of the Muslim peoples of Africa, though such influence cannot compare in any way with that which it has exercised upon pagan tribes. Islam, being a world religion, has its own material and social culture, which has assured a measure of cultural stability to African Muslims with a primitive background as well as those of the East with thousands of years of civilization behind them. In this region the peoples who came under European control were mainly Muslim and we need to consider what changes have been brought about in their lives by such rule.

The reasons which led European powers to take control of these largely barren territories were never exploitation, but on grounds of national prestige or because of strategic considerations. Consequently in their control these powers were primarily concerned with the maintenance of public security and took relatively little interest in effecting other changes in the mode of life of the people. The changes which have taken place are rather the incidental effects of the link thus forged with the Western world civilization than the deliberate intention of the Western rulers. The result is that these territories are many decades behind the more favoured regions of East and West Africa in material culture.

La Côte Française des Somalis is of importance to France simply as the port terminus of the railway which French enterprise built to the capital of Ethiopia. British Somaliland, similarly, is a barren land suitable only for the nomadic life. Zailaʿ, former port of Harar, Berbera, and Bender, retain some of their age-long value for the dhow commerce in gums and perfume, but most of their ancient transit trade with Ethiopia was destroyed in favour of Jibuti after the construction of the railway to Addis Ababa. What little external trade the Protectorate has is largely based on the export of hides and skins. So poor is the country that it has always had to be subsidized by grants-in-aid from the British treasury. Eritrea, the oldest Italian colony, is not only the most advanced but also the most populated since it includes highland regions suitable for the support of a settled agricultural population. It was the most favoured of the territories of the former Italian African Empire, where a considerable European settlement took place. But the cultivable area is less than one quarter of the whole, it is only self-supporting in foodstuffs for its own population and it always showed an adverse trade balance under Italian rule.[1] Whilst the greater part of Italian Somalia is semi-desert nomad country, certain parts along the perennial rivers Jūba and Wēbi Shabeli are suitable for agriculture and the Italians developed a system of modern agriculture in the hope of making Somalia self-sufficient. These schemes, however, were of little benefit to the people of the country and were based upon a system of exploitation of somalized Bantu labour.[2] In spite of these enterprises the colony was always a financial drain upon the administering authority and can only subsist with difficulty upon its own resources.

The inclusion of mutually antagonistic tribes under one administrative system gave Eritrea and the Somalilands separate, even if artificial, entities; but above all it provided their inhabitants with such security of life and property as had hitherto been unknown. New contacts were established between their peoples and the outside world, new material achievements came to be taken for granted, whilst peace, internal security, and medical services led to increases in their population.[3]

The aim of the Western rulers was, speaking generally, to co-ordinate the interactions of the two parties, the Western rulers and the peoples of the land, and thereby to reduce friction to the minimum and find compromise solutions to the problems which arose through their contact. The impact was reduced to the minimum because, taking a short-term view, the penetration of Western ideas and forms of economic exploitation was very slight compared with the complete dislocation of life which they had caused in parts of pagan Africa. The reasons for the weakness of the impact were that the rulers were dealing primarily with nomadic Islamic tribes and because Western commercial enterprise could find so little to exploit. Taking a longer view it meant that the standard of living of the peoples could be raised very little and that they would remain much more backward than Africans whose natural resources could be exploited to provide the economy upon which Western educational systems and social services could be based. In consequence of this policy the establishment of colonial governments was not felt by tribal groups, especially the nomads, as a very revolutionary political change. The governments have in general retained traditional

[1] S. H. Longrigg, *A Short History of Eritrea* (1945), p. 139.

[2] Lord Rennell, *British Military Administration in Africa 1941–47*, pp. 161–2.

[3] In 1900 the population of Eritrea was estimated at about 300,000, the census of 1931 gave a figure of 596,013; whilst in 1941 the population had risen to 760,000.

tribal chiefs and many of their former functions. They are taxed, it is true, and sometimes chiefs are arbitrarily changed, whilst the gradual suppression of inter-tribal raiding made life more drab. But, on the other hand, they have gained many advantages. They are richer, for their flocks and herds have increased. Life on the whole went on much the same as before. They did not regard foreign overrule as humiliating since it did not until recent years bring them the curse of a national consciousness. Whilst it is true that the culture of no people that has come under Western rule can be regarded as stationary, no root changes such as would revolutionize the whole structure of society are yet in motion. Changes are taking place under the conditions of Western rule, such as in the relationship between master and serf amongst the Tigrē-speaking tribes of Eritrea, but these are natural changes to which the social structure can accommodate itself gradually. The greatest changes are taking place in the towns, and that is due to the education and new ideas brought in by the occupying powers and has stirred in a minority the beginnings of a national consciousness. The quickening of the tempo of life by the extension of facilities for rapid communication, the acquiring of new internal security and of new social amenities, have created new needs in the lives of many, but the institutions of tribal life have moulded themselves to suit them without any basic change. The make-up of the tribes has never been static and under European rule some have been strengthened and united, others have weakened and disintegrated. All this has been regulated by Western legislation.

Islam has tended to claim the sympathy of Western rulers, partly because it represented a higher civilization, and it has been long before they realized how unappeaseably it is opposed to Western culture and that it is in danger of leading Africans up a blind alley. Consequently Islam has enjoyed special consideration by European rulers which has favoured both the consolidation of orthodox Islam and its spread amongst pagan peoples. Administrative necessities have tended to strengthen the Islamic system, as we have already pointed out, because, whilst the Western rulers introduced civil codes on European lines, they seized upon the *sharīʿa* as a ready-made code to regulate the religious and social life of any people who could, however superficially, be called Muslim. *Qāḍīs* were appointed over urban and rural communities and attempts were even made to extend their jurisdiction to many nomadic tribes, though this process was very gradual and tribal *qāḍīs*, if they were accepted, were obliged to apply a good deal of tribal law. In this connexion the contrast has often been noted between European governments' recognition of tribal law (e.g. the *lex talionis*) when they dealt with Muslim tribes and their prohibition of such practices when they had to deal with pagan peoples.

The new factor of secularist materialism has affected only a tiny minority who have been more deeply influenced by Western intellectual currents. Modern materialism, the enemy everywhere of religious faith, has not undermined the traditional moorings of the faith of the vast majority. The whole social and religious structure of these peoples remains fundamentally what it was. Changes are taking place, but it is only too easy to exaggerate their extent and profundity.

Whilst the standard of life of many of these people, especially the Eritreans and the townspeople everywhere, was definitely raised, European powers did little in the way of education and that little was intended merely to cope with their own administrative need to have local functionaries. Amongst the nomads nothing was done, nor could be done, in the way of education. Elders and chiefs alike were opposed to the spread of Western educational methods. One of the changes in British Somaliland brought about by the war was a modification in this attitude. Lord Rennell writes that, 'Before 1939 the introduction of education was opposed and in 1938 the Director of Education was stoned out of the one existing government school. Yet, in 1944, a full educational programme was initiated and increasingly welcomed.'[1] By 1945 seven elementary schools had been opened catering for 410 boys and at Shaikh a primary boarding-school was opened. An attempt was also made to improve the standards of Qur'ān-schools of the traditional type by providing them with grants-in-aid. The wave of enthusiasm for the development of self-governing institutions which swept British administrators after the war reached this territory. The first step towards associating the Somali in the government was taken in 1946 when an Advisory Council for the British Somaliland Protectorate held its first session at Shaikh. At this Council for the first time in history chiefs and akils with four shaikhs representing the religious community met under the presidency of the Military Governor to discuss wider aspects of the country's administration.[2]

In Italian Somaliland under the temporary British administration some desire for educational facilities manifested itself. In 1944 there were two Arab and Somali schools in Maqdishu attended by 290 Arabs and 190 Somali. The following year a nine-months teachers' course

[1] Lord Rennell, *British Military Occupation in Africa 1941–47*, p. 479.

[2] Ibid., pp. 483–7; cf. p. 185.

was started to help overcome the shortage of teachers, and schools were opened at Galkayu, Merka, Afgoi, and Lugh. Eritrea also experienced considerable educational progress under the British military administration and between 1943 and 1946 twenty-three schools with an attendance of 1,671 were provided for the Eritrean population.

The only nationality which these peoples could be regarded as possessing was the vague and general one constituted by the idea of common origin, by common language and customs, and adoption of the same religion. Such common factors could, if given the requisite stimulus, become the germ and core of more authoritative agglomerations. Since one of the results of the spread of the Western materialistic culture in most Islamic countries under Western rule has been the awakening of some form of nationalism it can scarcely be expected to have completely missed this region, large sections of which have come under the rule of Western powers. The development of nationalism has little to do with a basis of geographical unity. More generally it is ethnical and cultural unity which is the important element as in Turkey, Irān, and in the Arab countries of the Near East where the idea of nationality and of race fuse themselves. Another important element is a sedentary agricultural population, and a third is the existence of urban centres. The usual ingredients therefore for the growth of nationalism are urban centres with some Western-type schools in the midst of an agricultural population who possess a general ethnical unity. Egypt has all of these, as well as the geographical unity conferred by the sedentary region of the Nile valley from the Nubian reach to the Mediterranean.

But little of this is offered to the Muslims of our region. If we take ethnical unity first, we find it amongst the Galla, ʿAfar, and Somali. As we have seen, the Galla, who overflowed upon Ethiopia as nomadic invaders, proved themselves unable to unite to overthrow Amharan sovereignty. The only factor which could have unified them was Islam which has spread rapidly amongst them during the last 150 years. At the present time a gradual process of absorption of the Galla who settled in the highlands (the Christian Shoan and Muslim Wallo Galla) is going on and in time they will be practically indistinguishable from Amḥara. The Muslim Yajju and Rāya are an unstable element in the process towards unity for they have always been ready to burst out into rebellion, but they constitute provincial problems and are no real danger. The Muslim Galla of the south-west based on Jimma are no danger on their own, though they might act as a secondary centre of agitation based on Harar. It is the people of the south-east, who are predominantly Galla and Somali,[1] who are most likely to develop ideas of sectarian nationalism because of the influence of the permanent centre of Harar, regarded as the capital of the region; and in April 1948 there was considerable agitation in Harar for the regional independence of the whole province.[2]

The Somali have ethnical, linguistic, and religious unity, but they are chiefly nomads who could not normally set up a state unless they could flow over another sedentary society. Those who live in towns or have travelled abroad learnt new ideas, but above all the changes brought about by the war and the influence of social and political movements in other Muslim countries did not fail to exercise an increasing influence on the trend of affairs, and a Somali Youth League was formed which aimed at breaking down the barriers between the Somali and uniting the tribes and the lands in which they live. When the Committee of Investigation sent by the 'Big Four' Powers in 1947 visited Somalia this Youth League campaigned for the trusteeship of Somalia by the Four Powers for a period of ten years in preparation for independence and the union of all the Somalilands. It was well led and obtained support throughout the country from the educated and urban classes, and, through the influence of chiefs and elders, from almost all the tribes except the Sab confederacy who, because of deeper rivalries, were opposed to the Somali Youth League programme. It was this rivalry which resulted in the riot whilst the Commission was there in which fifty-one Italians and fourteen Somalis were killed.[3] The United Nations General Assembly agreed in November 1949 that Italy should administer her former colony of Somalia under United Nations trusteeship for ten years after which the territory will become independent.

As for the ʿAfar, they also are nomads, alike in religion, customs, and mode of life, but with no conception of ʿAfar unity at all. Even Abyssinian aggression could not unite the mutually hostile tribes. The one sedentary and permanently settled region is Aussa which has been

[1] The population of the Province of Harar was estimated by the Italians as 1,517,833 (F. Santagata, *L'Harar*, p. 92) made up as follows:

| | |
|---|---|
| Galla | 720,515 |
| Somali | 475,003 |
| Amhara | 306,170 |
| Arabs | 5,543 |
| Others | 10,602 |

[2] See *Al-Ahrām*, 4 Apr. 1948, translated in *O.M.* xxviii. 102.

[3] Cf. *International Affairs* (1949), pp. 50–52. A similar riot took place in October 1949, though with less loss of life.

able to maintain itself as a small independent principality. The ʿAfar present an administrative rather than a political problem.

Of the tribes of Eritrea only the Christian agriculturalists of the highlands are unified ethnically, linguistically, and geographically, and have been subject longer to Western influence. Through living under one administration they have developed a greater feeling of solidarity than have the Muslims, the majority of whom are nomads, divided in languages and customs. The Committee of Investigation which visited Eritrea in 1947 found little evidence of the growth of an Eritrean nationhood, and a movement for union with Ethiopia which began in 1942 had secured a strong hold upon the Christians of the plateau. Only the small educated group of Muslims in the towns amongst whom tribal allegiance is weakening and for whom Islam can provide the binding force, find themselves being brought more together by common interest and aspirations; and their opposition to the proposal for Ethiopian rule resulted in the formation of a Muslim League which succeeded in banding together many of the important tribal leaders. The Muslims' demand was for the ultimate independence of Eritrea after an interim period of trusteeship in which, since numerically Muslims and Christians are about equal, they could expect to have an equal share in the government.[1] The Committee estimated that some 45 per cent., that is the majority of the Christians of the plateau region, favoured union with Ethiopia, whilst 40 per cent., that is a majority of the Muslims, were followers of the Muslim League seeking an independent Eritrea. Serious questions of policy are involved in the question of its future and this is the reason why the question is not settled at the time these lines are being written.

[1] Ibid., p. 48.

# INDEX

Arabic names to which the definite article *al-* is prefixed will be found under the initial letter, e.g. -Maqrīzī for al-Maqrīzī. The letter *b.* between two names stands for *ibn* ('son of') and the letter T for 'tribe'. Arabic, Ethiopic, and other non-English words are printed in italics.